Why Are There Differences in the Gospels?

Why Are There Differences in the Gospels?

What We Can Learn from Ancient Biography

MICHAEL R. LICONA

Foreword by
CRAIG A. EVANS

OXFORD
UNIVERSITY PRESS

OXFORD
UNIVERSITY PRESS

Oxford University Press is a department of the University of Oxford. It furthers
the University's objective of excellence in research, scholarship, and education
by publishing worldwide. Oxford is a registered trade mark of Oxford University
Press in the UK and certain other countries.

Published in the United States of America by Oxford University Press
198 Madison Avenue, New York, NY 10016, United States of America.

Library of Congress Cataloging-in-Publication Data
Names: Licona, Michael, 1961– author.
Title: Why are there differences in the gospels? : what we can learn from
ancient biography / Michael R. Licona ; foreword by Craig A. Evans.
Description: New York : Oxford University Press, 2016. | Includes
bibliographical references and index.
Identifiers: LCCN 2016017896| ISBN 9780190264260 (cloth : alk. paper) |
ISBN 9780190264284 (epub)
Subjects: LCSH: Bible. Gospels—Criticism, interpretation, etc. |
Synoptic problem. | Plutarch. Lives.
Classification: LCC BS2555.52 .L53 2016 | DDC 226/.066—dc23
LC record available at https://lccn.loc.gov/2016017896

3 5 7 9 8 6 4 2

Printed by Sheridan Books, Inc., United States of America

To Craig Keener and John Ramsey, consummate scholars and dear friends.

Contents

Foreword

ALL WHO READ the New Testament Gospels carefully will observe a great many similarities and a great many differences. The similarities are what we expect. After all, the four Gospels are talking about the same person, Jesus of Nazareth. It is the observation of the differences that creates the problem. The wording of something Jesus says appears in two or three forms in the Gospels. Sometimes where Jesus says it differs from one Gospel to another. How is this to be explained? Should these discrepancies be regarded as errors? Were the Gospel writers poor historians? Have they told the truth about Jesus?

It is very understandable that modern readers of the Gospels raise these questions. If historians today produced parallel accounts of the life and accomplishments of a United States president or a British prime minister, which exhibited the kinds of discrepancies that we find in the Gospels, no doubt their work would be sharply criticized.

In large part this explains the problem. We moderns have very different expectations of what constitutes historiography, or the "writing of history." Most of us have no idea how the ancients understood history or how it should be written. Many of us probably assume that the ancients wrote their histories the way we moderns do, or at least tried to. If we think this, we are wrong. In fact, many of us have little idea how the ancients thought the life and teaching of a great man should be preserved and passed on. This is especially important in the case of someone like Jesus, who as a teacher (or "rabbi") taught disciples ("learners"). How he taught, what he expected his disciples to learn, and how he expected them to teach others all come into play in the writing of the Gospels. In other words, the pedagogy (manner of teaching) of Jesus is every bit as important as ancient historiography for understanding the Gospels and why they tell the story of Jesus differently.

To understand the New Testament Gospels and the kind of biography or history that they offer, it is necessary to compare them to the biographies and histories that were written in their time, not our time. This is what Michael Licona has done in his learned study *Why Are There Differences in the Gospels?* Dr. Licona addresses this important question by inquiring into how the ancients wrote history. He focuses on Plutarch, who flourished at the end of the first century and the first two decades of the second century and authored the *Lives*. The choice of Plutarch is a good one because in several biographies he frequently covers the same ground, thus creating a number of parallels or, we might say, "synoptic" accounts not unlike what we have in the New Testament Gospels, especially in the first three—Matthew, Mark, and Luke—which scholars call the Synoptic Gospels because of their many parallels.

What Dr. Licona shows is that the writers of the New Testament Gospels often edit their material in ways very similar to what Plutarch did with his material. This similarity enables us to evaluate the Gospels in their time and environment. Just as Plutarch compresses stories, sometimes conflates them, inverts the order of events, simplifies, and relocates stories or sayings, so do the authors of the New Testament Gospels.

However, compared to the compositional practice of Plutarch, the authors of the Gospels were far more conservative, especially when it comes to the editing and paraphrasing of the words of Jesus. Indeed, it has been observed that the authors of the New Testament Gospels are far more conservative in their paraphrasing of the words of Jesus than was Josephus in his paraphrasing the words of Israel's ancient Scripture. What the evidence seems to show is that while the authors of the New Testament Gospels exhibit many of the compositional practices of their day, they also had a very high regard for the stories of Jesus, especially for his words.

Many Christian readers of Dr. Licona's book will be surprised by his findings. Some will perhaps be troubled. Hopefully all will read his book with an open, teachable mind. Those who regard the Gospels as inspired and trustworthy, but are troubled by their apparent discrepancies, should be encouraged by Dr. Licona's careful, informed study. His work exposes the vapid assertions of the hacks, to the effect that the Gospels are filled with errors and contradictions and so cannot be trusted. At the same time, it cautions naïve conservatives who rely on simplistic harmonizations and pat answers that really do not do justice to the phenomena.

It is a pleasure for me to commend Dr. Licona's well-researched and well-written book to all readers.

Craig A. Evans, PhD, DHabil, John Bisagno Distinguished Professor of Christian Origins and Dean of the School of Christian Thought, Houston Baptist University.

Acknowledgments

I WOULD LIKE to express my gratitude to four classical scholars for their assistance: to John Ramsey most of all, who provided a great deal of assistance throughout the first half of this project, especially for pericopes #1–22 in chapter 3, a portion of chapter 5, and all of Appendix 4; to Christopher Pelling for reviewing the introduction, chapters 1–2, and pericopes #23–36 in chapter 3; to Rainer Hirsch-Luipold for reviewing portions of chapters 2–3, and pericopes #23–36 in chapter 3; and to Steven L. Jones, my colleague at Houston Baptist University (HBU), for reviewing the introduction through chapter 3.

I likewise wish to express my thanks to the following New Testament scholars for their part in this work: to Darrell Bock and Craig Keener for reviewing the entire manuscript except for chapter 5 and the conclusion; to Craig Blomberg and Darrell Bock for reading a paper I presented in 2015 at the Annual Meeting of the Evangelical Theological Society, which became the basis for chapter 5, and for providing response papers to it, which provided helpful ideas; to Craig Blomberg, Darrell Bock, Lynn Cohick, Gary Habermas, Randy Richards, and Dan Wallace for showing an interest in the thesis of this book while providing critical feedback to ideas they allowed me to run by them. I am also grateful to my son-in-law, Nick Peters, for his initial assistance.

I want to express my thanks to my HBU colleague Jerry Walls, who continuously pushed me to submit my book proposal to Oxford University Press (OUP) until I did; to Cynthia Read at OUP for being a pleasure to work with; to HBU for allowing me a flexible teaching schedule in order to complete my research for this volume; to William Lane Craig and Greg Monette, who both encouraged me to push forward with this research when I became weary of it; and to Craig Evans, Craig Keener, Greg Monette, my Doktorvater Jan van der Watt, and Dan Wallace, all of whom encouraged me to pursue truth no matter where it led when my observations made me uncomfortable.

I want to express my gratitude for the Support Team Members of Risen Jesus, Inc., who provided consistent financial assistance, to *Sola Scriptura* in Indonesia and its partners, who provided a research grant that gave me precious time to focus on my research for this book. I am grateful to Bryant Paul Richardson for creating the three graphics illustrating the three major solutions to the Synoptic Problem. I am grateful to Paul Brinkerhoff and Lois Stück of Grace and Truth Communications for editing the manuscript for this book. They greatly improved it. I am thankful to my wife, Debbie Licona, who patiently listened to me while I ran ideas past her and provided valuable feedback during the seven and a half years I was engaged in this project, and, having read a near-final draft, provided valuable comments and suggestions. She is truly a βοηθόν (Gen. 2:18).

My friend Paul Maier had intended to embark on a research project similar to what is contained in this volume but was unable to because of challenges he and his wife had to face concerning her health. I hope this volume satisfies his curiosity.

Abbreviations

IN THE TEXT AND NOTES, references to ancient authors and their works when abbreviated follow the abbreviations used in the *SBL Handbook of Style* (2nd ed.), supplemented by the *Oxford Classical Dictionary* (4th ed.), as are references to journals and other works of classical and biblical scholarship. Some alternate abbreviations are also included parenthetically as they appear in quoted material. For the reader's convenience, full Latin (or Greek) titles are provided along with their English titles. All references to Jewish, intertestamental, Greco-Roman, and patristic literature not mentioned below are given in full.

All English translations of Plutarch and all other quotations of ancient authors are from the volumes in the Loeb Classical Library, unless otherwise indicated. All English translations of Theon are from George A. Kennedy's *Progymnasmata*, unless otherwise indicated. Kennedy's English translation of Hermogenes and Aphthonius is based on the Greek texts provided by Hugo Rabe, *Prolegomenon Sylloge* (Leipzig: Teubner, 1931). For more detail on Rabe, see Kennedy, *Progymnasmata*, 90–91. Kennedy's English translation of Nicolaus is based on the Teubner text provided by Joseph Felton in 1913. All Scripture quotations, including the Septuagint (LXX), are the author's translation. Other English translation of quotations from ancient sources is indicated as such if translated by the author.

Author names are generally used in full along with works when first mentioned to avoid abbreviating too concisely for readers not specializing in classical or biblical studies. Whether abbreviated or used in full, other frequently cited works appear as follows (entries are grouped by category with works alphabetized by abbreviation under an author's name):

General and Bibliographic

ABC	Anchor Bible Commentary
ANF	*Ante-Nicene Fathers*

Antichthon	*Antichthon: Journal of the Australian Society for Classical Studies*
AYBRL	Anchor Yale Bible Reference Library (formerly called ABRL or Anchor Bible Reference Library)
AYBD	*Anchor Yale Bible Dictionary.* Edited by David Noel Freedman. 6 vols. New York: Doubleday, 1992 (formerly called *ABD* or *Anchor Bible Dictionary*)
BBR	*Bulletin for Biblical Research*
BEB	*Baker Encyclopedia of the Bible.* Edited by Walter A. Elwell. 2 vols. Grand Rapids: Baker, 1988
BECNT	Baker Exegetical Commentary on the New Testament
BDAG	Danker, Frederick W., Walter Bauer, William F. Arndt, and F. Wilbur Gingrich. *Greek-English Lexicon of the New Testament and Other Early Christian Literature.* 3rd ed. Chicago: University of Chicago Press, 2000 (Danker-Bauer-Arndt-Gingrich)
ECL	Early Christianity and Its Literature
Historia	*Historia: Zeitschrift für Alte Geschichte*
ICC	International Critical Commentary
IVPNTC	IVP New Testament Commentary
JBL	*Journal of Biblical Literature*
JGRChJ	*Journal of Greco-Roman Christianity and Judaism*
JRS	*Journal of Roman Studies*
Lampr. Cat.	Lamprias Catalogue
LCL	Loeb Classical Library
LNTS	Library of New Testament Studies
LXX	Septuagint
MS(S)	manuscript(s)
MT	Masoretic Text
NAC	New American Commentary
NCBC	New Cambridge Bible Commentary
NET	New English Translation
NIGTC	New International Greek Testament Commentary
NRSV	New Revised Standard Version
NTC	New Testament Commentary
NTS	*New Testament Studies*
OCD	*Oxford Classical Dictionary.* Edited by S. Hornblower, A. Spawforth, and E. Eidinow. 4th ed. Oxford, 2012

PNTC	Pillar New Testament Commentary
RSV	Revised Standard Version
Teubner	Bibliotheca Scriptorum Graecorum et Romanorum Teubneriana (1849–)
TJ	*Trinity Journal*
SymS	Symposium Series
VigChrSup	*Supplements to Vigiliae Christianae*
WBC	Word Biblical Commentary
GRW	Writings from the Greco-Roman World

Hebrew Bible/Old Testament (including Septuagint)

Gen.	Gen.
Deut.	Deuteronomy
1 Kings	1 Kings
2 Kings	2 Kings
Ezra	Ezra
Job	Job
Ps(s).	Psalm(s)
Eccles.	Ecclesiastes
Isa.	Isaiah
Jer.	Jeremiah
Dan.	Daniel
Mal.	Malachi

New Testament

Matt.	Matthew
Mark	Mark
Luke	Luke
John	John
Acts	Acts
1 Cor.	1 Corinthians
Gal.	Galatians
Col.	Colossians
2 Tim.	2 Timothy
Philem.	Philemon
James	James

1 Pet.	1 Peter
1 John	1 John
Jude	Jude

Deuterocanonical Works

1 Macc.	1 Maccabees
2 Macc.	2 Maccabees

Dead Sea Scrolls and Related Texts

4Q521	Messianic Apocalyse

Old Testament Pseudepigrapha

1 En.	1 Enoch (Ethiopic Apocalypse)
2 En.	2 Enoch (Slavonic Apocalypse)
4 Ezra	4 Ezra

New Testament Pseudepigrapha

Gos. Pet.	Gospel of Peter

Apostolic Fathers

1 Clem.	1 Clement
Mart. Pol.	Martyrdom of Polycarp

Rabbinic Works

Sipra
pq.	*pereq* (chapter)
VDDeho.	*Vayyiqra Dibura Debobah*

Other Ancient Sources

App.	Appian
Bell. civ. (or *B Civ.*)	*Bella civilia* (*Civil Wars*)
Celt.	*Celtica*

Ar.	Aristophanes
Eccl.	*Ecclesiazusae*
Ath.	Athenaeus
Deipn.	*Deipnosophistae* (*The Deipnosophists* or *The Banquet of the Learnèd*)
August.	Augustine
Cons.	*De consensu evangelistarum* (*Harmony of the Gospels*)
Caesar	
Bell. civ.	*Bellum civile* (*Commentaries on the Civil War*)
Bell. gall.	*Bellum gallicum* (*Commentaries on the Gallic War*)
Chiron	*Chiron: Mitteilungen der Kommission für Alte Geschichte und Epigraphik*
Chrysostom	John Chrysostom
Hom. Matt.	*Homiliae in Matthaeum*
Cic.	Cicero (Marcus Tullius)
Att.	*Epistulae ad Atticum* (*Letters to Atticus*)
Ep. Brut.	*Epistulae ad Brutum* (*Letters to Brutus*)
Fam.	*Epistulae ad familiares* (*Letters to Friends*)
Mur.	*Pro Murena* (*For Lucius Murena*)
Phil.	*Orationes philippicae* (*Philippics*)
Planc.	*Pro Plancio* (*In Defense of Gnaeus Plancius*)
Sest.	*Pro Sestio* (*In Defense of Publius Sestius*)
Cn.	Gnaeus (a name)
Dio (or Dio Cass.)	Cassius Dio
Hist. rom.	*Historia romana* (*Roman History*)
Euseb.	Eusebius
Cels.	*Contra Celsum* (*Against Celsus*)
Hist. eccl.	*Historia ecclesiastica* (*Ecclesiastical History*)
Hermog.	Hermogenes
Inv.	Περὶ εὑρέσεως (*On Invention*)
Joseph.	Josephus
Ant.	*Jewish Antiquitites*
J. W.	*Jewish War*
Life	*The Life*
Justin.	Justinian
Inst.	*Institutes*
Liv.	Livy
Epit.	*Epitomae*
Per.	*Periochae*

Lucan
   De bello civili   *De bello civili* (On the Civil War) (or *Pharsalia*)
Lucian
   Hist. conscr.   *Quomodo historia conscribenda sit* (*How to Write
                                  History*)
Mart.   Martial
   Spect.   *Spectacula*
Nic. Dam.   Nicolaus of Damascus (or Damascenus)
   Vit. Caes.   *Vita Caesaris* (*Life of Caesar*)
Origen
   Comm. Jo.   *Commentarii in evangelium Joannis*
Philostr.   Philostratus
   Vit. Apoll.   *Vita Apollonii* (*Life of Apollonius of Tyana*)
Pliny   Pliny the Elder
   Nat.   *Naturalis historia* (*Natural History*)
Polyb.   Polybius
   Hist.   *Histories*
Plut.   Plutarch
   Comp. Nic. Crass.   *Comparatio Niciae et Crassi* (*Comparison of Nicias
                              and Crassus*)
   Vit.   *Vitae Parallelae* (*Parallel Lives*)
     Alex.   *Alexander* (*Life of Alexander*)
     Ant.   *Antonius* (*Life of Antonius* or *Life of Antony*)
     Brut.   *Brutus* (*Life of Brutus*)
     Caes.   *Caesar* (*Life of Caesar*)
     Cat. Min.   *Cato Minor* (*Life of Cato Minor*)
     Cic.   *Cicero* (*Life of Cicero*)
     Cim.   *Cimon* (*Life of Cimon*)
     Cor.   *Marcius Coriolanus* (*Life of Marcius Coriolanus*)
     Crass.   *Crassus* (*Life of Crassus*)
     Luc.   *Lucullus* (*Life of Lucullus*)
     Nic.   *Nicias* (*Life of Nicias*)
     Pomp.   *Pompeius* (*Life of Pompey*)
     Publ.   *Publicola* (*Life of Publicola*)
     Sert.   *Sertorius* (*Life of Sertorius*)
     Sull.   *Sulla* (*Life of Sulla*)
   Mor.   *Moralia* (*Morals*)
   Mulier. virt.   *Mulierum virtutes* (*Virtues of Women*)

Quint.	Quintilian
Inst.	*Institutio oratoria* (*Institutes of Oratory*)
Rhet. Her.	*Rhetorica ad Herennium*
Sall.	Sallust
Cat.	*Bellum Catalinae* or *De Catilinae coniuratione* (*War with Catiline*)
Sen.	Seneca (the Elder)
Contr.	*Controversiae*
Suas.	*Suasoriae*
Spengel, *Rhet.*	L. Spengel, *Rhetores Graeci*, 3 vols.: 1/1 (1885), 2 (1854), 3 (1856)
Suet.	Suetonius
Caes.	*De vita Caesarum* (*Lives of the Twelve Caesars*)
Jul.	*Divus Julius* (*The Deified Julius*)
Tac.	Tacitus
Ann.	*Annales*
Theon	Aelius Theon of Alexandria
Thuc.	Thucydides
Hist.	*Histories*
Val. Max.	Valerius Maximus
Mem.	*Facta et dicta memorabilia* (*Memorable Deeds and Sayings*)
Vell. Pat.	Velleius Paterculus
Hist. rom.	*Historiae Romanae* (*Roman History*)

*Why Are There Differences in
the Gospels?*

Introduction

ANYONE WHO READS the Gospels carefully will notice that there are differences in the manner in which they report the same events. Julius Africanus (ca. late second to early third century) attempted to explain the different genealogies of Jesus provided by Matthew and Luke (*Letter to Aristides*; preserved by Eusebius in *Hist. eccl.* 1.7). In the early third century, Origen acknowledged the presence of differences. On one occasion he harmonized*[1] them (*Cels.* 5.56),[2] while on another he suggested that at least one of the evangelists* (i.e., the authors of the canonical Gospels) was communicating spiritual rather than literal truth (*Comm. Jo.* 10).

At the end of the fourth century, Chrysostom addressed Gospel differences, saying if the Gospels agreed in every detail, their authors would be accused of collusion. But if a difference amounted to a discrepancy (i.e., a contradiction) on minor matters such as times, places, and the very words, this by no means would discredit the major matters in them (John Chrysostom, *Hom. Matt.* 1.6). In the late fourth and early fifth centuries, Augustine recognized differences in the Gospels but made great attempts to resolve them through harmonizations. Notwithstanding, he concluded at one point that it is often impossible to determine the original *logion** or teaching of Jesus in question, and it is useless to ask, since the meaning is present in spite of some differing details (Augustine, *Cons.* 3.3.8). These attempts to deal with the presence of differences in the Gospels inform us that the differences troubled some even during the early centuries of the church.

The presence of differences in parallel accounts is not unique to the Gospels. Gerald Downing identified many differences in the manner Josephus retold a story that originally appeared in the Jewish Scriptures. R. A. Derrenbacker took Downing's work even further, while Jordan

Henderson identified many differences in the manner Josephus reported autobiographical material in the *Jewish War* and the *Life*.[3] Brian McGing observed how Philo adapted the biblical texts when writing about Moses.[4] Differences in how authors reported the same event are part and parcel of classical literature studies. D. A. Russell assessed how Plutarch adapted his lone source, Dionysius of Halicarnassus, when writing his *Life of Coriolanus*.[5] Charles Hill surveys works assessing how Homer, Herodotus, Philo, Josephus, Plutarch, Porphyry, Justin, and others quoted and/or used their sources.[6] Craig Keener noted numerous differences in the manner Tacitus, Suetonius, and Plutarch report the suicide of the Roman emperor Otho—differences quite similar to those we observe in the Gospels.[7] Modern commentaries on classical literature also discuss differences that appear when the same event is reported by different ancient authors and even by the same author.

There are numerous reasons why differences exist: a slip of memory,[8] the use of different sources, the elasticity of oral tradition,[9] the flexibility of the biographical genre, redaction, adaptation within *chreia**,[10] reporting the event from different vantage points, one author featuring content omitted by another,[11] and the use of idioms that are now foreign to us.[12] It is also possible that an author may have altered his source(s) in order to render the story in a manner he regarded as being more plausible than as it was told in his source(s).[13] We can often make a good guess pertaining to why one text differs from another. But it is also the case that we are often left scratching our heads in bewilderment.

There are at least two additional causes responsible for differences that have received comparatively little attention, and they pertain to ancient compositional devices.[14] The first involves rhetorical devices taught in the *progymnasmata* (i.e., preliminary exercises in rhetoric) that appear in the compositional textbooks written by Theon, Hermogenes, and others.[15] The second involves compositional devices employed by ancient biographers and historians. Unfortunately, there are no extant ancient manuals providing the proper techniques to be employed when editing the work of another.[16] Only a little literature has survived from antiquity describing how history was written. Lucian's tractate *How to Write History* (*Quomodo historia conscribenda sit*) is one of the very few. Thucydides (*Hist.* 1.22.1–3), Polybius (*Hist.* 2.56), and Lucian of Samosata (*Hist. conscr.* 58), inform us about the process of reporting speeches. Accordingly, aside from the very little extant literature describing literary conventions for writing history, scholars have had to resort to educated guesswork based on inference when considering literary devices in ancient history writing.

This volume will pursue the identification of several techniques employed in the writing of ancient history and biography that can be gleaned from compositional textbooks and inferred from observations of the differences in how Plutarch reported the same events in nine of his *Lives*. We will also observe how the employment of these techniques by the evangelists would result in precisely the types of differences we often observe in the Gospels. This book is not a Rosetta Stone for understanding all of the differences in the Gospels. Its aim is rather to investigate compositional devices that are often inferred by classical scholars and by some New Testament scholars in order to see if the existence of those devices may be more firmly established and provide insights into many of the differences in the Gospels.

Gospels as Biography

In the middle of the twentieth century, most New Testament scholars regarded the Gospels as *sui generis**. Then in 1977, Charles Talbert proposed that the Gospels belong to the genre of Greco-Roman biography, and others made similar proposals in the years that followed.[17] Richard Burridge believed their conclusions were mistaken and set out to refute them. To his surprise, he concluded that the Gospels indeed belong to Greco-Roman biography, and his resulting book, *What Are the Gospels?*, has become the definitive treatment on the subject.[18] Today, a growing majority of scholars regard the Gospels as Greco-Roman biography.[19]

One may rightly ask why the Gospels have been classified as Greco-Roman rather than Jewish biography. There are several reasons. First, the Gospels contain many of the characteristics of Greco-Roman biography. For example:

1. They are written in continuous prose narrative.
2. Stories, logia, anecdotes, and speeches are combined to form a narrative.
3. The life of the main character is not always covered in chronological sequence.
4. Attention is focused on a main character rather than on an era, event, or government as in a history.
5. Little to no attention is provided for psychological analyses of the main character.

6. We learn something of the main character's ancestry and then move rapidly along to the inauguration of his public life.

7. Ancient biographies were of the same general length, with shorter works being under 10,000 words, medium length between 10,000 and 25,000 words, and longer length over 25,000 words. Because a scroll would normally hold a maximum of 25,000 words, most biographies fell in the medium length category so they could be read in a single sitting.[20]

8. 25 to 33 percent of the verbs are "dominated by the subject, while another 15 to 30 percent occur in sayings, speeches or quotations from the person."[21]

9. Lives of philosophers and teachers are usually "arranged topically around collections of material to display their ideas and teachings."[22]

10. The main subject's character is illuminated through his words and deeds as a model for readers either to emulate or to avoid.[23]

Second, with the possible exception of Philo's *Life of Moses*, which many scholars do not regard as biography, there are no clear examples of biographies of Jewish sages written around the time of Jesus. Burridge writes, "Philip Alexander concludes his study of 'Rabbinic Biography and the Biography of Jesus' thus: 'there are no Rabbinic parallels to the Gospels as such. This is by far the most important single conclusion to emerge from this paper. ... There is not a trace of an ancient biography of any of the Sages. ... This is a profound enigma.' "[24] Jacob Neusner similarly writes, "There is no sustained biography of any [Jewish] sage."[25]

The objective of Greco-Roman biography was to reveal the character of the subject through the person's sayings and deeds. Writing around the same time as some of the Gospels were written, Plutarch provided the clearest statement in this regard in his *Life of Alexander*:

For it is not Histories that I am writing, but Lives; and in the most illustrious deeds there is not always a manifestation of virtue or vice, nay, a slight thing like a phrase or a jest often makes a greater revelation of character than battles where thousands fall, or the greatest armaments, or sieges of cities. Accordingly, just as painters get the likenesses in their portraits from the face and the expression of the eyes, wherein the character shows itself, but make very little account of the other parts of the body, so I must be permitted to devote myself rather to the signs of the soul in men, and by means of these to portray the life of each, leaving to others the description of their great contests. (*Alex.* 1.2–3 [Perrin, LCL])[26]

The tone of Plutarch's statements suggests he was following the existing objective of biography rather than amending or even inventing it. Plutarch makes similar statements in his *Life of Nicias* (*Nic.* 1.5), *Life of Pompey* (*Pomp.* 8.7), and *Life of Cimon* (*Cim.* 2.3–5). In his *Life of Cato Minor*, Plutarch tells the story of Cato's offensive treatment of and reconciliation with his friend Munatius (*Cat. Min.* 37.1–5). He then adds, "I have spent time on this because I think it just as telling as Cato's great public actions in giving the reader illumination and insight into the man's character."[27] So the primary objective of biography appears to have been to reveal the character of the biography's subject.[28]

Greco-Roman biography was a broad and flexible genre. The biographies often differ from one another so much that scholars often divide the genre into various subsets.[29] Complicating matters for us moderns, the lines distinguishing some ancient genres were fuzzy and were often crossed, producing hybrid literature. Beth Sheppard observes that the lines separating biography and history were often blurred and cites as examples Varro's *De vita populi Romani* and Dicaearchus's *Life of Greece*.[30] Plutarch's *Caesar* contains elements that are often closer to the genre of history writing than biography.[31] Some biblical scholars view Luke's Gospel as history rather than biography.[32] They recognize that the prologues to his Gospel and its sequel, Acts, reflect Luke's familiarity with Greco-Roman historiography. That is, he knew and was probably writing in a manner that had strong affinities with Hellenistic or Greco-Roman histories. Therefore, some ancient biographies, including one or more of the Gospels, may be said to resist firm grouping within a genre.[33] For our purposes, we only need to recognize that the New Testament Gospels bear a strong affinity to Greco-Roman biography. Accordingly, we should not be surprised when the evangelists employ compositional devices similar to those used by ancient biographers. In fact, we should be surprised if they did not.

Burridge and Gould say Bultmann was correct in asserting that the Gospels do not look anything like modern biography. What Bultmann neglected to observe, however, is that neither do any other ancient biographies.[34] Differing from modern biography, which is a product of the nineteenth century, ancient biographical conventions provided authors a license to depart from the degree of precision in reporting that many of us moderns prefer.

Generally speaking, ancient authors took fewer liberties when writing histories than when writing biographies. However, there are plenty of exceptions when even the more careful historians of that era engaged in history writing using the same liberties we observe in biographical writing. A history was meant to illustrate past events whereas a biography was meant to serve as a literary portrait of its main character. Accordingly, if an adapting or bending of details would serve to make a historical point or illuminate the qualities of the main character in a manner that rendered them clearer, the historian and biographer were free to do so, since their accounts would be "true enough."[35]

Ancient historians and biographers varied in their commitment to historical accuracy. Whereas Tacitus is regarded as a fairly accurate historian, Lucian of Samosata reported that when the Greek historian Aristobulus of Cassandreia read to Alexander a story he had invented concerning a battle between Alexander and Porus, in which Alexander had single-handedly killed an elephant, Alexander discarded the book and said Aristobulus should be treated in like manner (*Hist. conscr.* 12). Plutarch's *Lives* and Suetonius's *Lives of the Caesars* (*De vita Caesarum*) are regarded as more accurate literary portraits of their main characters than Philostratus's *Life of Apollonius of Tyana* (*Vita Apollonii*), which is a combination of history and fiction.[36]

The historical accuracy of ancient literature may be viewed in a manner similar to what we observe in movie theaters today. Some movies claim at the beginning to be "based on true events" while others claim to be "inspired by true events." The latter will involve more dramatic license than the former. Even in the former, however, we expect reenacted conversations to be redacted to varying degrees for clarity, dramatic impact, and artistic improvement.[37]

Observations of a Student of the New Testament

Conducting research in a different discipline requires a very steep learning curve. This research involved more than I had anticipated. Being engaged in historical Jesus research combined with a growing understanding of early Christianity does not necessarily provide one with knowledge about the late Roman Republic. Emperors, proconsuls, prefects, and Jewish tetrarchs were only a few of the political positions held in the world in which the earliest Christians lived and the New Testament authors wrote. Augustus led Rome at a time when the Republic was in the beginning stages of a transition toward empire, a process that continued throughout Jesus's lifetime. The role of the senate, the various political posts, and the varying dates on which the posts were to be taken and vacated were just a few of many matters that impacted my research and had to be learned.

There are bound to be some errors in this volume, despite the fact that four classical scholars and two New Testament scholars graciously viewed it with the intent of catching the more obvious ones. Of course, I alone am responsible for any errors that remain.

The Loeb Greek text of Plutarch's *Lives* has been tagged and is available for all to view at the Perseus Project (online)[38] and within Logos Bible Software. But that edition is nearly a century old. I learned that a more recent version of the Teubner text is available and is the preferred critical Greek text used by classical scholars. Unfortunately, the current Teubner text is pricey. Plutarch's *Lives*, at least the nine I am considering in this volume, appear in six volumes and cost approximately $600 USD. In light of this, one comes quickly to appreciate the affordability of critical Greek New Testaments, which are far more extensive than Teubner's Greek texts of Plutarch's *Lives* and may be purchased for less than $50 USD.[39] Though using the most current Teubner text for Plutarch's *Lives*, I will be employing the reference system of verse numbering found in Loeb unless otherwise indicated, since the Loeb Greek text is readily available to so many and this book is written primarily for students of the canonical Gospels.

My work in Plutarch's *Lives* has provided me with a much greater appreciation for what those of us who study the New Testament have available to us. Commentaries on the New Testament literature are found in an abundance that truly overwhelms. It is a sobering thought that when my life is over I will not have consulted as much as one-third of the commentaries on the New Testament literature. Such abundance is far from the case when we come to Plutarch. Furthermore, the manuscript support for our present critical Greek text of the New Testament is superior to what we have for any of the ancient literature. As of the time I am writing this chapter, there are 5,839 Greek manuscripts of the New Testament.[40] A dozen or so of these manuscripts have been dated to have been written within 150 years of the originals, and the earliest (P[52]) has been dated to within ten to sixty years of the original.[41] In contrast, of the nine *Lives* of Plutarch we will be considering, only a few dozen Greek manuscripts have survived. The earliest of these is dated to the tenth or eleventh century, or roughly eight to nine hundred years after Plutarch wrote them. Moreover, while the wealth of manuscripts for the New Testament literature leaves us very few places where uncertainty remains pertaining to the earliest reading or at least the meaning behind it, there are few if any places where a gap in the manuscripts forces scholars to amend the text with a reading that appears in no Greek manuscript or even one that is contrary to what we read in the manuscripts.[42] This is not the case with Plutarch's *Lives*.

In short, this research project has humbled me concerning my initial lack of understanding of the late Roman Republic (an understanding that, of course, is still growing) and has greatly increased my appreciation for the wealth of both the available resources for the study of the New Testament literature and the available Greek manuscripts. This project also kindled in me a strong interest in the events leading to the fall of the Roman Republic for their own sake. The personalities involved, the events themselves, and their outcomes are fascinating.

Some final comments must be made in terms of some content of this volume. It contains research that may be of interest to both students of the Gospels and students of classics. Because many of us who are students of the New Testament are largely unfamiliar with matters pertaining to Roman history, I must include some content that will be quite elementary to students of classics. Likewise, many students of classics will be deficient in their understanding of the New Testament. Accordingly, some of the content will be quite elementary to students of the New Testament. Because many readers may not be familiar with some of the Roman characters in Plutarch's *Lives*, biosketches of the main characters are provided in appendix 4. Many readers can profit from reading that appendix before reading chapter 3. A glossary is provided for nontechnical readers, and an asterisk (*) appears after the first occurrence of terms included. All dates are BCE unless otherwise indicated. All English translations of Plutarch are from the volumes in the Loeb Classical Library, unless otherwise indicated.

These preliminary comments made, let us proceed on our lightly traveled road toward identifying various literary devices that contribute to the presence of differences in the Gospels.

I

Compositional Textbooks

RHETORIC COMPRISED a significant portion of the education received by the fortunate in antiquity. Beginning students learned preliminary exercises or *progymnasmata*. There are seven textbooks of progymnasmata that have survived from antiquity, five of which were written in Greek and two in Latin. Of the five Greek textbooks, the earliest is attributed to Aelius Theon of Alexandria. There is uncertainty pertaining to the date of composition. Most scholars date it to sometime in the first century CE and believe it is the earliest surviving work of its kind.[1] The next earliest is attributed to Hermogenes of Tarsus and is tentatively dated to the third or fourth century CE. Then Libanius wrote one in the middle to late fourth century. Even later is the progymnasmata of Aphthonius of Antioch, who studied rhetoric sometime during the second half of the fourth century CE and must have written shortly thereafter. We then have a textbook written by Nicolaus of Myra, who probably wrote during the second half of the fifth century CE. Of the five, Nicolaus is least helpful, since he largely quotes verbatim from the earlier textbooks and is often confused when offering commentary on them.[2] The two textbooks that were originally written in Latin are *Institutes of Oratory*, composed by Quintilian about 94 CE,[3] and *Rhetorica ad Herennium*, whose authorship is unknown.

Since Theon's textbook of progymnasmata may be the earliest and the closest to when the evangelists wrote, this chapter will focus on his exercises. Theon himself says he did not invent most of the rhetorical exercises he describes but rather claims to have provided definitions for each and how to distinguish one from another as well as when, where, and how to use them (Preface 59 [3]).[4] Therefore, the techniques for rhetorical writing provided by Theon would probably have been known and employed during earlier times. And there is some evidence this was the case. We observe most of the compositional textbooks making use of a particular anecdote for instruction. Theon (98–99 [17]) writes, "When Diogenes the cynic philosopher saw a boy eating fancy food, he beat his pedagogue with his staff." Hermogenes (6 [76]) renders it, "Diogenes, on seeing an undisciplined youth, beat his pedagogue," while Nicolaus the Sophist (20 [140]) says, "When Diogenes saw a disorderly youth in the marketplace, he beat his pedagogue with his staff." Libanius wrote, "Diogenes, upon seeing a child misbehaving, struck his pedagogue, adding, 'Why do you teach such things?'"[5] Before any of these Greek textbooks were written (save possibly Theon), the Latin author Quintilian used the same anecdote. Related to the writing of moral essays, he wrote, "Crates on seeing an ill-educated boy, beat his pedagogue" (*Inst.* 1.9.5). Instead of "Diogenes," Quintilian used "Crates" and relates it to moral essay rather than an example of chreia (Theon, Hermogenes, Nicolaus) or as a sample that may be altered in various exercises in anecdote (Libanius).

Learning rhetoric was essential for delivering speeches as well as for writing everything from poetry to history. Theon wrote,

> Now I have included these remarks, not thinking that all are useful to all beginners, but in order that we may know that training in exercises is absolutely useful not only to those who are going to practice rhetoric but also if one wishes to undertake the function of poets or historians or any other writers. These things are, as it were, the foundation of every kind (*idea*) of discourse. (70 [13])[6]

Theon goes on to devote much space to teaching paraphrase, since "all ancient writers seem to have used paraphrase in the best possible way, rephrasing not only their own writings but those of each other" (62 [6]). Many of Theon's progymnasmata are relevant to our discussion related to differences between reports of the same event. And it is to these that we now turn.

Chreia: "A chreia (*chreia*) is a brief saying or action making a point, attributed to some specified person or something corresponding to a person" (96 [15]). A chreia is always attributed to a person and can include what the person said, did, or a combination of both (96–97 [15–16]).[7] Hermogenes adds that it often takes the form of a question and answer (7 [77]). Theon provides the example of an active chreia: "When Diogenes the Cynic philosopher saw a boy eating fancy food, he beat his pedagogue with his staff" (99 [17]). In this case, the action of Diogenes alone communicates the point. Chreia can be offered in the form of a jest (99 [18]). Plutarch preserves a number of these in his *Life of Cicero*, of which the following is an example:

> When many in the senate were displeased at Caesar's having got a vote passed that the land in Campania should be divided up among the soldiers, and Lucius Gellius, who was about the oldest [of the senators], said that this would not happen while he was alive, Cicero said: "Let us wait, for the postponement Gellius is asking for is not a long one." (*Cic.* 26.3)

This is an example of a chreia in terms of what a person had said rather than did. A chreia involving a combination of what a person both said and did is when "Alexander, the king of the Macedonians, was asked by someone where he kept his treasures. 'Here,' he said, pointing to his friends" (Theon 100 [18]).

Theon observes that chreia can be altered by inflection. Among other things, this can involve "restatement, grammatical inflection, comment, and contradiction, and we expand and compress the chreia, and in addition (at a later stage in study) we refute and confirm" (101 [19]). Theon explains that inflection can also include changing the number of persons involved. For example, we can change the number of people speaking from one to two or even more. The converse may likewise occur, changing a plurality of persons speaking to only one. The same may be said of the number of persons being addressed (101 [19]).

On a regular basis, we observe Plutarch employing inflection when mentioning two or more persons speaking in one *Life* while only mentioning one speaking in another *Life*. However, many if not most of these do not appear within a chreia. We will look at this in detail in chapter 3.

Narrative: "Narrative (*diegema*) is language descriptive of things that happened or as though they had happened" (Theon 78 [28]).[8] Theon discusses how there is a substantial amount of flexibility involved when reconstructing speeches, and the imagination of the writer is welcomed. However, the narration must be credible and suitable to the speakers, audience members, and occasion (84–85 [33–34]).[9] Theon discusses other techniques by which one may vary a narrative:

> Sometimes as making a straightforward statement and sometimes as doing something more than making a factual statement, and

sometimes in the form of questions, and sometimes as things we seek to learn about, and sometimes as things about which we are in doubt, and sometimes as making a command, sometimes expressing a wish, and sometimes swearing to something, sometimes addressing the participants, sometimes advancing suppositions, sometimes using dialogue. (87 [35])

It is then interesting to observe how Theon takes a statement from Thucydides and varies it using a number of the above techniques (87–90 [36–38]). Thucydides wrote,

A force of Thebans a little over three hundred in number made an armed entry during the first watch of the night into Plataea in Boeotia, a town in alliance with Athenians. (*Hist.* 2.2.1)

Theon restates these words of Thycydides as something more than making a factual statement:

The arrival at Plataea of the Thebans was, it seems, the cause of great troubles for Athenians and Lacedaimonians and the allies on each side; for a force of Thebans a little over three hundred in number made an armed entry during the first watch into Plataea in Boeotia.

He then turns it into a question:

Is it really true that a force of Thebans a little over three hundred in number made an armed entry during the first watch into Plataea in Boeotia?

Theon also expresses the original statement as a command:

Come, O Plataeans, be worthy of your city and of your ancestors who contended with Persians and Mardonius, and of those who lie buried in your land. Show the Thebans that they do wrong in thinking you should harken to them and be slaves and in forcing those unwilling to do so, contrary to oaths and treaties, when, a little more than three hundred in number, they entered under arms during the first watch into our city, an ally of Athenians.

He then imagines some people talking to create dialogue about what has occurred:

A. Often in the past it occurred to me to ask you about what happened to the Thebans and Plataeans at Plataea, and I would gladly hear now if this is a good opportunity for you to give a narrative account.
B. By Zeus, it is a good opportunity, and I shall tell you now if, as you say, you have a desire to hear about these things. The Thebans, always at odds with the Plataeans, wanted to seize hold of Plataea in peace time. A force of them, therefore, a little more than three hundred in number, went under arms about the first watch into the city, an ally of Athenians.
A. How then did they easily escape notice, going in at night when the gates were shut and a guard posted?
B. You slightly anticipated what I was going to say, that some men, Naucleides and those with him, opened the gates, there being no guard posted because of the peace.

Theon turns to the matter of paraphrase proper and very briefly describes four kinds (108–10 [70–71]).[10] Because he does not provide examples for half of them, I will provide a statement of my own and alter it in the four manners described by Theon:

I am reading a book that discusses why there are differences in the Gospels.

1. Writers can alter the syntax of a sentence. In Greek, the options are exceedingly abundant. Here is one way of altering the syntax:

A book that discusses why in the Gospels there are differences I am reading.

2. Writers can add to the original words or thoughts for clarification, further description, or artistic improvement. Theon is thinking in terms of only a very few additional words. However, he follows up his section on "Paraphrase" with one on "Elaboration," in which a text is expanded in order to add what was lacking in thought and expression (110–11 [71–72]). The following example is an addition followed by another example illustrating expansion:[11]

I am reading an interesting book that discusses why there are so many differences in the Gospels.

I am reading a book that discusses ancient rhetorical exercises and compositional devices in order to gain insights pertaining to why the Gospels may often differ when they describe the same events.

3. Writers can subtract words or thoughts from the original:

I am reading a book.

4. Writers can substitute words in the original:

I am perusing a volume that converses on why there are discrepancies in Matthew, Mark, Luke, and John.

Writers may combine any number of the above. Thus, the aspiring writer in antiquity would have had many options before him.

The compositional textbooks of antiquity provided exercises meant to assist aspiring writers in the development of their writing skills. In these exercises, students improved their skills by altering the wording of their sources. Although the textbooks do not specifically state this was the manner in which they handled their sources when writing professionally, it is a very small step of faith to surmise they would employ such alterations. Referring to the progymnasmata in the textbooks that have survived, Gerald Downing opines,

> The procedures are always so similar that it would be absurd to suppose without massive supporting evidence that the NT evangelists could have learned to write Greek and cope with written source material at all while remaining outside the pervasive influence of these common steps toward literacy.[12]

We will not be disappointed when a careful viewing of ancient literature bears out our hunch.

2

Who Was Plutarch?

L. MESTRIUS PLUTARCHUS, or Plutarch, was born into a wealthy family in Chaeronea (ker-uh-NEE-uh) sometime prior to 45 CE and died sometime after 120.[1] Chaeronea is located in central Greece and was the site of two major battles. In 338 BCE, Philip II of Macedonia, the father of Alexander, defeated the Greek states led by Athens and Thebes. And in 86 BCE, Sulla defeated Archelaus in the First Mithridatic War, which was pivotal for Rome in obtaining supremacy over Greece.[2] In fact, Plutarch attests that the trophy Sulla had set up to commemorate his victory remained and the weapons and armor that had belonged to the enemy were still being found in the mud nearly two hundred years later (*Sull.* 19.5; 21.4).

In early September of 31 BCE, the inhabitants of Chaeronea had also been pressed into hard labor by Antony to assist him in his fight against Octavian. Plutarch reports that his great-grandfather Nicarchus used to tell the story of how Antony's soldiers forced them to carry certain quantities of wheat on their shoulders to the sea and hurried them along with whips until news of Antony's defeat at Actium arrived (*Ant.* 68.4–5).

Plutarch was among the affluent in his town. He studied rhetoric and then became a philosopher of the Academy founded by Plato. His friend L. Mestrius Florus, who was of consular rank and whose name Plutarch took, obtained Roman citizenship for him.[3] Another of Plutarch's friends was Quintus Sosius Senecio (consul 99 and 107), and it is to him that Plutarch dedicated his *Parallel Lives*.[4]

Most of Plutarch's life was spent in Chaeronea and Delphi, and he served as a priest at Delphi during the last three decades of his life. Trajan bestowed on him the honorary title *ornamenta consularia*, which designated him as an advisor of emperors, and he served as imperial procurator in Achaea under Hadrian, which, if true, was probably also an honorary title.[5]

Plutarch was an avid writer. The Lamprias Catalogue (possibly third or fourth century CE) lists 227 items written by Plutarch, of which roughly one half are extant and are usually grouped as *Moralia* and *Lives*.[6] A few additional works of Plutarch are not mentioned in the Catalogue. He wrote more than sixty biographies, of which fifty have survived and are referred to as Plutarch's *Lives*. They were written between 90 CE and around 120, when Plutarch died. Of the fifty, forty-six appear in pairs: a *Life* of a prominent Greek with a *Life* of a prominent Roman. These are referred to as the *Parallel Lives* and were all written after 96 CE.[7] Plutarch provides a short *Comparison* following nineteen of the twenty-three pairs, in which he compares and contrasts the Greek and Roman he has just featured. D. A. Russell comments that the *Lives* "have been the main source of understanding of the ancient world for many readers from the Renaissance to the present day."[8] The *Lives* may have been known by Tacitus and Suetonius and may have been one of their sources, but certainty is not possible.

The practice of writing history and biography as we know them today is a product of the nineteenth century. Modern historians critically assess their sources, mine them for facts, and report in a detached and objective manner. At least this is their goal and claim. So modern historians came to devalue Plutarch's *Lives* because he had a bias favoring the Romans and because he was willing to sacrifice precise historical truth in order to provide greater illumination of his main character's moral qualities.

Since the middle of the twentieth century, however, the study of ancient historiography has undergone a significant transformation. Modern historians came to understand that the objectives of ancient historians differed from their modern counterparts and that these objectives, though different, were not necessarily inferior. Accordingly, there is now a greater appreciation for what ancient historians, or at least some of them, produced. As a result, studies in Plutarch's literature have thrived during the ensuing decades, to the point that Plutarch has been called "the greatest Greek writer of the post-Classical era."[9] He has been read extensively over the ages, and although opinions of him as a historian and moralist have differed, modern scholars view him as "a thinker whose view of the classical world deserves respect and study."[10]

Plutarch and History

J. L. Moles writes,

> Despite the panoply of modern scholarship (excellent libraries and
> communications, a vast scholarly literature, dictionaries, lexica,
> word-processors and computers), Classical scholars continue to
> make errors; of course their seriousness varies according to the
> competence of the individual but no one is immune from error and
> even the greatest scholars are capable of howlers.[11]

Since modern scholars are far from perfect, it should be of no surprise to
observe Plutarch making factual errors on occasion. These often result
from his less than perfect understanding of the Roman political system
and faulty memory. While we should not make light of the errors, the
importance of their presence should not be exaggerated.[12]

Plutarch gave considerable thought to how biography and history
should be written. Pelling writes, "*On Herodotus' Malice* is sufficient dem-
onstration of that, and the Lamprias Catalogue attests a work on *How We
Are to Judge True History* (Lampr. Cat. 124)."[13] When composing his *Lives*,
Plutarch followed the literary conventions of his day for the biographical
genre. His primary objective was to illuminate the character of the person
who was the subject of that *Life* on which his readers were meant to con-
template. Cato Uticensis was dedicated to philosophy, acted on his principles, could not be persuaded by compliments or bribes, was far more
moderate in his conduct and lifestyle than most of the Roman elite, and
was dedicated to resisting tyranny. He could be too harsh at times, and his
unbending devotion to his principles led to tragic consequences for the
Republic he strove so hard to preserve. Readers of Plutarch's *Cato Minor*
can identify these character traits they are meant to emulate or eschew.

In order to accomplish his objective, Plutarch occasionally bends the
facts to support the portrait he is painting—a portrait that is largely true
though not always entirely so in the details. He does not bend to mislead
his readers but rather to emphasize an important *deeper truth* about his
main character that readers can now grasp more fully and emulate. Like
every biographer of his day, he had no commitment to present the facts
with photographic accuracy or legal precision; nor would his intended
readers have expected that of him or of any biographer.[14] Accordingly,
Plutarch's commitment to the truth in his *Lives* is genuine but qualified.[15]

Like most other historians of his day, Plutarch takes liberties with his sources that would make us uncomfortable in modern biography, adding details or scenes in order to reconstruct what *must have* happened, or to emphasize a quality that may not have been as matured in the main character as he portrays, or to improve the story for the delight of his readers.[16] This mixture of history and conjecture presents a challenge for historians who desire to get behind such "improvements" to the *real* person or event.

In an age when shorthand was in the infant stages of its development (and the invention of recording devices would not occur until a half century prior to the advent of flight), transcriptions of speeches were not possible except on rare occasions when the notes of the speaker were extant.[17] Accordingly, there were literary conventions in place for the reporting of speeches that were almost universally adopted by those writing history and biography.[18] For the most part, the author did not provide a transcript of a speech but rather the gist of what was spoken on that occasion. If the content was unknown, the historian was given the license to creatively reconstruct what must have been said given the occasion and the person. Historians were expected to depict the spirit of the actual message or, at the very minimum, narrate a speech that was likely to have occurred on such an occasion with historical verisimilitude*.[19]

There are limits to the extent Plutarch would go to accomplish his biographical objective. Conjecture is present, but it is "never very extensive."[20] While Plutarch felt free to invent an occasional scene, he did not invent entire episodes.[21] He does not engage in lying by attributing to the subject of his *Life* behavior that would have been foreign to that person.[22] He does not engage in deliberate falsehood.[23] When compared to other biographers of his day, Plutarch is less concerned than some to preserve precise historical truth and more concerned than others.[24] Pelling observes, "On the whole Plutarch seems to belong with the more scrupulous group; and we can certainly see him operating in a similar way to the great historians who survive."[25]

In sum, ancient biographers, including Plutarch, did not always write as we would today because their objectives of writing biography differed somewhat from the objectives of modern biography. They would sacrifice a degree of precise historical truth in order to accomplish their objectives. Accordingly, modern readers must be prepared to recalibrate their expectations when reading ancient biography and history. There are similarities, but there are also important differences.

Dating of the Lives

As stated earlier, most scholars hold that Plutarch wrote his *Lives* between ca. 90 to 120 CE. However, the chronology in which Plutarch penned them is difficult to establish.[26] Since our present research focuses on only nine of Plutarch's fifty extant *Lives*, we may be able to provide a narrowed dating of those *Lives*. Appealing to Plutarch's increasing knowledge, around fifty cross-references to another *Life* within the nine, and cross-fertilization in which Plutarch exploits a story in the *Life* he is writing and that he mentioned in a previously written *Life*, Pelling concludes that *Cicero* and *Lucullus* were the first of the nine to be written, while "*Pompey, Cato Minor, Crassus, Caesar, Brutus*, and *Antony*—stand closely together, and show peculiarities which are best explained in terms of simultaneous preparation."[27] *Sertorius* may have been the last of the nine to be written.[28]

For purposes of this project, I will assume the following dates and order of composition:

100–110 CE: *Lucullus* and *Cicero*[29]

110 CE and perhaps a bit later: *Pompey, Cato Minor, Crassus, Caesar, Brutus*, and *Antony* (or *Antonius*)[30]

115–20 CE: *Sertorius*

Since Plutarch's biographical project took approximately three decades, there is a possibility, even a likelihood, that he discovered more reliable data that he used when writing the set of six than what he had before him a few years earlier when writing *Lucullus* and *Cicero*. This could, though not necessarily, account for some of the differences between the accounts. Accordingly, we are able to detect Plutarch's use of compositional devices with greater confidence when identifying how he tells the same story differently within the set of six *Lives*.

Compositional Devices of Plutarch

In addition to the liberties previously mentioned, classical scholars have recognized a number of compositional devices that are "practically universal in ancient historiography."[31] Although not always identified by the same terms, the following are some of the compositional devices we will observe in Plutarch's *Lives*, at least the nine *Lives* we will be considering.[32]

Transferal: When an author knowingly attributes words or deeds to a person that actually belonged to another person, the author has transferred the words or deeds.

Displacement: When an author knowingly uproots an event from its original context and transplants it in another, the author has displaced the event. Displacement has some similarities with *telescoping*, which is the presentation of an event as having occurred either earlier or more recently than it actually occurred. Plutarch displaces events and even occasionally informs us he has done so. In *Cat. Min.* 25.5, having told the story of Hortensius's request of Cato that he be allowed to marry Cato's wife, Marcia, Plutarch adds, "All this happened later, but as I had mentioned the women of Cato's family it seemed sensible to include it here."[33]

Conflation: When an author combines elements from two or more events or people and narrates them as one, the author has conflated them. Accordingly, some displacement and/or transferal will always occur in the conflation of stories.

Compression: When an author knowingly portrays events over a shorter period of time than the actual time it took for those events to occur, the author has compressed the story.

Spotlighting: When an author focuses attention on a person so that the person's involvement in a scene is clearly described, whereas mention of others who were likewise involved is neglected, the author has shined his literary spotlight on that person. Think of a theatrical performance. During an act in which several are simultaneously on the stage, the lights go out and a spotlight shines on a particular actor. Others are present but are unseen. In literary spotlighting, the author only mentions one of the people present but knows of the others.

Simplification: When an author adapts material by omitting or altering details that may complicate the overall narrative, the author has simplified the story.

Expansion of Narrative Details:[34] A well-written biography would inform, teach, and be beautifully composed. If minor details were unknown, they could be invented to improve the narrative while maintaining historical verisimilitude. In many instances, the added details reflect plausible circumstances. This has been called "creative reconstruction" and "free composition."[35]

Paraphrasing: Plutarch often paraphrased using many of the techniques described in the compositional textbooks. I had initially considered creating a synopsis of Plutarch's parallel pericopes* that we will be examining in the next chapter, which would be arranged in a manner similar to Kurt Aland's *Synopsis of the Four Gospels*.[36] However, I decided against including a synopsis because Plutarch paraphrases so often; plus we do not observe in his *Lives* anything close to the near "copy and paste" method that is very often employed by Matthew and Luke.

Law of Biographical Relevance

Throughout his *Lives*, Plutarch employs the *law of biographical relevance*.[37] A story is told in a manner that is most relevant to the main character. This can take the form of relaying a matter from the perspective of the main character in a particular *Life*, but when telling the same story in a different *Life*, the author shifts to a new perspective suited to the main character of that *Life*.[38] For example, in Plutarch's *Cato Minor*, Caesar is power hungry, deceptive, and conniving, whereas in Plutarch's *Caesar* he is a patient diplomat who does much good for the state and the *demos**.

Biographical relevance also plays out when details of an event pertaining to a person in one *Life* do not appear when the same event is reported in another, since those details possess little significance related to the main character of that *Life*. Plutarch mentions Caesar's assassination in his *Caesar, Brutus, Antony*, and *Cicero*. In *Brutus* and *Antony*, Plutarch devotes far less attention to the assassination itself than in his *Caesar* and then moves along to describe the aftermath, since this is the beginning of the most prominent part of the *Lives* of Brutus and Antony. In *Cicero*, Plutarch merely mentions the assassination and then devotes only a little space to the immediate aftermath, since Cicero's role in it was relatively small.

The Relevance of Plutarch's Lives to Understanding Gospel Differences

I decided to take a focused look at differences in the canonical Gospels. I began by reading them several times in Greek and making a list of the differences I observed. To my surprise, the resulting document grew to more than fifty pages. Of course, most of the differences were insignificant, but I began to notice a few patterns related to the type of differences that surfaced. Since patterns can be seen in virtually anything, I sought to discern whether the patterns I observed were coincidental or intentional. Perhaps the answer could be found by reading other biographies written by rough contemporaries of the evangelists and looking for similar patterns of differences in the way some of them told the same stories. I made a list of all of the extant biographies written within roughly 150 years on each side of the life of Jesus. There are less than one hundred, of which Plutarch is responsible for writing fifty.

Upon concluding my first read of Plutarch's *Lives*, I noticed that nine of them feature characters who had lived at the same time, and most of them had known each another. Sertorius, Lucullus, Cicero, Pompey, Crassus, Caesar, Younger Cato, Brutus, and Antony were all involved in events that ultimately led to the fall of the Roman Republic.

There are only a few examples of literature from the period we are considering in which the author's source or sources are easily discerned.[39] On occasion, the author identifies his sources, while in other cases we can observe very close verbal agreement with another source. However, with only a few exceptions, the source(s) used by an ancient author is difficult to access, if not impossible.[40] Plutarch provides historians with a unique opportunity. Because these nine figures participated in many of the same events, there is extensive overlapping of content in the *Lives* featuring them. For example, Plutarch reports Caesar's assassination in his *Lives* of Caesar, Cicero, Brutus, and Antony. So rather than comparing how four authors told the same story, we are able to compare how the same author told the same story on multiple occasions while often using the same sources.[41] Many differences appear, and when the same type of difference recurs repeatedly, it suggests Plutarch's alterations were intentional and that, in such cases, the differences may have resulted from a compositional device he was employing.

Pelling and Moles have conducted some initial work in this matter.[42] Until now, Pelling's essay has been the most extensive work comparing how Plutarch tells the same story differently, and it provides a very nice springboard into our present research.

3

Parallel Pericopes in Plutarch's Lives

IN THIS CHAPTER we will note differences within thirty pericopes that appear on two or more occasions within the nine *Lives* written by Plutarch. Each pericope takes the following format: References are provided for all instances or portions of a given pericope's location in Plutarch's *Lives*.[1] A short narrative summarizing the pericope follows these references. Because differences exist in each of these accounts, I have either harmonized the accounts in my narratives or preferred the narrative as Plutarch has presented it in one of the accounts. Finally, an analysis and summary of the differences between the accounts is given. The same format will also be used in the next chapter, which examines a number of pericopes appearing in two or more of the canonical Gospels.

Constraints, Cautions, and Clarifications Pertaining to This Research

Before proceeding, I want to articulate six matters for us to keep in mind as we proceed throughout this chapter:

1. We will only be comparing how Plutarch reports the same events in nine of his *Lives*. Of course, one could profitably assess how Plutarch tells a certain story differently than another biographer. For example, Suetonius and Cassius Dio narrate Caesar weeping at the statue of Alexander, but Plutarch says that Caesar wept when he read of Alexander. He also places the event later in Caesar's life.[2]

One may also benefit from comparing how Plutarch alters his source material when his sources are extant. For example, Plutarch speaks of

Brutus's anger toward Cicero after he had aligned himself with Octavian Caesar in *Cic.* 45.2 and, to an even greater extent, *Brut.* 22.3. Because some of Brutus's letters are extant, we can compare what Plutarch reports Brutus wrote with what Brutus actually wrote (Cicero, *Ep. Brut.* 1.106–7). In another example, Cicero was returning to Rome from his quaestorship in Sicily. Cicero himself said he conversed with two strangers and was disappointed to learn they knew nothing of his distinguished service in Sicily (*Planc.* 65). However, Plutarch alters what Cicero reported, saying Cicero's conversation had been with a distinguished man who was one of Cicero's friends (*Cic.* 6.3). Plutarch's altering of his source material is perhaps most noticeable when comparing his *Life of Coriolanus* with the account as told by Dionysius of Halicarnassus. D. A. Russell estimates that Plutarch was so dependent on Dionysius in writing that *Life* that perhaps only 20 percent of it is non-Dionysian material.[3]

Since one must limit the scope of a project, those interested in comparing how Plutarch reports a story differently than other historians of his period or comparing Plutarch's use of his sources may consult commentaries on Plutarch's *Lives*.[4] Thus, it is important to keep in mind that the *narrative* component provided for each pericope is, almost exclusively, a summary of how Plutarch alone told the story. Only rarely will we consider how contemporaries of Plutarch reported the same events.

2. Roman historians and Plutarch specialists will notice numerous occasions where Plutarch employs compositional devices I have not mentioned. For example, there are numerous occasions when Plutarch is possibly or even probably expanding narrative details through inventing.[5] I have not given attention to such instances, since one must almost always go outside of Plutarch to justify such a conclusion. Moreover, identifying instances of invention often involves a greater amount of conjecture, since we cannot be certain Plutarch did not have a written or oral source for the details he provides. Therefore, I will focus attention on those compositional devices for which examples are most clear.

3. I have often devoted little or no attention to narrating details in a pericope that lack overlapping material in another *Life*, since it would contribute little if anything toward the objective of the present research.

4. We must be very careful to avoid the temptation to see a compositional device lurking behind every difference. And once we identify a

difference that probably results from the use of a compositional device, we must recognize that any reason we may propose for why Plutarch or an evangelist utilized it is tentative and provisional. It would be wonderful if we could get into a time machine, return to the past, and interview Plutarch and the evangelists on why the differences are present. Because we cannot, we must be content with making educated guesses and are humbled by the knowledge that some of our speculations are probably incorrect. Accordingly, our objective will be to identify *probable* compositional devices in Plutarch's *Lives* and provide examples in the Gospels where it is possible, plausible, or perhaps probable that the evangelists employed similar devices.

5. Various biographers of the era in which Plutarch and the evangelists wrote varied in their commitment to accuracy. The sole objective of this research is to identify various compositional devices employed by Plutarch that resulted in differences in the pericopes he reported in two or more *Lives* and to examine the possibility that the evangelists employed similar devices. Accordingly, I am making no suggestions that the evangelists were more or less accurate than Plutarch.

6. The thirty-six pericopes related to Plutarch are arranged in a general chronological order. There are no differences in six of the thirty-six. Only the thirty with differences will be afforded attention in the main text. An outline including all thirty-six is provided in appendix 1. The number introducing each pericope corresponds with the number in which it appears in the appendix. Some of the pericopes in Plutarch may be floating stories that were originally known outside a particular context and for which Plutarch included where he thought appropriate, for example, Antioch's faux pas with Cato (#8). Moreover, it is possible to define where a pericope begins and ends in a different manner than I have done in this volume. For example, the conspiracy to assassinate Caesar, the assassination itself, and the aftermath appear in a single pericope (#33), but they could have been divided into several pericopes. For purposes of this volume, it is not so important how the pericopes are defined as it is a convenient way to observe the differences between Plutarch's accounts. Others may certainly define the parameters of a pericope differently. Readers will observe that the differences in the pericopes become more pronounced and abundant as time progresses and the pericopes become more involved.

#3 *Pompey Fights Sertorius (*Sert. *12.1–5; 19.1–6; 21.5–6; 23.1–24.4; 26.1–27.3;* Pomp. *10.1; 17.1–18.1; 19.1–5; 20.1–3;* Luc. *5.1–2; 8.5)*

Narrative

A Roman ex-praetor named Sertorius had lost faith in the ability of the current Roman government to win the civil war being waged against Sulla. Since Sertorius had fought against Sulla, he decided to leave Rome for his assigned province, Nearer Spain, and settled there with three thousand troops in 83 BCE.

Sulla won the war in 82 and issued proscriptions*.[6] Sulla was not satisfied with the voluntary exile of his enemies, since as long as they lived, they posed a threat to his rule. So he dispatched others to hunt down and execute those on his proscription list. Sertorius was the ablest of generals and posed the greatest threat of those who had been proscribed. In time, several Roman generals were sent after Sertorius, and each suffered defeat.

After Sulla's death in 78, Metellus became the leading Roman. He was a great and famed general, though now old. He went to fight Sertorius, who consistently got the best of him in most battles. Roman generals were used to standing toe-to-toe with their enemies on the battlefield. Sertorius, however, used his knowledge of the land to his advantage, and because his armies were greatly outnumbered, he developed fighting strategies involving a degree of agility seldom experienced by Roman generals. Finally, in 77, Pompey was dispatched to Spain to assist Metellus.

When news of Pompey's arrival in Spain made its way to Metellus's province, Further Spain, Metellus's troops were encouraged, and some of the cities who had sided with Sertorius went over to Pompey and Metellus. Another Roman general whose name appeared on the proscription lists was Perpenna; he had also fought against Sulla.[7] When Perpenna's troops heard Pompey's army was near, they forced him to join Sertorius, who had been a far better and more successful general.

Pompey found himself outgeneraled by Sertorius at Lauron. He then experienced some victories when engaging some of Sertorius's generals in battle. Since he was closer to Sertorius at that time than Metellus and desired a quick victory in order to gain all the glory for himself, he challenged Sertorius to a battle at Sucro. Sertorius agreed, knowing it was to his advantage to fight Pompey now rather than wait for Metellus to arrive and join Pompey's forces. The battle commenced and both sides experienced some success. But Sertorius had the better day because his forces routed those directly under Pompey's direction. Pompey was almost killed and narrowly escaped.

The clever Sertorius then cut off supplies for Pompey and Metellus, who were forced to leave the region for a season as a result. In the winter of 75/74, a frustrated Pompey sent word to Rome of his need for funding and threatened to return to Rome with his armies if he did not receive it.

In 74, L. Licinius Lucullus was consul* in Rome and was less afraid of the threat to Rome posed by Sertorius than he was of losing his appointment to conduct a war against Mithridates in Asia Minor.[8] So Lucullus raised the funds for Pompey to continue his conflict with Sertorius. Meanwhile, Sertorius made an agreement with Mithridates, sending him his general Marius and some troops, while in turn Mithridates sent Sertorius ships and money.

The rigors of war took its toll on Sertorius, making him difficult and brutal. Some of his men formed a conspiracy to kill him. And an ambitious Perpenna was all too willing to lead it. In 73, while reclining one evening at a banquet given in his honor, Sertorius was attacked and killed by some of his own men. So in 72 Perpenna led Sertorius's army, but the inferior general was immediately defeated by Pompey, who had him executed.

Analysis

Plutarch relates portions of the above narrative in his *Lives* of *Sertorius*, *Pompey*, and *Lucullus*. Not surprisingly, we find far more detail of these events reported by Plutarch in his *Sertorius* than in his *Pompey* or *Lucullus*, since the events are what made Sertorius famous, whereas they were only a small element in the life of Lucullus and were relevant to only one among the many campaigns of Pompey. The accounts agree with one exception; Plutarch reports Sertorius making a sarcastic statement in which he refers to Pompey as a "boy" and Metellus as an "old woman":

> But as for this boy, if that old woman had not come up, I should have given him a sound beating and sent him back to Rome. (*Sert.* 19.6)

Sertorius disseminated haughty speeches against Pompey and scoffingly said he should have needed but a cane and whip for this boy, were he not in fear of that old woman, meaning Metellus. (*Pomp.* 18.1)

Two differences stand out in this logion. The first concerns wording. Plutarch provides a direct statement in *Sertorius* and an indirect statement in *Pompey*, which also includes details absent from the direct wording. The second difference concerns context. In *Sertorius*, he uttered the statement after the Battle of Sucro. In *Pompey*, he utters the statement upon learning of Pompey's arrival in Spain prior to the Battle of Sucro. Plutarch may have *displaced* the event in one of the *Lives* or the logion may have been free-floating and Plutarch placed it where he desired in each *Life*.

Summary

In this pericope, we observed Plutarch either displacing a logion or placing a free-floating logion in a plausible context.

#6 Pompey and Crassus Serve as Consular Colleagues for the First Time
(Pomp. 22.1–23.2; Crass. 12.1–4)
Narrative

Pompey and Crassus constantly competed against each other for who would become Rome's leading man.[9] After Pompey's military successes over the army of Sertorius and, to a much lesser extent, Spartacus, he stood for consul in 71 BCE, and Crassus asked him to support him in his bid to serve as his consular colleague (i.e., co-consul). Pompey seized the opportunity to do something for Crassus that would make him indebted to him. So he whole-heartedly endorsed Crassus in his bid to serve Rome as his consular colleague. Both won. However, these two chief magistrates disagreed and quarreled so much that they accomplished very little for the Roman state.

As their term in office drew to a close in December 70, Pompey and Crassus were delivering their final speeches to the people when a Roman knight addressed the crowd. He said Jupiter had appeared to him while he slept and ordered him to address the crowd, encouraging them not to allow Pompey and Crassus to leave office until they had reconciled. Pompey was stunned. And when the Roman people expressed approval of the knight's message, Crassus took the initiative, and he and Pompey reconciled.

Analysis

This pericope appears in *Crassus* and *Pompey*. We notice slightly different wording of Crassus's statement of reconciliation toward Pompey:

> Oh, Men! Citizens! I think that I do nothing humiliating [ταπεινὸν, *tapeinon*] or unworthy [ἀνάξιον, *avaxion*] of myself in taking the initiative of good-will and friendship toward Pompey, whom, before he had grown a beard, you proclaimed "Great," and, to whom, before he became a senator, you voted a triumph. (*Crass.* 12.4b)[10]

> I think I do nothing base [ἀγεννὲς, *agennes*] or humble [ταπεινὸν, *tapeinon*], Oh, Citizens, in yielding first to Pompey, whom before he had grown a beard, you thought it worthy to call "Great," and, to whom, before he became a senator, you voted two triumphs. (*Pomp.* 23.2b)[11]

The wording in both accounts differs slightly. Plutarch uses synonyms: In *Crassus*, his action is neither humiliating nor unworthy, whereas it is neither base nor humble in *Pompey*. Moreover, in *Crassus*, a single triumph is mentioned, whereas in *Pompey* there are two. The latter is correct. Pompey had indeed celebrated his second triumph only two days prior to assuming his first consulship at which time he became a senator. There is also one difference between the accounts regarding the name of the knight. In *Crass.* 12.3, the name of the knight is Onotius Aurelius, whereas it is Gaios Aurelios in *Pomp.* 23.1. This difference appears in the Loeb text. In the more recent Teubner text of *Crassus*, Onotius has been emended to Gaios.[12] The emendation is without any manuscript support but was made to agree with the knight's name in *Pomp.* 23.1. It is worth observing that there are a few differences of names in the writings of Josephus. In *J.W.* 2.481, Noarus took care of public affairs in Agrippa's kingdom, whereas it is Varus in *Life* 48–49. In *J.W.* 628, Joazar, Ananias, Simon, and Judas are sent to turn the people against Josephus, whereas it is Jonathan, Ananias, Jozar, and Simon in *Life* 197.[13] It is difficult to know why Josephus changed Judas to Jonathan. That all of the differences pertain to autobiographical data written relatively recently after the events make them even more interesting as well as unique. Therefore, there are occasions when it is possible that something we are unaware of is behind the differences of names. Perhaps the author did not know the name of the person or was uncertain about it, and he thus either crafted one or provided readers with the various options circulating at the time. Perhaps the author was following different sources in each account and preserved the name as it appeared in the source he was following at that moment. Perhaps he was using different names within a person's *tria nomina** (three names: *praenomen, nomen, cognomen*),[14] since we observe other ancient authors doing this elsewhere.[15] Accordingly, caution is required before emending the text without any manuscript support.

Summary

- Plutarch uses synonyms for terms he has used in another *Life*.
- Plutarch is here careful to be more specific pertaining to the accomplishments of Pompey in his *Pompey*.
- If one rejects the textual emendation in the current Teubner text, the different names might be explained by Plutarch's mentioning various names by which the knight was called or that were reported was his name or by a simple slip of Plutarch's memory.

#7 Pompey Replaces Lucullus
(Luc. 21–35; Pomp. 30–31)
Narrative

The Roman general Lucullus enjoyed several important military successes. He defeated Mithridates VI, the Parthian king who challenged Roman expansion. Then in 69 BCE, with an army one-twentieth the size of his enemy's, he defeated the powerful King Tigranes II in battle and captured the city named after him, Tigranocerta.

Although Lucullus had defeated both Mithridates and Tigranes in battle and had come close to winning the war against them, complete victory remained just outside his grasp. Lucullus did nothing to endear himself to his troops, who came to believe the battles he continued to wage resulted from his quest for personal glory and wealth rather than for Roman interests. They resented him for putting their lives at risk and causing them to endure the hardships of war away from their families without sharing the spoils of battle to anywhere near the extent Pompey had enriched his soldiers.

In 66, the tribune Gaius Manilius transferred command of the war from Lucullus to Pompey. Roman aristocrats believed Lucullus was being wronged by this move and feared Pompey's newfound power. Pompey reassigned most Roman soldiers to fall under his generalship, including those serving under the command of Lucullus. So that everyone would be clear on who possessed ultimate authority, Pompey reversed numerous edicts as well as rewards and punishments that had been issued by Lucullus.

Lucullus was disappointed at losing command of the war and infuriated by Pompey's strong-arming. A meeting in Galatia between the two generals was arranged. When it occurred, they praised each other in public for their successes. However, when they met in private, their praises turned to insults. Afterward, Pompey took away all but 1,600 of Lucullus's worst soldiers. To add to Lucullus's frustrations, Pompey completed the fight against Mithridates, and so it was him rather than Lucullus who was granted the coveted triumph. Thus, Pompey again enjoyed the public recognition for a war that had been largely won either by another (e.g., Crassus over Spartacus) or by circumstance not of his own doing (e.g., the murder of Sertorius by one of his own generals, Perperna). Lucullus was given a triumph, but it was not of the magnitude of the one enjoyed by Pompey.

Analysis

This pericope appears in two *Lives*: *Pompey* and *Lucullus*. There are only a few differences between the accounts. These amount to one *Life* reporting minor information not included in the other.

The senate believed Lucullus had been treated wrongly by the people and Pompey, since Pompey enjoyed a triumph for a victory that had been largely achieved by Lucullus (*Luc.* 35.7; *Pomp.* 30.3). *Pomp.* 30.3 adds that the Roman aristocrats were even more concerned with the power given to Pompey.

Pompey took away rewards and punishments Lucullus had issued and reversed his edicts (*Pomp.* 31.1; *Luc.* 36.1). *Luc.* 36.1 adds that Pompey instilled fear in others by having his larger army nearby.

Friends of Lucullus and Pompey brought them together in Galatia. As they approached each other, their lictors carried laurels signifying their victories. Since Pompey had come through a dry region, his laurels were withered, so the lictors of Lucullus gave some of their laurels to the lictors of Pompey (*Luc.* 36.2–3; *Pomp.* 31.2–3). *Luc.* 36.3 says this was interpreted by Pompey's friends as a sign that the victories of Lucullus adorned Pompey, whereas *Pomp.* 31.3 says this was thought to be a sign that Pompey came to take the victory and glory from Lucullus.

Luc. 36.4 says their conference ended with neither yielding, and they left even more estranged. *Pomp.* 31.4 agrees and adds that they abused one another with words and had to be separated by friends with difficulty.

Pomp. 31.5 says Pompey took from Lucullus all but 1,600 soldiers who were of such character as would be useless to Pompey and who were stubborn and hostile toward Lucullus. *Luc.* 36.4 says Pompey led off all of Lucullus's soldiers except 1,600 whom he allowed to remain but who were not very eager to follow Lucullus.

Summary

In this pericope, Plutarch occasionally includes details in one *Life* not included in another.

#8 Antioch's Faux Pas with Cato
(Pomp. *40.1–3;* Cat. Min. *13.1–3)*
Narrative

Pompey's good reputation continued to grow to the point that even his freedman Demetrius was held in very high regard. In 66 BCE when Cato Uticensis approached the city of Antioch to inspect it, he saw a huge throng of people waiting to greet a celebrity. Concluding that the crowd had assembled to pay him honor but never one to flaunt his high standing around others, Cato proceeded on foot and ordered his friends to do likewise. As they approached the city gate, they saw the multitude standing on each side of it. A leader of the welcoming delegates approached them and, to Cato's astonishment, asked where they had left Pompey's freedman Demetrius and when he would come. The citizens of Antioch had prepared a lavish reception for him, while failing to recognize the Roman citizen from a consular family who stood before them. Seeing the irony, Cato's men broke out in laughter. Cato only offered a short comment, speaking of the city in negative terms.

Analysis

In both texts, the pericope is a floating anecdote, not situated in any chronological context. Only a small difference is present and pertains to the way Cato described Antioch. In *Cat. Min.* 13.3, Cato says, "O, cursed [κακοδαίμονος, *kakodaimonos*] city," whereas in *Pomp.* 40.3, he says, "O, miserable [ἀθλίας, *athlias*] city!"

Summary

Plutarch uses a synonym to substitute a term.

#9 *Sayings about Cato*
(Cat. Min. *19.4–5;* Luc. *40.1–3)*
Narrative

There are two texts in the nine *Lives* under consideration that contain anecdotes about Cato's character, specifically, his reputation among the Romans for his integrity and honesty. So highly esteemed was Cato for his honesty that a lawyer once told jurors that a single witness was insufficient for convicting someone, even if that witness were Cato. When relating a story that seemed unbelievable and extraordinary, others would say the story should not be believed even if Cato had told it. Another anecdote describes a man who lectured the senate on its need to be thrifty and self-controlled while he himself lacked these qualities. This elicited a response from someone present who pointed out the man's hypocrisy while attempting to sound like Cato.

Analysis

The third anecdote mentioned above is of interest. *Cat. Min.* 19.4 narrates a dishonest and extravagant man who proposed a decree for the senate to be thrifty and self-controlled. Amnaeus[16] opposed him, saying, "O, Man! Who can endure you, eating as Lucullus, building as Crassus, and pontificating as Cato?" A similar logion appears in *Luc.* 40.3, where Plutarch writes of a young senator who made a long and pompous speech in the senate concerning thriftiness and self-control. Cato rose in resistance saying, "Do you not cease? You have wealth like Crassus, are living like Lucullus and speaking like Cato!" Plutarch then adds that some say these words were spoken, although not by Cato.

That both accounts refer to the same event is suggested by the following: (a) the setting, which is a meeting of the senate; (b) the nature of the proposal being about "thriftiness" and "self-control" (εὐτελεία, *euteleia* and σωφρονισμός, *sōphronismos* in both accounts); and (c) the rebuke of the senator that followed in both is very similar in that it refers to the lavish dinners and life of Lucullus, the real estate and wealth of Crassus, and the public pronouncements of Cato.

The accounts differ in a few minor details. In *Cato Minor*, the rebuke comes from Amnaeus, whereas it is credited to Cato himself in *Lucullus*, although Plutarch adds that some did not attribute it to Cato. Why did Plutarch assign Amnaeus the rebuke in his *Cato Minor* but attribute it to Cato with a disclaimer in his *Lucullus*? If *Lucullus* was written years earlier, as Pelling argues, Plutarch may have since learned that Amnaeus was the rebuker and updated his account accordingly. But Pelling argues that "it is evidently better to make someone else the speaker [in *Cato Minor*]: the point is how others regarded Cato, not how he regarded himself."[17] The opening address of the rebuke to the orator differs: "Do you not cease?" vs. "O, Man! Who can endure you."

The order of the three names differs in the accounts (*Lucullus*: Lucullus, Crassus, Cato; *Cato Minor*: Crassus, Lucullus, Cato).

Summary

- Plutarch may have transferred a statement in *Cato Minor*.
- Plutarch recasts a logion in different terms (paraphrase).
- Plutarch inverts the order of names. This could be intentional. However, it is difficult to know whether Plutarch consulted his earlier *Lucullus* or his notes on which it was based while writing *Cato Minor* or was drawing upon his memory. It is likely that he consulted his notes at minimum and inverted the order in which they appeared in one of his *Lives*.

#10 Lucullus's Triumph
(Luc. 37.1–4; Cat. Min. 29.3–4)
Narrative

In 66 BCE, the command for the war against Mithridates and Tigranes was transferred from Lucullus to Pompey, who celebrated a triumph in 61 for his victory in that war—a war some claimed had been largely won by Lucullus. It was Pompey's third triumph.[18]

Lucullus returned to Rome in 66 and was blocked for the next several years from receiving the honor of a triumph for his contribution to the war. His brother Marcus was in the midst of being prosecuted by Gaius

Memmius for his service to Sulla. After Marcus was acquitted, Memmius redirected his attention against Lucullus, charging him with diverting the spoils of war for his own use and for needlessly protracting war in his region. Memmius's efforts against Lucullus were unsuccessful, thanks to the efforts of several leading citizens, including Cato, who intervened on Lucullus's behalf and persuaded the people not to stand in the way of a triumph, which was granted and celebrated in 63.

Analysis

This pericope appears in *Lucullus* and *Cato Minor*. In *Lucullus*, Plutarch provides information pertaining to Lucullus's brother Marcus and the specific formal charges against Lucullus, which he omits in *Cato Minor*. However, *Cato Minor* provides the motivation behind Memmius's actions, which are absent in *Lucullus*. While both texts inform us that Lucullus celebrated a triumph, only *Lucullus* provides a description of the event. This is to be expected, given its biographical relevance, since Plutarch would have no reason for doing so in *Cato Minor*.

A few differences exist between the two texts. First, *Lucullus* states that Memmius successfully persuaded the people not to grant Lucullus a triumph. *Cato Minor* states that Lucullus *almost* lost his triumph. There is no mention that Memmius's attempts were initially successful in *Cato Minor*. Plutarch compresses the account and focuses on the end result in *Cato Minor*, apparently being more concerned with relaying the part his subject played in the event than in providing full details of an event that belonged primarily in another *Life*.

Second, in *Lucullus* many of the leading and powerful men of the city worked hard in the cause of Lucullus and were able to persuade the Roman people to reverse their decision and grant Lucullus a triumph. In *Cato Minor*, Plutarch shines his literary spotlight on Cato so that readers have a clear impression that he alone stood with Lucullus. In that *Life* we expect Plutarch's description of the event to focus on the part his subject, Cato, played in the event. But in *Lucullus*, the mention of the "leading and powerful men of the city" includes Cato among others.

Summary

· Plutarch provides more details pertaining to the event in *Lucullus* than in *Cato Minor*, since Lucullus is the main character in that *Life*.

- Plutarch compresses the account in *Cato Minor* in order to maintain focus on his main character.
- Plutarch shines his literary spotlight on his main character in *Cato Minor*.
- Plutarch includes an event related to the main character in *Lucullus* that he omits in *Cato Minor*. This is in accordance with the law of biographical relevance.

#11 Catilinarian Conspiracy (Cic. 10.1–22.5; 23.1–3; Caes. 7.1–8.4; Cat. Min. 22.1–24.3; 26.1–4; Crass. 13.2–4; Brut. 5.2–3; Ant. 2.1–2; Luc. 38.3)

Narrative

Sulla's constitutional reforms had notable deficiencies. Combined with widespread corruption in the city, these deficiencies provided fertile ground for a revolution. While Pompey was out of the country fighting Mithridates and Tigranes, some revolutionaries decided to take advantage of his absence and change the Roman government for their own benefit. Leading them was Lucius Sergius Catilina (known in English as Catiline), a man of poor character and a patrician[19] who had served under Sulla.

In order to lead a revolt from a position of power, Catiline stood for consul in 64 BCE but was defeated by Cicero. The following year when he heard that Mithridates had been defeated by Pompey, who was expected to return soon with his army, Catiline knew he had to act quickly. With many of Sulla's ex-soldiers coming to Rome to support him, Catiline sought the consulship a second time in 63 and planned to kill Cicero the day of the consular elections. But Cicero received news of Catiline's plans, postponed the elections, and summoned Catiline before the senate for questioning. Although Catiline defended himself adequately to escape conviction, he ended up losing in his second bid for a consulship in mid-July.[20]

Since the people would not have Catiline lead Rome as a consul, he planned to attack the city and take it by force. As his fellow conspirators began to assemble, Crassus received a number of letters at his house— one for him and the others were to be forwarded to some senators. Since Catiline was his friend, Crassus had been under suspicion. But he joined Marcus Marcellus and Metellus Scipio and went to Cicero's house on the night of 20 October and had him awakened in order to bring the letters to his attention. In the morning (21 October), Cicero called a meeting of the senate and revealed the plot.[21] News then came that Catiline's army in Etruria was under arms. Both consuls, Cicero and Antonius, were authorized to do whatever was necessary to protect the city.

Still in the city, Catiline sent two men to kill Cicero at his home. When word of the plot came to Cicero through a spy, he avoided the would-be assassins and called the senate together on 7 or 8 November.[22] Catiline attended in order to offer a defense, believing many senators would support him. But they instead kept their distance and Cicero ordered him to leave the city. Catiline joined his forces and worked toward gathering support from other cities. The war had begun.

Others interested in overthrowing the city remained in Rome and came together under Lentulus, whose own ambition was for the Roman monarchy. Lentulus and his co-conspirators plotted to kill all of the senators and as many Roman citizens as possible, then burn the city. However, Cicero learned of the plot, secured the written evidence, and called another meeting of the senate on 3 December. The information he provided was confirmed by reports from several others. Lentulus and the other conspirators were then arrested.

That evening Cicero was at his home, pondering his options. If he executed the conspirators, some would accuse him of an excessive use of his power. However, if he did not execute them, they would only rebel again, and others would regard him as being weak. Cicero's wife and friends advised him to put the conspirators to death. When the senate met the next morning, the first senator to speak opined that the conspirators should all be executed. All of the other senators followed until Caesar argued instead that the property of the conspirators should be confiscated and the conspirators should remain under arrest until Catiline had been defeated, and then they would be tried. Caesar's speech persuaded most of the senators, including Cicero. However, Lutatius Catulus opposed Caesar's proposal and was followed by Cato, who argued so passionately against the conspirators that they turned the senate's opinion. The conspirators were condemned and put to death. Moreover, suspicion of siding with the conspirators was so strongly cast on Caesar that he had to be rescued.

During the debate in the senate between Caesar and Cato over what should happen to the conspirators, Caesar received a note from Servilia, the wife of Lucullus and sister of Cato.[23] Cato suspected that Caesar was aligned in some manner with the conspirators and suggested that the note Caesar just received had come from them. So he demanded that Caesar read the note aloud. Caesar merely handed the note to Cato, who read it, only to discover it was a love letter to Caesar from Servilia. Cato returned the note to Caesar saying, "Take it, you drunkard!"[24]

On 5 December, Lentulus and the other conspirators were executed and the city celebrated Cicero as a savior of their country.[25] A few days later, Caesar had to appear before the senate to defend himself against the suspicion now cast upon him. Even at this early stage of his political career, Caesar was so popular among the people that they intimidated the senate into releasing him. Cato feared the populace and, as tribune of the plebs, persuaded the senate to pass a bill increasing the monthly allowance of grain for the poorer citizens.[26]

On 10 December 63, Metellus Nepos and Calpurnius Bestia took their new offices as tribunes of the plebs. Together they unsuccessfully attempted to prevent Cicero from delivering his final oration as consul on 29 December. On 3 January, Metellus introduced a bill providing for the recall of Pompey to Italy to protect Rome from the threat of Catiline's army, which was still to the north. But his measure was strongly opposed by Cato and failed to pass in the assembly.

Analysis

Plutarch tells this story in three *Lives* (*Cicero, Caesar, Cato Minor*), a portion of it in another three (*Crassus, Brutus, Antony*), and merely mentions it in another (*Lucullus*). By dividing our pericope into three sections, we can more easily observe how Plutarch narrated the story differently.

1. On 20 October 63, Crassus went to Cicero and informed him of letters delivered to him with warnings of Catiline's plans for imminent violent action against Rome (*Crass.* 13.3; *Cic.* 15.1–4).

   In *Cic.* 15.1–4, (a) Marcus Crassus, Marcus Marcullus, and Scipio Metellus went to Cicero at night and (b) gave multiple letters to him, although Crassus read to him only the letter addressed to himself. However, in *Crass.* 13.3, (a) only Crassus is mentioned coming to Cicero at night, and (b) only one letter is mentioned: the letter to Crassus. Plutarch shines his literary spotlight on Crassus, but he is aware of the others who had accompanied him and that many letters were delivered to Cicero.

2. The punishment of Lentulus and his co-conspirators was debated in the senate. Most of the senators recommended executing them, until

Caesar delivered a persuasive speech advocating imprisonment until they could receive a proper trial. But Catulus and Cato answered with speeches strongly opposing Caesar's suggestion and won the day. The senate condemned the conspirators, who were then executed the evening of 5 December (*Cat. Min.* 22.2–24.2; 26.1; *Caes.* 7.4–8.2; *Brut.* 5.2–3; *Ant.* 2.1–2; *Cic.* 19.2–22.5. *Cic.* 30.2 merely says Caesar was an object of suspicion in the Catiline affair). Because of the suspicion cast on Caesar, he had to defend himself before the senate and did so successfully.[27]

There are numerous differences in this section. In *Caesar*, Cato and Catulus opposed Caesar's proposal. In *Cicero*, Catulus was the first to oppose Caesar, followed by Cato. However in *Cato Minor*, Plutarch does not mention Catulus, leaving the reader with the impression that Cato alone opposed Caesar, since Plutarch shone his spotlight on him.

In *Caes.* 7.4, Plutarch says it is uncertain whether Caesar was aligned with Catiline. In 7.5, Caesar was compassionate and prudent. And in 8.3, when Caesar defended himself against the suspicion Cato cast on him, Plutarch makes no mention of Caesar appealing to the base element of the populace. Thus, Caesar was presented in a favorable light at this point in *Caesar*. In *Cic.* 20.3–4, however, Plutarch shows there were reasons for suspecting that Caesar was in some way affiliated with the conspirators. And in *Cat. Min.* 22.4–23.2, Plutarch exposes Caesar's secret plans for Rome and has Cato castigate him in front of the senate. To a degree, Plutarch chooses to represent the subject of his *Life* from his subject's viewpoint, rather than taking a consistent position of his own. This is in accordance with the law of biographical relevance.

In *Cicero*, Caesar said the men should not be executed but rather be imprisoned outside of Rome and their property confiscated. In *Cato Minor* and *Caesar*, Caesar said the men should not be executed *without trial* but rather be imprisoned until after the rebellion had been defeated. The confiscation of their property was not mentioned. Plutarch merely provides more information in a *Life* than he does in another.

In *Cic.* 19.1–22.2, the arraignment of Lentulus and Cethegus occurred on one day (3 December), and their punishment was determined and carried out on the next.[28] In *Caes.* 7.3–5, Plutarch describes the summons of Lentulus and Cethegus before the senate and the discussion of their punishment, which resulted in their executions being carried out as though on the same day. Plutarch has compressed the account in *Caesar*.

In *Cat. Min.* 26.1, the cost of the corn dole was 1,250 talents year. In *Caes.* 8.4, it was 7,500,000 drachmas. Since there were approximately 6,000 drachmas per talent, this is the same amount.[29] Plutarch substitutes one monetary measurement for another.

One clearly sees Plutarch's use of the law of biographical relevance in his narrations of the Catilinarian conspiracy. Pelling comments,

> The scale of the treatment naturally varies: the conspiracy was central to Cicero's career, less material to Cato and to Caesar, and barely relevant at all to Crassus. *Cicero* consequently gives the fullest treatment—though even there he dismisses the military side swiftly, for Cicero had no part in it. . . . *Caesar* gives the most detail of Caesar's speech; *Cato* develops the arguments used by Cato. Both ignore the speech of Cicero, to which *Cic.* 21.2–3 had given a full treatment.[30]

3. Metellus proposed to the senate that they recall Pompey and his armies to Rome (*Cic.* 23.1–3; *Cat. Min.* 26.2–4).

In *Cic.* 23.1–3, Metellus and Bestia became tribunes and, with Caesar's support, introduced a law to recall Pompey and his army in order to put down Cicero's political power. Cato opposed the tribunes and extolled the office of Cicero to the people, resulting in their voting him the greatest honors.

In *Cat. Min.* 26.2–4, Metellus became tribune and held tumultuous assemblies. He proposed a law to recall Pompey and his army to Italy in order to preserve Rome because Catiline imperiled it. Metellus's actual motive was to hand over the supreme power to Pompey. Cato replied with praise of Metellus and provided advice with an uncharacteristically restrained passion. But when Metellus became emboldened and threatened to carry his proposal through in spite of the senate, Cato altered his approach and gave a vehement speech saying that while he lived Pompey would not enter the city with his army. *Cato Minor* mentioned nothing about Cato laboring to rescue and honor Cicero. Both accounts report the same event, since (a) Metellus had just become tribune in December 63, and (b) he introduced a law to recall Pompey and his army to Rome. However, a number of differences appear:

In *Cato Minor*, Metellus introduced the law, whereas in *Cicero* it is Metellus and Bestia. Caesar is likewise involved. Greater detail is provided in *Cicero* to show the extent of opposition against the main character of that *Life*.

In *Cato Minor*, the proposal to recall Pompey was to preserve Rome from the threat of Catiline, whereas in *Cicero* its aim was to put down Cicero's political power.[31]

In *Cato Minor*, Cato's opposing speech concerned Pompey returning with his army to Rome, whereas in *Cicero*, Cato extolled Cicero, and this led to honors being conferred on him. Neither mentions the reason provided in the other. The emphasis in *Cato Minor* and in *Cicero* is very different. Plutarch is consistent in his presentations of the character qualities of his main characters. In *Cato Minor*, Cato is always more interested in thwarting attempts to place too much power in the hands of Pompey, Crassus, and Caesar than in his friendships, while Cicero's accomplishments are remembered in spite of the opposition he faced in *Cicero*. This is in accordance with the law of biographical relevance.

Summary

- In *Crassus* and *Cato Minor*, Plutarch shines his literary spotlight on his main characters.
- In *Cicero*, *Caesar*, and *Cato Minor*, Plutarch employs the law of biographical relevance by representing the main character of each *Life* from that character's viewpoint, rather than taking a consistent position of his own.
- Plutarch employs compression in *Caesar*.
- Plutarch describes monetary values in different manners.

#12 Cicero Defends Murena
(Cic. 35.3; Cat. Min. 21.5)
Narrative

In 63 BCE, Murena canvassed for a consulship and won. In November he was prosecuted for election bribery but was successfully defended by Cicero.

Analysis

In *Cic.* 35.3, Cicero was so concerned to outdo the opposing advocate Hortensius that he spent the entire night before the trial in preparation. At the trial, Cicero was not as impressive as usual because of his excessive anxiety and lack of sleep. However, Plutarch paints a different picture in *Cat. Min.* 21.5. There he writes that Cicero's strategy paid off and he had the jurors laughing. And there is not even a hint that Cicero's performance was not up to par, nor is there mention of his concern to outperform Hortensius. This omission is Plutarch's observance of the law of biographical relevance, since he is not concerned with Cicero's oratory ambitions in *Cat. Min.*

Summary

In *Cicero*, Plutarch focuses on a weakness in the main subject's character in the interest of its biographical relevance.

#13 Pompey Attempts to Form a Marriage Alliance with Cato (Pomp. 44.1–5; Cat. Min. 30.2–5; 45.1)
Narrative

In 62 BCE Pompey returned to Rome as victor in his war with Mithridates and Tigranes. While waiting outside the city to celebrate his triumph, he desired to support Piso's candidacy for the consulship of 61, but he was prohibited from entering the city until after his triumph. So he requested that the senate postpone the midsummer elections until after his triumph. Cato objected and persuaded the senate to reject Pompey's request. Pompey then attempted to ally himself with Cato by arranging to marry one of Cato's nieces and have one of his sons marry the other niece. Knowing Pompey's motives behind the proposal, Cato declined, to the displeasure of his wife and sister(s). A year later, Pompey offered money for votes to secure the election of Lucius Afranius to the consulship of 60. Afranius won the office, but Pompey gained a bad reputation for his shady acts. Cato's wife and sister(s) told Cato his assessment of Pompey was correct.

Analysis

This pericope appears in two *Lives*, *Cato Minor* and *Pompey*, with three differences. In both accounts, Pompey's motive behind his proposal to Cato was to foster friendship with him. In *Cat. Min.* 30.2, Pompey's motive behind the friendship was to make Cato a friend so he would not be a stumbling block to his plans. In *Pomp.* 44.2, Pompey's main motive behind his proposal was out of his admiration of Cato's integrity, although his desire to remove Cato so he would no longer be a hindrance to his goals was ever present. Given the law of biographical relevance, we might expect the mention of Cato's integrity to appear in *Cato Minor* rather than *Pompey*.

In *Cat. Min.* 30.3–4, Cato's wife and sisters (plural) were displeased when he rejected Pompey's proposal. In *Pomp.* 44.3, it was Cato's wife and sister (one). Perhaps this is a change of inflection from singular to plural or vice versa.

In *Cat. Min.* 30.2 and *Pomp.* 44.2, Pompey's proposal involved Cato's nieces. However, Pompey's proposal concerned Cato's daughter in *Cat. Min.* 45.1. In *Cat. Min.* 30.3, Plutarch mentions the existence of conflicting reports that Pompey's proposal involved Cato's daughters rather than his nieces.

Summary

Plutarch possibly employs a change of inflection from singular to plural or vice versa.

#15 *Pompey Was Sick and Refused to Get a Thrush from Lucullus* (Pomp. 2.5–6; Luc. 40.2)
Narrative

The spoils of war had made Lucullus very wealthy, and he was known for his extravagant living. On one occasion when Pompey was sick, his physician prescribed that he eat a thrush. Because it was summer and thrushes were out of season, Pompey's servants could not obtain this delicacy. Someone suggested that he request one from Lucullus, who kept these birds in captivity year round. Pompey answered, "So if Lucullus did not live a life of extravagance, Pompey would not live?" He then asked his servants to prepare a meal for him comprised of readily accessible ingredients.

Assessment

Pompey's statement concerning Lucullus's thrush in both accounts has very similar wording, although there is one difference. In *Lucullus*, Pompey's statement begins with "So" (οὐκοῦν, *oukoun*), whereas in *Pompey*, it is "then" (εἶτα, *eita*).[32] It is difficult to know whether Plutarch is altering his own account by substituting another term or is recalling the gist of the logion from memory and used a different term.

Summary

There are no clear compositional devices in view.

#16 Caesar, Pompey, and Crassus Form a Coalition; Caesar's First Consulship (Caes. 13.1–14.9; 15.3; Pomp. 46.2–4; 47.1–48.7; 67.6; Crass. 14.1–3; Cat. Min. 31.1–35.5; Luc. 42.4–6; 43.1; Cic. 26.3)
Narrative

Lucullus had largely retired from politics and was enjoying a life of luxury from the rewards of his military victories. Because Pompey had replaced him as commander at the end of the Mithridatic War, tensions remained between them in 60 BCE.

Lucullus seized an opportunity for a little revenge. Just as Pompey had nullified Lucullus's war-time rulings, Lucullus, with the assistance of Cato, worked in the Forum* and successfully nullified Pompey's rulings that had replaced his. Pompey then proposed a generous distribution of land to his soldiers. But that, too, was successfully blocked by Lucullus and Cato. Now significantly weakened, Pompey aligned himself with a bold and immoral popular leader named P. Clodius Pulcher and later with Caesar.

During the same year, Caesar returned to Italy from governing Further Spain and awaited his triumph. He desired to run for consul but faced a hurdle with which Pompey was familiar.[33] Candidates for office were required to be present in the city, and those waiting to celebrate a triumph had to remain outside it. Caesar requested permission from the senate to stand for the consulship in absentia. But Cato persuaded the senate to reject the request. Forced to choose between glory and political power, Caesar pursued the latter and entered Rome.

Caesar recognized an opportunity to assist him in being elected consul. Pompey was in need of a powerful friend and was at odds with Crassus, who competed with him for power and prestige. So Caesar proposed to both that the three unite and fight their opposition, namely Cicero, Cato, and Catulus. Moreover, Caesar promised to get for them what they desired if they would assist him in his bid for consul. Pompey and Crassus agreed, the alliance was formed, and Caesar was elected consul for 59.[34]

Upon taking office on 1 January 59, Caesar immediately sought to endear himself to the lower classes by proposing to give them land. He also revived Pompey's previous proposals that had been blocked by Lucullus and Cato. These proposals were opposed by Caesar's consular colleague, Bibulus, and by Cato, Bibulus's father-in-law. So Caesar went before the people, with Pompey and Crassus standing on either side, and asked them whether they approved of his proposed laws. After Pompey and Crassus voiced their approval, Caesar asked them whether, if the laws were adopted, they would defend them against any who might oppose them by force. Both said they would.

Before Caesar's proposed laws were put to a vote, he formed a marriage alliance with Pompey by betrothing his daughter Julia to him. Shortly after the wedding in spring 59, Pompey filled the Forum with soldiers. A crowd attacked Bibulus as he went into the Forum, broke the fasces of his lictors, and wounded some of those with him.[35] Someone also threw a basket full of dung on his head. Seeing the violence done to a consul, Cato, Lucullus, and all of the senators fled from the Forum.

With none present to oppose Caesar's proposed laws, they were passed with an added clause requiring each senator to take an oath that he would uphold the new laws and imposing heavy penalties on any senator who refused to take the oath. Caesar was awarded both Cisalpine and Transalpine Gaul and Illyricum as his consular province with four legions for five years instead of the usual one year.

Encouraged by his successes obtained with the support of Pompey and Crassus, Caesar proposed a second agrarian law in late April, distributing more land to the poor. As to be expected, Cato objected, and Caesar had him led off to prison. Cato surprised Caesar by going peacefully, and Caesar observed that many of the most influential men were displeased at this treatment while many of the populace present were troubled and followed Cato in silence as he was led off. So Caesar secretly ordered a tribune to have Cato released.

When Bibulus later realized that his continuous actions to block Caesar's laws were ineffective and exposed him to grave danger, he locked himself in his house throughout the remaining eight months of his consulship and from there issued proclamations against Caesar and Pompey.

Analysis

This pericope appears in six of Plutarch's *Lives*. He employs a number of compositional devices, and this results in numerous differences in the narratives. In *Luc.* 42.5–6, Lucullus nullified [A] the dispositions Pompey made after his conquest of the kings and [B] Pompey's proposal for generous distribution of lands to his soldiers. Cato assisted with [B] in *Lucullus*. But *Cat. Min.* 31.1–2 reports Cato assisted with both [A] and [B]. This difference might have resulted from Plutarch applying the law of biographical relevance so he could focus his attention on the actions of his main character in each *Life*.

In *Luc.* 42.5–6, Pompey found refuge in an alliance with Caesar and Crassus. However, no mention is made of Caesar becoming consul as we observed in *Pompey, Caesar, Cato Minor*, and *Crassus*. There is no mention of Pompey going to Clodius as in *Cat. Min.* 31.2. This is consistent with biographical relevance.

In *Cat. Min.* 31.4, Caesar is painted as attaching himself to Pompey rather than the other way around in *Luc.* 42.6. And there is no mention made of Crassus in the agreement in *Cato Minor*.

In *Luc.* 42.6b, when Pompey filled the Forum with soldiers and got his measures ratified, there is no mention that he did this through Caesar's consulship as in *Pompey* and *Caesar*. Caesar and Crassus are only support. Plutarch simplifies in *Lucullus*, since Pompey alone is Lucullus's nemesis in that *Life*.

The extent to which Lucullus was living a life of luxury and pleasure, only briefly mentioned in *Pomp.* 46.3, is described in detail in *Luc.* 39.2–42.4 in accordance with its biographical relevance.

In *Cat. Min.* 31.1–33.3, Plutarch gives treatment to the two agrarian laws that were presented on different occasions (January and late April 59).[36] However, in *Pomp.* 47.3–48.3 and *Caes.* 14.1–7, Plutarch conflates the two occasions and presents the proposal and ratification of the laws as though on one occasion. And in *Pompey*, Plutarch conflates a third event—the proposal and ratification of the law extending Caesar's provincial command for five years.

In *Caes.* 14.1–3, Caesar brought Crassus and Pompey before the people to have them declare their support for his proposed laws. In *Pomp.* 47.4–5, the participation of Crassus was omitted. This may be explained by Plutarch shining a spotlight on the main character of that *Life*. But it is worth observing that Plutarch likewise omitted Crassus's participation in *Cat. Min.* 31.4, where he merely states that Caesar would introduce the laws and Pompey would support them. Although Plutarch elsewhere says Pompey and Crassus were the two greatest Romans of the day (*Caes.* 13.2), he certainly views Pompey as being of far greater value (and threat) to

Caesar, since it was with Pompey that Caesar formed a marriage alliance by betrothing his daughter Julia to him (*Caes.* 14.4; *Pomp.* 47.5–6; *Cat. Min.* 31.4).

In *Pomp.* 47.3–48.3 and *Caes.* 14.1–6, at least the first agrarian law was proposed prior to Caesar giving his daughter Julia in marriage to Pompey. However, in *Cat. Min.* 31.4–32.3, Pompey's marriage to Julia precedes the introduction of the agrarian laws. Plutarch displaces the proposal of the first agrarian law in *Cato Minor* to simplify.[37]

Caesar and Pompey used violence to clear the Forum of those opposing them. *Pomp.* 48.1 suggests Bibulus was accompanied by Lucullus and Cato when they were attacked as they entered the Forum. In *Cat. Min.* 32.2, Bibulus was attacked as he entered the Forum where he would meet Lucullus and Cato, and the violence caused the senators to flee from the Forum at a run, while Cato left last at a walk.

Only in *Cat. Min.* 32.3–6 does Plutarch report that when Caesar's agrarian law was passed, a provision was included requiring every senator to take an oath to uphold the law and imposing heavy penalties on any senator who refused to take this oath. For some time, Cato refused to take the oath; then he did so at the pleading of his wife and daughters but especially at that of Cicero. Plutarch includes this element in *Cato Minor* given its biographical relevance.

Plutarch gives differing accounts of how Cato was led off to prison on Caesar's order. In *Caes.* 14.7, Plutarch gives the impression that Cato was arrested and taken away for objecting to the first agrarian law in January. He does not mention the second agrarian law proposed in April. However, in *Cat. Min.* 33.1–2, Cato's arrest occurred in April after he voiced his objections when Caesar introduced his second agrarian law. Since other ancient authors who report these events also differ among themselves about the occasion on which Cato was arrested, Plutarch either displaced Cato's arrest in one of the accounts or took a floating anecdote and set it within a plausible context.[38] Moreover, in *Cat. Min.* 33.1–2, while Cato was escorted to prison, he continued to speak out against the law and urged the people to stop these things. However in *Caes.* 14.7, Cato was led off without uttering a sound. Pelling observes that Plutarch often invents "dramatic silence" for effect and has, accordingly, changed Cato's response to silence in *Caesar* as well as portrayed a supportive crowd following him in silence (see e.g., *Caes.* 60.2; 67.4; *Cic.* 22.1).[39]

In *Crassus*, Plutarch does not relate these events with the level of detail we find in *Pompey, Cato Minor,* and *Caesar*. Plutarch mentions that troops

were voted to Caesar for his provincial command, but he does not spec-
ify how many (four legions in the other *Lives*). He neglects to mention
Illyricum as part of the territory awarded Caesar and does not include the
term of five years during which Caesar was to have them. It is possible that
Crassus's role in these events was far less than Pompey's, and Plutarch
omits them in *Crassus* given their lack of biographical relevance.

Summary

- Plutarch includes and omits according to biographical relevance in
  Lucullus, *Cato Minor*, and *Crassus* (possibly).
- Plutarch simplifies in *Lucullus* and *Cato Minor*.
- Plutarch conflates in *Pompey* and *Caesar*.
- Plutarch shines a literary spotlight in *Pompey* and possibly in *Cato Minor*.
- In either *Caesar* and/or *Cato Minor*, Plutarch displaces an event, per-
  haps for simplification, or sets a floating anecdote in a plausible context.
- Plutarch occasionally narrates events with slightly differing details.
  This may be the result of a faulty memory or only the gist of the events
  rather than that precise details were known and Plutarch narrated the
  gist differently.

#17 The Tribune P. Clodius Pulcher Abuses Cicero, Cato, and Pompey (Cic. 30.1–33.2; Cat. Min. 31.2; 32.5; 33.3–4; 34.1–39.4; Caes. 14.9; Pomp. 46.4–7; 48.5–7; Brut. 3.1–2)
Narrative

In 59 BCE, Caesar was consul, thanks to the alliance formed the previous
year with Pompey and Crassus. The three pushed to have a ruthless patrician named Clodius transferred to plebian status by lending their aid to
an adoption. This permitted Clodius to stand for tribune of the plebs later
that year.[40] He won, and on 10 December 59, Clodius assumed the office
and began passing laws that pleased the people.

Clodius turned on Cato and Cicero, since they opposed the plans of
the alliance between Caesar, Pompey, and Crassus. He began by accusing Cicero of executing Romans without trial, referring to the Catilinarian
conspirators, and forced Cato to accept both an administrative command
in Cyprus and a mission in Byzantium. With Cato about to leave Rome,

he would be unable to support Cicero, allowing Clodius to turn his full attention toward his efforts against Cicero. Cicero asked for advice from Cato and others, who urged him to refrain from violence, some adding he might once again become savior of Rome, rescuing her from Clodius just as he had in the matter of the Catilinarian conspiracy.

Because Cicero had used his influence to assist Pompey on many occasions, he turned to him for assistance against Clodius. However, Caesar had recently given his daughter Julia in marriage to Pompey, who was very much enjoying his new wife. So Caesar asked Pompey to refrain from assisting Cicero. When Cicero sent others to Pompey to request assistance, Pompey refused to see them. And when Cicero himself sought an interview with Pompey, Pompey shamefully slipped away. Without any support, Cicero was forced to leave the city, probably on 20 March. Shortly thereafter, Clodius banished him from Italy.[41]

Emboldened by his successes and his popularity with the people, Clodius then turned on Pompey. He attempted to repeal some of the arrangements Pompey had made after his conquests in the Third Mithridatic War, took away Pompey's prisoner from that war, the son of King Tigranes, and put a number of Pompey's friends on trial.

While this was occurring in Rome, Cato was in Rhodes and sent Canidius to Cyprus in order to persuade King Ptolemy to yield his kingdom to the Romans. But Ptolemy committed suicide by poisoning himself, and Canidius was left in charge of Ptolemy's wealth. Although Cato initially trusted Canidius with the task, he soon suspected he may have been corrupted by Ptolemy's enormous wealth. So Cato asked his nephew Brutus to sail quickly to Cyprus and take part in the confiscation of Ptolemy's estate. Cato then sailed to Byzantium where he reconciled the exiles. He then sailed to Cyprus where, with the assistance of Brutus, he successfully liquidated Ptolemy's estate. In May or June 56, Cato returned to Rome with great wealth for deposit in the public treasury and was offered great honors.

Analysis

This pericope appears in its entirety or in part in five of Plutarch's *Lives*. We observe Plutarch's use of a few compositional devices that result in differences between the narratives. In *Pomp.* 46.5, Clodius requested Pompey to refrain from assisting Cicero, whereas in *Cic.* 30.4 and 31.3 it was Caesar who made the request. This need not be a contradiction, since both Caesar and Clodius desired to have Cicero removed from Rome and both may have made requests of Pompey on the matter. There are additional plausible solutions. Caesar may have communicated his wishes to Pompey via the tribune Clodius (transferal via substitution). It is also possible that Plutarch transferred the request from Caesar to Clodius in *Pompey*, since Clodius was the villain at that point in that *Life* and he would very soon turn on Pompey as well. Another possibility is Plutarch, since writing *Cicero*, may have discovered a more reliable report that attributed the request to Clodius and corrected it in *Pompey*.

Cicero sought counsel from his friends while Clodius was attempting to have him banished. In *Cic.* 31.1–4, the consul Piso advised Cicero to yield to the change in power and not to resist Clodius with force, for in doing so, Cicero would spare Rome from violence and save her once again. However in *Cat. Min.* 35.1, it was Cato who counseled Cicero in this manner. Perhaps both offered similar counsel. Perhaps Plutarch corrected what he believed to have been an error in *Cicero*. Perhaps Plutarch transferred the counsel to Cato, since that would have been consistent with Cato's character. It is difficult to know.

There is a difference pertaining to whom Clodius attacked first: Pompey or Cicero. In *Pomp.* 46.4–5, Plutarch reports that Clodius "even went so far as to ask a reward for his services from Pompey [i.e., for Pompey to betray Cicero], as if he were helping [Pompey] instead of disgracing him." In *Cic.* 33.1–2, Plutarch gives the reader the impression that only after Clodius had succeeded in banishing Cicero did he turn his attention against Pompey.

There is no mention of Clodius's ill-treatment of Pompey in *Cato Minor*, presumably because it has little biographical relevance in that *Life*.

Although not observed by comparing Plutarch's works, in *Brutus* he omits a story mentioned by Cicero (Cic. *Att.* 5.21) of Brutus exerting his political influence while in Cyprus to allow a loan to be made to Cyprus at a crippling interest rate of 48 percent. It would have complicated his portrait of the fair and highly principled Brutus.[42] Pelling mentions that "Plutarch discreetly avoids mentioning that Brutus discarded his first wife, Claudia (daughter of Appius Claudius Caecus, consul 54), in order to marry Porcia."[43] Plutarch has simplified his portrait of Brutus.

Summary

· Although certainty is not possible, Plutarch may transfer action and/or counsel from one person to another in *Pompey* and *Cato Minor*.

- Plutarch presents narrative chronologies in *Cicero* and *Pompey* that are in conflict.
- Plutarch omits elements of the pericope in *Cato Minor*, since it bore little biographical relevance.

#18 Pompey Returns Cicero from Banishment; Cicero Reconciles Pompey to the Senate; Cicero Wants to Nullify Deeds of Clodius, but Cato Objects (Pomp. 49.1–7; Cat. Min. 40.1–2; Cic. 33.1–34.2)

Narrative

There is overlap between this pericope and the previous one. In 58 BCE, Caesar was in Gaul and Cicero was banished from Italy. Clodius flexed his new political muscle as tribune of the plebs and began to challenge Pompey's power by vilifying him. But Pompey found no support from the senators, who were pleased to see him experiencing difficulty after his betrayal of Cicero. In fact, Pompey was bullied so much by Clodius that he feared for his safety and retreated to his home, where he stayed for the remainder of the year. There is irony in this, since in the previous year the actions of Pompey, Caesar, and Crassus had forced the consul Bibulus to remain confined to his home for the remainder of the year out of fear for his safety. The bully is now the one bullied.

The following year (57), Clodius was no longer tribune, and violent crime in Rome was increasing. Pompey began to petition the people and the senate to recall Cicero from banishment. Clodius objected, but Pompey and his supporters drove Clodius from the Forum and summoned the people for a vote on the matter of Cicero. A law was passed to recall Cicero on 4 August, and he entered Rome on 4 September. During the spring of the following year (56), Cicero seized and destroyed Clodius's records concerning his acts as tribune, claiming they were illegal because Clodius was illegally transferred from patrician status to plebian. Having recently returned from his mission in Cyprus, Cato spoke against Cicero's actions, and their disagreement led to a cooling of their friendship.

Analysis

This pericope appears in three *Lives*. There are three differences that appear in the accounts in *Pompey* and *Cicero*. In *Cic.* 33.1–5, Pompey's actions to recall Cicero from banishment occurred in three stages: (1) Pompey and Cicero's friends attempted to have Cicero returned, but Clodius opposed them. (2) After Clodius's time in office expired, violence occurred in the Forum on 23 January 57 where Cicero's brother (among others) was injured and believed to have been killed.[44] (3) In response, one of the tribunes prosecuted Clodius for violence, and many people began changing their minds and came from the cities surrounding Rome to join Pompey. With these, Pompey drove Clodius from the Forum and summoned the people for a vote, which occurred on 4 August 57.[45] However, when Plutarch tells the same story in *Pomp.* 49.1–4, he compresses and conflates the action into one stage: Pompey escorted Cicero's brother with the people into the Forum, where some were wounded, others killed, and Clodius was defeated.

In *Pomp.* 49.3, Pompey followed the advice of others to work toward having Cicero returned from banishment. In *Cic.* 33.2, Pompey blames himself for betraying Cicero and works toward having him returned from banishment.

When Cicero and Cato argued over Cicero's seizure and destruction of Clodius's tribunal records, Plutarch reports in *Cicero* that a crowd of supporters accompanied Cicero to seize the tablets and destroy them.[46] In *Cato Minor*, however, Plutarch shines his literary spotlight on Cicero, mentioning only him as the one seizing the tablets.

Also worth observing is that Cato's arguments against Cicero are more fully explained in *Cato Minor*, since that detail has greater biographical relevance in that *Life*.

Summary

- Plutarch compresses and conflates in *Pompey*.
- Plutarch provides slightly different motivations for Pompey's actions.
- Plutarch shines a literary spotlight on his main character in *Cato Minor*.

#19 Luca Meeting; Carrying Out the Agreement (Caes. *21.1–4;* Pomp. *51.1–52.3;* Crass. *14.5–15.5;* Cat. Min. *41.1–43.6)*
Narrative

In the winter of 57–56 BCE, Caesar had successfully put down multiple rebellions throughout his province and had crossed the Alps to spend the winter in Cisalpine Gaul. Many went to meet him to request his assistance in getting them elected to various offices. By giving them money for their campaigns, Caesar forged friendships he would call upon in the future.

Caesar's most important meeting that year took place in April with Pompey and Crassus in Luca. They renewed the alliance they had previously formed in 60. This time, however, it was for the three of them to gain control over Rome and change its constitution.[47] The plans were for Pompey and Crassus, consular colleagues in 70, to sue for a joint consulship in 55 and for Caesar to provide assistance in assuring that they succeeded. In return, Pompey and Crassus would push to get funding for the new legions Caesar had put together in Gaul and introduce a law extending Caesar's provincial command in Gaul for another five years.

In late May to early June, additional funding for Caesar was approved. But word of the alliance leaked. The consul Marcellinus and Cato's brother-in-law Domitius rose in the senate and asked Pompey and Crassus if they intended to stand for the consulships. Pompey answered with arrogance that he may or may not. Seeing that his answer had provoked others, Crassus answered with political astuteness, saying he would abstain from pursuing a consulship unless he deemed it to be in the best interest of Rome.

The consular elections of 56 were delayed due to acute political unrest in Rome. Pompey and Crassus then announced they would seek consulships. Caesar called upon his network of friendships, and in the winter of 56 he sent many of his soldiers into the city to cast their votes for Pompey and Crassus. Intimidated by the political stature of those two candidates, others desirous of standing for the consulship desisted. But Cato encouraged Domitius to stand for the consulship, saying the liberty of Rome was now at stake. Others joined Cato in his support for Domitius. However, when the election was finally held in January 55, Pompey and Crassus sent armed thugs to attack Domitius, Cato, and their supporters while on their way to the Forum, killing the torch bearer and wounding others, including Cato. In fear, Domitius fled to his home. With none now left to oppose Pompey and Crassus, both were elected consuls for 55.

In order to be in a position to oppose the plans of the new consuls, Cato pursued a praetorship but was thwarted by the underhanded tactics of Pompey and Crassus. The tribune Trebonius proposed a law assigning provinces to Pompey and Crassus for five years rather than the typical one year.[48] Cato objected so strongly that Trebonius had him taken away to prison. As he was led off, a crowd followed him, listening to his pleas that the proposed law should not be ratified. When Trebonius observed the people's support for Cato, he became alarmed and released him. When it came time to ratify the law, Pompey filled the Forum with armed men who drove out Cato and attacked those who openly opposed the bill. The law was passed, and Pompey received both Spains (i.e., Nearer and Further Spain) and Northern Africa as his consular provinces while Crassus was given Syria and Egypt.

Shortly thereafter, Trebonius passed a law that extended Caesar's command in Gaul for another five years. In reaction, Cato warned Pompey that he was empowering Caesar to an extent he would come to regret.

Analysis

This pericope appears in four *Lives*, all of which were written around the same time (*Caesar, Pompey, Crassus*, and *Cato Minor*). Plutarch employs a number of compositional devices when retelling the story.

There are occasions where Plutarch chooses to omit portions of the story, in part or whole, in one or more of his *Lives*. That Caesar was planning all along to thwart Pompey's plans for Rome is mentioned in *Pomp.* 51.1–2 but not in *Caesar*. In *Pomp.* 52.3, there is no mention of Pompey filling the Forum with armed men who drive Cato out and attack those in opposition in order to have the proposed laws concerning consular provinces ratified. In *Pomp.* 52.3, Crassus was awarded Syria as his consular province and was given the campaign against the Parthians, while Pompey was awarded all of Libya (i.e., Northern Africa), both Nearer and Further Spain, and four legions. In *Cat. Min.* 43.1, Pompey was awarded both Spains and Libya, while Crassus received Syria and Egypt, and both could wage war on whomever they wished. In *Crass.*15.5, Syria was awarded to Crassus and both Spains to Pompey—Egypt and Northern Africa are not mentioned. The legions are mentioned only in *Pomp.* 52.3b. Only in *Crassus* is Libya omitted when referring to Pompey's consular provinces while only in *Cato Minor* is Egypt mentioned as one of the consular provinces awarded to Crassus. Since *Pompey, Crassus*, and *Cato Minor* were probably written simultaneously, the differences most likely result from either an error on the part of Plutarch or his lack of concern to report every detail in each account.

Plutarch shines his literary spotlight on occasion. In *Crass.* 15.1, Marcellinus and Domitius ask Pompey and Crassus whether they intend to be candidates for the consulship. In *Pomp.* 51.5, only Marcellinus is mentioned. Plutarch employs spotlighting, perhaps because Marcellinus was consul that year. In *Cat. Min.* 43.1–6, Trebonius introduced the first law, and it is not stated who brought the second law to a vote. In *Pomp.* 52.3, Pompey and Crassus had both laws passed by means of Trebonius. In *Crass.* 15.5, Pompey and Crassus had the laws passed with no mention of Trebonius. Thus, in *Crassus*, Plutarch shines his spotlight on Pompey and Crassus, since they were ultimately responsible for the passing of the laws. On occasion, Plutarch loosely paraphrases. In *Crass.* 15.3, the supporters of Cato and Domitius asked, "Why should Pompey and Crassus desire a second consulship? And why serving again together? Why not with others? Are there not many other men among us who are worthy of co-ruling with Pompey or Crassus?" In *Cat. Min.* 41.3, their discussion is summarized, saying that the consular power must not become haughty and heavy as a result of Pompey and Crassus serving as consular colleagues. One could serve, but not both. The opposition of some to Pompey and Crassus becoming consular colleagues is stated in *Crassus* and *Cato Minor*, although the reasons they provided for their opposition differ slightly. In *Cat. Min.* 43.1–6, Trebonius the tribune proposed laws awarding the consular provinces for five years. Cato opposed these laws, although unsuccessfully. Afterward, Trebonius proposed another law concerning Caesar's provinces and army. At this time, Cato only shared his warnings with Pompey. However, in *Pompey* 52.3 and *Crass.* 15.5, the laws concerning the consular provinces and Caesar's second term as proconsul of Gaul are mentioned as though they had been proposed and ratified together. In fact, in *Crass.* 15.5, the law extending Caesar's province is placed with the awarding of consular provinces, giving the impression these occurred at the same time.[49] Accordingly, in *Pompey* and *Crassus*, Plutarch conflates the two occasions during which the laws were ratified into one.

Inclusion of details appears only in *Cato Minor* on three occasions due to their biographical relevance. First, when Trebonius introduced the laws for assigning consular provinces for five years, Cato so strenuously objected that Trebonius had him led off to jail, but then released him. Second, only in *Cat. Min.* 43.1–4 is a fuller account of Cato's objections provided. Third, when it came time to ratify the law, Pompey and Crassus filled the Forum with armed men who drove out Cato and wounded some of those who resisted, even killing some, and thereby passed the law. Only *Cato Minor* includes the detail that Cato warned Pompey of the consequences of his friendship with Caesar. However, in *Pomp.* 60.5 and *Cat. Min.* 52.2, Cato reminded Pompey at a later time that he had warned him of the danger. It is also worth observing that Cato's bid for a praetorship and the actions of Pompey and Crassus against it are reported in *Pomp.* 52.2 and *Cat. Min.* 42.1–5 but omitted in *Crassus*, where Cato is rarely mentioned. *Cato Minor* provides more details related to the events, since they evidently have greater biographical relevance in that *Life*.

Summary

· Plutarch omits often for convenience or brevity in *Caesar*, *Pompey*, and *Crassus*.
· Plutarch shines a literary spotlight in *Pompey* and *Crassus*.
· Plutarch loosely paraphrases in *Crassus* or *Cato Minor* or both.
· Plutarch has conflated certain events in *Pompey* and *Crassus*.
· Plutarch often includes details for their biographical relevance in *Cato Minor*.

#20 Caesar Conquers Germans during a Truce *(*Caes. *22.1–4;* Cat. Min. *51.1); Pompey Loans Troops to Caesar (*Caes. *25.1;* Pomp. *52.3;* Cat. Min. *45.3)*
Narrative

The agreements devised at Luca between Caesar, Pompey, and Crassus had thus far proven effective in achieving the desired results for all three. Caesar then returned to his military campaigns in Transalpine Gaul, received additional troops loaned to him by Pompey, then attacked the Germans in 55 BCE, handing them a crushing defeat. The senate approved celebratory sacrifices, but Cato argued that they should instead hand over Caesar to the Germans whom he had wronged.

Analysis

Three differences appear in these accounts. In *Caes.* 22.2, Plutarch cites Caesar's journal, which asserts that it was the Germans who had broken the truce, forcing him to engage them in battle. However, in *Cat. Min.* 51.1, no mention is made of the Germans striking first. It is the warmongering Caesar who had broken the truce. Plutarch observes the law of biographical relevance in *Caesar* and *Cato Minor* by telling the story from the perspectives of each.

The other two differences result from errors on the part of Plutarch. In *Caes.* 22.3, 400,000 Germans were slain. However, in *Cat. Min.* 51.1, 300,000 Germans were slain. Pelling says the 400,000 figure is closest to being accurate and is probably a rounded number. Caesar's own account (*Bell. gall.* 4.15.3) places the number at 430,000, while Appian (*Celt.* 1.4, 18) gives the number of 400,000. The difference in *Cato Minor* is probably due to a slip of memory on the part of Plutarch.[50] The other error occurs in *Caes.* 25.1 and *Pomp.* 52.3, where Plutarch mistakenly reports that Pompey loaned Caesar two legions. In *Cat. Min.* 45.3, he correctly reports that Pompey loaned Caesar one legion.[51]

Summary

- Plutarch applies the law of biographical relevance in *Caesar* and *Cato Minor*.
- Plutarch has numerical errors on two occasions in *Caesar, Pompey*, and *Cato Minor*.

#22 Crassus and His Son Publius Are Killed by Parthians (Crass. 25.1–12; 30.1–33.5; Cic. 36.1; Caes. 28.1; Pomp. 53.6; Ant. 34.1–2; 37.1)

Narrative

In June 53, Crassus and his son Publius were in battle with the Parthians, who outnumbered them. While the Parthians were attempting to surround them, Crassus ordered Publius to force an engagement before the circle could be completed. Publius suffered a great defeat and was severely wounded in the process. He and the survivors were forced to retreat to a hill where he and his army were attacked. Because his hand was wounded, Publius ordered his shield bearer to kill him with his own sword. When the Parthians found Publius, they cut off his head and then turned their attention to Crassus.

Crassus was also losing to the Parthians at Carrhae. On 9 June, when everything was all but lost, the Parthian general Surena misled the Romans, telling them Parthian King Hyrodes desired a truce and would assist them with their withdrawal if they would leave the area. Crassus was familiar with Parthian treachery and did not trust Surena. But his army had lost patience and threatened Crassus if he chose not to give the Parthian proposal a chance. So fearing his own soldiers, Crassus reluctantly agreed to meet with Surena. When they met, Crassus was killed. He was then beheaded and his right hand cut off. Surena sent Crassus's head and hand to Parthian King Hyrodes. When his head was presented to the king, all sorts of revelry erupted.

Fifteen years later in the spring of 38, the Romans avenged the treachery and disrespect shown to Crassus when they again engaged in war with the Parthians. Pancorus, a son of Hyrodes, faced the Roman general Ventidius in Syria and was defeated and killed in battle. Shortly afterward, Hyrodes became jealous of Surena and executed him. Hyrodes then contracted a disease that resulted in dropsy. Not wanting to wait to inherit his father's throne, his son Phraates gave him poison. But it had no effect, and Hyrodes was restored to health. So Phraates strangled his father and took possession of his kingdom in late 38 or 37.[52]

Analysis

As one may expect, Plutarch provides the greatest amount of detail on these events in *Crassus*, given their biographical relevance to its main character. Worth noting is that *Cicero* mentions the death of the "younger Crassus" in passing, and it completely passes over the death of Crassus. Both *Caesar* and *Pompey* only mention that the Parthians killed Crassus and that paved the way for Caesar and Pompey (the main characters of those *Lives*) to battle one another for supremacy. In a similar manner, in *Crassus* Plutarch has no reason to mention that Crassus's death was the final obstacle removed that prompted Caesar and Pompey to battle one another for supremacy. We observe the law of biographical relevance at play.

In *Crassus* and *Antony*, there is a disparate amount of attention given to the fates of those who killed Crassus and celebrated it. In *Crass.* 33.5, Plutarch says Phraates tried to poison Hyrodes. When that was ineffective, he strangled him. In *Ant.* 37.1, Plutarch merely states that Phraates executed Hyrodes and took possession of his kingdom. Plutarch provides more detail in *Crassus*, since he is interested in reporting how the infamous death of his main character was avenged. We again observe biographical relevance at play.

Summary

Plutarch provides additional details of an event in *Crassus* given their biographical relevance.

#23 Rome in Chaos; Pompey Elected Sole Consul to Establish Order; Pompey Delivers Illegal Encomium (Caes. 28.1–5; Pomp. 53.1–55.7; Cat. Min. 47.1–48.5)

Narrative

Caesar, Pompey, and Crassus—three strong personalities. Each desired to become Rome's monarch and had been awaiting the right opportunity.[53] Crassus had been waiting for Pompey and Caesar to fight each other before he would challenge the victor. Caesar had given his daughter Julia to Pompey in marriage in order to strengthen their alliance, at least for the time being. However, in August 54 BCE, Julia died in childbirth, and on 9 June 53 Crassus was killed after the disastrous Battle of Carrhae against the Parthians.[54] The stage was then set for Caesar and Pompey to vie for supreme power.

The concept of monarchy was repugnant to most Romans. But Rome was then in a state of such violent chaos that some of its citizens began to suggest, even publicly, that a monarchy was needed in order to bring about order and that Pompey should be chosen for the role.

With the politically ambitious Caesar in Gaul accompanied by his battle-hardened troops, Cato and his colleagues understood that drastic action had to be taken. In early 52, they proposed that Pompey be made sole consul. That would give him power just short of what he desired while preserving the Republic; it would be a legal way of expanding his power as consul without dismantling the Republic. The measure was approved, and in late February 52 Pompey became sole consul, and his tenure for holding his consular provinces was extended. He would govern alone for at least two months after which he could choose a colleague if he so desired.

Pompey invited Cato to visit him. When Cato arrived, Pompey expressed his gratitude, acknowledged that he was indebted to him for the favor, and invited him to be his counselor. Cato replied that Pompey owed him nothing, since he helped secure the sole consulship for Pompey because it was in the best interest of Rome. He added that he would be happy to advise Pompey when asked and, if not asked, he would make his opinions public if needed.

Pompey was inconsistent in his leadership. He worked to restore order to the city and ensure others received fair trials. But he showed partiality to his friends and relatives. He brought pressure to bear on the jury when his father-in-law Quintus Caecilius Metellus Pius Scipio was on trial. And he broke his own law and delivered an encomium* at the trial of his friend Plancus between 10 December 52 and the end of January 51.

Analysis

This pericope appears in three *Lives: Caesar, Pompey,* and *Cato Minor.* There are three major differences that appear throughout the accounts: In *Pomp.* 54.3 and *Cat. Min.* 47.2–3, Cato and his party decided to allow Pompey a special office. Cato's son-in-law Bibulus made the proposal to the senate, and Cato provided his support. In *Caes.* 28.5, Cato discerned Pompey's scheme and persuaded the senate to elect him sole consul. The involvement of Bibulus and other members of Cato's party are omitted. Plutarch shines his literary spotlight on Cato, perhaps for simplicity, since he was ultimately the driving force behind the proposal.

In *Pomp.* 55.4–6, Plutarch reports that Pompey broke the very laws he had established when he extended special treatment to his friends and relatives who were on trial. He provides two examples: (1) He describes Pompey's corruption of the jury when his father-in-law Scipio was on trial. (2) He then tells of an occasion when Pompey had an encomium read illegally at the trial of Plancus. In *Cat. Min.* 48.4, Plutarch reports that Cato sharply rebuked Pompey for his inconsistency in upholding the law of fair trials, and he offered the example of Pompey providing an encomium at the trial of Plancus. As one may expect given the law of biographical relevance, this example is featured in *Cato Minor,* since Cato is directly involved. However, the story of Pompey corrupting the jury in the trial of Scipio does not appear in *Cato Minor,* since Cato was not involved. Thus, we observe additional information being included when it has biographical relevance.

Plutarch reports the reading of Pompey's encomium differently. In *Cat. Min.* 48.4, Pompey wrote the encomium and had it read at the trial but was not present. This is confirmed by other historians.[55] Therefore, it is interesting to observe that in *Pomp.* 55.5, Plutarch reports that Pompey himself appeared in court and delivered his encomium. Plutarch transfers the action of reading the encomium from Pompey's emissary to Pompey himself, since Pompey was ultimately behind it.

Summary

- Plutarch shines his literary spotlight on Cato in *Caesar*.
- Plutarch provided additional details for their biographical relevance in *Cato Minor* and *Pompey*.
- We observe transferal via substitution occurring in *Pompey*.

#24 No Compromise Reached between Caesar, Pompey, and the Senate (Caes. 29.1–31.2; Pomp. 56.1–59.4; Ant. 5.1–4; Cat. Min. 51.4–5; Cic. 36.6–37.1)

Narrative

Rome remained in an unsettled state. Pompey was still the most powerful Roman, but Caesar had plans for changing that. Making use of the massive wealth he had obtained from his military expeditions, Caesar gave lavish gifts to men of influence. In 50 BCE, he desired to pursue a second consulship. However, he faced the same challenge of a decade earlier when standing for consul: generals with their army were not permitted to enter the city, while those who desired the office of consul had to sue for it inside the city. He requested that an exception be made for him so that he could stand for consul in absentia, but his request was denied.

The extension of his command obtained as a result of the Luca agreement was then about to expire, so Caesar requested another extension. But the senate denied this request as well. One of Caesar's centurions was in the city at the time, and when he learned of the senate's decision, he slapped the handle of his sword and said, "But this will give it!" The senate then recommended that Caesar lay down his arms and return to the city, and Pompey asked him to return the legion he had loaned him.

Caesar returned the borrowed legion, giving each soldier a generous gift as he left. As a result, the borrowed soldiers remained loyal to him. Once they arrived in Rome, their officers began spreading the lie that all of Caesar's soldiers were fed up with their commander and would gladly fight for Pompey against Caesar should Pompey merely show up. The deception increased Pompey's confidence to the extent that he took little precaution preparing forces to protect Rome from a possible attack by Caesar. And at one point, when some senators were alarmed because they could see no forces to protect the city, Pompey told them not to worry, for he merely needed to stomp on the ground and both soldiers and horses would spring up from it.

Caesar understood that his situation was quickly worsening. If he laid down his arms, Pompey would have the upper hand. So he attempted to level the Roman political playing field with a proposal: if he was to disarm, so should Pompey. The Roman people could then decide which of the two they preferred. Of course, Caesar knew he would gain the upper hand in such an arrangement, since he had been purchasing the friendships of many for years.

Major debates occurred in the senate pertaining to what was to be done with Caesar. The first debate occurred on 1 December 50 during which the consuls put to a vote two options before the senate. The first was for Pompey to dismiss his troops. Only a few senators voted for that option. The second was for Caesar to dismiss his troops. All but a few voted for that option. But then the tribune Curio suggested a third option: both Caesar and Pompey dismiss their troops. To this, almost all of the senators agreed. Elated, Curio left the senate and informed the people of the senate's opinion. But the consuls refused to allow an official vote on Curio's option.

On 10 December, Antony, who was a partisan of Caesar, replaced Curio as tribune. And on 1 January 49, Lentulus and Marcellus assumed their new offices as consuls, and the second debate occurred when Curio brought another letter from Caesar with a proposal to the senate. However, the consuls would not permit Antony to read it. Pompey's father-in-law, Scipio, proposed that Caesar disarm by a certain date or be declared a public enemy. Lentulus said there was a need for arms against a bandit like Caesar. With tensions heating to a boil, Cicero returned to Rome on 4 January and attempted to broker an agreement between Pompey and Caesar in order to avoid a civil war.[56] Caesar made some concessions: He wished to maintain his command in Cisalpine Gaul and Illyricum and would return all of his troops with the exception of two legions until he could stand for a consulship the following year. Pompey countered that Caesar could keep his two provinces but must relinquish all of his troops. Cicero then countered with a proposal that Caesar maintain his two provinces while keeping only one legion. Pompey appeared ready to agree, but Cato scolded him for allowing himself once again to be deceived by Caesar, and the consul Lentulus would not permit any agreement.

On 7 January, the senate voted to replace Caesar in his provincial command and declined his request to stand for a consulship in absentia. Antony and Curio vetoed the decision and were warned by Lentulus to leave the senate and the city. Antony, Cassius, and Curio then fled to Caesar. The consuls asked Pompey to put together forces and protect Rome. He began the process but quickly learned he had underestimated how difficult the task would be. The people knew that Caesar was making concessions and desired a compromise, so they had no stomach for joining Pompey in the hardships of a war they regarded as unnecessary.

Analysis

The pericope appears in five of Plutarch's *Lives: Cicero, Caesar, Pompey, Antony,* and *Cato Minor.* Several differences are present, and it is easy to see why Pelling refers to this pericope as "the most bewildering example of Plutarch's simplifications and displacements."[57]

Who gave false information to Pompey? In *Caes.* 29.4, it is the officers who returned the soldiers Pompey had loaned Caesar. In *Pomp.* 57.4, it is Appius who returned the soldiers Pompey had loaned Caesar.

Three options were put before the senate: (1) Pompey disarm, (2) Caesar disarm, or (3) both disarm. When did this occur? In *Pomp.* 58.4–5 and 59.1, it was before 10 December, because Curio was tribune and Lentulus was consul elect. (This is the correct timing.) In *Caes.* 30.3, it was in January because Lentulus was consul. In *Ant.* 5.2, 4, it was after 9 December because Antony was tribune rather than Curio.[58]

Who made that proposal to the senate? In *Pomp.* 58.4–5, Curio, strengthened by Antony and Piso, asked the senate for its opinion on all three options prior to 10 December. In *Caes.* 30.3, the consuls asked the senators for their opinion on the first two options, and Antony asked their opinion on the third option. In *Ant.* 5.4, Antony rose and asked their opinion on the third option, while no mention is made of who stated the first two options. In *Cat. Min.* 51.5, friends of Caesar were only said to suggest the third option. No mention is made of the first two options. This proposal was made either (a) by Curio prior to 10 December 50 and Antony after 9 December 50 or (b) by Curio prior to 10 December with Plutarch displacing the event to a later date in *Caesar* and *Antony* while also transferring the proposal from Curio to Antony.[59]

Antony read a letter from Caesar with his proposal in a popular assembly. When did this reading occur, and what did Caesar propose? In *Caes.* 30.2, it was after 9 December because Antony was tribune at the time. (It is also prior to the proposal of three options before the senate.) The details of Caesar's proposal are not provided. In *Ant.* 5.2–3, it was after 9 December because Plutarch lists three ways in which Antony assisted Caesar's partisans upon entering the office of tribune on 10 December. (It is also possibly prior to the proposal of three options before the senate.)[60] The details of Caesar's proposal are not provided. In *Pomp.* 59.2–3, it was in January because Lentulus is consul, an office he took on 1 January. (It is also after the proposal of three options before the senate.) Caesar's proposal is that he and Pompey should both give up their provinces and armies and put themselves in the hands of the people.

Actions against Caesar were proposed. Who made them? In *Caes.* 30.2, Scipio introduced a motion that Caesar be declared a public enemy if he did not disarm by a certain date (no indication of the date this was uttered is provided). In *Caes.* 30.3, Lentulus the consul said there was a need for arms against a bandit. Since Lentulus took office on 1 January, the event is said to have occurred that month in *Caesar.*[61] In *Pomp.* 58.4, Marcellus called Caesar a bandit and urged that he be declared a public enemy if he refused to lay down his arms.[62] (Plutarch portrays this as occurring before 10 December since Curio was still tribune and Lentulus was consul designate [59.1]. Transferal and displacement are present.)

When Cicero started another series of negotiations by bringing to Pompey another proposal from Caesar with further concessions, what were the initial concessions proposed? In *Caes.* 31.1, Caesar was to give up all except Cisalpine Gaul and Illyricum and keep two legions. In *Pomp.* 59.3, Caesar was to give up all except Illyricum and two legions.

When a final attempt at a compromise was offered, Pompey was willing to agree to it. What was the compromise? In *Caes.* 31.1, Caesar was to give up all except Cisalpine Gaul, Illyricum, and one legion. In *Pomp.* 59.3–4, Caesar was to give up all except Illyricum and one legion.

Whom did Lentulus drive from the senate? In *Caes.* 31.2, Lentulus drove Antony and Curio from the senate. In *Ant.* 5.4, Lentulus drove Antony from the senate (spotlighting). Antony then joined Quintus Cassius and went to Caesar.

When did the city go into mourning? In *Caes.* 30.3, it was in January, since Lentulus was consul. In *Pomp.* 59.1, it was in December, since Lentulus was consul elect.

Because other sources of the period likewise report these events, historians have been able to determine a general chronology for some of them. For example, the sitting in which two votes were put before the senate— should Pompey disarm and should Caesar disarm—and the tribune Curio suggesting a third option—asking that both should disarm—occurred on 1 December 50.[63] At the sitting on 1 January 49, Scipio proposed that Caesar should disarm by a certain date or be declared a public enemy. Caesar sent a letter with further concessions (i.e., keep his two provinces and two legions until he stood for a consulship). Curio delivered a letter of Caesar's to the senate on 1 January 49 suggesting he and Pompey both relinquish their provinces and armies and entrust themselves to the people. Antony insisted that it be read.[64] When the consuls refused, Antony read the letter to the people.

Cicero returned from his proconsulship in Cilicia on 4 January and immediately attempted to broker a compromise between Caesar (via his friends Antony, Cassius, and Curio) and Pompey. Intense debates in the senate on a proposed compromise occurred on 5–6 January, ending with Lentulus rejecting it.[65] Finally, on 7 January, the senate decided to replace Caesar in Gaul and rescind his right to stand for the consulship in absentia. The tribunes Antony and Cassius vetoed the decision, resulting in the consul Lentulus warning them to leave the senate and the city immediately. In view of this chronology, Pelling is spot on when he describes Plutarch's differing accountings of these events as "bewildering."[66]

Although Plutarch's use of compositional devices is clearly observed in some instances, it is foggy in others. For example, as stated earlier, were the three options (i.e., Pompey disarm, Caesar disarm, both disarm) made (a) by Curio prior to 10 December 50 and Antony after 9 December 50, or (b) by Curio prior to 10 December in *Pompey*, with Plutarch displacing the event to a later date in *Caesar* and *Antony* and transferring the proposal from Curio to Antony? It is difficult to know.

Plutarch places in different contexts the event of Curio informing the people of Caesar's proposal, them lauding him, and them placing garlands of flowers on him. In *Caesar*, Curio's act occurs prior to Caesar's proposal being offered to the senate, whereas it is afterward in *Pompey*. Noteworthy is that when Antony proposed the third option, the senate not only agreed but also gave him shouts of praise (*Ant.* 5.3). It is possible that Plutarch has here conflated this story with the people praising Curio in *Pomp.* 58.4–5. We may likewise observe that the nature of Curio's act changes. In *Pompey*, the people celebrate Curio *because* he has brought them news the senate had reached a compromise. In *Caesar*, however, Curio could not be celebrated for this reason because Caesar's proposal had not yet been brought before the senate, since Plutarch places the event after Antony became tribune. Instead, Curio was celebrated merely upon informing the people that Caesar had offered a compromise. Plutarch altered details in his narrative to accommodate his altered chronology.

In *Caesar*, and possibly in *Antony*, Antony read Caesar's letter to the people prior to the three options being presented to the senate. However, in *Pompey*, he read the letter after the three options were presented to the senate. Plutarch also provides a different chronology pertaining to when the city went into mourning. In *Caesar*, it was in January. But in *Pompey*, it was in December. Plutarch displaces the event in *Pompey*.

Plutarch appears to conflate the logia uttered against Caesar by Scipio and Lentulus and transfer them to Marcellus. He has also displaced at least one of them. For in *Caesar*, the logion by Lentulus was uttered in January, whereas Marcellus uttered it prior to 10 December in *Pompey*.

In *Antony*, Curio is mentioned as the one who assisted Antony in obtaining his political post and was then brushed out of the remainder of this pericope. Antony read Caesar's letter to the people, and it was Antony rather than Curio who presented the third option to the senate. And it was Antony who was driven out of the city, whereas in *Caesar*, Lentulus forced Antony and Curio to leave the senate and the city.

If Plutarch is employing displacement and transferal when reporting Antony's presentation of three options to the senate in *Caes.* 30.3 and *Ant.* 5.4, he is likewise shining a spotlight on Antony, who supports Curio in his presentation in *Pomp.* 58.4–5. Plutarch spotlights elsewhere in this pericope. In *Pompey*, he shines his spotlight on Appius, who spoke with Pompey and deceived him, whereas it was the officers performing the deceit in *Caesar*. It is possible that Appius is mentioned because he was the commander of the troops being returned to Pompey and personally passed along the misinformation to Pompey, whereas in *Caesar* the officers misinformed Pompey and the people.

Scholars propose various reasons why Plutarch employed these compositional devices in this pericope. Sometimes they disagree on which compositional device Plutarch employed, while on other occasions some contend there were similar but separate events. If they were separate events, Plutarch has placed focus on different events within his varying renditions of the same story rather than employing displacement and conflation.[67]

If we exclude occurrences where Plutarch may be employing a compositional device that resulted in differences, there is one occasion in this pericope where he probably contradicts himself. The difference appears in the terms of the compromise to which Pompey was willing to agree. In *Caesar*, Caesar is to give up all except Cisalpine Gaul, Illyricum, and one legion. However, in *Pompey*, Caesar is to give up all except Illyricum and one legion.

Noteworthy is that all of these differences appear in four *Lives* that were written at the same time within a set. Pelling opines that, in this pericope, Plutarch employs many of these changes in order to lay stress on different events in different *Lives*.[68] Whatever reasons Plutarch had in this pericope for employing so many instances of conflation, displacement, transferal, literary spotlighting, and altering narrative details, historians remain perplexed over his different ways of telling the same story in accounts that he wrote at the same time.

Summary

Because correct details pertaining to the events in this pericope are difficult to know with certainty, all that can be said with certainty is that Plutarch has displaced events, conflated them, transferred what one person said to another, and shined his literary spotlight on occasion, although not always on his main character.

#25 Caesar Crosses the Rubicon and Attacks Ariminum; Rome in Panic (Caes. 32.1–34.4; Pomp. 60.1–61.4; Cat. Min. 52.1–5; Ant. 6.1–3; Cic. 37.1–3)
Narrative

In January 49 BCE, final attempts to forge a compromise between Caesar and the senate had failed, and civil war appeared inevitable. The bulk of Caesar's army was beyond the Alps, but he had three hundred cavalry and five thousand soldiers with him. Deciding to use this smaller force to capitalize on the elements of speed and surprise, Caesar led his small force toward Italy.

Caesar came to a small river called the Rubicon. This was the border between Cisalpine Gaul and Italy. Once crossed, there would be no turning back. For he would be breaking the law and invading Italy. He paused and deliberated with his friends. Then, as if throwing caution to the wind, he crossed the river, marched through the night of 11 or 10 January, and took possession of Ariminum before sunrise.

Caesar's surprise attack caused panic in Rome. Pompey was caught off guard, and some began blaming him for strengthening Caesar while others denounced him for being unwilling to compromise. Tullas asked

Pompey if he had enough forces to defeat Caesar. Pompey hesitated and then answered that he had the forces Caesar had just sent and that he could enlist and train another thirty thousand rather quickly. But Pompey appeared to lack confidence in his answer, and this caused alarm. Favonius sarcastically told Pompey to stomp on the ground in order to bring forth the troops he had said would spring up at his bidding. And Cato reminded Pompey he had predicted Caesar would one day attempt to establish himself as Rome's monarch. Pompey replied that Cato's words were prophetic whereas his own approach was friendlier.

Cato advised the senate that Pompey should be made general with unlimited powers and be charged with solving the problem he had created. The senate agreed. Although Pompey's forces were more numerous than Caesar's, the people lacked confidence in his judgment. Rumors of Caesar's whereabouts and actions were everywhere. Influenced by the panic of the moment, Pompey declared a civil war to be in effect and left the city on 17 January, commanding the senate and everyone who was not a partisan of Caesar to follow. Unable to decide which side to take, Cicero remained in Rome, hoping somehow to help the city, but he was regarded by some as a partisan of Caesar for not leaving with Pompey. Caesar treated with grace those who sided with Pompey, and when some returned to him, he forgave them.

Analysis

This pericope appears in five of Plutarch's *Lives: Caesar, Pompey, Cato Minor, Antony*, and *Cicero*. Two differences appear between them. The first concerns who Cato reminded that he had been warning them all along of Caesar's intentions. In *Pomp.* 60.5, he reminded Pompey. But in *Cat. Min.* 52.2, he reminded many who were present, including Pompey, and then looked to him for advice on what to do with Caesar who was now on his way to Rome. It is entirely possible that both accounts are correct and that Plutarch is shining his literary spotlight on his main character in *Pompey* who in turn explained the different nature of their approaches.

The second difference concerns what Pompey said about those who decided to remain in the city. In *Caes.* 33.5, those citizens who preferred country and freedom to tyranny were to follow him. In *Pomp.* 61.3, Pompey would regard those who remain in the city to be a partisan of Caesar. Pelling observes that in his *Commentaries on the Civil War*, Caesar himself reported that Pompey said, "He would regard those who stayed in Rome in the same light as those who fought for Caesar"—a statement very similar to what we find in Plutarch's *Pompey*.[69] Therefore, Pompey's statement recorded in *Pompey* may be closer to what he actually uttered than how it appears in *Caesar*. If Pelling is correct, Plutarch redacted Pompey's statement in *Caesar* to give it the appearance of encouraging Roman citizens to leave the city in the cause of patriotism rather than in fear of Pompey.

Summary

- Plutarch may be spotlighting in *Pompey*.
- Plutarch may have redacted a statement in *Caesar* in a manner that is less favorable to its main character.

#26 Caesar Conquers Italy, Pursues Pompey, and Ends Up Being Pursued by Him
(Caes. *15.3; 35.1–37.5; 39.1–41.3;* Pomp. *62.1–67.6;*
Cat. Min. *53.3–55.2;* Ant. *6.1–4; 8.1–2;* Cic. *38.1–6;*
Brut. *4.1–4)*

Narrative

In March 49 BCE, Pompey, the consuls, most of the senate, and much of the city's population left the city. Pompey arrived in Brundisium, from where on 4 March he sent the consuls and many of his forces ahead of him to Dyrrhachium. Caesar arrived at Brundisium on 9 March, and on 17 March Pompey left the city quickly and crossed the sea to join the others. When Caesar discovered Pompey had left, he desired to pursue him but did not have ships for his forces. So he turned and went to Rome where, arriving in late March, he found the city in a less chaotic state than he expected. While there, he attempted to access funds from the treasury and was hindered by the tribune Metellus. However, Metellus backed down when Caesar threatened to kill him. At this point, Caesar had become master of Italy without having had to engage in a single battle.

Now in possession of additionally needed funds from the treasury, Caesar left Rome on 6 or 7 April and headed off to Spain, where he intended to defeat Pompey's legates and win over their troops.[70] This would provide him with additional forces and eliminate the prospects of being attacked from behind while pursuing Pompey.[71] Having accomplished this objective, Caesar once again returned to Rome, where he was appointed dictator in December 49. After attending to a number of matters, he abdicated his sole power and left the city, having spent only eleven days there.

Caesar then obtained adequate transportation, returned to Brundisium, and crossed the sea on 4 January 48 to engage Pompey in battle. Pompey was well fortified and supplied in Dyrrhachium, while Caesar was in a disadvantaged position and running out of food.[72] In mid-to-late April, Antony arrived with reinforcements to assist Caesar, and Cato arrived from Syracuse in late April to assist Pompey. While Cato counseled Pompey to delay battle with Caesar, Caesar attempted to lure Pompey out into battle by having his battle-hardened soldiers engage Pompey's in continual skirmishes. Caesar won all but one of those skirmishes. Then in mid-July 48, Pompey and Cato incited the troops to engage in battle with Caesar and so soundly defeated him they could have ended the civil war that day. But a cautious Pompey stopped short. Because Caesar's army was low on supplies and worn out from the rigors of many military campaigns, Pompey decided to delay and continue to impose hardships on Caesar's army rather than risk a decisive battle with Caesar's highly skilled and battle-hardened troops.

Caesar seized the opportunity to escape and left for Macedonia to engage in battle with Scipio, hoping he would entice Pompey to leave his strong position for a less favorable one in which to engage Caesar in battle. Emboldened by their rout over Caesar, Pompey's army desired to pursue Caesar and end the war. Pompey's experience as a general told him to stick to his strategy and wait. And Cato affirmed Pompey of the wisdom in his decision. But when Pompey's army began to speak negatively of what they perceived as Pompey being overly cautious and loving command, he was moved by the pressure and convinced himself of the need to pursue Caesar. He left Cato and some others behind in Dyrrhachium and began the pursuit, intending to avoid battle while keeping Caesar's troops in a weak position. When Pompey arrived in Macedonia, he was joined by Brutus.

Analysis

Plutarch narrates the chronology of events in this pericope in a far more consistent manner than in the preceding one. However, differences are still present. In *Caesar* and *Antony*, the chronology of events appears in the following order: (a) Caesar pursued Pompey to Brundisium. (b) When he learned that Pompey had fled across the sea, he went to Rome because he did not have the means for sea travel. Once in Rome, Caesar invaded the treasury. (c) He then went to Spain in order to defeat Pompey's legates and absorb their troops. However, in *Pompey*, Caesar (a) stopped first in Rome, where he invaded the treasury. (b) He then went to Brundisium in pursuit of Pompey. (c) When he learned that Pompey had fled across the sea, he went to Spain in order to defeat Pompey's legates and absorb their troops. In *Pompey*, the first two events have been inverted. Plutarch has displaced Caesar's trip to Rome and transplanted it prior to the siege of Brundisium.[73]

Both *Pompey* and *Antony* compress their accounts and omit Caesar's second trip to Rome that occurred after his campaign in Spain and prior to returning to Brundisium from where he would cross the sea to meet Pompey at Dyrrhachium.

The suggestion of Cato, adopted by Pompey, that their forces would neither kill any Roman except on the battlefield nor plunder any city subject to Rome is reported in *Pompey* and *Cato Minor* and omitted in *Caesar, Antony,* and *Cicero.* This is to be expected given its biographical relevance.

In *Pomp.* 67.3–4, Domitius Ahenobarbus, Favonius, and Afranius offered three specific jests aimed against Pompey for declining to pursue Caesar. Plutarch adds that many similar speeches were given. In *Caes.* 41.1–2, Favonius and Afranius are assigned the same jests found in *Pompey.* But it is "all the others" except Cato who are assigned with the words attributed to Ahenobarbus in *Pompey.* Does Plutarch transfer what others were saying to Ahenobarbus (or from Ahenobarbus to others), or does he employ inflection by changing a plural in *Caesar* to a singular in *Pompey* (or change a singular in *Pompey* to a plural in *Caesar*)?

Of interest are two reports that some *Lives* have omitted. *Pompey* reports that Caesar sent Numerius, a prisoner of war and friend of Pompey, to Pompey in Brundisium, requesting reconciliation between himself and Pompey. But Pompey ignored the request and crossed the sea. Later, when Caesar crossed the sea in pursuit of Pompey, he sent another prisoner of war and friend of Pompey named Vibullius, proposing that they have a conference, disband their armies, and renew their friendship. Once again, Pompey ignored the proposal and went to Dyrrhachium. These reports are provided because it is Pompey's friends who were sent to initiate a peace agreement that Pompey rejected rather than what could be an emphasis on Caesar's continuous efforts to avoid civil war. We may expect for this to be reported in *Caesar* but instead find it in *Pompey.* The second report pertains to Antony's arrival with troops from Brundisium to assist Caesar. It is reported in *Antony* and *Caesar* but is absent in *Pompey.*

Numerical differences are present. How many did Caesar conquer? In *Caes.* 15.3, Plutarch reports that Caesar took by storm more than eight hundred cities, subdued three hundred nations, and fought battles at different times with three million, of whom he killed one million and took as many prisoners. However, in *Pomp.* 67.6, Plutarch says that Caesar took by storm one thousand cities, subdued more than three hundred nations, took one million prisoners, and killed as many on the battlefield. In *Pompey*, Plutarch has perhaps rounded up the number of cities attacked (one thousand vs. more than eight hundred). Caesar subdued "three hundred nations" in *Caes.* 15.3, whereas it is "more than three hundred nations" in *Pomp.* 67.6. Also of interest is that Plutarch has placed this data at different points in *Caesar* and *Pompey*. In *Caesar*, it appears in reference to Caesar's military accomplishments and is placed after he is elected for his first consulship and prior to the Luca meeting. In *Pompey*, it appears in the context of the overconfidence of Pompey's commanders after his near victory over Caesar. Their success gave them overconfidence as though they had gained the upper hand against a powerful king but not one as successful as Caesar. This is not displacement but merely applying the data where Plutarch thought most appropriate in that particular *Life*. The numbers are slightly higher in *Pompey*. Perhaps this may be since they relate to a later time, which included Caesar's additional accomplishments.[74]

In *Caes.* 36.1, after Caesar had defeated Pompey's legions in Spain, the leaders of those legions escaped (φεύγοντες, *pheugontes*) to Pompey. However, in *Pomp.* 65.2, Caesar took Pompey's soldiers into his own command and sent away (ἀφῆκε, *aphēke*) their commanders. The version in *Pompey* agrees with Appian (*Bell. civ.* 2.43.171–74) and Cassius Dio (*Hist. rom.* 41.23.1–2).[75] Did they escape to Pompey or did Caesar send them back to Pompey? Unless there was a competing version that has left no other trace than in Plutarch's *Caesar*, Plutarch redacts the story in *Caesar* in order to put the main character's adversary in the stronger light.

Summary

- Plutarch inverts the order of events, displaces them, and transplants them in *Pompey*.
- *Pompey* and *Antony* employ compression.
- Biographical relevance is observed in *Pompey* and *Cato Minor*.
- Plutarch transfers or inflects in *Caesar* or *Pompey*.
- Plutarch omits stories.

- Numerical differences are present.
- Plutarch may redact a detail in *Caesar* in order to place the main character's adversary in a stronger light.

#27 Caesar Defeats Pompey at Pharsalus; Pompey Flees; Brutus Goes Over to Caesar; Cato Rescues Cicero from Pompey's Son; Caesar Pardons Cicero (Caes. *42.1–47.2;* Pomp. *68.1–73.7;* Cat. Min. *55.2–3;* Brut. *5–6; 8.3;* Cic. *39.1–5;* Ant. *8.2–3)*

Narrative

After being nearly destroyed close to Dyrrhachium, Caesar continued his flight from Pompey southward and arrived in Thessaly. He intended to continue onto Scotussa when Pompey decided to engage him in battle at Pharsalus on 9 August 48. Pompey's force outnumbered Caesar's more than two-to-one, and his leaders were very confident of a victory, although their inexperienced soldiers were not. Conversely, Caesar's soldiers were ready and anxious to fight, declining Caesar's option to wait for additional troops commanded by Calenus and presently stationed at Athens and Megara. Caesar instructed his soldiers to spare Brutus if they confronted him. He did this out of regard for Servilia, Cato's sister,[76] who was in love with Caesar and because he suspected Brutus might be his son through her.

Caesar divided his forces into three divisions with Dimitius Calvinus in the center, Antony on the left wing, and Caesar taking the right wing. Pompey also divided his forces into three divisions to face Caesar's: Scipio (Pompey's father-in-law) in the center, Lucius Domitius with cavalry on the left to oppose Caesar and his powerful tenth legion, and Pompey on the right to oppose Antony. Pompey's strategy was to allow Caesar's troops to make the charge while his own troops remained steady in place. Pompey's left wing, led by Domitius, would send his cavalry against Caesar's strongest wing (where Caesar was), surround them, and gain a quick victory. Caesar, therefore, brought over to his wing approximately three thousand reserve troops and instructed them to meet the cavalry, get alongside their horses, and use their javelins to jab upward in the horsemen's faces. Because the horsemen were young, they would not want to emerge from the conflict with disfigured faces and would not have the fortitude to remain in battle.

As the battle began, a centurion named Crassinius told Caesar that their side would be victorious that day and that, whether he lived or died in battle, Caesar would praise him. With that the centurion took his men into battle, killed many, but was then killed when someone thrust a sword through his mouth with such force that it came out the back of his neck.

Once the center division clashed, Domitius's cavalry began to encircle Caesar's right wing. But Caesar's reserve cohorts did as he had instructed them, thrusting their spears at their faces. This threw the cavalrymen into confusion, and they protected their faces and fled. Caesar's reserve cohorts and tenth legion then surrounded and destroyed Domitius's infantry on Pompey's left wing.

When Pompey observed his strongest division being defeated, he walked away from the battlefield without saying a word, returned to his tent, changed his clothes to those of a fugitive, and fled when Caesar's soldiers breached the camp. With Pompey now defeated in this decisive battle, Brutus fled and went to Caesar, who welcomed him joyfully and obtained from him valuable information that would lead him to Pompey. Caesar chose Antony to be Master of the Horse and sent him to Rome while he pursued Pompey.[77]

When Cato learned of Pompey's defeat at Pharsalus, he was determined to keep Pompey's existing fleet together if Pompey survived. He offered the command of the fleet to Cicero. But he declined and decided to return to Italy with some others. When Pompey's older son learned of Cicero's intentions, he determined to kill him and the others leaving for Italy. But Cato intervened, saving them and sending them off. Cicero crossed the sea and arrived in Brundisium by mid-October, where he waited for Caesar. When he learned that Caesar had landed in Tarentum, he went to him in late September 47 and Caesar pardoned him.

Analysis

There are three items worth noting in this pericope. The first concerns the spelling of a name. In *Pomp.* 71.1, the name of the centurion Caesar addressed prior to the battle is Crassianus. But his name is Crassinius in *Caes.* 44.6. Caesar gives the name "Crastinus" in *Bell. civ.* 3.91.[78] This appears to be either a lapse of memory or carelessness on Plutarch's part.

In *Cat. Min.* 55.3, Cato rescued Cicero and others who were about to return to Italy from the younger Pompey, who wanted to kill them.

However, in *Cic.* 39.1–2, the others are not mentioned. Plutarch is shining a literary spotlight on his main character in *Cicero*.

After describing Pompey's defeat at Pharsalus and Pompey's initial flight from the area, Plutarch writes in *Caes.* 45.5, "As for his later fortunes, and his death after entrusting himself to the Egyptians, we tell that story in his own *Life*."[79] Biographical relevance is in play here, since a detailed description of Pompey's last days is relevant in *Pompey* but not in *Caesar*.

Summary

- Plutarch errs in the spelling of a name.
- Plutarch shines a literary spotlight on his main character in *Cicero*.
- Plutarch omits a story due to its lack of biographical relevance in *Caesar*.

#28 Pompey Killed; Caesar in Egypt; Caesar Defeats Pharnaces *(Caes. 48.1–50.2;* Pomp. *74.1–80.6;* Cat. Min. *56.1–4;* Brut. *33.1–4)*
Narrative

Pompey and his advisors assessed their situation. In Attaleia, he joined some of his war ships, some of his soldiers, and sixty senators. He also learned that his fleet was still intact thanks to Cato. So he began raising funds and rebuilding his army. However, Caesar was in pursuit, and Pompey needed to find refuge.

It was decided that his best course of action was to flee to Egypt, where the thirteen-year-old boy-king Ptolemy XIII would most likely provide him assistance. Pompey arrived in Pelusium, where Ptolemy was at war with his sister Cleopatra. The eunuch Potheinus was actually running Egypt until Ptolemy grew old enough. When Pompey requested entrance, Potheinus called together a council to discuss their options. Theodotus convinced the council members that it was in their best interest to execute Pompey. So Pompey was deceived into believing he would be given safety, killed, and then beheaded, probably on 28 September 48.

Cato took Pompey's fleet and headed toward Egypt, hoping to find Pompey there. In late 48, after landing just east of Egypt somewhere in Libya, he met Pompey's younger son, who informed him of Pompey's death. So Cato took command of the fleet and sailed to Cyrene. In the winter of 48/47, Cato marched east on land to Numidia, where Scipio had joined Varus, who had been appointed by Pompey to govern Libya and, thus, had an army. Moreover, they had the support of Juba, king of Numidia. Cato's forces then amounted to nearly ten thousand.

While Cato and his allies were fortifying their forces, Caesar arrived in Alexandria, Egypt, around 1 October 48. When Theodotus presented him with Pompey's head, Caesar turned away in disgust. Caesar was also given Pompey's seal ring, which he received with tears. Caesar began executing those involved in Pompey's inglorious death and then went to war with Ptolemy and defeated him on 27 March 47. Theodotus escaped and fled Egypt. A few years later, Brutus found him and put him to death. Caesar placed Cleopatra on the throne, and later that year she bore him a son, whom she named Caesarion.

When Caesar learned that Domitius had been defeated by Pharnaces, the son of Mithridates, he went north to Pontus, engaged Pharnaces in a great battle near the city of Zela on 2 August 47, and crushed Pharnaces's army. Caesar described this battle with the now-famous words: *Veni, vidi, vici* ("I came, I saw, I conquered").

Analysis

Portions of this pericope appear in four *Lives: Caesar, Pompey, Cato Minor,* and *Brutus.* A few differences are present. On two occasions Plutarch omits details due to their lack of biographical relevance. On the first occasion, he provides details pertaining to Pompey's death in *Pomp.* 77.1–80.1. However, in *Caes.* 48.2, Plutarch reports that Caesar arrived in Alexandria shortly after Pompey's death while providing no details pertaining to the deception of Pompey or the manner in which he died. The second occasion appears in *Brut.* 33.1–4, where Plutarch describes the deception of Pompey, states that he was killed, and explains that the person who had recommended that course of action, Theodotus, had escaped Caesar's vengeance on Pompey's behalf for a time but was later captured by Brutus and punished. Potheinus and Achillas were not mentioned by name but only as the others who paid the penalty for killing Pompey and were executed in a severe manner. Once again, little attention is given to Pompey's death. It is only mentioned in order to provide some background for Brutus's discovery of one of Pompey's murderers.

In *Pomp.* 80.6, Plutarch reports that after Brutus assassinated Caesar and fled from Rome, he discovered Theodotus, who had escaped from Caesar a few years earlier. Brutus put Theodotus to death using all sorts of tortures. However, in *Brut.* 33.4, Plutarch reports that Brutus discovered

Theodotus and punished him without mentioning that he did so in the cruelest manner. This is an example of Plutarch employing simplification. Since Plutarch's *Brutus* paints a portrait of Brutus as a mild and moderate person, mentioning Brutus's cruel execution of Theodotus would complicate that portrait. So he omits the detail.[80] In *Pompey*, however, it fits Plutarch's point that Pompey's murderers received just reward for their treachery.

In *Caes.* 49.2–5, Caesar learned that Achillas and Potheinus were plotting against him, so he executed Potheinus. Achillas escaped and fled to his camp, waged war on Caesar, and nearly defeated him. Ptolemy then joined Achillas; then Caesar attacked and defeated them. Achillas's ultimate fate is not mentioned, and Ptolemy disappeared. However, in *Pomp.* 80.5–6, Plutarch provides no hint that self-defense was the cause of Caesar's actions against Potheinus, Achillas, and Ptolemy. He instead gives the impression that Caesar avenged Pompey's inglorious death by executing Achillas and Potheinus, and then proceeded to defeat Ptolemy in battle, while Theodotus was able to escape.[81] In *Pompey*, Plutarch simplifies by omitting any hint that Caesar's acts against the Egyptians were in self-defense, and he merely reports the fates of those who had killed Pompey, doing so in a manner that is brief and meant to communicate that Pompey's inglorious death was avenged.

Summary

- In *Caesar* and *Brutus*, Plutarch omits details for their lack of biographical relevance.
- Plutarch simplifies in *Brutus* by omitting details that would complicate the portrait he is painting of his main character.
- Plutarch simplifies in *Pompey* by omitting details in order to cast a different and slightly distorted picture pertaining to why Caesar fought Ptolemy.

#29 Caesar Returns to Rome during His Second Dictatorship; Caesar Elected to Third Consulship (Caes. 51.1–2; 57.4; Cic. 40.1–4; Ant. 10.1–3; 21.2)

Narrative

Caesar returned to Rome in October 47 BCE and was proclaimed dictator for a second time. He was to be consul for the year 46. But there was unrest throughout the empire. Moreover, the actions of Caesar and many within his camp affected public opinion, and many began to speak poorly of Caesar. When some of his soldiers mutinied and killed two praetors, Caesar let them off with a mere slap on the hand. Antony's conduct was also inappropriate for a Roman of high standing. He was often drunk, and when the house of the beloved Pompey was auctioned, Antony purchased it.

Analysis

Various elements of the narrative are provided in *Caesar, Cicero,* and *Antony* with at least one difference. That Antony angered the people for purchasing Pompey's house is reported in *Caes.* 51.2 and *Ant.* 21.2,[82] yet the reason for their anger differs. In *Caes.* 51.2, it is because Antony refurbished Pompey's house, thinking it was not good enough for him in its present state.[83] In *Ant.* 21.2, it is because Antony was inviting persons of ill-repute to his house, which was contrary to Pompey's practice of entertaining guests of high standing. Both reasons may be correct, and Plutarch may have provided the reason he regarded as most germane at that point in his narrative rather than provide a complete account in one or both *Lives*.[84]

Summary

In *Antony,* Plutarch either emphasizes one element of the story over another or he slightly alters the story to add to the portrait of his main character. Even if Plutarch had no credible reports supporting his alteration, he believed the behavior that was typical of his main character supported his alteration.

*#30 Scipio Ignores Cato's Advice Not to Attack Caesar and Is Defeated; Cato Commits Suicide; Deaths of Cato's Son, His Daughter Porcia, and His Friend Statilius (*Caes. *52.1–54.3;* Cat. Min. *58.1–66.7; 73.3–4;* Brut. *49.5; 51.4; 53.4–5)*
Narrative

Overlap exists between this pericope and the previous one. In the spring of 46 BCE, Caesar learned that Cato had united with Metellus Scipio and

King Juba in Libya, and he launched a campaign against them. Cato was in the well-fortified city of Utica with a Council of 300 from Utica and some Roman senators. Scipio was in command of their army, and after a battle occurred in which Caesar was almost defeated, Scipio proposed that he leave Afranius and Juba and go after Caesar to engage him in a decisive battle. Cato counseled him not to press fortune but rather to allow time to soften the emotions and resolve of their enemy. But Scipio called Cato a coward, engaged Caesar in battle at Thapsus, and was utterly defeated.[85] Then Caesar defeated Afranius and Juba.

Finally, Caesar turned his attention toward Cato. The people of Utica panicked when news arrived that Caesar was headed there. But Cato calmed the people and worked hard to ensure the Roman senators and many of his friends in the city could escape to safety. After this was accomplished, Cato used his sword and took his own life on 12 April 46. When Caesar received word of Cato's death, he said, "Oh, Cato! I grudge you your death, because you grudged me your salvation."

Plutarch goes on to ask whether Caesar would actually have spared Cato's life if provided the opportunity. He then tells of the fates of Cato's son, who had remained with him in Utica, his daughter Porcia, and Statilius, who hated Caesar and was trying to emulate Cato.

Cato's son had been lazy and had morally questionable relationships with women. But these reports were forgotten after the manner of his death became known. He fought with Cassius's army with Brutus in the first battle at Philippi[86] against Octavian Caesar and Antony. And when the line was breaking and he was exhausted, he decided to stand his ground and encouraged those with him to stand and die alongside him. With sword in hand, he told the enemy he was Cato's son. He was killed, and his enemies marveled at his courage.

Analysis

There are a few differences in this pericope. However, all of them are quite minor. There is a very slight difference in Caesar's words uttered upon learning that Cato had taken his own life. The meaning is so similar that an English translation will not differ: "O, Cato! I grudge you your death. *For also you grudged me your salvation*" (*Caes.* 54.1: καὶ γὰρ σύ μοι τῆς σωτηρίας ἐφθόνησας, *kai gar su moi tēs sōtērias ephthonēsas, also for you to me salvation grudged; Cat. Min.* 72.2: καὶ γὰρ ἐμοὶ σὺ τῆς σαυτοῦ σωτηρίας ἐφθόνησας, *kai gar emoi su tēs sautou sōtērias ephthonēsas, also for to me you your salvation grudged*).

Plutarch describes the death of Cato's son using different terms. In *Cat. Min.* 73.3, Plutarch explains that Cato's son had not lived a life like his father until his death and that he changed from a lazy womanizer to one who died a valiant death in the cause of freedom. His enemies marveled at his courage. This data is included in *Cato Minor*, but Plutarch omits it in *Brut.* 49.5 given its lack of biographical relevance. In *Cat. Min.* 73.3, Cato's son decided not to "flee or hide when the line was breaking." In *Brut.* 49.5, he would not "flee or yield to the enemy when exhausted." In *Cat. Min.* 73.3, Cato's son challenged the enemy. In *Brut.* 49.5, with sword in hand, Cato's son told his enemies who he was.

The death of Cato's daughter Porcia is described in greatest detail in *Brut.* 53.4–5, where Plutarch describes Porcia's suicide as reported by Nicolaus of Damascus. After learning of Brutus's death, she desired to die, but her friends prevented her from taking her life. So she snatched up some live coals from a fire, swallowed them, and died. Plutarch adds that there is an extant letter from Brutus, although its authenticity is uncertain. The letter suggests Porcia died prior to Brutus. Thus, Nicolaus was mistaken in the timing of her death. More details are provided in *Brutus*, since it is of greater importance in that *Life*. In *Cat. Min.* 73.4, Plutarch only says Porcia committed suicide in a manner worthy of her noble birth and virtue, as he had written in his *Brutus*.

In *Cat. Min.* 73.4, Statilius desired to take his own life when defeat was imminent but was prevented from doing so. However, he later joined Brutus and was both trustworthy and beneficial to him. He died in Philippi. In *Brut.* 51.4, when Brutus desired to return to his camp after battle, Statilius offered to make his way through the enemy, since there was no other way. He would reconnoiter the camp and raise a torch if it was safe and then return to them. Statilius reached the camp and raised a torch. But while returning, he fell among the enemy and was killed. More detail is provided in *Brutus*, since its relevance is greater in that *Life*.

Summary

- Plutarch alters the syntax of a logion.
- Plutarch describes an event using different yet compatible language.
- Plutarch provides more details in the *Life* where it bears greater relevance. In this case, it is in *Brutus*.

#31 More Victories and Challenges for Caesar
(Caes. 56–57; 62; Cic. 40.4; Brut. 7.1–9.3;
10.2–4; Ant. 11)

Narrative

After defeating Scipio, Juba, and Cato, Caesar returned to Rome in April 46 BCE where he celebrated his victories. After being declared consul for the fourth time (in 46 for 45), he left Rome for Spain, where in March 45 he defeated Pompey's two sons, who had amassed a powerful army (*Caes.* 56.1–3).[87] Caesar returned once again to Rome (October 45), celebrated a triumph, was chosen consul for the fifth time (in 45 for 44), and chose Antony for his consular colleague (*Ant.* 11.2; cf. *Caes.* 61.3). In early 44, Caesar was appointed dictator for life (*Caes.* 57.1).

Cicero proposed honors for Caesar in the senate (*Caes.* 57.2; *Cic.* 40.4). Caesar pardoned many who had fought against him, gave honors and offices to Brutus and Cassius (*Caes.* 57.3; *Brut.* 7.1–3; cf. 6.6), and set up the statues of Pompey, which had been thrown down (*Caes.* 57.4; *Cic.* 40.4).

Caesar desired to relinquish his office of consul to Dolabella. However, Antony objected and Caesar abandoned his efforts. At this point two anecdotes are told. On one occasion, a man was heaping accusations against Dolabella and Antony. Caesar said he did not fear them, being fat with long hair, but rather feared those pale and thin ones, referring to Brutus and Cassius (*Caes.* 62.5; *Brut.* 8.1; *Ant.* 11.2–3). On another occasion when some were accusing Brutus, Caesar replied, "Brutus will wait for this shriveled skin" (*Caes.* 62.3; *Brut.* 8.2).

Many Romans were upset that Caesar had become dictator and encouraged Brutus to overthrow him. Because Brutus was thought by some to be related to the Brutus who was reputed to have expelled Tarquinius Superbus from Rome in the late sixth century BCE,[88] some were leaving notes on his praetorial tribune and chair saying, "You are sleeping, Brutus," and "You are not Brutus" (*Caes.* 62.1, 4; *Brut.* 9.3; cf. 10.3). But Brutus's opposition to Caesar had been softened because Caesar had pardoned him, pardoned many of his friends at his request, bestowed honors and the urban praetorship to him in spite of Caesar's opinion that Cassius was the more deserving of the two, and chosen Brutus over Cassius to be consul in three years (*Caes.* 62.1–2; *Brut.* 7.1–4). But Cassius observed that Brutus was stirred by the people turning to him and prodded Brutus to take action against Caesar (*Caes.* 62.4; *Brut.* 8.3; 10.2–4).

Analysis

There are a several differences in how Plutarch reports this pericope. Plutarch alters how he tells the story using synonyms and changing a statement to a question (or vice versa). Caesar is reported to describe Brutus and Cassius as being pale and thin (*Caes.* 62.5; *Brut.* 8.1; *Ant.* 11.2–3). In *Caesar* and *Antony*, Plutarch uses the synonym λεπτοὺς, *leptous* (small, thin), whereas in *Brutus* he uses ἰσχνοὺς, *ischnous* (thin, lean, weak). In *Caes.* 62.3, Plutarch has Caesar express his reply in a statement: "Brutus will wait for this skin" (Ἀναμενεῖ τοῦτο τὸ δέρμα Βροῦτος, *anamenei touto to derma Broutos*). In *Brut.* 8.2 he poses it as a question: "What? Does it not occur to you that Brutus thinks to wait for this flesh?" (τί δέ; οὐκ ἂν ὑμῖν δοκεῖ Βροῦτος ἀναμεῖναι τουτὶ τὸ σαρκίον, *ti de? ouk an humin dokei Broutos anameinai touti to sarkion?*). In *Caes.* 62.3, Plutarch says "skin" (δέρμα, *derma*), whereas he substitutes with "flesh" (σαρκίον, *sarkion*) in *Brut.* 8.2.

In *Caes.* 62.3, Brutus is worthy of ruling because of his virtue (ὡς ἄξιον μὲν ὄντα τῆς ἀρχῆς δι᾽ ἀρετήν, *hōs axion men onta tēs archēs di' aretēn*), whereas in *Brut.* 8.2, no one other than Brutus was able to rule with such power in his hands (ὡς οὐδενὶ προσῆκον ἄλλῳ μεθ᾽ ἑαυτὸν ἢ Βρούτῳ δύνασθαι τοσοῦτον, *hōs oudeni prosēkon allō meth' heauton ē Broutō dunasthai tosouton*). In other words, it is Brutus's virtue that qualified him as Caesar's natural successor in *Caesar*, whereas the virtue of being able to handle such power is specified in *Brutus*.

In *Caes.* 62.4, the praetorial tribune and chair of Brutus were covered with graffiti, whereas in *Brut.* 9.3 Plutarch abbreviates and only mentions his tribunal.[89]

In *Caes.* 62.4, the graffiti says, "You are sleeping, Oh, Brutus," and "You are not Brutus" ("καθεύδεις, ὦ Βροῦτε," and "οὐκ εἶ Βροῦτος," "*katheudeis, ō Brute*" and "*ouk ei Brutos*"). In *Brut.* 9.3, it is "Brutus, you are sleeping," and "You are not really Brutus" ("Βροῦτε, καθεύδεις;" and "οὐκ εἶ Βροῦτος ἀληθῶς," "*Brute, katheudeis*" and "*ouk ei Brutos alethōs*"). It is possible that Plutarch changed a statement ("You are sleeping, Oh, Brutus") in *Caesar* to a question ("Brutus, are you sleeping?") in *Brutus*. However, with no punctuation in Plutarch's Greek, we cannot be certain what punctuation, if any, was assigned by the Latin graffiti artist.[90] At minimum, Plutarch paraphrased via syntax and the use of slightly different wording.

In both *Caes.* 62.2 and *Brut.* 7.3, Plutarch says Brutus was awarded the best of the praetorships (the urban praetorship). In *Caesar*, Plutarch adds that Brutus was also selected by Caesar to be consul in three years. Plutarch gives the impression in *Caesar* that Brutus was chosen over

Cassius to be consul, whereas in *Brutus*, it is the praetorship for which Brutus is preferred over Cassius. It cannot be decided whether both are true and Plutarch emphasizes different positions in *Caesar* and *Brutus*, or whether Plutarch has altered the details in one of his accounts.[91]

In *Caes*. 62.4, it is mentioned briefly that Cassius motivated Brutus to assist him in a conspiracy, whereas much more detail of Cassius's arguments is provided in *Brut*. 10.2–4 where its reference to persuading Brutus to act against Caesar possesses greater biographical relevance.

In *Caes*. 62.4, it is Cassius's hatred for Caesar that motivates him to organize a rebellion against him. Plutarch refers his readers to his *Brutus* (8.3) for the reasons why he hated Caesar; specifically, Caesar had taken his lions. In *Brut*. 9.1–2, Plutarch adds that Cassius's primary reason for organizing the conspiracy against Caesar was his hatred for tyrannical leaders, an animosity going back to his childhood and Sulla.

In *Caes*. 62.4, it is Brutus's love of honor (φιλότιμον, *philotimon*) that initially motivates him to rebel, whereas in *Brut*. 8.3 and 10.2 it is his objection to Caesar's monarchy. Thus, in *Brutus* Plutarch seeks to portray the conspirators as being motivated by noble reasons, whereas their reasons lay in their self-interests in *Caesar*.

Summary

- Plutarch alters by using synonyms, different wording, different syntax, and changes a statement to a question (or vice versa).
- Plutarch is more specific in a *Life* when it carries greater biographical relevance.
- Plutarch simplifies in *Brutus*.
- Plutarch portrays motivations differently and in a manner that favors the main character of a *Life*.

#32 Caesar Hailed as King; Lupercalia Festival; Diadems Placed on Statues of Caesar; Caesar Removes Marullus and Flavius from Their Offices; Caesar Insults Politicians Honoring Him; Exposes His Neck and Invites Another to Kill Him (Caes. 60.2–61.5; Ant. 12.1–4; Brut. 9.4)

Narrative

In early 44 BCE, Caesar was enjoying a certain, though diminished, popularity among the common people. Rumors abounded that Caesar would like to be king. But Rome was a republic, and despite consistent power struggles among the leading politicians, the Roman people still found the concept of kingship to be a repugnant idea, preferring power to remain with the people and the senate.

On 26 January 44, some hailed Caesar as king as he was returning to Rome from the Alban Mount.[92] When Caesar observed that this troubled some of those present, he said, "My name is Caesar, not king."

The Lupercalia festival occurred a few weeks later on 15 February, and Caesar was seated on the Rostra* in regal attire. An event occurred in which young nobles and magistrates ran through the city virtually naked, slapping people with leather thongs as they passed. Women stood in the way, hoping to be slapped in order to bring good luck for conceiving or having a smooth pregnancy.

Antony was Caesar's consular colleague and one of the runners. At the event's end as he entered the Forum, he carried a diadem that was intertwined in a wreath and placed it on Caesar's head—a gesture suggesting he should be made king. This was a daring move. When Antony's gesture did not receive the enthusiastic response from the people for which he had hoped, Caesar removed the crown. When he did, the people responded with hearty applause. Antony again attempted to place the crown on Caesar's head, to which some in the crowd responded with approval. But when Caesar again declined the crown, the majority expressed their strong approval. Caesar then rose from his seat disappointed, ordered the crown to be taken to the Capitol, and departed.

Several of Caesar's statues were later discovered adorned with diadems. Two of the tribunes of the Plebs, Marullus and Flavius, had them removed. They also arrested and imprisoned those who had hailed Caesar as king a few weeks earlier. The people applauded and praised the tribunes, calling them "Brutuses," after Lucius Iunius Brutus, who had removed the last king Tarquinius Superbus five centuries earlier. Caesar became angry with Marullus and Flavius, removed them from their offices, and referred to them and those praising them as "Brutuses" and "Cumaens." Here there is a play on the word "Brutus," which had come to mean "stupid," after the Brutus of old feigned stupidity in order to avoid being feared by the tyrants (see Plutarch, *Publ.* 3.4). "Cumaens" were a people known for their simple-mindedness.[93]

During another event, perhaps in late 45 and earlier than the previously mentioned event at the Lupercalia, all of Rome's elite politicians approached Caesar in an impressive processional in order to confer extravagant honors upon him. Caesar paid little attention to them and even failed to stand in respect to receive them as would be appropriate. The politicians and Roman people were insulted by Caesar's arrogance, and many left. When Caesar became aware of his gaffe, he pulled back the toga from his neck and invited any who desired to strike and kill him.

Analysis

Plutarch reports these stories in *Caesar, Brutus,* and *Antony* with a few differences. In *Ant.* 12.2, Antony placed the diadem on Caesar's head. In *Caes.* 61.3–4, he attempted to do so. But it is not revealed whether he was successful. Indeed, readers are left with the impression he was not.

In *Caes.* 61.4–5, Caesar ordered the diadem he had rejected to be taken to the Capitol. Some placed diadems on the statues of Caesar, and the tribunes removed them. In *Ant.* 12.4, the diadem refused by Caesar was placed on one of his statues and was removed by the tribunes. No mention is made of the other diadems placed on statues of Caesar. In *Brut.* 9.4, Caesar's flatterers placed diadems on Caesar's statues during the night. No mention is made of their removal by the tribunes or of the Lupercalia event.

In *Caes.* 60.3–5, Caesar offered his neck after realizing his gaffe at the procession.[94] However, in *Ant.* 12.1–4, Caesar offered his neck when the people at the Lupercalia indicated they did not want a king. When describing the events that led up to Caesar's assassination in *Antony,* Plutarch does not concern himself with events not involving Antony. However, he appears to like the story of Caesar offering his neck. So Plutarch has perhaps displaced that element of the story of the procession and transplanted it at the Lupercalia, conflating a portion of one event with another event in order to emphasize Caesar's negative emotions resulting from the people's response to the suggestion that he be made king.

In *Caes.* 61.4–5, after Marullus and Flavius imprisoned those who had hailed Caesar as king, Caesar removed them from their offices. In *Ant.* 12.4, their removal from office by Caesar was not tied specifically to their imprisoning of the others but as a result of their removing the diadem that had been declined by Caesar and placed on one of his statues. In *Brut.* 9.4, the positive response of the people to the tribunes' action is mentioned. However, no reference is made to Caesar's depriving the tribunes of their office. We might speculate that Plutarch included elements of the story that fit the portrait he was painting of his main character while not feeling obligated to include all of the details that were circulating or were known. In this instance, Plutarch's dominant interest in Caesar's popularity with the demos (i.e., common people, populace) in *Caesar* is well illustrated with their hailing him as king, while Plutarch keeps the attention on Antony when citing the diadem that his main character had presented Caesar in *Antony* and the positive response of the people to the tribunes' actions in *Brutus* that serves to encourage the main character of that *Life* to move against Caesar.

Was the diadem offered to Caesar taken to the Capitol or placed on one of Caesar's statues? Were Marullus and Flavius removed from their offices for imprisoning those who had hailed Caesar as king or for removing the diadem that had been placed on Caesar's statue? These are questions that remain after reading Plutarch's different versions of the story. However, additional differences surface when other sources are considered and raise further questions such as these: Did Plutarch conflate two or even three events regarding the placement of diadems? Or are different events being described? Although beyond the scope of our research, we will take a brief excursus (rare in this project) to consider how some other ancient historians report the same events.

Differences Reported by Ancient Historians
Regarding the Same Events

Many of the elements in this pericope are likewise reported by Cicero, Nicolaus of Damascus, Livy, Velleius Paterculus, Suetonius, Appian, and Cassius Dio. And differences appear in abundance. The number of diadems, the number of Caesar's statues on which they were found, who placed them there, the motives for placing them there, and when they were placed are only a sampling of elements where differences are present. It is not clear whether varying traditions are responsible for the differences or whether different events are being described. That the differing elements are rarely, if ever, included by only one author may suggest the existence of different traditions.

Dio (*Hist. rom.* 44.9.1–2), Appian (*Bell. civ.* 2.108), Suetonius (*Caes.* 79), and Nicolaus of Damascus (*Vit. Caes.* 130.21) speak of one diadem placed on one statue, whereas Plutarch (*Brut.* 9.4; *Caes.* 61.4) mentions "diadems" on "statues" of Caesar. Appian (*Bell. civ.* 2.108) and Suetonius (*Caes.* 79.1) tell of a man who placed a diadem on Caesar's statue, whereas Dio (*Hist. rom.* 44.9.1–2), Plutarch (Plut. *Brut.* 9.4), and Nicolaus of Damascus (*Vit. Caes.* 130.21) speak of multiple people being involved.

Dio (*Hist. rom.* 44.9.1–2), Appian (*Bell. civ.* 2.108), and probably Plutarch (*Brut.* 9.4) have the diadem(s) placed on Caesar's statue(s) to cause trouble

for Caesar, whereas Nicolaus of Damascus (*Vit. Caes.* 130.21) has Antony
hand the diadem to others and instructs them to place it on a nearby statue
of Caesar when Caesar refuses it.

Dio (*Hist. rom.* 44.9.1–2) says a diadem was placed on Caesar's statue
prior to Caesar's visit to the Alban Mount, while Suetonius (*Caes.* 79.1)
situates it when Caesar returned to Rome from the Alban Mount and prior
to the event at the Lupercalia. Nicolaus (*Vit. Caes.* 130.21) situates it immediately after the Lupercalia event.[95]

At the Lupercalia event, Antony placed a diadem on Caesar's head.
However, differences are present in the peripheral details. The manner
in which Antony approached Caesar differs. Appian (*Bell. civ.* 109) says
he leapt onto the Rostra. Plutarch (*Ant.* 12.1–4) says his fellow runners
lifted him up and onto the Rostra. Cicero (*Phil.* 2.33.84–2.34.87) says
Antony ascended to the Rostra dressed as a priest and with a diadem he
had brought from his home. Nicolaus and Dio each present the story differently than the others. Nicolaus (*Vit. Caes.* 130.21) tells us that the event
having concluded, Licinius presented a wreath with a diadem inside to
Caesar, laying it at his feet. Cassius Longinus removed the diadem from
the wreath and placed it on Caesar's lap. Caesar continued rejecting it.
Then Antony rushed up, grabbed the diadem, and placed the diadem on
Caesar's head. However, Dio (*Hist. rom.* 44.11.1–3) portrays Antony and his
fellow priests saluting Caesar as king at the Lupercalia. (Dio makes no
mention of the running event.) Then Antony placed a diadem on Caesar's
head and said, "The people offer this to you through me."

Nicolaus (*Vit. Caes.* 130.21), Appian (*Bell. civ.* 2.108), Suetonius (*Caes.*
79.1), and possibly Plutarch (*Ant.* 12.1–4) narrate Antony placing the diadem on Caesar's head at least twice. However, Plutarch (*Caes.* 61.1–4) tells
us Antony approached Caesar and held a diadem out for him. Caesar
pushed it away and declined it when Antony offered it again.

Two tribunes of the plebs engaged in raising up trouble for Caesar
who deposed them from their office. Although there are no contradictions pertaining to their identity, their names are reported differently.
Dio (*Hist. rom.* 44.9) gives us their tria nomina: Gaius Epidius Marullus
and Lucius Caesetius Flavius. Suetonius (*Caes.* 79.1), Livy (*Per.* 116.2),
and Velleius Paterculus (*Hist. rom.* 68.4) give us their second and third
names (*nomina* and *cognomina*): Epidius Marullus and Caesetius Flavus.
(Velleius Paterculus [*Hist. rom.* 68.4] lists their *cognomina* prior to their
nomina: Marullus Epidius and Flavus Caesetius.) Nicolaus (*Vit. Caes.*
130.20) provides us with only their first names (*praenomina*), Lucius and

Gaius, while Plutarch (*Caes.* 61.4–5) provides only their last names (*cognomina*), Flavius and Marullus, and spells "Flavius" instead of "Flavus." Appian (*Bell. civ.* 2.108) gives us the *cognomen* (Marullus) for the first tribune and the *nomen* (Caesetius) for the second.[96] As we observed in an earlier pericope (#6), ancient authors could select different components of a person's name to provide.

There is a difference pertaining to who was arrested by orders of the tribunes. Plutarch (*Caes.* 60.2; 61.4–5) says it was the people who had hailed Caesar as king when he returned to Rome from the Alban Mount. Dio (*Hist. rom.* 44.10.1) says it was the first man to do so on that occasion. Suetonius (*Caes.* 79.1) says it was the man who placed a diadem on Caesar's statue while people were hailing him. Appian (*Bell. civ.* 2.108) says they arrested both the first man to hail Caesar as king and the man who had placed a diadem on Caesar's statue.

There is a difference pertaining to when the arrest(s) was made. Suetonius (*Caes.* 79.1), Dio (*Hist. rom.* 44.10.1; 11.1), and Appian (*Bell. civ.* 2.108–9) place them prior to the Lupercalia festival, while Plutarch (*Caes.* 60.2; 61.4) puts it afterward.

Differences occur related to the reasons why Caesar deposed the tribunes. Appian (*Bell. civ.* 2.108) tells us it was for imprisoning the man who had placed a diadem on Caesar's statue (to which Caesar was agreeable) and then punishing the man who had begun hailing Caesar as king when he entered the city. Caesar, therefore, accused Marullus and his faction of conspiring to slander him cunningly as though he were seeking a tyranny. Suetonius (*Caes.* 79.1) says it was because they imprisoned the man who had placed the diadem on Caesar's statue (either because Caesar was offended they had rejected the suggestion that he be given regal power or because, as Caesar claimed, they had robbed him of the glory of refusing it). Recall that Appian said Caesar was agreeable to this action. Nicolaus (*Vit. Caes.* 130.20) says Caesar charged them with secretly placing the diadem there so that in removing it they might insult him and look brave to the people, all as a means of stirring up the people against him. Yet Appian and Suetonius tell us Caesar knew they had arrested the man who had placed the diadem on the statue, and Appian adds that he was agreeable to their action. Dio (*Hist. rom.* 44.9.1–10.3) says Caesar became angry with the tribunes when they removed the diadem that others had placed on his statue and then punished a man who had hailed him as king. But, in agreement with Appian, Dio reports that Caesar refrained from any actions against them at this point. It was when they then issued a proclamation stating they were not able to speak freely and safely for the public good that he had them banished. Plutarch (*Ant.* 12.1–4) tells us they were deposed for removing Antony's diadem that had been placed on Caesar's statue at the Lupercalia. However, in *Caesar* (60.2; 61.3–5), Plutarch says it was for removing diadems that had been placed on statues of Caesar[97] and imprisoning those who had hailed Caesar as king. Livy (*Per.* 116.2) and Velleius Paterculus (*Hist. rom.* 68.4–5) abbreviate, stating succinctly that they were deposed for creating hostility toward Caesar by asserting he was working toward becoming king.

Differences also occur in describing the fates of the tribunes. Suetonius (*Caes.* 79.10), Plutarch (*Ant.* 12.4; *Caes.* 61.5), and Livy (*Per.* 116.2) tell us they were deposed from their office, while Appian (*Bell. civ.* 2.108) and Dio (*Hist. rom.* 44.10.3) add that they were also removed from the senate. Nicolaus (*Vit. Caes.* 130.20) and Velleius Paterculus (*Hist. rom.* 68.4–5) tell us they were banished.

Finally, differences exist pertaining to when the tribunes were deposed. Suetonius (*Caes.* 79.1), Nicolaus (*Vit. Caes.* 130.20–21), and Dio (*Hist. rom.* 44.10.2–11.3) situate it prior to the Lupercalia, while Plutarch (*Caes.* 60.2; 61.4; *Ant.* 12.1–4) places it afterward.[98]

These accounts differ so much between the sources that it is difficult to know precisely what occurred and when.[99] Why are there differences? Some of the sources may have been more careful than others in their recollection and/or recording of details. Some may have altered the details in order to make certain desired emphases. Many of the differences suggest there were components of the narrative that belonged in an original context that was unknown by the time that particular historian wrote. So each placed it where he thought most plausible or expedient for emphasizing a point.[100] Stated differently, at least some of the authors may have used synthetic chronological placement in order to keep the narrative moving along. And there is reason to think this was an accepted practice.

In his short book *How to Write History*, Lucian of Samosata instructed,

> Now after the preface, the transition to the narrative, whether long or short, should be unforced and compliant, proportionate to the content. For all of the remaining body of a history is simply a long narrative. So, let it be adorned with the virtues of narrative, writing in a manner that is smooth, even, and consistent, not with bumps or potholes. Then, for style, let its clarity bloom, as I said, having been engineered even in the interconnection of its content matter.

For the historian will make everything distinct and complete. And after he has described the first topic he will introduce the second, holding and linking both together as a chain, neither with breaks nor as merely a collection of many stories. Instead, the first and second topics should not only be neighbors but also share content and overlap to the uttermost.[101]

Quintilian offers similar instructions:

History does not so much demand full, rounded rhythms as a certain continuity of motion and connection of style. For all its members are closely linked together, while the fluidity of its style gives it great variety of movement; we may compare its motion to that of men, who link hands to steady their steps, and lend each other mutual support. (*Inst.* 9.5.129 [Butler, LCL])[102]

The point made by Lucian and Quintilian is that historians should connect pericopes in an artistic manner by interweaving content and linking one story to another. This interweaving and linking could be especially useful when the order of events and some specific details pertaining to them are unknown. In such a scenario, we might speculate that historians were also free to create narrative details, and that this would include synthetic chronological links. Indeed, classical scholars have often suggested these types of flexibilities when the ancients wrote history.[103]

Such a practice may be why we observe so many differences, even contradictions, in the way a pericope is reported by several authors. In the present pericope we are assessing, perhaps some vague details were known about one or more diadems being discovered on one or more of Caesar's statues, that some had hailed Caesar as king as he entered the city, that Antony presented a diadem to Caesar at the Lupercalia, and that this angered others, including two tribunes. Some people were arrested as a result. In time, the two tribunes pushed beyond what Caesar was willing to endure and he deposed them from their office. Historians may have taken these vague reports and creatively reconstructed events in a narrative that flowed smoothly, filling in the blanks and linking the events together to make for a good read that was largely accurate though not in every detail. In the end, we can only speculate, leaving us with questions pertaining to a number of peripheral details while a historical core is discernable.

We have observed how Plutarch has narrated this pericope with many differences. Although plausible solutions were suggested, in a few cases we can have no certainty pertaining to which solution reflects what Plutarch was doing. We then observed in an excursus how other historians of that era reported the same events and did so in a manner that included even more differences. A number of these are contradictory in nature, although plausible explanations for the differences are available in most cases.

Summary

- Plutarch exhibits minor flexibility in the way he reports peripheral details.
- Plutarch displaces an element of one event from its original context, whether known or unknown, and transplants it in another context to which it is conflated.
- Plutarch often includes elements of the story that best serves his portrait of the main character in that particular *Life* while omitting other elements possessing less value for his portrait.
- Ancient historians and biographers may craft peripheral details in a narrative and connect events synthetically in order to produce a narrative that flows smoothly. This may especially be present when numerous details were unknown.

*#33 Conspiracy Against and Assassination of Caesar; Aftermath with Assassins (*Caes. *64.1–68.1;* Cic. *39.5b–6; 42.3;* Ant. *13.2–15.1;* Brut. *11.1–21.1)*
Narrative

As discontent with Caesar grew, a team of conspirators formed. Cassius and others enlisted Marcus Brutus, whose participation motivated still others to join when asked. Trebonius had previously hinted to Antony of a conspiracy to kill Caesar. While Antony had no interest in joining them, he would not stop them. The conspirators decided not to include Cicero in their plot because of his natural timidity and for fear that his need for great caution would keep them from acting quickly when an opportunity arose.

As the Ides of March (15 March) approached, certain portents occurred: there were apparitions, lights in the sky, crashing sounds, and strange actions of birds; multitudes of men on fire were seen rushing up; an animal was found without a heart when sacrificed; a seer warned

Caesar about the Ides of March. Moreover, while Caesar and his wife slept, the windows and doors of their bedroom flew open. He awakened and observed his wife, Calpurnia, uttering words and groaning because of a dream. In the morning, Calpurnia begged Caesar not to go to the senate that day. Since he knew Calpurnia was not a superstitious person, he feared going and consulted a few seers, who informed him the omens were unfavorable. He decided to send Antony to dismiss the senate. But one of the conspirators, Decimus Brutus Albinus, persuaded Caesar to go.

The senate meeting was to take place in a room adjacent to a theater erected by Pompey. Ironically, there was a statue of Pompey in this room toward which Cassius turned and silently invoked it for assistance. This was uncharacteristic of Cassius, who tended not to believe in an afterlife. Trebonius delayed Antony outside while several others were designated to attack Caesar. Before the senate meeting could begin, the assassins surrounded Caesar under the pretext of asking him to return the brother of Tillius Cimber from exile. When a suitable moment presented itself, Tillius Cimber seized Caesar's toga with both hands and tore it down from his neck, which was a sign to the other assassins, who then commenced the attack with their daggers. Casca struck first from behind with a blow from his dagger that failed to go deeply into Caesar. Caesar turned quickly, grabbed Casca's hand, and yelled in Latin, "Filthy Casca! What are you doing?" Casca then yelled in Greek for his brother to join him. The other conspirators joined in the attack and began stabbing Caesar with their daggers. Caesar tried to escape, but they had surrounded him. When Caesar saw Brutus approaching with his dagger, he pulled his toga over his head and surrendered himself to their blows.[104] He was stabbed twenty-three times and died at the foot of Pompey's statue.

After killing Caesar, Brutus attempted to speak to the senators amid the commotion and confusion. But the senators and the consul Antony fled in fear. The conspirators then walked confidently to the Capitol proclaiming freedom to the people as they went. Later, many senators and common people went up to the Capitol and Brutus delivered a speech, his first. The audience applauded and invited him to come down from the Capitol. The next day, he and the other conspirators walked to the Forum, where Brutus addressed the people from the Rostra, his second speech. They gave silent and respectful attention to his words. But when Cinna spoke afterward and denounced Caesar, the people were so outraged that the conspirators feared for their lives and fled back to the Capitol.

On the following day, the senate met. Antony, Cicero, and Plancus spoke in favor of avoiding civil war and for granting amnesty to the conspirators. The senate agreed, Antony offered his son as hostage to the conspirators as a guarantee for their safety, and the conspirators came down from the Capitol. That evening, Antony entertained Cassius at his home and Lepidus hosted Brutus. On the following day, the senate met again and thanked Antony for his leadership in avoiding a civil war, commended the conspirators, granted provinces to some of them, granted Caesar divine honors, and ensured that none of his rulings would be rescinded.

Shortly thereafter, Caesar's will was read. He left every Roman a notable monetary sum. Caesar's body was then prepared for cremation and burial. Antony read a eulogy and played into the people's sentiments toward Caesar, displaying Caesar's torn, blood-stained robe and denouncing the assassins. This incited the people's anger against the conspirators. A friend of Caesar named Cinna was present at the funeral. When some heard that "Cinna" was present, they assumed he was the conspirator by the same name, and they attacked and killed him. After Caesar's pyre was set ablaze, the people took up wood from the fire and went to the homes of the conspirators to set them ablaze, but they were prevented from carrying out the deed. Soon afterward, the conspirators fled from the city.

Analysis

Nicholas Horsfall writes, "On the Ides more varied and abundant information survives, I believe, than on any other day in Roman or Greek history. But this evidence is full of obscurities and inconsistencies, largely unexplored."[105] Due to the nature of this project, only Plutarch's four accounts of the events will be considered here. But we will not be disappointed, since there are several differences even between Plutarch's accounts.

On two occasions, there is a difference involving a name. *Cic.* 39.5b–6 names "Quintus Ligarius" as one of the conspirators, whereas it is "Gaius Ligarius" in *Brut.* 11.1. Pelling says *Quintus* is correct and that textual corruption in *Brut.* 11.1 is more likely than a mistake on the part of Plutarch.[106] There is a difference pertaining to who delayed Antony from entering the room in which Caesar was to be killed. In *Brut.* 17.1, it is Trebonius. In *Ant.* 13.2b, it is "by several of the conspirators." However, it is D. Brutus Albinus in *Caes.* 66.3. Has Plutarch had a slip of memory? Pelling suggests Plutarch is correct in *Brutus* (in agreement with all other ancient sources who mention the act),[107] has made a mistake in *Caesar*, of which he later became aware and sought to accommodate his error when writing *Antony*.[108] However, Pelling also observes that Plutarch does not mention Trebonius elsewhere in his *Caesar*, whereas he is mentioned not only here in *Brut*. 17.1 but also a little later in 19.3. So Pelling thinks it is possible that Plutarch substituted one of his existing characters for Trebonius in *Caesar* in order to avoid confusion. This latter option may be more than merely possible because D. Brutus Albinus would be a convenient substitution, since Plutarch has just had him lead Caesar to the room of senators (*Caes*. 64.1–4). So he was already there and available to detain Antony in 66.3. Plutarch simplifies.

The term used to identify the location of the first strike delivered to Caesar differs. According to *Caes*. 66.4, Casca delivered the first strike near Caesar's neck (παρὰ τὸν αὐχένα, *para ton auchena*). But according to *Brut*. 17.2, it was near the shoulder (παρὰ τὸν ὦμον, *para ton ōmon*). "Near the neck" and "near the shoulder" could certainly be describing the same location. We may ask, however, could Plutarch in *Caesar* have in mind Caesar's earlier invitation for anyone who wished to strike his neck and intentionally referred to Caesar's neck as the recipient of the first strike to create irony (*Caes*. 60.5; cf. *Ant*. 12.1–4)? Plutarch notes details for their irony elsewhere in that same *Life* (e.g., *Caes*. 69.3).

Plutarch alters logia by substituting words with synonyms. When attacked, in *Caes*. 66.5, Caesar yelled in Latin, "Vilest [μιαρώτατε, *miarōtate*] Casca, what are you doing?" and Casca yelled to his brother in Greek, "Brother, help!" In *Brut*. 17.3, Caesar yelled in Latin, "Profane [ἀνόσιε, *anosie*] Casca, what are you doing?" and Casca yelled to his brother in Greek to come to his assistance. When Caesar was killed, in *Ant*. 14.1, Antony put on a servant's clothing (θεράποντος, *therapontos*) and hid (ἔκρυψεν, *ekrupsen*). In *Brut*. 18.3, Antony put on clothing of a common person (δημοτικὴν, *dēmotikēn*) and fled (ἔφυγεν, *ephugen*).

The chronology of events differs in *Caesar* and *Brutus*. In *Brutus*, Plutarch narrates the initial progression of events more rapidly than in *Caesar*, compressing them. There we read that Caesar's assassination, the conspirators' trip to the Capitol, Brutus's speech to the people from the Capitol, their invitation for him to come to the Forum, the conspirators' trip to the Forum, Brutus's second speech, Cinna's speech and the people's angry response, and the conspirators' flight back to the Capitol all occurred on 15 March. In *Caesar*, Brutus's first speech (in the Capitol) is not mentioned and his second speech (in the Forum) occurred on 16 March.

The number of senate sittings differs. In *Brutus*, there are two senate sittings. On 16 March, the senate met for the first time while the conspirators remained at the Capitol. The senate voted and approved immunity for the conspirators and determined that the consuls would propose a measure to the people for granting honors to the conspirators.[109] On 17 March, the senate met for the second time, and this time the conspirators were present. The senate voted to commend the conspirators and distributed provinces to some of them. In *Caes.* 67.4, there is only one senate sitting: 16 March. Cinna's speech to the people is omitted, so there was no negative response of the people or the conspirator's necessary flight back to the Capitol. The senate met and voted to grant Caesar divine honors, not to change any of Caesar's measures, and to give honors and provinces to the conspirators. *Ant.* 14.2 likewise speaks of only one senate sitting.[110]

Caesar's assassination itself is mentioned in four *Lives: Caes.* 66.3–7, *Brut.* 17.2–4, *Ant.* 14.1, and *Cic.* 42.2. As we might expect, Plutarch provides his most detailed description in *Caesar* given its biographical relevance. In *Brutus* and *Antony*, far less attention is devoted to the assassination itself before Plutarch moves along to describe the aftermath, since this is the beginning of the most prominent part of the lives of Brutus and Antony. And in *Cicero*, Plutarch merely mentions the assassination and then devotes only a little space to the immediate aftermath, since Cicero's role in it was relatively small.

The manner in which amnesty for the conspirators was proposed differs in the accounts. In *Cic.* 42.2, Antony called the senate together and spoke *briefly* on the need for unity, while Cicero gave a *long* speech and persuaded the senate to decree amnesty and assign provinces to Brutus and Cassius. Cicero's role is emphasized in this *Life*. In *Ant.* 14.2, Antony called the senate together and spoke in favor of amnesty and a distribution of provinces to Brutus, Cassius, and their associates. Antony left the meeting that day as a hero because he was thought to have avoided civil war and to have handled a difficult situation with great prudence and as a statesman. Cicero's participation was not even mentioned, for this is a *Life of Antony*. So Plutarch emphasizes the roles played by the main characters in his *Cicero* and *Antony* and shines his literary spotlight in *Antony* when omitting Cicero's role. He may also have conflated the speeches of Antony and Cicero in *Antony* and assigned the ideas in them to his main character. In *Brut.* 19.1, it is the combined efforts of Antony, Plancus, and Cicero who propose amnesty and unity, with no emphasis being placed on any of the three. In *Caes.* 67.4, it is the senate that votes for amnesty for the conspirators, that Caesar should be honored as a god, that none of his decrees should be altered, and that provinces and honors be given to Brutus and his associates. None of the individuals who led the efforts to bring about amnesty and unity are named, because the story is about Caesar and the role of others in the aftermath have little biographical relevance in this *Life*.

Reasons differ pertaining to why the people turned against the conspirators. In *Caes.* 68.1, it is Caesar's goodwill and final act of kindness toward the Roman people manifested in the monetary gift he had willed to them. No mention is made of Antony's eulogy. In *Ant.* 14.3–4, no mention is made of Caesar's will, and it is Antony's eulogy alone that turns the people against the conspirators. In *Brut.* 20.2–4, it is both Caesar's kindness to the people, realized in the gifts he had willed to them, and Antony's eulogy. In *Cic.* 42.3, it is the pity the people feel when viewing Caesar's body in the Forum and Antony's showing Caesar's torn and bloody clothing. No mention is made of Caesar's gifts to the people or of Antony's eulogy. In both *Caesar* and *Antony*, Plutarch spotlights the reason having the greatest amount of biographical relevance to their main characters. In *Cicero*, Plutarch's focus is on the emotions that led the people to turn against the conspirators.

Differences appear in Antony's eulogy. In *Brut.* 20.3–4, when Antony observed that the people were moved by his eulogy, he changed his tone to be compassionate toward Caesar, unfolding (ἀνέπτυξεν, *aneptuxen*) his clothing (τὴν ἐσθῆτα, *tēn esthēta*) and displaying its bloodstains and piercings.[111] In *Ant.* 14.3–4, when Antony observed that the people were moved by his eulogy and his words of praise for Caesar, he expressed sorrow and indignation over the assassination, displayed and shook (ἀνασείων, *anaseiōn*) Caesar's torn and bloodstained garments (τοὺς χιτωνίσκους, *tous chitōniskous*), and called the conspirators villains and murderers. The account in *Antony* portrays Antony being more dramatic than in *Brutus*, shaking rather than merely unfolding Caesar's clothing and vilifying the assassins. Plutarch also adds that Antony verbally attacked the conspirators in order to put down Brutus so that he would be the first man in Rome.[112] In *Antony*, Antony's eulogy receives greater attention, and perhaps Plutarch's redaction, in order to support Plutarch's portrait of his main character.

There are differences pertaining to whom provinces were awarded. In *Cic.* 42.2 it is Cassius and Brutus. In *Brut.* 19.2–3, it is Brutus, Cassius, Trebonius, Cimber, and D. Brutus Albinus. In *Ant.* 14.2, it is Brutus, Cassius, and their colleagues. In *Caes.* 67.4, it is Brutus and his colleagues. More specifics are provided in *Brutus*, perhaps because they were more closely aligned with the main character of that *Life*.

The conspirators' reasons for killing Antony and sparing his life differ. In *Brut.* 18.2–3, when the conspirators were discussing their plans, all but

Brutus wanted to kill Antony along with Caesar because (a) Antony was a violent man, (b) he desired a monarchy, (c) he had strength because of his favor with the soldiers, and (d) it was especially because of his arrogance and ambition resulting from taking the consular office as Caesar's colleague. Brutus opposed killing Antony because (aa) he wanted to take a righteous course, and (bb) he was hoping Antony would have a change of heart and follow their example. In *Ant.* 13.1–2, when the conspirators were discussing their plans, all but Brutus wanted to kill Antony along with Caesar because they were afraid of Antony's strength and his influence as consul (i.e., only "d" is mentioned). Brutus opposed killing him because the deed must be pure and free from injustice since it would be done on behalf of law and justice (i.e., only "aa" is mentioned). Because this was a decision that was debated by Brutus and his colleagues, Plutarch provides more details pertaining to the elements they considered in *Brutus* for their biographical relevance, whereas he abbreviates in *Antony*.

When Caesar saw Brutus approaching with his dagger, he released Casca's hand, pulled his toga over his head and resigned himself to the blows at Pompey's statue (*Caes.* 66.6–7; *Brut.* 17.3). That Caesar fell dead at Pompey's statue is mentioned only in *Caesar* in order to note the irony of a perceived vengeance from the one whom Caesar had defeated. This observation is absent in *Brutus*, since it bears no biographical relevance to its main character. Plutarch likes irony here. Later in *Caes.* 69.3 he reports that Cassius killed himself using the same dagger he had used to kill Caesar.

Many of the conspirators were wounded by one another in the process (*Caes.* 66.7). In *Brut.* 17.4, Plutarch shines a spotlight on Brutus's wounds without mentioning that some of the others were likewise wounded in the process.

Brutus is the only *Life* to mention Brutus's first speech after the assassination and Cinna's provocative speech following Brutus's second.

When reporting the conspirators' first trip from the Capitol to the Forum, *Brut.* 18.5 adds that Brutus and the conspirators were escorted honorably by the people, even by many eminent citizens, emphasizing Brutus's high standing and favor with the people. This is precisely what we would expect given the literary portrait Plutarch is painting of Brutus.

The amount Caesar left each Roman citizen in his will is described differently. In *Caes.* 68.1, he leaves them a sizeable (ἀξιόλογος, *axiologos*) gift, whereas in *Brut.* 20.2, he left them seventy-five drachmas and donated his gardens beyond the Tiber River for public use.[113] We might expect this extra detail to appear in *Caesar* rather than in *Brutus* where it does.

From where did the people get the wood for the pyre on which Caesar's body was laid? In *Caes.* 68.1, it is from the Forum (ἀγορᾶς, *agoras*), whereas *Brut.* 20.3–4 is more specific, saying it is from the shops (τῶν ἐργαστηρί- ων, *tōn ergastēriōn*) in the Forum.

Plutarch's *Caesar* ends with the report that Caesar's great daimon[114] avenged his death by pursuing the conspirators until they all had been punished. He then provides details of the deaths of Cassius and Brutus.

Summary

- Plutarch may have transfered the action of one character to another in order to avoid confusion in *Caesar*.
- Plutarch may have selected a specific term in order to create irony in *Caesar*, since he notes irony elsewhere in that *Life*.
- Plutarch alters logia by substituting words with synonyms in *Caesar, Brutus*, and *Antony*.
- Plutarch compresses in *Caesar*.
- Plutarch includes additional details for their biographical relevance in *Caesar* and *Antony*.
- Plutarch shines his literary spotlight in *Antony* and *Brutus* and on elements having the greatest amount of biographical relevance in *Caesar, Antony*, and *Brutus*.
- Plutarch emphasizes the roles played by his main characters in certain events in *Cicero* and *Antony*.
- In *Cicero*, Plutarch focuses on the emotions that led to certain events.
- In *Antony*, Plutarch perhaps redacts elements of a story in order to support the portrait he is painting of his main character.
- Plutarch abbreviates in *Antony*.

#34 Octavian Arrives in Rome, Disputes with Antony, and Forms Friendship with Cicero (Cic. 43.6–45.2; Brut. 22.1–4; Ant. 16.1–4)
Narrative

Having learned of his uncle's death and that Caesar had adopted him in his will, in May 44 BCE Octavian returned to Rome from Apollonia, where he had been studying. He engaged in a dispute with Antony over Caesar's inheritance and the 25 million drachmas held by Antony, out of which seventy-five drachmas was to be paid to every Roman citizen in accordance with Caesar's will. Antony insulted Octavian, despising his youth, but Octavian would not be denied. Tensions between the two escalated when Antony threatened Octavian after he began pushing his way into the political arena, enlisting the support of Cicero, eventually the senate, and Caesar's former soldiers. Antony then feared Octavian and was motivated to reconcile with him at a meeting between the two at the Capitol that was held in late July or early August.

Brutus was angry with Cicero for forming a friendship with Octavian, whom he asserted was as much a tyrant as Antony. Cicero and Antony both experienced dreams about Octavian. Cicero's dream convinced him to support Octavian, while Antony's led him to distrust him. Antony's suspicion soon led to the dissolution of his friendship with Octavian, and he left Rome to take up his province of Cisalpine Gaul.

Analysis

Plutarch describes dreams that both Cicero and Antony had of Octavian and does so in the same context even though Cicero's dream occurred years earlier while Octavian was a boy. Cicero's dream suggested Octavian was sent by Zeus to end civil war in Rome (*Cic.* 44.2–4). Antony's dream suggested Octavian would attack him (*Ant.* 16.3–4). So Cicero's dream motivated him to form a friendship with Octavian, whereas Antony's dream gave him reason to distrust him.

The reasons provided pertaining to why Cicero formed a friendship with Octavian differ. In *Cic.* 44.1–45.1, it is (a) for Cicero's protection, (b) because Cicero had a dream in which Octavian was chosen by Zeus to rule, (c) due to his hatred for Antony, and (d) because of his ever-present desire for honor. In *Brut.* 22.3a, Plutarch simplifies and says it is out of Cicero's hatred for Antony (c). In *Ant.* 16.3, no reasons are provided. It is of interest that in *Ant.* 16.3, Octavian joined ("gave himself to") Cicero and others who hated Antony, whereas in *Cic.* 44.1, Octavian's stepfather Philippus, brother-in-law Marcellus, and Octavian came to Cicero and proposed a mutually beneficial friendship.

The reasons for Brutus's anger toward Cicero are described differently. In *Cic.* 45.2, Brutus said that in befriending Octavian out of his fear of Antony, he was clearly not accomplishing liberty for his country but rather wooing to himself a benevolent tyrant. In *Brut.* 22.3, Brutus asserted that Cicero was not so much opposed to a tyrant as it was that he hated a tyrant whom he feared. Moreover, by declaring in his letters and speeches that

Octavian was a good man, Cicero was actually recommending a government of benevolent slavery. He then reminded Cicero that their forefathers would not tolerate even gentle tyrants. Plutarch refers to Brutus's letters to Cicero, which are extant (*Ep. Brut.* 1.16 and 1.17). When we compare those letters with Plutarch's representation of their contents, we observe that Plutarch has summarized and paraphrased.

Cic. 44.1, *Brut.* 22.2, and *Ant.* 16.1–4 all tell of Octavian's return to Rome and entry into politics and say that he had many of Caesar's former soldiers serving under his command. Octavian disputed with Antony over the funds his uncle had willed to the Roman people and Antony had not distributed. Octavian ended up forming an alliance with Cicero and others who hated Antony. Antony eventually allowed the funds to be distributed. Only certain of these elements are told in each *Life*. In *Cic.* 44.1, Octavian disputed with Antony over the funds and formed an alliance with Cicero. *Brut.* 22.2 does not mention that Octavian sought out a friendship with Cicero nor Octavian's dispute with Antony over the funds, but reports that Octavian distributed them. And since Brutus's part was minimal here, Plutarch moves the story along more quickly in *Brutus* than in *Cicero* and *Antony*, given the lack of its biographical relevance to Brutus. In *Ant.* 16.1–3, we are informed that Octavian formed an alliance with Cicero and others who hated Antony. Antony's dispute with Octavian is mentioned while the distribution of funds is not.

Summary

· In *Brutus*, the arguments of the main character are articulated with more detail.
· Plutarch paraphrases and summarizes in *Brutus*.
· Plutarch abbreviates and moves the narrative along more rapidly when the events have less biographical relevance.

#35 Antony Declared a Public Enemy and Driven out of Italy; The Triumvirate Is Formed; Cicero Is Killed; The Conspirators Are Condemned (Cic. 45.3–46.4; 48.4–49.1; Ant. 17.1; 19.1–20.2; Brut. 24.2; 26.2–27.5)

Narrative

Antony's brother Gaius was leading an army against the conspirators and endured many difficulties. When he called on soldiers near Apollonia to assemble under him and fight Brutus, they instead went over to Brutus.

Gaius then engaged in battle against an army led by Cicero's son, who was one of Brutus's generals, and Gaius lost. His soldiers then went over to Brutus and surrendered Gaius to him. Brutus treated Gaius with honor, but Gaius attempted to persuade Brutus's officers to revolt. When Brutus learned of this, he placed him on a ship under guard.

Back in Rome, Antony had left for his province of Cisalpine Gaul, while Cicero had persuaded the senate to declare him a public enemy and sent Octavian and the consuls Hirtius and Pansa to drive him out of Italy. In April 43 BCE, they defeated Antony near the city of Mutina. However, both consuls were killed in the process, and their forces joined Octavian's. The senate became alarmed with the very young Octavian now leading such a powerful army. So it attempted to lure the soldiers away from him on the grounds that there was no longer a need for such a large army with Antony no longer offering a significant threat. The senate also confirmed Brutus's command of his provinces. When Octavian learned of these actions, he became fearful, and with the help of Cicero, he obtained a consulship at the age of only twenty on 19 August 43.

Like his uncle, Octavian's ambition was for complete power. Knowing that Cicero was committed to the Republic, Octavian abandoned him and invited Antony and Lepidus to become his friends. In late October or November, Octavian, Antony, and Lepidus met for three days on an island in the middle of a river near Bononia, formed a triumvirate, and divided the provinces among themselves.[115] At the demand of the soldiers, Octavian agreed to marry Antony's stepdaughter Clodia to seal their friendship. After this, the three created proscriptions. Antony demanded that Cicero's name be added, but Octavian declined. When Antony refused to agree to any terms apart from Cicero's death and Lepidus sided with Antony, Octavian acquiesced.

Soldiers were dispatched to kill Cicero. After the deed was done on 7 December 43, at Antony's command, Cicero's head and hands were cut off and returned to Rome. When they were presented to Antony, he laughed with great joy and ordered that they be placed on the Rostra.

When Octavian took the consular office in January 42, he started a prosecution against those who had conspired against his uncle and they were subsequently condemned.

Analysis

In this pericope, there are a few matters worth observing and a few differences. The consuls engaged Antony in battle and defeated him but were killed in the process. In *Cic.* 45.3 and *Ant.* 17.1, the senate sent Octavian and the consuls Hirtius and Pansa to war against Antony and drove him from Italy. However, in *Brut.* 27.1, Octavian is said to have driven Antony out of Italy, and no mention is made of the consuls for whom Octavian had provided assistance. Plutarch shines his literary spotlight on Octavian in *Brutus.* Also, Plutarch has inverted the order in which the names of the consuls are given. In *Cic.* 45.3, it is Hirtius and Pansa, whereas in *Ant.* 17.1, it is Pansa and Hirtius.

In *Brut.* 27.1–2, Octavian pressed for a consulship contrary to the law and no mention is made of Cicero's role. However, in *Cic.* 45.5–46.2, Octavian relied on Cicero to obtain the consulships for both of them, and there is no suggestion that it was sought contrary to the law. In *Brutus,* Plutarch highlights the corruption of the power-hungry opposition faced by the main character, whereas it is the events in the life of the main character that are in focus in *Cicero.*

There is a difference in the number of names that appeared on the proscriptions. In *Cic.* 46.2, there were "more than two hundred." In *Brut.* 27.5, there were "two hundred." In *Ant.* 20.1, there were "three hundred."[116]

Were one or both of Cicero's hands cut off? In *Cic.* 48.4, Herennius killed Cicero and cut off his head and hands. In *Ant.* 20.2, Cicero's head and right hand were cut off. Only in *Antony* does Plutarch report Antony's laughter and rejoicing upon seeing them. Other ancient sources differ in their reports, some saying the right hand was amputated whereas others say both were.[117] Perhaps Plutarch was providing one known version in *Cicero* and another in *Antony.* It is possible that those ancient authors who only mentioned Cicero's right hand were employing a sort of spotlighting by placing emphasis on the hand that was used to write the *Philippics* against Antony.

What Antony's act revealed is described from different angles. In *Cic.* 49.1, the Romans shuddered, because they did not think they saw the face of Cicero but rather an image of Antony's soul. In *Ant.* 20.2, Plutarch opines that Antony thought he was maltreating the dead with this deed, whereas, in fact, he was displaying his insolence and abuse of power in a time when he had experienced good fortune. In both *Lives,* Plutarch approaches the response to Antony's deed from different angles. But the message is the same: Antony's act may have displayed Cicero's body parts, but it more brightly (or darkly) displayed his own character in the process.

In *Cic.* 46.2, Octavian abandoned his friendship with Cicero and formed friendships with Antony and Lepidus. In *Ant.* 19.1, Plutarch also provides the reason: Octavian knew that Cicero was devoted to liberty. Thus, they were on different paths pertaining to the form of government Rome was to have.

In *Cic.* 46.2, the triumvirate divided the empire among themselves as a piece of property. In *Ant.* 19.1, they divided the empire among themselves as if it were an inheritance from their ancestors. In *Brut.* 27.5, they simply distributed the provinces among themselves.

In *Ant.* 19.1–2, Plutarch says the triumvirate disputed over the proscriptions. In *Cic.* 46.2–4, the proscription of Cicero was what caused the greatest dispute. An emphasis on Cicero can be expected in Plutarch's *Cicero*.

Plutarch provides his thoughts on the proscriptions agreed upon by the triumvirate. In *Cic.* 46.4, he says such anger and madness on their part resulted in their casting human reasoning aside and showing that no wild animal is more uncontrolled than man when power is added alongside of passion. In *Ant.* 19.3, he says, "I do not think anything can be as savage or as wild as this exchange. For this exchanging of blood for blood made them guilty of killing those they had handed over to the others as if actually doing the deed itself. On another point it was worse because they killed their friends whom they did not hate."

Only *Ant.* 20.1 mentions the agreement that Octavian should marry Antony's stepdaughter Clodia.

Cic. 47.1–49.1 provides an extensive description of the events leading to the death of Cicero that we do not find in the other *Lives*. This is expected given its biographical relevance in that *Life*.

In *Cic.* 45.2, Brutus enlisted into his service Cicero's son while he was studying philosophy at Athens. Brutus gave him a command, and he achieved many successes for him. In *Brut.* 24.2, Brutus brought into his service all the young Roman men studying at Athens, one of which was Cicero's son. Brutus praised him because of his noble spirit and because he hated tyranny; Brutus wished Cicero possessed more of the latter quality. In *Brut.* 26.2–3a, Cicero's son served as a general for Brutus, and he won many battles for him, one of which was against Antony's brother Gaius. Thus, the deeds of Cicero's son are described with more detail in *Brutus* than in *Cicero*.

Summary

· Plutarch shines his literary spotlight on someone who is not the main character in *Brutus*.

- Plutarch presents names in an inverted order in either *Cicero* or *Antony*.
- Numerical differences exist in *Cicero*, *Brutus*, and *Antony*.
- Plutarch either provides differing reports that were circulating, one in *Cicero* and one in *Antony*, or he shines a spotlight on an element to make a point.
- Plutarch often provides more details in *Cicero* for their biographical relevance.

*#36 Deaths of Gaius, Cassius, and Brutus (*Brut. *25.2b–3a; 26.2–5; 27.5–28.2a; 36.3–4; 41.1, 4; 42.2b–3a; 43.5–6; 48.1; 52.4b–5; 53.3;* Caes. *69.3–8;* Ant. *19.1–20.2; 22.1–4)*

Narrative

When Brutus learned that Cicero had been killed on orders of Antony, he avenged Cicero by executing Antony's brother Gaius, whom he had been keeping under guard (December 43 BCE or early 42).

The fate of the Republic was then decided in two final battles at Philippi between Brutus and Cassius, who were being pursued by Antony and the young Octavian. This is the same city in which the apostle Paul would start a local church about a century later and to which he would write a letter that has survived. Prior to the first battle, Brutus was alone in his tent when he was visited by a phantom that frightened him and told him he would see him at Philippi.

The first battle was fought in early October 42.[118] Brutus enjoyed a sound victory that came very close to utterly defeating both Antony and Octavian. Cassius heard false reports of Brutus's death, was then defeated by Antony, and fled. While hiding, Cassius sent a group to meet some soldiers who were approaching them, not knowing whether the troops were allies. They were from Brutus, but when Cassius's soldiers greeted them with embraces, Cassius's poor eyesight led him to believe the enemy had captured his soldiers. Thinking his cause was now without hope, he ordered his freedmen Pindarus to kill him.

On the night prior to the second battle (23 October), the phantom appeared once again to Brutus.[119] When it said nothing to him this time, Brutus resolved himself to his impending death.

Brutus's army was defeated, and he fled with some friends and hid for the evening. He asked a number of his soldiers to assist him in his suicide.

All refused until Strato agreed and helped Brutus run his sword through his chest.

When Antony came to Brutus's corpse, he scolded him for ordering the killing of his brother Gaius. But he placed most of the blame on Hortensius, who had performed the deed at Brutus's command, and Antony executed Hortensius on Gaius's tomb. Antony then wrapped Brutus's corpse with one of his costly scarlet cloaks and entrusted one of his freedmen with the responsibility of providing Brutus with an honorable funeral. But the freedman stole the cloak Antony had placed on Brutus along with some of the funds Antony had provided for the funeral. When Antony learned of this, he executed the thief and sent Brutus's ashes to his mother, Servilia.

Analysis

There are numerous differences in the manner in which Plutarch relates this pericope. Cassius's death is described in more detail in *Brutus* (43.5–6; cf. 45.1b). Cassius took one of his freedmen named Pindarus into a tent. He drew his robes over his face, laying bare his neck for Pindarus. Cassius's head was discovered severed. Because Pindarus was not seen afterward, some believed he killed Cassius without being asked. In *Ant.* 22.3b, Cassius ordered one of his trusted freedmen, Pindarus, to kill him. In *Caes.* 69.3, Plutarch merely mentions Cassius's suicide. There is no mention of Pindarus's assistance in the deed. However, Plutarch adds the interesting detail that Cassius used the same dagger to kill himself that he had used to kill Caesar.[120]

The first appearance of the phantom to Brutus is described with only slight differences. In *Caes.* 69.5, the phantom first appeared to Brutus in Abydus. In *Brut.* 36.3, he was in Asia. There is no contradiction here; Pelling says Brutus would cross the Hellespont from Abydus.[121] In *Caes.* 69.6, the phantom is described as "a terrifying [φοβερὰν, *phoberan*] appearance of an unnatural [ἐκφύλου, *ekphulou*] man having a great and troublesome form." In *Brut.* 36.3, the phantom is described as having "a terrifying [δεινὴν, *deinēn*] and strange [ἀλλόκοτον, *allokoton*] appearance with an unnatural [ἐκφύλου, *ekphulon*] and terrifying [φοβεροῦ, *phoberou*] body." In *Caes.* 69.6, the phantom stood silently by Brutus's couch (παρὰ τὴν κλίνην, *para tēn klinēn*). In *Brut.* 36.3, it stood silently by Brutus (παρεστῶτος αὐτῷ, *parestōtos autō*). In *Caes.* 69.6, Plutarch says Brutus asked the phantom who or what sort of (ὅστις, *hostis*) person he is, using an indirect question.

In *Brut.* 36.4, Brutus asks a direct question: "Are you of men or gods? What do you want that you have come as us?"

The second visit of the phantom to Brutus is reported in *Caes.* 69.8 and *Brut.* 48.1. Both accounts report that the phantom appeared on the night prior to the second battle and said nothing to Brutus this time. *Caesar* adds that Brutus understood what his fate in battle would be, while *Brutus* adds that the philosopher Publius Volumnius was with Brutus from the beginning and made no mention of the phantom, although he mentioned other portents. This may suggest Plutarch did not believe the story of the phantom. Elsewhere, Plutarch reports events for which he doubts their authenticity (e.g., *Cic.* 49.2).

Brutus's death is described differently. In *Brut.* 52.4b–5, Plutarch provides two accounts: (1) Brutus firmly grasped the handle of his sword with both hands, fell onto it, and died. (2) Some say that at Brutus's request Strato held the sword and looked away while Brutus threw himself upon it so that it went through his chest and he died quickly. In *Caes.* 69.8, Brutus took his sword and struck his chest while a certain friend helped him by strengthening the blow, and Brutus died. Plutarch may have conflated both versions mentioned in *Brutus*.[122] In *Ant.* 22.4a, Plutarch merely says Brutus killed himself after he was defeated. No descriptions of the manner in which the deed was carried out are provided. Plutarch provides more details in *Brutus*, due to its biographical relevance.

There is a difference pertaining to whether Antony and Octavian were present at the first battle. In *Brut.* 41.1 and 42.2b–3a, neither Antony nor Octavian were with their armies in the first battle. At the beginning of the battle, Antony went away to a marshy area, and Octavian was nowhere to be seen after his friend Marcus Artorius described to him a dream in which Octavian was commanded to leave the camp. However, in *Ant.* 22.1–4, Antony was victorious everywhere (22.1), and Caesar (the name given here rather than Octavian) narrowly escaped secretly when his camp was overrun by Brutus. Plutarch reports that Caesar (i.e., Octavian) says in his *Memoirs* that he had left camp prior to the battle as a result of a friend's dream (22.2; cf. *Brut.* 41.4). He adds that some assert that Antony was also absent from that battle but came afterward while his soldiers were chasing the enemy (*Ant.* 22.3; cf. *Brut.* 42.2b–3a). A few days later, Antony defeated Brutus in a second battle while Caesar (Octavian) was sick (22.4). So there were conflicting reports pertaining to whether Antony and Octavian were present with their armies when they were victorious. In *Brutus*, Plutarch says Antony and Octavian were absent from the first battle, whereas they were present in *Antony*. Pelling observes that reports of a general's absence from the battlefield originated with enemies attempting to diminish the achievement of the general.[123] He asserts that Antony was indeed present and had led decisively.[124] While this may be true of Antony, if Octavian had written in his *Memoirs* that he was absent from the first battle, that report at least would not have originated with his enemies. Accordingly, if Pelling is correct, Plutarch provides the competing report in *Brutus* that casts the main character's antagonist in a negative light.

In *Brut.* 53.3, when Antony discovered Brutus's corpse, he ordered that it be clothed in one of his most costly scarlet cloaks. Upon learning afterward that the cloak had been stolen, he executed the thief and sent Brutus's ashes to his mother, Servilia. In *Ant.* 22.4b, when Antony stood by Brutus's corpse, he uttered very few words of reproach to it for executing his brother Gaius in Macedonia to avenge the murder of Cicero. But Antony blamed Hortensius rather than Brutus and ordered him to be slain on Gaius's tomb. However, he threw his own very costly scarlet cloak over the corpse of Brutus and gave instructions to one of his freedmen to take care of burying Brutus. When he later learned he had not burned the cloak with Brutus but had kept it and much of the funds that had been assigned for Brutus's burial, Antony executed the man. Only in *Brutus* does Plutarch mention that Brutus's ashes were sent to his mother, Servilia, although more details are provided in *Antony*, such as Brutus having Antony's brother Gaius executed and that the thief who had stolen Antony's cloak was his freedman who had also taken for himself some of the funds Antony had designated for the funeral. In *Ant.* 22.4, Antony's scarlet cloak is "very costly" (πολλῶν χρημάτων ἀξίαν, *pollōn chrēmatōn axion*), whereas the noble main character in *Brutus* is worthy of Antony's "most costly" (τῇ πολυτελεστάτῃ τῶν ἑαυτοῦ, *tē polutelestatē tōn heautou*) scarlet cloak. Plutarch alters his description of the cloak using a synonym in one of the accounts. If one had to choose, we might guess the value was upgraded in *Brut.* 53.3 in order to emphasize the greatness of the main character.

The reason why Brutus executed Gaius differs. In *Brut.* 28.1, it was to avenge the death of his friend Cicero and his kinsman D. Brutus Albinus.[125] In *Ant.* 22.4, Plutarch abbreviates, saying it was to avenge the death of Cicero. It is surprising to find *Cicero* lacking mention of this. In *Pomp.* 80.6, Pompey's murder was avenged when Brutus captured Theodotus and put him to death with every sort of torture. In *Caes.* 69.2, Caesar's murder was avenged when his great daimon tracked down all of the conspirators until every one of them had been punished. Therefore, we would expect to find a report of Brutus avenging the death of Cicero in *Cicero*.

In *Brut.* 28.1, Brutus ordered Hortensius to execute Gaius, whereas in *Ant.* 22.4, Brutus does the deed. In *Brut.* 28.1, Antony slayed Hortensius, whereas in *Ant.* 22.4, he ordered Hortensius to be slain. In both instances, we observe transferal and spotlighting. In the Gospels, this is similar to reporting that Pilate crucified Jesus. Although Pilate ordered the deed, we do not imagine him as the one who drove the nails through Jesus's hands and feet. This form of transferal and spotlighting is so common to us even in modern times that we would not give it a thought any more than the ancients did.

Summary

- In *Brutus*, Plutarch shows more care for detail where a report has greater biographical relevance than in parallel accounts in other *Lives*.
- Plutarch provides the competing report in *Brutus*, perhaps in order to cast the main character's antagonist in a negative light.
- Plutarch uses a synonym, perhaps in *Brutus* in order to emphasize the greatness of his main character.
- Plutarch abbreviates in *Antony*.
- Transferal and spotlighting appear in *Brutus* and *Antony*.

Chapter Summary

In the fifty *Lives* written by Plutarch that have survived, we have focused our attention on nine, since they feature main characters who, for the most part, knew the main characters in the other *Lives: Sertorius, Lucullus, Cicero, Crassus, Pompey, Cato Minor, Caesar, Brutus,* and *Antony*. Of these, we identified thirty-six pericopes that appear in two or more of these *Lives*. Of the thirty-six, thirty contain many differences worth noting.

We often observe Plutarch writing in accordance with the law of biographical relevance. He provides more details of a story in a *Life* where it bears greater biographical relevance for the main character. When the relevance to the main character is minimal, Plutarch abbreviates, omits, and moves the story along more rapidly. He often emphasizes the roles played by his main characters in certain events while minimizing the roles of others involved. Sometimes he represents the main character of each

Life from that character's viewpoint, rather than taking a consistent position of his own (especially compare *Caes.* 7.4–5; 8.3 // *Cic.* 20.3–4 // *Cat. Min.* 22.4–23.2).

To be expected, Plutarch employs numerous techniques observed in the compositional textbooks.[126] He alters using synonyms, using different wording, different syntax, and changes a statement to a question (or vice versa). He describes monetary values in different manners (compare *Cat. Min.* 26.1 with *Caes.* 8.4) and inverts the order of names presented. There are two occasions in which Plutarch possibly uses inflection, changing a singular to a plural or vice versa (*Pomp.* 67.3–4 // *Caes.* 41.1–2; *Pomp.* 44.3 // *Cat. Min.* 30.3–4). On occasion, Plutarch substitutes a term in order to emphasize a point, such as the greatness of his main character (e.g., *Brut.* 53.3 // *Ant.* 22.4). He paraphrases logia and content, sometimes by summarizing a large amount and recasting it. For the most part, his paraphrasing appears to have had no objective other than to follow the literary conventions of his day.

Plutarch often shines a literary spotlight on a character. It is usually, though not always, on the main character. He simplifies by omitting details that would complicate either his narrative or the portrait he is painting of his main character, or to cast a slightly distorted picture in order to make a point about his main character. He often compresses and conflates accounts. He also takes the words or actions he had assigned to a certain character in one *Life* and transfers them to a different character in another *Life*. On occasion, Plutarch displaces an event or logion from its original context and transplants it in a different one, sometimes conflating elements from both contexts. In a few of those instances, it is difficult to determine whether the events or logia were intentionally displaced or if they were free-floating, orphaned from a known context, and set by Plutarch within a context he deemed appropriate.

Sometimes Plutarch will redact elements of a story in order to support the portrait he is painting of his main character. This may result in placing the main character or his adversary in a light that is more or less favorable. Even if Plutarch had no credible reports supporting his redaction, he still believed the point he was emphasizing was true. Plutarch may also have altered a detail slightly to create irony. He occasionally portrays motives differently, usually in a manner that provides some illumination on the protagonist's character in that *Life*.

On a few occasions there are differences pertaining to the names provided in the narratives. In one instance, it is clear Plutarch was using different components of the person's *tria nomina*. In the others, the differences may be due to the same reason (using different components of the person's full name), a slip of memory, a different spelling, textual corruption, or a reason unknown to us. Numerical differences exist in six of the nine *Lives* we are considering: *Cicero, Brutus, Antony, Caesar, Pompey,* and *Cato Minor.* While some of these differences probably result from Plutarch's rounding a number or providing a general figure, a few of them appear to be erroneous. There is a difference pertaining to the location of an event. And he occasionally narrates events with conflicting chronologies. Plutarch sometimes acknowledges the existence of conflicting reports. Though not always, these often relate to the main character. We observed that numerous differences in details were not limited to the manner in which Plutarch reported a story in multiple *Lives*, but also appear when the same pericope is reported by other historians of that era (see especially pericopes #32, #33).

In light of instructions for good literature writing by Lucian and Quintilian, we determined that historians were permitted to craft peripheral details and connect events synthetically in order to produce a narrative that flows smoothly. We deduced that this might have been practiced especially when numerous details were unknown, and we suspect that this may be the reason behind many of the differences that appear when Plutarch reports the same pericope in multiple *Lives*. This hypothesis gains even more plausibility when the same pericopes are also reported with differences by additional historians of that era. Accordingly, we plausibly conjectured that the creative reconstructions of different historians may have resulted in a number of the differences we observed between their accounts.

Having carefully analyzed the differences that appear when the same story is told in two or more of Plutarch's *Lives*, we are now prepared to render some final conclusions for this section. On occasion, Plutarch errs. Only rarely do his accounts disagree on so many details that we are left puzzled and entirely unaware of what he was doing (e.g., pericope #24). The differences we observe almost always could have resulted from Plutarch's use of the compositional devices that have been noted by classical scholars for some time and who have contended that these were standard conventions for writing history and biography of that day and were practiced by virtually all. Moreover, these differences appear to occur only in the peripheral details. And we must consider the possibility that, in many instances, the differences result from Plutarch's recalling the story from memory rather than checking his source(s) and even what he had written earlier in another *Life*.

With these observations in mind, we will now turn our attention to the Gospels in the New Testament and assess a number of pericopes that appear in two or more of them. We will look for differences in how they report the same story and assess whether it seems likely that the authors were using compositional devices similar to those employed by Plutarch.

4

Parallel Pericopes in
the Canonical Gospels

FROM AN EARLY time in its history, the Christian church came to regard
the Gospels of Matthew, Mark, Luke, and John as possessing authority far
surpassing other Gospels written during that period. Even today, most New
Testament scholars agree that these four Gospels command far greater
historical value pertaining to our knowledge about Jesus of Nazareth than
any of the Gospels that were not included in the New Testament canon.
Bart Ehrman writes,

> [I]f historians want to know what Jesus said and did they are more
> or less constrained to use the New Testament Gospels as their
> principal sources. Let me emphasize that this is not for religious
> or theological reasons. ... It is for historical reasons, pure and
> simple.[1]

Ehrman likewise asserts "the noncanonical Gospels are of greater importance for understanding the diversity of Christianity in the second and
third and later centuries than for knowing about the writings of the earliest Christians."[2] In reference to the discovery of the Nag Hammadi Library
and the *Gospel of Thomas*, Luke Timothy Johnson says,

> [T]hese discoveries are of interest for the patristic period more than
> for the period of Christianity's birth and first expansion. Despite all
> the excitement and expectation, it turns out that the canonical writ-
> ings of the New Testament remain our best historical witnesses to
> the earliest period of the Christian movement.[3]

Craig Keener similarly writes,

> Although scholars may differ with this or that aspect of the portrayal, I believe that on the whole there is much that we can know about Jesus historically, and that the first-century Gospels preserved by the church remain by far the best source for this information.[4]

Accordingly, in this section I will limit my analysis to the canonical Gospels.

Scholars also draw a sharp distinction between the first three Gospels and the Gospel of John. The first three are referred to as the Synoptic Gospels. The term *synoptic* derives from two Greek words: *syn* (with) and *opsis* (see). Thus, the Synoptic Gospels can be "viewed together." Of course, it is possible to view all four Gospels together. However, Matthew, Mark, and Luke are far more similar in the order in which they present their stories and even in the very words they use than when compared with John. They are so similar that scholars for a long time have recognized there are literary relationships between them.

Although there is no consensus on what those relationships are, the large majority of New Testament scholars hold one of three positions. Most hold the *Two-Source Hypothesis*, or Two-Document Hypothesis, which states that Matthew and Luke used Mark as their primary source and supplemented Mark with at least one other source. The most common way that another source is detected is by recognizing the significant amount of material absent from Mark but appearing in both Matthew and Luke (roughly 20 percent of their Gospels), often with precise verbal agreement, and all of it belonging to the sayings of Jesus. The Two-Source Hypothesis holds that this material was drawn from a common source that scholars have named Q (from the German *Quelle*, meaning "source"; see Fig. 4.1). Most, though not all, hold this was a written source rather than oral tradition. Were these notes of Jesus's teachings his disciples had carried with them? It is impossible to know. The Q source is entirely hypothetical since other ancient authors do not mention it,[5] and no manuscripts of it have ever been discovered. Notwithstanding, the Two-Source Hypothesis explains a lot, although it is by no means perfect or assured.

The second major position taken to explain the literary relationships between the Gospels is commonly referred to as the *Farrer Hypothesis*, first proposed by Austin Farrer in 1955.[6] This view also holds that Mark was written first and that Matthew wrote next, using Mark as his primary

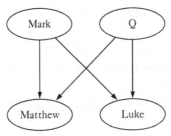

FIGURE 4.1 Two-Source hypothesis solution to the Synoptic problem.

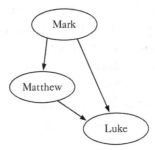

FIGURE 4.2 Farrer hypothesis solution to the Synoptic problem.

source and supplementing him with his own material. Luke then wrote and used Mark and Matthew (see Fig. 4.2). So there is material common to Matthew and Luke because Luke used Matthew as one of his sources.[7] In this view, there is no need to posit a Q source. The Farrer Hypothesis also explains a lot, although it, too, is by no means perfect or assured. A significant minority of scholars holds it.

The third major position is the *Griesbach Hypothesis*, which asserts that Matthew wrote first and that Luke wrote next, using Matthew and supplementing him with his own material. Mark wrote third, using and abbreviating Matthew and Luke (see Fig. 4.3). A small minority of scholars holds this view today.

There is a vast amount of literature on the literary relationships between the Gospels.[8] None of the positions posited to date are without problems. That is why the matter is referred to as "the Synoptic Problem." Although a majority of scholars hold the Two-Document Hypothesis, many scholars have serious reservations about it, and some significant scholars prefer the Farrer Hypothesis.

Before moving along, I must say some things about the Gospel of John. John's Gospel is quite different than the Synoptics. Almost all historians of Jesus agree that he taught using parables and astonished crowds by

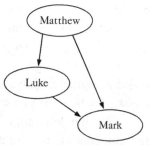

FIGURE 4.3 Griesbach hypothesis solution to the Synoptic problem.

performing deeds that he and his disciples claimed were divine exorcisms.[9] Yet Jesus's parables and exorcisms are surprisingly absent in John. When it comes to Jesus's miracles, his feeding a crowd of five thousand is the only miracle in John that can be said with confidence to appear also in the Synoptics. Although Jesus's words in John often contain the same gist of what we read him saying in the Synoptics, they are often stated quite differently and appear in a style and vocabulary similar to what we find in the letter of 1 John. Many scholars think what we are reading in John reflects years of either the author's or editor's reflections and provide fuller theological implications of Jesus's teachings.[10] John often chose to sacrifice accuracy on the ground level of precise reporting, preferring to provide his readers with an accurate, higher-level view of the person of Jesus and his mission.[11]

There is no agreement today on the identification of the author of John's Gospel. Almost all of the early church tradition attributed its authorship to John the son of Zebedee, who was one of Jesus's three closest disciples. Although most of today's New Testament scholars reject that tradition, they still think the Beloved Disciple mentioned in John's Gospel was the eyewitness source of much of the information contained in John. Many think him to be one of Jesus's minor disciples; others continue to maintain that the author was in fact John the son of Zebedee.[12]

The relationship of the Gospel of John to history and to the Synoptic Gospels continues to perplex scholars. In the United States at the Annual Meeting of the Society of Biblical Literature—the largest society in the field of biblical scholarship—numerous papers are read every year in a section titled "John, Jesus, and History." Moreover, almost all scholars, including theologically conservative ones, acknowledge that John often adapted his source material and rewrote it in his own idiom.[13] N. T. Wright's humorous comment accurately summarizes the thoughts of many New Testament scholars: "I feel about John like I feel about my wife; I love her very much, but I wouldn't claim to understand her."[14] Clement of Alexandria referred to John as a "spiritual Gospel."[15] Origen noted several narratives in John having parallels in the Synoptics that he regarded as impossible to harmonize in a historical sense and that often their truth must be sought for not in the letter but in the message, which must be spiritually interpreted.[16]

I have no objective to solve the Johannine puzzle in this volume. Therefore, on most of the occasions where John differs from one or more of the Synoptics, only the difference will be noted with little or no attempt to account for why it exists. Those interested in pursuing Johannine differences further may consult the commentaries.

Dealing with Differences in the Gospels

In many cases it is difficult, if not impossible, to determine if an evangelist has altered his source or is using another. We must also be open to the possibility that there were multiple recensions of the Gospels and that Luke used an earlier or later recension of Mark than the one possessed by Matthew. Different recensions may have existed for a variety of reasons, such as multiple drafts or authorial redaction to accommodate a different recipient.

It is also possible, perhaps probable, that some differences may carry the appearance of being in greater tension with one another than is actually the case because the Gospel narratives are not exhaustive. The discussions between Jesus and Pilate are described in much greater detail in John (18:33–38; 19:8–11) than in the Synoptics. It could be suggested that much of the dialogue between Pilate and Jesus is a Johannine creation, since the Synoptic narratives do not suggest that anyone else was present to overhear the exchanges, much less any of Jesus's disciples. Of course, this suggestion can neither be confirmed nor disconfirmed. However, it is worth observing what Luke 23:3–4 says: "Pilate asked Jesus, 'Are you the king of the Jews?' And Jesus answered, 'Yes.' Then Pilate said to the chief priests and the crowd, 'I find no cause for guilt in this man.'" Luke's report seems implausible if read independently of John. Would the Roman governor respond in such a manner after Jesus had just affirmed himself as a king?[17] Yet Pilate's response to Jesus's claim to be a king is entirely plausible if a dialogue had occurred between the two that was at least somewhat similar to what we read in John. Since John was probably written after Luke and is largely independent of Luke, both evangelists must have known a tradition such as we read in John. Whether John received detailed information from someone who had been present at Jesus's dialogue with Pilate or whether he knew a very basic gist of what was said and creatively reconstructed the dialogue with literary artistry is impossible to know.

Jesus almost certainly preached the same messages and told the same parables on multiple occasions over the course of his ministry. Like any good teacher, he would adapt his teachings to his particular audience. When a story with striking similarities appears in different contexts and contains differences, it is often difficult to discern whether (a) we are reading about two similar but different events and a few of the details from one have cross-pollinated to the other; (b) one of the evangelists displaced the pericope from its original context, redacted it, and transplanted it in another; (c) the pericope was free-floating outside of any context and each evangelist planted it where he thought fitting; or (d) we are reading a "stump speech" that Jesus gave on many occasions.[18]

It is safe to assume that nearly every conversation narrated in the ancient literature, if historical, is a summary of content recalled by the author and/or his sources. In some cases, the text may come very close to reflecting the actual wording used on that occasion (*ipsissima verba**). However, in most cases, we are reading the voice or gist of what was said (*ipsissima vox**), that is, a paraphrase.[19]

There are many observations of differences in the pericopes that follow for which potential devices are neither described in the compositional textbooks nor observed being employed by Plutarch. We will keep in mind that many of the compositional devices in use by Plutarch are likewise not found in the compositional textbooks. Nor are they taught in any of the ancient literature that has survived. Accordingly, much of what an ancient author did and why he did it will remain in the realm of informed guesswork for modern historians. We must keep in mind that since we cannot enter a time machine, return to the first and early second centuries, and interview the evangelists and Plutarch pertaining to their compositional practices, I am only surmising some of their compositional techniques, given what we learn from the compositional textbooks, a few other sources, and the rare opportunities where we can compare how an ancient author redacted the source we know he used.

This chapter and the one that follows contain nineteen pericopes that appear on two or more occasions throughout the canonical Gospels. Although there are many more than those that follow, I have limited myself to those pericopes I regard as having the best chance of containing differences resulting from the same type of compositional devices described in the compositional textbooks and inferred from the pericopes we examined in Plutarch's *Lives*. On the rare occasion when I have touched on a lengthy discourse of Jesus, I have only mentioned one or a few elements in that discourse.

I assume Markan priority in this study and that Matthew and Luke often use Mark as their source. This is most clearly detected when significant verbal similarities are present. Since Mark predates Matthew and Luke, Mark will usually appear prior to Matthew and Luke in the references. When Mark is probably the source used by Matthew and/or Luke, I place double forward slashes between them (e.g., Mark 16:6 // Matt. 28:5–6). Although I hold the Two-Source Hypothesis with the present majority of scholars, I recognize this position does not enjoy anything near a consensus and numerous significant scholars are in dissent. For convenience, I often use Two-Source terminology.

This chapter is not meant to serve as a commentary on specific texts. Accordingly, I will rarely offer comments pertaining to the historicity of an event or logion and/or its possible theological implications. Unfortunately, it is often difficult, if not impossible, to discuss Jesus of Nazareth in a sense that is neutral of metaphysical commitments. Naturalist scholars will tend to regard stories of Jesus's miracles in the Gospels as being entirely legendary in character, since miracles do not occur in their estimation. Christian scholars who are to varying degrees committed to tradition have no problems with the occurrence of miracles. Therefore, they tend to view miracle reports appearing in the Gospel narratives with more confidence in their historicity. I have unashamedly chosen membership in the latter camp. However, I have attempted to describe the Gospel texts in a manner that is largely neutral of partisan theological and philosophical commitments, focusing on their differences while making judgment calls pertaining to historicity only on occasion. If the nearly universal consensus of scholars is correct that Jesus's earliest followers remembered him as a miracle-worker and exorcist, he very likely performed acts that led to these memories. Of course, that is not to say we can know those acts were divine miracles and exorcisms. Nor is it to say the events occurred precisely as described in the Gospels. It is to say that there are probably historical events that lay behind many of the stories of miracles and exorcisms we read in the Gospels. Even many of those holding that some of the stories have been substantially revised and embellished maintain that historical kernels lay behind them.

Each pericope follows a format similar to what we observed with the pericopes in Plutarch in the preceding chapter: References are provided in which all or portions of the pericope are located. A short narrative summarizing the pericope follows. Because differences exist in each of these accounts, I have either harmonized the accounts in my narratives or preferred the narrative as presented by one of the evangelists. I then provide an analysis of the differences between the accounts. Finally, I summarize our findings. One difference concerns the numbers that appear at the top of each pericope. These are numbered one through nineteen and are immediately followed by numbers in parentheses. The latter coincide with the pericope numbers found in the primary text used for viewing parallel Gospel texts: *Synopsis of the Four Gospels*, edited by Kurt Aland.[20]

My proposed solutions are tentative. Others have offered different solutions. Some New Testament scholars may prefer to view some of the differences as resulting from an evangelist redacting the tradition in order to make a theological point rather than seeing the use of a compositional device. Such an approach may sometimes be preferable. In these pericopes, I am primarily attempting to view the differences in light of compositional devices to see if a greater understanding of what lays behind the differences may be obtained in some instances.

#1 (#13–16, 18) John the Baptist and Jesus's Baptism (Mark 1:2–11; Matt. 3:1–17; Luke 3:1–18, 21–22; John 1:19–34)

Narrative

John the Baptist came in fulfillment of Isaiah's prophecy (Isa. 40:3–5) to prepare the way for the Messiah. He was "a voice of one crying out in the wilderness, 'Prepare the way of the LORD. Make his paths straight.'" John the Baptist lived off the land in the wilderness by the Jordan River. His clothes were made from camels' hair, and he had a leather belt. Locusts and wild honey were his food. Many came to see him, confessed their sins, and were baptized by him. Even some of the Jewish leaders came to be baptized, and John the Baptist had a strong warning for them:

> Offspring of vipers! Who warned you to flee from the coming wrath? Therefore, bear fruit worthy of repentance and do not think to say to yourselves, "We have Abraham for our father." For I tell you that God is able to raise children of Abraham from these stones. And

even now the ax is laid to the root of the trees. Therefore, every tree not bearing good fruit is cut down and thrown into the fire. (Matt. 3:7–10; Luke 3:8–9)

The Jewish leaders in Jerusalem sent some people to ask John the Baptist whether he was the Messiah. He told them he was not and that one greater than he was coming whose sandals he was not worthy to untie. He baptized with water, but the one who was coming would baptize with the Holy Spirit and bring judgment. Therefore, all should repent of their sins and live righteously.

One day while John the Baptist was baptizing, Jesus came from Galilee to be baptized by him. When Jesus was baptized, the heavens opened, the Holy Spirit descended upon him like a dove, and a voice from heaven said, "You are my Son. I am well pleased with you."

Analysis

There are numerous differences within this pericope, and it will quickly become apparent that the evangelists employed many of the devices found in the compositional textbooks discussed in chapter 1. So often are these observed in this pericope that I will limit the number of examples provided in the pericopes that follow so as not to burden readers with too much minutia and to direct our focus on the larger differences.

All four Gospels tell us John the Baptist was chosen by God to prepare the way for Jesus. Immediately after writing, "As it is written in Isaiah the prophet," Mark 1:2 first quotes Malachi, "Behold, I am sending my messenger before you, who will prepare your way" (3:1a), then follows by quoting Isaiah, "A voice of one crying out in the wilderness, 'Prepare the way of the LORD. Make his paths straight'" (40:3).

Mark 1:2 slightly alters Mal. 3.1a, from "behold, I am sending my messenger and he will oversee the way before me" (ἰδοὺ ἐγὼ ἐξαποστέλλω τὸν ἄγγελόν μου καὶ ἐπιβλέψεται ὁδὸν πρὸ προσώπου μου, *idou egō exapostellō ton angelon mou kai epiblepsetai hodon pro prosōpou mou*, LXX), to "behold, I am sending my messenger before you, who will prepare your way" (ἰδοὺ ἀποστέλλω τὸν ἄγγελόν μου πρὸ προσώπου σου, ὃς κατασκευάσει τὴν ὁδόν σου, *Idou apostellō ton angelon mou pro prosōpou sou hos kataskeuasei tēn hodon sou*). There are three alterations:

- Mal. 3:1a: sending out, ἐξαποστέλλω, *exapostellō*; Mark 1:2: sending, ἀποστέλλω, *apostellō*.

- Mal. 3:1a: oversee, ἐπιβλέψεται, *epiblepsetai*; Mark 1:2: prepare, κατασκευάσει, *kataskeuasei*.
- Mal. 3:1a: The messenger will oversee "the way *before me*." God is speaking to the people and says he will send a messenger to prepare for his coming. Mark 1:2: God is speaking to another person, the Messiah, and says he will send a messenger who will prepare "your way."[21]

Mark also quotes Isa. 40:3 almost verbatim: "A voice of one crying out in the wilderness, 'Prepare the way of the LORD, make straight his paths'" (make straight his paths, εὐθείας ποιεῖτε τὰς τρίβους αὐτοῦ, *eutheias poieite tas tribous autou*). This differs slightly from the Isaiah text, which has "make straight the paths of our God" (εὐθείας ποιεῖτε τὰς τρίβους τοῦ θεοῦ ἡμῶν, *eutheias poieite tas tribous tou theou hēmōn*). Mark changes "the paths of our God" to "his paths."

Luke 3:5–6 alone quotes Isa. 40:4–5 (LXX) and alters the text slightly:

Isa. 40:4–5: "Every ravine will be filled and every mountain and hill will be brought low and *all* the crooked places will become straight and the uneven *place* will become *fields*. *And the glory of the* LORD *will appear,* and all flesh will see the salvation of God. *For the* LORD *has spoken.*"

Luke 3:5: "Every ravine will be filled and every mountain and hill will be brought low, and the crooked places will become straight and the uneven *places* will become *smooth roads*, and all flesh will see the salvation of God."

The italicized words indicate where there is a difference in the Greek texts. Luke omits the word "all" (πάντα, *panta*) and changes the singular word "place" (ἡ τραχεῖα, *hē tracheia*) to the plural "places" (αἱ τραχεῖαι, *hai tracheiai*) (inflection). Luke substitutes "smooth roads" (ὁδοὺς λείας, *hodous leias*) for "fields" (πεδία, *pedia*) and deletes "and the glory of the LORD will appear" and "for the LORD has spoken."

Whereas the Synoptic authors tell their readers that John the Baptist is the messenger of whom Isaiah spoke, John 1:23 narrates John the Baptist claiming he is the messenger of whom Isaiah spoke. All four Gospels give the same message while John offers it as the words of John the Baptist. Perhaps John transferred the message of Isaiah to the lips of John the Baptist. It is impossible to know. And there is no reason why John the

Baptist could not have made such a claim about himself and the Synoptics chose to communicate the role of John the Baptist by citing the Scriptures he allegedly fulfilled.

Particular elements in John the Baptist's message are presented in the same order in three of the four Gospels. We are surprised, however, to observe it is Mark (1:7–8) rather than John who presents a different order. The order in Matthew (3:11), Luke (3:16), and John (1:26–27, 30, 33) appears as follows:

a. I baptize you with water.
b. But someone mightier than I is coming after me of whom I am not worthy, having stooped, to untie the strap of his sandals.
c. He will baptize you with the Holy Spirit and with fire.

Mark's order is b-a-c. We observe Mark and Luke using similar wording for b with only three minor differences: (1) Since Mark is following a different order, he does not include the word "but" (δὲ, *de*). (2) Only Mark includes "having stooped" (κύψας, *kupsas*). (3) Luke omits the redundant "after me" (ὀπίσω μου, *opisō mou*). For b, the wording of John 1:27 is surprisingly similar to Mark and Luke with only four minor differences: (1) John substitutes a synonym for "worthy" (ἄξιος, *axios*, instead of ἱκανὸς, *hikanos*). (2) John substitutes the verbal "in order that I may loose" (ἵνα λύσω, *hina lusō*) for the infinitive "to loose" (λῦσαι, *lusai*). (3) John places the possessive pronoun "his" (αὐτοῦ, *autou*) prior to "the strap of sandals," while Mark and Luke place it afterward. While this would seem odd for English, it is not at all odd for ancient Greek. (4) John *substitutes* the singular "sandal" (τοῦ ὑποδήματος, *tou hupodēmatos*) for the plural "sandals" in the other three Gospels (Mark // Luke: τῶν ὑποδημάτων, *tōn hupodēmatōn*; Matt.: τὰ ὑποδήματα, *ta hupodēmata*) (inflection).

In Mark 1:7, Luke 3:16, and John 1:27, John the Baptist says he is unworthy even to loose the strap of his sandal(s), while Matt. 3:11 substitutes "to carry his sandals."[22] Mark 1:8, Matt. 3:11–12, and Luke 3:16–17 have John the Baptist say, "He will baptize you with the Holy Spirit," while only Matthew and Luke add the apocalyptically flavored "and with fire. His winnowing fork is in his hand and he will clean out his threshing floor and gather his wheat into his barn. But he will burn the chaff with unquenchable fire."

In Mark 1:7–8 and Matt. 3:11–12, John the Baptist's words are merely part of his message to those coming to him, confessing their sins and being baptized by him. In Luke 3:15–17 and John 1:24–31, John the Baptist says the above in response to those asking him if he is the Christ ("Christ" is the Greek rendition of the Hebrew "Messiah"). In Luke 3:15, "all" are asking if he is the Christ, while in John 1:19–25, those asking him are specifically identified as the priests and Levites from Jerusalem who had been sent from the Pharisees, and they are asking if he is the Christ, Elijah, or the Prophet.[23]

Only Matt. 3:7–10 and Luke 3:7–9 report John the Baptist's stern rebuke and do so with a few differences. For example, in Matthew, the rebuke is directed toward many of the Pharisees and Sadducees who had come to be baptized by John the Baptist, while in Luke it is directed toward the crowds who had come to be baptized by him. The rebuke is reported by Matthew and Luke with a nearly word-for-word similarity with only four Greek words out of sixty-three in Matthew and sixty-four in Luke (including articles) differing:

1. In Matt. 3:8, the "fruit worthy" is in the singular (καρπὸν ἄξιον, *karpon axion*), while Luke 3:8 uses the plural (καρποὺς ἀξίους, *karpous axious*) (inflection).
2. In Matt. 3:9, John the Baptist says, "Do not *think* [δόξητε, *doxēte*] to say to yourselves," whereas Luke 3:8 has "do not *begin* [ἄρξησθε, *arxēsthe*] to say to yourselves" (substitution).
3. In Matt. 3:10, John the Baptist says, "And now [ἤδη δὲ, *ēdē de*] the ax is ready to start chopping." Luke 3:9 intensifies the urgency of John the Baptist's message by adding "even" (καὶ, *kai*): "and even now" (ἤδη δὲ καὶ, *ēdē de kai*) (addition).

Matthew 3:11b–12 and Luke 3:16b–17 are likewise rendered virtually word-for-word in the Greek (Matt.: thirty-four words; Luke: thirty-three words): "He will baptize you with the Holy Spirit and fire. His winnowing fork is in his hand and he will clean out his threshing floor and gather his wheat into his barn. But he will burn the chaff with unquenchable fire." Luke 3:17 uses two aorist active infinitives: "to clean out" (διακαθᾶραι, *diakatharai*) and "to gather" (συναγαγεῖν, *sunagagein*) instead of Matthew's addition of "and" (καὶ, *kai*) that introduces two future active indicative verbs "he will clean out" (διακαθαριεῖ, *kai diakathariei*) and "he will gather" (συνάξει, *sunaxei*). Because the verbal agreement is so close, Matthew or Luke appears to alter syntax. Matthew 3:12 connects the possessive pronoun "his" (αὐτοῦ, *autou*) to the "wheat" ("he will gather *his wheat* into the barn"), whereas Luke 3:17 connects it to the "barn" ("to gather the wheat into *his barn*").

Only Mark 1:6 and Matt. 3:4 mention John's clothing and diet. Only Matt. 3:13–15 reports that when Jesus asked John the Baptist to baptize him, John refused and said it was he who needed to be baptized by Jesus. But Jesus asked John to allow it, and John baptized him. Only Luke 3:21 adds that Jesus was praying when the Holy Spirit descended on him.

In Mark 1:10 and Matt. 3:16, the Spirit descends from the heavens (plural), whereas in Luke 3:21 and John 1:32 it is from heaven (singular) (inflection). In Matt. 3:16 and Luke 3:21 the heavens are "opened" (Matt.: ἠνεῴχθησαν, ēneōchthēsan [aorist passive indicative]; Luke: ἀνεῳχθῆναι, aneōchthēnai [aorist passive infinitive]), while Mark 1:10 uses the more dramatic "torn open" (σχιζομένους, schizomenous [present passive participle]). In John, there is no mention of the heavens opening.

In Mark 1:10, Matt. 3:16, and Luke 3:22, the Spirit descended from heaven like a dove and came upon Jesus. Luke 3:22 adds the Holy Spirit was "in bodily form [σωματικῷ εἴδει, sōmatikō eidei] as a dove." In John 1:32, the Spirit descended from heaven like a dove and remained (ἔμεινεν, emeinen) on Jesus. In Mark 1:10 and John 1:32, it is the "Spirit" (cf. Matt. 3:16, "Spirit of God"; Luke 3:22, "Holy Spirit").

In Mark 1:10 and Matt. 3:16, Jesus saw heaven open and the Holy Spirit descend upon him like a dove. In John 1:32, John the Baptist testifies that he saw the Spirit coming from heaven upon Jesus as a dove. Luke 3:21–22a does not state who saw it.

In Mark 1:11 and Luke 3:22b, the voice addressed Jesus: "You are my beloved Son. In you I am well pleased." In Matt. 3:17, the voice addressed the people: "This is my beloved Son. In him I am well pleased." Either Matthew or Mark followed by Luke has changed (i.e., transferred) the addressee to whom God spoke.[24]

In all three Synoptics (Mark 1:11; Matt. 3:17; Luke 3:22b), God's voice testifies that Jesus is his Son. However, in John 1:32–34, there is no mention of a voice from heaven (nor is there a mention of heaven being opened). Instead, John the Baptist says God told him he would provide him with a sign. The Spirit would descend and remain upon the one he had chosen to baptize others with the Holy Spirit.[25] And it is John the Baptist rather than God who directly testified that he saw the sign and testified that Jesus is God's Son. Therefore, in the Synoptics, the voice from heaven directly testifies that Jesus is God's Son, whereas in John, it is John the Baptist.

While the Synoptics are clear that John the Baptist baptized Jesus (Mark 1:9; Matt. 3:13–15; Luke 3:21), John 1:29–34 does not state Jesus was baptized. It could very well be that John's account assumes Jesus's baptism (and temptation) had already taken place and that John the Baptist is recalling what had occurred at his baptism.

In John 1:31, 33, John the Baptist says he did not know/understand the identity of the one greater than he until he saw the sign from God. However, Luke 1:24–56 reports that John the Baptist and Jesus were relatives. Jesus's mother Mary was told she would conceive by the Holy Spirit. Her son would be the promised Messiah and would be called the Son of God. Elizabeth, the mother of John the Baptist, is said to be Mary's relative ("your relative," ἡ συγγενίς σου, *hē sungenis sou*) whose conception was also miraculous (1:5–25). In Luke 1:43, Elizabeth tells Mary she is the mother of her Lord. And Mary stays with Elizabeth for about three months (1:56). There is an understanding between them that both of their sons have been miraculously given for divine purposes. Therefore, according to Luke, it is possible that John the Baptist would have known about Jesus and his coming role for many years. In Matt. 3:14, John the Baptist initially refuses to baptize Jesus, saying it is Jesus who should instead baptize him. Matthew is at least suggesting on the surface that John knew something about the greatness of Jesus prior to seeing him at his baptism.

Summary

In this pericope, we have observed a number of actual or potential compositional devices being employed.

- Mark mentions a prophecy by Isaiah then proceeds to quote Mal. 3:1a prior to Isa. 40:3 (Mark 1:2).
- Mark substitutes terms in Scripture without changing their meaning (Mark 1:2–3).
- Luke feels free to omit and substitute words when quoting Scripture (Luke 3:5).
- Matt. 3:9 or Luke 3:8 substitutes a term.
- Mark 1:10 or Matt. 3:16 and Luke 3:21 substitute a word.
- John 1:27 or Mark 1:7, Matt. 3:11, and Luke 3:16 substitute a word.
- Matt. 3:11 substitutes a phrase.
- Matt. 3:8 or Luke 3:8 alters inflection by changing a singular to a plural or vice versa.
- Either Mark 1:10 and Matt. 3:13–16 or Luke 3:21 (two times) and John 1:32 change inflection.
- John has a different inflection (John 1:27).

- Luke adds to intensify (Luke 3:9) or adds a thought (Luke 3:21–22).
- John 1:27 has a different syntax than Mark 1:7, Matt. 3:11, and Luke 3:16.
- John 1:19–25 provides a more specific identity of an audience.
- Luke 3:15 provides a more specific identity of an audience.
- John 1:32 provides additional thought.
- John 1:23 possibly transfers the message of Isa. 40:3 of a coming messenger to have John the Baptist state he is the messenger spoken of by Isaiah.
- Matt. 3:12 or Luke 3:17 alters syntax.
- There may be multiple traditions of what John the Baptist said that present his statements in a slightly different order, with Mark following one tradition while the other three Gospels follow another (Mark 1:7–8; Matt. 3:11; Luke 3:16; John 1:26–27, 30, 33).
- Mark 1:7 may add words.
- Either Matt. 3:16 and Luke 3:22 are more descriptive, or Mark 1:10 and John 1:32 are less descriptive.
- Matt. 3:7 or Luke 3:7 changes the recipient being addressed.
- Either Mark 1:11 and Luke 3:22b or Matt. 3:17 change the recipient being addressed.
- John 1:29–34 either assumes his audience is already aware of an event and leaves it unstated, or he intentionally does not mention it (simplification).

#2 (#20) The Temptation of Jesus (Mark 1:12–13; Matt. 4:1–11; Luke 4:1–13)
Narrative

After Jesus was baptized, the Spirit led him into the wilderness, and he ate nothing during that time. After being there for forty days, the Devil came and tempted him three times. For the first, he challenged Jesus to turn some stones into bread if he truly was God's Son. Jesus replied by quoting Deut. 8:3: "Man will not live by bread alone, but by every word that proceeds from the mouth of God." For the second temptation, the Devil took him inside Jerusalem, set him on the highest point of the temple, and challenged him to throw himself down if he truly was God's Son, since the Scriptures promised angels would be sent to protect the one who lives with God (Ps. 91:11–12). Jesus replied by quoting Deut. 6:16: "You will not tempt the LORD your God." For the third temptation, the Devil took Jesus to a place and displayed the world's kingdoms to him and all of their glory and told Jesus he would give all of it to him if he would worship him. Jesus replied by quoting Deut. 6:13: "You will worship the LORD and serve him only." The Devil then left, and angels came and ministered to Jesus.

Analysis

There are a few differences of interest in this pericope. Mark 1:13 and Luke 4:2 have Jesus in the wilderness for forty days, whereas Matt. 4:2 has forty days and forty nights. Matthew and Luke omit that Jesus was with wild animals during the forty days, while Mark does not mention that Jesus fasted during this time. Mark also does not describe the temptations but only says Jesus was tempted by Satan. Matthew or Luke inverted the order of the second and third temptations. In Matt. 4:4 and Luke 4:4, Jesus told the Devil, "It is written, 'Man will not live by bread alone,'" while Matthew adds, "but by every word coming from the mouth of God." The quote is from Deut. 8:3, of which Matthew provides a fuller version. The Devil's words are stated differently pertaining to the temptation to give Jesus all of the world's kingdoms. In Matt. 4:9, the Devil said, "All these I will give you, if you will fall down and worship me." In Luke 4:6–7, it is "to you I will give all this authority and their glory; for it has been handed over to me, and I give it to whomever I want. Therefore, if you will worship before me, all of it will be yours."

We observe a few alterations prescribed in the compositional textbooks. Matthew and Luke name the tempter the "Devil," whereas Mark has "Satan." Accordingly, one of the sources may have substituted the synonym. Matthew or Luke appears to inflect words, changing a singular to a plural or vice versa. Matthew 4:3 has the Devil challenge Jesus to turn stones into loaves of bread, whereas Luke 4:3 has the singular "stone" and a singular loaf of bread.

Summary

- We observe substitution.
- We observe inflection.[26]
- We observe inversion.

#3 (#47, 112) The Man with the Withered Hand (Mark 3:1–6; Matt. 12:9–14; Luke 6:6–11)

Narrative

Jesus entered a synagogue on the Sabbath. A man was there whose right hand was withered. Some Pharisees were also present, and they observed

Jesus closely to see if he would heal on the Sabbath so they would have a cause to accuse him. Jesus knew their thoughts, so he asked the man with the withered hand to come and stand before him. Jesus then asked the Pharisees, "Is it lawful on the Sabbath to do good or to harm, to save a life or destroy it?" But they were silent. Jesus then said to the man, "Stretch out your hand." When he did, his hand was restored to health. At this, the Pharisees left and discussed how they might kill Jesus.

Analysis

There are a few differences in this pericope. Matt. 12:9 gives readers the impression that Jesus went directly from the grain fields where his disciples had picked grain on the Sabbath to a synagogue: "And going down from there, he went into their synagogue" (Καὶ μεταβὰς ἐκεῖθεν ἦλθεν εἰς τὴν συναγωγὴν αὐτῶν, *kai metabas ekeithen ēlthen eis tēn sunagōgēn autōn*).[27] Although the grammar employed does not require the event to have occurred immediately after, the chronology is implied.[28] Mark 3:1 is not as clear: "And he entered again into the synagogue" (Καὶ εἰσῆλθεν πάλιν εἰς τὴν συναγωγήν, *kai eisēlthen palin eis tēn sunagōgēn*). However, Luke 6:6 is clear that this event occurred on a different Sabbath: "And on another Sabbath he entered their synagogue and taught" (Ἐγένετο δὲ ἐν ἑτέρῳ σαββάτῳ εἰσελθεῖν αὐτὸν εἰς τὴν συναγωγὴν καὶ διδάσκειν, *egeneto de en heterō sabbatō eiselthein auton eis tēn sunagōgēn kai didaskein*).

Luke is the only evangelist to add that Jesus not only entered their synagogue but also taught and that scribes were likewise present (Luke 6:6; Mark and Matthew only mention the Pharisees). Luke also specifies that it was the man's right hand that was withered.

Most interesting is that in Mark 3:2–5 and Luke 6:7–10 the Pharisees are portrayed as being silent throughout the entire event while observing Jesus to see if he would heal the man, thereby breaking the Sabbath and providing them with grounds to accuse him. But Jesus knew their thoughts and asked them whether it was lawful on the Sabbath to do good or to save a life. In Matt. 12:10–13, the Pharisees were not silent. Instead, Matthew takes the thoughts of the Pharisees and converts them into a dialogue with Jesus: "They asked him, 'Is it lawful to heal on the Sabbath?' in order that they might accuse him." Elsewhere, Matthew turns Jesus's statements into a brief dialogue with his opponents.[29] This may very well be what is occurring here.[30]

Luke reports this story as well as a different one in Luke 14:1–6, although there are similarities between both. In the second story Jesus was dining at the house of a ruler of the Pharisees on a Sabbath. Because there was a man with dropsy in attendance, they watched Jesus closely to see if he would break the Sabbath and heal the man.[31] Jesus asked the lawyers and Pharisees who were present, "Is it lawful to heal on the Sabbath?" When they were silent, Jesus healed the man, sent him away, and said to them, "Which of you having a son or an ox that has fallen into a well on a Sabbath will not immediately pull him up?" (Luke 14:5). Matthew provides a similar logion of Jesus in our earlier pericope: "What man among you who having only one sheep and it falls into a pit on the Sabbath will not take hold of it and lift it out?" (Matt. 12:11).[32]

It could be that Matthew knew of both stories and, given his tendency to abbreviate, redacted portions of Luke's second story and then conflated those portions with the first story.[33] Consider this logion from the first component in Luke (the healing) when compared with the pericope in Matthew:

> Which of you having a son or an ox that has fallen into a well on a Sabbath will not immediately raise him up [ἀναπάσει, *anaspasei*]? (Luke 14:5)

> What man among you who having only one sheep and it falls into a pit on the Sabbath will not take hold of it and lift it out [ἐγερεῖ, *egerei*]? How much more value is a man than a sheep! So it is lawful to do good on the Sabbath. (Matt. 12:11–12)

However, teachers in antiquity as well as today often vary an illustration, anecdote, parable, or fable. Accordingly, as is often the case, it is difficult if not impossible to discern whether an author is reporting a separate event or has heavily redacted an existing one.

Minor differences appear pertaining to the actions of the Pharisees. In Mark 3:6 and Matt. 12:14, the Pharisees "counseled" (συμβούλιον ἐδίδουν, *sumboulion edidoun*) with the Herodians pertaining to how they could "destroy" (ἀπολέσωσιν, *apolesōsin*) Jesus, while in Luke 6:11, they (i.e., the scribes and Pharisees) "discussed" (διελάλουν, *dielaloun*) with one another what they might "do" (ποιήσαιεν, *poiēsaien*) to Jesus.[34]

Summary

- It is possible that Matthew locates this event on a different day than Luke.
- Matthew converts Jesus's one-sided address to the Jewish leaders into a dialogue with them.
- Luke substitutes some terms found in Mark and Matthew.

#4 (#85) Healing the Centurion's Servant
(Matt. 8:5–13; Luke 7:1–10)[35]
Narrative

There was a centurion in Capernaum who had a slave who was valuable to him but was sick and near death. After Jesus entered Capernaum, the centurion sent Jewish elders to ask Jesus to come and save the life of his slave. They came to Jesus and asked him on behalf of the centurion to heal his servant, adding that the centurion loved the Jews and had built their synagogue. So Jesus went with them. When they were not far from the house, the centurion sent friends to Jesus who told him the centurion said he was not worthy for him to come into his house. But he knew that Jesus, like himself, was a man of authority who issued commands and they were carried out. Therefore, Jesus only needed to issue the command and he knew that his slave would be healed. Jesus marveled at the centurion's faith and turned to the others with him and said, "Truly I tell you, not even in Israel have I found such faith!" And the slave was healed.

Analysis

There is one major difference between the accounts. In Luke, the centurion sent elders and friends to Jesus but never saw him. Matthew brushes out the elders and friends from his narrative and instead has the centurion go to Jesus in person. Because Matthew tends to present abbreviated versions of stories paralleled in Mark and Luke, this is likely an example of Matthew compressing the narrative and transferring what a messenger had communicated to the literal mouth of the one who had sent the messenger. This pericope has a nice parallel in pericope #23 in chapter 3 in which Pompey appears in person rather than sending an emissary to read an encomium on behalf of his friend Plancus, who is on trial.

Summary

·   Matthew compresses the story and transfers via substitution.

#5 (#91, 137) The Gadarene Demoniacs
(Mark 5:1–20; Matt. 8:28–34; Luke 8:26–39)
Narrative

After Jesus had stilled the storm,[36] they came to the other side of the Sea of Galilee to the country of the Gerasenes. A man lived there who had been demon-possessed for a long time. He was naked, lived among the tombs, and was so violent that no one could pass that way. To that day, he had resisted being subdued, even breaking shackles and chains with which others had restrained him. All throughout the night and the day, among the tombs and in the mountains, he would cry out and cut himself with stones.

As Jesus stepped onto land, the demoniac ran up and fell before him. Jesus said, "Come out of the man, unclean spirit!" The demoniac cried out loudly, "What have you to do with me, Jesus, Son of the Most High God? I implore you by God! Do not torment me!" Jesus asked him, "What is your name?" And he answered, "Legion," for there were many demons in him. And they begged him not to send them out of the country. Now a large herd of around two thousand pigs were feeding on the hillside, so the demoniac begged Jesus to allow them to go and enter the pigs. He said to them, "Go," and they came out of the man and entered the pigs. Then the herd rushed down the steep bank into the sea and drowned.

Those tending the herd fled into the city and country and announced what had happened. When the people came to the area, they saw the man who had been possessed now clothed, sane, and sitting with Jesus. The people feared Jesus greatly and begged him to leave. As Jesus was getting into the boat, the man who had been possessed begged him to allow him to come and remain with him. But Jesus declined his request and instructed him to return to his house and announce what God had done for him. The man did as instructed, and the people were amazed.

Analysis

There are a few differences in this pericope that will be of interest to us. In Mark 5:1 and Luke 8:26, the location is the country of the Gerasenes. Luke adds that it was on the opposite side of Galilee, placing it in the country on the east side of the Sea of Galilee. Matthew 8:28 locates it in the country of the Gadarenes.[37]

Of greater interest, however, is that there is one demoniac in Mark and Luke, whereas there are two in Matthew. Thus, in Mark's version, the demoniac's question was, "What have *I* to do with you" (Mark 5:7 // Luke 8:28, emphasis added), rather than, "What have *we* to do with you" (Matt. 8:29, emphasis added). In Mark 5:9, when Jesus asked the demoniac to tell him his name, he replied, "My name is Legion, for *we* are many." Matthew does not include this element. The verbal agreement between Matthew, Mark, and Luke in this pericope is not nearly as close as we find in many other pericopes. Was Matthew using a different source? Or did he seek to illustrate multiple demons by adding a second demoniac? Or did he understand the "we" in Mark, whom Luke follows, to refer to two demoniacs and that Mark had shone his spotlight on the demoniac who was speaking? It is difficult to know. Furthermore, for reasons unknown to us, Matthew doubles up elsewhere when the other Gospels present one figure. A blind beggar in Mark 10:46–52 and Luke 18:35–43 becomes two beggars in Matt. 20:29–34.[38] A donkey in Mark 11:1–11 // Luke 19:29–34 // John 12:12–15 becomes a donkey and her colt in Matt. 21:1–11.

There is another possible solution. Matthew is prone to abbreviate stories found in Mark. He narrates this particular story using a mere 135 words compared to 324 used by Mark.[39] Perhaps Matthew has doubled up the demoniac in order to compensate for not telling the story of Jesus healing another demoniac mentioned earlier in Mark 1:21–28.[40]

Summary

- Matthew may have used a different source or illustrated multiple demons through creating an additional person or conflated two stories. However, it could also be that Mark, followed by Luke, has shone a literary spotlight on the main demoniac whom Matthew reveals.

#6 (#95, 138) Jairus's Daughter and the Woman with a Hemorrhage (Mark 5:21–43; Matt. 9:18–26; Luke 8:40–56)
Narrative

Jesus crossed over the Sea of Galilee again, and a crowd welcomed him. A ruler of the synagogue there named Jairus knelt before Jesus and asked him to come to his house and heal his twelve-year-old daughter, who was about to die. Jesus agreed, and as they were on their way, a woman who had suffered from a hemorrhage for twelve years came to Jesus. She was broke, having spent all that she had on physicians who had been unable to help her. After hearing reports about Jesus, she thought if she could get close enough just to touch his garment she would be healed. So she came up and touched the fringe of his robe, and immediately she felt in her body that she was healed. But Jesus, perceiving that power had gone forth from him, stopped and turned to the crowd around him, asking who had touched him. The woman realized that her act was not hidden. So she came before Jesus and fell down before him with fear and trembling and explained why she touched him and how she was healed. Jesus said to her, "Daughter, your faith has healed you. Go in peace."

While Jesus was still speaking to the woman, some people from Jairus's house came with the bad news that his daughter had just died. But Jesus told Jairus not to fear but to believe and that she would be well. When they arrived, Jesus took Peter, James, and John with Jairus and his wife into the house. Some inside were weeping loudly. Jesus told them not to weep because the girl was only asleep. But they laughed at him. He then went in to where the girl was, took her hand, and said, "Little girl, arise!" Immediately, she returned to life and got up.

Analysis

There are a number of interesting differences in this pericope. The first one concerns the context in which it occurs. This will be discussed in the next chapter. In Mark 5:35, people (plural) from Jairus's house came and told him, "Your daughter is dead [ἀπέθανεν, *apethanen*]. Why trouble the Teacher any further?" But in Luke 8:49, a man (singular) came from Jairus's house and said, "Your daughter is dead [τέθνηκεν, *tethnēken*]. Do not trouble the Teacher any longer." Thus, Mark has a plurality of people announce her death, while Luke has a single man do it. Luke may have shone his spotlight on the man who made the announcement to Jairus. Moreover, whereas Mark states a portion of the announcement as a question, Luke casts it as a statement.

The most interesting difference in the pericope pertains to the timing of the girl's death. In Mark and Luke, Jairus's daughter apparently died sometime after Jairus left his house to find Jesus.[41] However, in Matthew, Jairus was aware that she had already died when he left his house to find Jesus.[42] Typical of Matthew, he abbreviates his account, describing in nine verses what Mark does in twenty-three verses and Luke in seventeen. Matthew compresses his account and narrates Jairus's daughter as already dead when Jairus comes to Jesus.

In Mark 5:30, Jesus asked, "Who touched my garments?" In Luke 8:45 he asked, "Who touched me?" In Mark 5:39, Jesus said to those mourning, "Why the commotion and weeping? The child did not die but is sleeping." In Luke 8:52, he said, "Do not weep. For she did not die but is sleeping." Luke changed Jesus's question in Mark to a statement. In Matt. 9:24, he said, "Leave. For the girl did not die but is sleeping." Matthew likewise changed Jesus's question in Mark to a command.[43]

Summary

· Luke shines his literary spotlight.
· Luke twice casts a question as a statement.
· Matthew compresses the story.
· Matthew alters a question to a command.
· Luke substitutes terms.

#7 (#96, 264) Two Blind Men (Mark 10:46–52; Matt. 20:29–34; Luke 18:35–43; cf. Matt. 9:27–31)
Narrative

Jesus was near Jericho with his disciples and a crowd who was following him. Sitting by the road was a blind beggar named Bartimaeus, the son of Timaeus. When he heard that Jesus was passing by, he began crying out, "Jesus, Son of David! Have mercy on me!" Some began to rebuke him and told him to be quiet. But he called out even more. Jesus stopped and commanded Bartimaeus to be brought to him. Jesus asked him, "What do you want me to do for you?" Bartimaeus answered, "Rabbi, that I may see again." Jesus said, "Go. Your faith has healed you." And immediately he received his sight and followed Jesus along the way.

Analysis

That all three Synoptics are reporting the same event is clear. Matthew and Luke appear to be using Mark as their primary source given the order of the preceding events: the little children and Jesus, the rich and the kingdom of God, the parable of the laborers in the vineyard (Matt. only), Jesus's prediction of his death, the request of James and John (absent in Luke), and a blind beggar just outside Jericho receives sight (Mark 10:13–52 // Matt. 19:13–20:34; Luke 18:15–43).

There are a few differences of interest. In Mark 10:46, Jesus had come to Jericho and was now leaving the city when the blind beggar cried out to him. In Matt. 20:29, he was also leaving Jericho. But in Luke 18:35, Jesus was approaching Jericho. Various solutions to this difference in Luke have been proposed.[44] If Luke is using Mark as his primary source at this point, which he appears to be doing given the order of the preceding events,[45] he may have preferred to narrate the event prior to Jesus entering Jericho and then include a story unique to Luke about a tax collector in that city named Zacchaeus. Of course, Luke could have narrated Jesus healing the blind beggar after the story of Zacchaeus in order to maintain chronological accuracy with Mark. However, as we have observed elsewhere, chronological precision does not appear to have been very important to ancient biographers, including Luke.[46]

The most striking difference, however, pertains to the number of blind men in this pericope. There is one in Mark and Luke, whereas there are two in Matthew.[47] Thus, Mark and Luke have the beggar cry out, "Son of David, have mercy on *me*," and Matthew has, "Have mercy on *us*, Son of David!" As we observed in the preceding pericope, Matthew, who was given to abbreviating Mark, may have doubled up on the number of blind men in order to include another story from Mark 8:22–26 of Jesus healing the blind that Matthew will not otherwise mention.[48]

But Matt. 20:29–34 may have a doublet* in 9:27–31. In that context, Jesus healed a leper (8:1–4), healed a paralyzed man (8:5–13), healed others and cast out demons (8:14–17), healed two demoniacs (8:28–34), healed another paralytic (9:1–8), raised a dead girl (9:18–26), healed two blind men (9:27–31), and healed a demoniac who was mute (9:32–34). John the Baptist was imprisoned and appeared to be in doubt about Jesus. So he sent a few of his disciples to ask Jesus, "Are you the one who is to come, or should we wait for another?" (11:3). Jesus told them, "Go and report to John what you hear and see: the blind receive sight and the lame are walking, lepers are cleaned and the deaf hear, even the dead are raised, and the poor have the good news proclaimed to them" (11:4–5). John the Baptist could thus be assured Jesus was the Messiah, since he was doing the very things expected of the Messiah (Isa. 61:1; 4Q521). Accordingly, Matthew may have included the doublet (although with variations) he would repeat later in 20:29–34 to provide an example of Jesus healing the blind as evidence for Jesus being the Messiah.[49] If the healing of two blind men in Matt. 9 is a doublet, it could weaken the proposal that Matthew added another blind man to Bartimaeus in order to account for another story of Jesus healing the blind man mentioned in Mark but not covered in Matthew. But there was no need to do so if Matthew twice narrated this story of Jesus healing two blind men.

Yet we should also consider the possibility that there were two blind beggars in this story and that Mark was shining his literary spotlight on the one known by Mark's readers, whose name he provides: Bartimaeus, the son of Timaeus. Later in his Gospel, Mark mentions another person who might be familiar to his readers: Simon of Cyrene, the father of Alexander and Rufus (15:21).[50] This could suggest either Mark's readers were familiar with these men[51] or that Mark is citing his sources. One can only speculate.

The interaction between Jesus and the blind man also differs. In Mark 10:51, the blind man answered Jesus, "Rabbi, that I may see again." In Luke 18:41 it is, "Lord, that I may see again." In Matt. 20:33 it is, "Lord, in order that our eyes may be opened." One of the evangelists may have substituted a term, or Matthew and Luke may have used a different source (e.g., Q or Luke follows Matthew).

In Mark 10:52, Jesus said, "Go. Your faith has healed you." In Luke 18:42, he said, "Receive your sight. Your faith has healed you." In Matt. 20:34, Jesus touched their eyes.

Summary

- Luke shows a disinterest in chronological precision and inverts events as he does elsewhere (Matt. 4:5–11 // Luke 4:5–13; Matt. 12:41–42 // Luke 11:31–32; Matt. 27:50–51 // Luke 23:45–46).
- Matthew may be doubling up and conflating two healings in order to abbreviate, or Mark is either shining a spotlight on a person known to his readers or identifying his source.
- At least one evangelist is substituting a term or using a different source.
- At least one evangelist paraphrases freely.

#8 (#146–48) Feeding the Five Thousand; Walking on Water; Healings at Gennesaret (Mark 6:31–56; Matt. 14:13–36; Luke 9:10b–17; John 6:1–25)
Narrative

When Jesus heard that John the Baptist had been executed, he and his disciples entered a boat and went to a lonely place. The crowds followed him, and Jesus felt compassion for them. He taught and healed them. When it grew late, the disciples encouraged Jesus to send the people away to the villages in order to purchase food for themselves. But Jesus instructed his disciples instead to give them something to eat. They answered that they only had 200 denarii, which would not be enough. Jesus asked what food they had available now. They checked and answered five loaves of barley bread and two fish. Jesus then instructed his disciples to have the people sit down in groups of fifty or one hundred. Then Jesus looked up to heaven, blessed and broke the loaves and fish, and gave them to his disciples to give to the crowds. All ate until they were full. Jesus then ordered his disciples to pick up the food that was left over, and they filled twelve baskets. There were five thousand men who had eaten, not including the women and children.

Jesus then ordered his disciples to get in the boat and cross over the sea ahead of him. He dismissed the crowd and went up on the mountain to pray. Around the fourth watch of the night, Jesus saw his disciples struggling against the wind in the boat, and he came to them walking on the water. When they saw him near the boat, they thought it was a ghost and were afraid. But he told them not to be afraid because it was he. Peter then said, "Lord, if it is you, command me to come to you on the water." Jesus said, "Come!" Peter got out of the boat and began walking on the water toward Jesus. But he became fearful when he observed the wind and began to sink. So he cried out to Jesus, "Lord, save me!" Jesus reached out, caught him, and said, "Man of little faith, why did you doubt?" And when they got in the boat, the wind ceased and they were immediately at the land where they were going. And the disciples were amazed.

Analysis

There are a few differences in the accounts, most of which are minor. In Mark 6:34, Jesus taught the people. In Matt. 14:14, he healed them. In Luke 9:11, he taught and healed them. In John 6:2, the people came to him because he had healed some. In the Synoptics, the issue of feeding the crowd does not arise until the end of the day *after Jesus had taught and healed them*, whereas in John, Jesus asked Philip where they would buy bread for the crowd *before they arrived.*[52] It is possible that the earliest tradition or recollection of the event was imprecise pertaining to when the issue of feeding the crowd arose and that the evangelists used their literary artistry to work it into their narratives in different manners. However, one might posit that the issue arose on both occasions, that John focused on the earlier while the Synoptics followed the latter, and that John compressed the story and omitted Jesus's teaching and healing the crowd on this occasion.

In Luke 9:14, the people were to sit in groups of about fifty. In Mark 6:40, they sat in groups of fifties and hundreds. In Matthew and Luke, the twelve baskets were full of leftover "pieces" (κλασμάτων, *klasmatōn*). In Mark, the twelve baskets were full of leftover "pieces and fish." In John, they were full of leftover "pieces from the five barley loaves."

Only Matt. 14:28–31 reports that Peter also walked on water. Only Mark 6:51 // Matt. 14:32 report the wind stopped when Jesus (Matt.: and Peter) entered the boat. Only John 6:21 reports they were immediately at their destination when Jesus entered the boat. Mark 6:51 says the disciples were "greatly amazed," whereas Matt. 14:33 says the disciples "worshipped [προσεκύνησαν, *prosekunēsan*] him, saying, 'Truly you are God's Son!'"

The largest difference concerns the location where Jesus fed the five thousand. In Mark 6:32 // Matt. 14:13, it was in a "lonely place" (ἔρημον τόπον, *epēmon topon*) where Jesus and his disciples had withdrawn. In Luke 9:10, Jesus had withdrawn to a town named Bethsaida. The Sea of Galilee is not exactly round but is wider in its upper third. If we view this large lake as a clock, Bethsaida is located at 12:30 and a little inland. In John 6:1, they crossed to the other side of the Sea of Galilee, although it is not stated from where they came or where they went.

After Jesus had fed the five thousand, he ordered his disciples to get into a boat and cross the Sea of Galilee. In Mark 6:45, Jesus urged his disciples to get into a boat and go ahead of him "to the other side, to Bethsaida" (εἰς τὸ πέραν πρὸς Βηθσαϊδάν, *eis to peran pros Bēthsaidan*). This appears to be in conflict with Luke 9:10, which places the feeding at or near Bethsaida. In Matt. 14:22, Jesus urged his disciples to get into a boat and go ahead of him to the other side. Given the verbal similarities, it seems probable that Matthew's source is Mark. But Matthew may be aware of a problem with Mark's "to Bethsaida" and omits it. In John 6:16–17, the disciples got into a boat and were crossing to the other side of the sea "to Capernaum" (εἰς Καφαρναούμ, *eis Capharnaoum*), which is located at 11:00 on our clock.[53]

Next we observe where the evangelists tell us they landed. Mark 6:53 and Matt. 14:34 say they landed at Gennesaret (10:00).[54] John 6:21 says they landed where they had intended, Capernaum (6:17), which bordered on the region of Gennesaret (11:00).[55]

Harmonizing the accounts in order to reconcile the differing details pertaining to the location of the feeding is difficult. Luke places it at or very close to Bethsaida, whereas Mark places it anywhere but Bethsaida, since after the feeding Jesus tells his disciples to cross over to Bethsaida.

Matthew, Mark, and John tell us they landed on the west side of the lake, and John tells us that is where they had intended to land. Accordingly, it will not work to harmonize the accounts by asserting the disciples intended to go to Bethsaida but were blown off course and landed in Capernaum.[56]

Summary

- The evangelists paraphrase slightly.
- Either John slightly compresses or one or more of the evangelists artistically weave elements into their narrative that were not remembered in a precise manner.

#9 (#166, 263, 313, 253) Who Is the Greatest? (Mark 9:33–37; 10:13–16, 35–45; Matt. 18:1–6; 19:13–15; 20:20–28; Luke 9:46–48; 18:15–17; 22:24–30)
Narrative

There are two occasions when Jesus deals with discussions pertaining to the supremacy of one or more of his disciples and a third occasion that is related. On the first occasion, while Jesus and his disciples were walking on a road to Capernaum, his disciples debated among themselves which of them was the greatest. When they arrived in Capernaum, Jesus asked them what they had been discussing along the way, but they were silent and did not answer. So he called them together and sat down. Jesus then called a child and had him stand beside him and said, "Unless you are like children, you will never enter the kingdom of heaven. Whoever humbles himself like this child is the greatest in the kingdom of heaven. Whoever receives such a child in my name receives me. And whoever receives me receives the one who sent me."

The second occasion occurs at a different time during Jesus's ministry. The wife of Zebedee comes to Jesus with her two sons, James and John. She kneels before him and requests that when he is glorified in his kingdom he will grant that her sons will sit on his right and left. Jesus replied to all three, "You do not know what you are asking. Are you able to drink the cup that I am about to drink or to be baptized with the baptism with which I am baptized?" He was referring to his suffering and death. The brothers answered, "We are able." Jesus said, "You will drink my cup and be baptized with my baptism. But it is not mine to grant who will sit on my right and left, but it is for those for whom it has been prepared by my Father."

When the other ten disciples heard this, they became indignant with the two brothers. Jesus called them all together and said, "You know that the rulers of the Gentiles lord it over them, and their great men exercise authority over them. It will not be so among you. But whoever would be great among you must be your servant. And whoever would be first among you must be your slave. For I did not come to be served but to serve, and to give my life as a ransom for many."

On the third occasion, people were bringing their children to Jesus so that he might lay his hands on them and pray. But his disciples began to rebuke them. Jesus became indignant with his disciples and said, "Allow the children to come and do not hinder them. For to such belongs God's kingdom. I tell you truly that whoever does not receive God's kingdom like a child will not enter it."

Analysis

There are a number of items of interest here. On the first occasion, in Mark 9:33–34 Jesus's disciples had been discussing which of them was the greatest. When Jesus asked them what they had been discussing, they were silent. However, in Matt. 18:1, it was the disciples who came to Jesus and asked him who among them was the greatest. In Luke 9:46–47, after the disciples had discussed which of them was the greatest, Jesus perceived the thoughts/disputings of their hearts, appearing to imply no question was asked by either. Thus, Jesus asked the question in Mark while the disciples asked the question in Matthew, and no question is mentioned in Luke. Matthew transferred by having the disciples initiate the discussion rather than Jesus.

All three Synoptics report that when Jesus placed a child in their midst he said, "Whoever receives one such child in my name receives me." Only Matt. 18:3 includes, "Truly I say to you, unless you turn and become as children, you will never enter the kingdom of heaven." Mark and Luke locate these words in a different context, the third occasion to be assessed below (Mark 10:15 // Luke 18:17).

In Mark 9:37b and Luke 9:48b Jesus said, "And whoever receives me, receives the one who sent me." John 13:20 is familiar with this logion but places it at the end of Jesus's ministry, during the Last Supper.

In Luke 9:48c, Jesus said, "For the one who is least among you all is the one who is great." Mark 9:35 has, "If anyone desires to be first, he will be last of all and servant of all." In Matt. 23:11, Jesus said something similar just prior to his Olivet Discourse: "The greater one among you will be a servant." Because this principle would have been especially profound in that culture, we should expect that Jesus would have said it on many occasions. Accordingly, it is unnecessary to suggest each evangelist redacted the tradition and placed it where he thought fitting, although such a solution is plausible and equally possible.

We will now proceed to a second occasion when some of Jesus's disciples pursued supremacy. In Mark 10:35, James and John the sons of Zebedee came to Jesus and asked him to allow them to sit on his right and left when he would reign. However, in Matt. 20:20, the wife of Zebedee makes the request while accompanied by her sons, James and John. Mark may have brushed the mother out of the story and transferred the request to her two sons since they were present and perhaps motivated their mother to ask Jesus on their behalf. However, it could instead be that Matthew added the mother in order to cast James and John in a better light.[57]

In Mark 10:37b // Matt. 20:21b, the request is to sit on each side of Jesus in his "glory" (Mark) // "kingdom" (Matt.). Given the close verbal similarities in the narrative, Matthew appears to be using Mark as his source. Therefore, Matthew substitutes "kingdom" for "glory."

Luke omits the request of James and John. However, he appears to have taken Jesus's statement pertaining to Gentile rulers lording it over others, that the disciples are rather to exercise humble servant leadership, and that he has set the example by coming to serve and give his life as a ransom for many, and has situated it in the first occasion described above, although that occasion occurs in a different context (Last Supper), perhaps a week later than we find in Mark // Matthew. Of course, it is possible that Jesus addressed a similar dispute pertaining to which of the disciples was the greatest on multiple occasions. However, there are enough verbal similarities between Jesus's answer in Mark and Luke to suggest Jesus's reply could derive from the same tradition. If Mark is Luke's source for this tradition, Luke's redaction of and displacement of the tradition to a different context gives us an idea of the extent of Luke's flexibility with the tradition.

In Mark 10:43–45 // Matt. 20:26–28, Jesus says, "Whoever desires to be great among you must be your servant [διάκονος, *diakonos*], and whoever desires to be first will be your slave [δοῦλος, *doulos*]." Luke 22:26–27 either paraphrases or makes use of a different source when Jesus says, "Let the greater one among you be as the youngest [ὁ νεώτερος, *ho neōteros*] and the leader as the one serving [ὁ διακονῶν, *ho diakonōn*]. For who is the greater, the one reclining [at a meal] or the one serving? Is it not the one reclining? But I am among you as the one serving." The final portion of Jesus's logion preserved by Luke may also suggest familiarity with Jesus's act of foot washing, which John also narrates during the Last Supper (John 13:3–16).

In Luke 22:28–30, Jesus continues, "You are those who have remained with me in my trials. And I grant to you, just as my Father has granted to me, a kingdom, in order that you may eat and drink at my table in my kingdom and will be seated on thrones judging the twelve tribes of Israel." This is similar to the tradition in Matt. 19:28: "I tell you, truly, when the Son of Man is seated on his glorious throne in the new world, you also who have followed me will be seated on twelve thrones judging the twelve tribes of Israel." Luke locates this logion at the Last Supper, while Matthew locates it on an earlier occasion.

We come to the third occasion. Mark 10:14b // Luke 18:16b render "the kingdom of God," whereas Matt. 19:14b renders "the kingdom of heaven" (substitution).[58] Mark 10:15 // Luke 18:17 report Jesus saying, "Truly, I tell you, whoever does not receive the kingdom of God as a child will never enter it." Matthew 18:3 has a similar statement placed in an earlier context (the first occasion just considered above): "Truly, I tell you, unless you turn and become like children, you will never enter the kingdom of heaven." Matthew may have redacted and displaced this teaching to an earlier context (the first situation in this pericope), or Jesus taught it on both occasions.

Summary

- Matthew transfers by having the disciples initiate the discussion rather than Jesus.
- Matthew displaces a portion of Jesus's teaching and transplants it in a different context.
- Mark transfers the mother's request to her sons, since they were probably the initiators or Matthew adds her in order to cast James and John in a better light.
- Matthew substitutes "kingdom" for "glory."
- Luke probably paraphrased a teaching of Jesus before displacing and transplanting it in a different context.
- Luke either paraphrases and substitutes terms or uses a different source.
- Mark or Matthew substituted a term.

#10 (#271–76 [cf. #25]) Jesus in Jerusalem (Cleansing of the Temple); Cursing a Fig Tree; Return to Bethany (Mark 11:12–14, 20–26; Matt. 21:18–22; Luke 19:45–46)

Narrative

Jesus entered Jerusalem, went into the temple, and looked around. But since it was late in the day, he and his disciples left and went to Bethany (Mark 11:11). On the following day, Jesus was hungry when he and his disciples were returning to Jerusalem. He noticed a fig tree by the road and walked up to it. Although the tree had leaves, there were no figs on it, so Jesus cursed it. Then they continued their journey into the city.

Upon entering the temple, Jesus saw people buying and selling inside. He drove them out and overturned their merchant tables, quoting Isa. 56:7 and alluding to Jer. 7:11, "It is written, 'My house will be called a house of prayer.' But you have made it a robbers' den.'" That evening, Jesus and his disciples left Jerusalem and returned to Bethany. The Jewish leaders felt threatened by Jesus because the people were impressed by his teachings. So they sought for a way to have him killed.

The following morning, Jesus and his disciples returned to Jerusalem. On their way they came upon the fig tree Jesus had cursed on the previous day and observed it had since withered and died. Peter was astonished and said, "Look, Rabbi! The tree you cursed has died!" Jesus told them to have faith in God and that if they had enough faith they could order a mountain to be thrown into the sea and it would obey them. Whatever they asked for in prayer, it would be granted if they believed it.

They arrived in Jerusalem, and Jesus once again entered the temple. The Jewish leaders approached and asked him on whose authority he had acted on the previous day. Jesus answered by offering a *quid pro quo*. If they would tell him whether John's authority to baptize was from God or man, he would tell them on whose authority he had cleansed the temple. When they refused to answer, Jesus likewise refused to answer their question.

Analysis

There are numerous differences in how the evangelists tell this story. The chronology of events differs. All four Gospels narrate Jesus's triumphal entry on Sunday. In Mark, Jesus's temple cleansing occurs on the following day, Monday, while in Matthew and Luke, it appears to have occurred on Sunday. If Matthew and Luke have Sunday in mind, they (or their source) have probably compressed the story. Unless John 2:13 is referring to an earlier temple cleansing, he has displaced the event to the early days of Jesus's ministry where it was also near the Passover but not related to his triumphal entry.

Mark is clear that Jesus performed the temple cleansing on Monday, then observed the tree had died on Tuesday. In Matthew, Jesus entered Jerusalem and cleansed the temple on Sunday, then cursed the fig tree on Monday, and he states that the tree withered "immediately" (παραχρῆμα, *parachrēma*).[59] Thus, Matthew has compressed that element of the story. It is grammatically possible to read Matthew (with Mark) as having Jesus cleanse the temple on Monday. If we were to understand Matthew in this manner, he narrates Jesus cursing the fig tree on Tuesday, since according to Matt. 21:17–28, Jesus left Jerusalem after cleansing the temple, spent the night in Bethany, then returned to Jerusalem in the morning. And it is during the latter trip that Jesus cursed the tree. However we understand Matthew, he compressed the account of the fig tree so that it withered on the spot when Jesus cursed it.

In Mark, the Jewish leaders challenged Jesus's authority on Tuesday. In Matthew, it was probably on Monday but perhaps on Tuesday. In Luke 19:47–48, Jesus was teaching daily in the temple while the Jewish authorities were seeking to have him killed. Luke 20:1–8 then follows, saying that "on one of those days" (ἐν μιᾷ τῶν ἡμερῶν, *en mia tōn hēmerōn*)[60] while teaching the people in the temple (connecting this event chronologically to the two verses immediately preceding them), the Jewish authorities asked him on whose authority he had acted. Thus, Luke does not narrate the challenge to Jesus's authority with the precision offered by the other evangelists. John's chronology differs even more if we understand the temple cleansing in John 2:13–22 as the same event.

Jesus's words to those he drove out differ slightly among the Synoptics and even more in John. In Mark 11:17, he says, "Is it not written, 'My house will be called a house of prayer for all nations?' But you have made it a robbers' den!" Matthew 21:13 reads, "It is written, 'My house will be called a house of prayer.' But you are making it a robbers' den!" Luke 19:46 reads, "It is written, 'My house will be a house of prayer.' But you made it a robbers' den!" Finally, in John 2:16, Jesus said, "Take these from here! Do not make my Father's house a house of business!" In Mark, Jesus's first statement is a rhetorical question, whereas it is a statement in Matthew and Luke and a command in John. The tenses of "make" (ποιέω, *poieō*) differ.

In Mark 11:17, it is the perfect tense. In Luke 19:46, it is the aorist tense. In Matt. 21:13 and John 2:16, it is the present tense. In all three Synoptics, Jesus quotes Isa. 56:7 and alludes to Jer. 7:11. In John 2:17, Jesus does not quote Scripture; however, the disciples remember Ps. 69:9.

The reply of the Jewish leaders to Jesus's actions differs slightly. In Mark 11:27, the chief priests, scribes, and elders approached Jesus while he was *walking* in the temple, whereas in Matt. 21:23 // Luke 20:1 they approached him while he was *teaching* in the temple. In Mark 11:28 // Matt. 21:23, the chief priests, scribes, and elders *asked* Jesus by what authority he did these things and who gave it to him. In Luke 20:1–2, the chief priests, scribes, and elders *ordered* Jesus to inform them by what authority he did these things and who gave it to him. Luke changed a question to a command. In John 2:18–22, the Jewish leaders (not further identified) *asked* Jesus what sign he would provide them in order to prove he had the authority to cleanse the temple.

Jesus answered the Jewish leaders differently. In all three Synoptics (Mark 11:29–33 // Matt. 21:24–27 // Luke 20:3–8), Jesus replied with a *quid pro quo*. If they would tell him on whose authority John baptized, God's or man's, he would tell them on what authority he cleansed the temple.[61] In John 2:19, instead of replying with a *quid pro quo*, Jesus told them the sign he offered was that if they "destroy this temple" (i.e., his body; see 2:21–22), he would rebuild it in three days.[62] In both the Synoptics and John, the requests of the Jewish leaders possessed the same gist: prove that you have the authority to do what you have just done. But Jesus's reply differs. In the Synoptics, he offered them a *quid pro quo*, whereas in John he told them his future resurrection would be the sign they sought.

Summary

- Matthew has certainly compressed at least one element in the pericope (cursing the fig tree) and perhaps (with Luke) another (Jesus's entering Jerusalem and the temple cleansing to have occurred on the same day).
- John may have displaced the temple cleansing to the beginning of Jesus's ministry.
- Mark presents a question where Matthew and Luke render it as a statement and John as a command.
- Mark and Matthew present a question that Luke changes to a command. If John is referring to the same temple cleansing, he alters the nature of the command and Jesus's reply.

#11 (#278) Parable of the Vineyard and Wicked Tenants (Mark 12:1–12; Matt. 21:33–46; Luke 20:9–19)

Narrative

After the Jewish authorities questioned Jesus's authority, he replied by telling a parable against them. A man prepared a vineyard and leased it to tenants before going away for a considerable time. When the proper time came, the owner of the vineyard sent some of his servants to collect what the tenants owed him. But the tenants mistreated the servants. So the owner sent other servants, whom they also mistreated in various ways, even killing some. Finally, the owner sent his son, thinking the tenants would listen to him. But the tenants conspired with one another and killed the son, thinking the vineyard would become theirs since the son was the heir.

Jesus asked what the proper response of the owner would be and answered that he would kill the tenants and hand over the vineyard to others who would keep their promise to give the owner what is due. Jesus then quoted Ps. 118:22–23: "The very stone which the builders rejected has become the cornerstone. This was the LORD's doing and it is marvelous in our eyes." He continued, "Therefore, I tell you the kingdom of God will be taken from you and given to a people who will produce its fruit. The one falling on this cornerstone will be broken to pieces and the one on whom it falls will be crushed." The Jewish authorities knew Jesus had spoken the parable against them, so they sought to arrest him. However, because they feared the people, they left and planned how they might trap him in his words.

Analysis

Since Jesus told this parable in the same context in all three of the Synoptics, the same event is certainly in view. Yet numerous differences appear. Matthew is the only evangelist to include, "Therefore, I tell you the kingdom of God will be taken from you and given to a people who will produce its fruit."

In Mark and Luke, the owner sends a different servant on three occasions. On each occasion, the tenants mistreat the servant. They beat and send away the first servant. On the second occasion, they beat

(Mark: head strike) and shamefully treat the servant (Luke: then send him away empty-handed). The owner then sends a third servant, whom they kill (Luke: wound and cast out of the vineyard). Matthew compresses the three occasions into one, saying the owner sent three servants whom the tenants beat, killed, and stoned. He is referring to one rather than a combination of occasions, since in 21:36 Jesus said the owner then sent more servants than he had *the first time* (πλείονας τῶν πρώτων, *pleionas tōn prōtōn*). In Mark, after these three rounds, the owner continued to send more servants in what appears to be several additional rounds, whereas in Matthew the owner sent more than three servants in a second round. Luke is silent on these. Finally, the owner sent his son. In Mark, the tenants killed him and cast him out of the vineyard, while Matthew and Luke invert the order by casting him out of the vineyard first and then killing him.

In Mark 12:9 and Luke 20:15–16, Jesus asked what the owner of the vineyard would do. He then answered his own question, saying the owner would kill those tenants and give the vineyard to others. However, Matt. 21:41 takes Jesus's statements and creates a dialogue with his interlocutors, adding words for effect: "They said to him, 'He will put those evil men to a miserable death and will rent the vineyard to other tenants who will give to him what he is due at the appointed time!' " In doing so, Matthew transfers the answer from Jesus to the chief priests and Pharisees and adds for effect. Of course, the differences could result from the flexibility allowed within the handing on of oral tradition or because only the core of the story was known to one or more of the evangelists who then creatively reconstructed the scene, each differently. However, we must keep in mind that Matthew and Luke probably have Mark's Gospel in front of them and often quote it verbatim. Accordingly, it may be more likely that the differences here result from Matthew and Luke altering Mark than from the flexibility of oral tradition.

The following chart (Figure 4.5) lists most of the differences.

Summary

- Matthew compresses the story throughout.
- Matthew and Luke (or their source) invert the order of details.
- Matthew takes Jesus's teaching and creates a dialogue with his interlocutors. He also adds for effect.

Table 4.1 Parable of Vinyard and Wicked Tenants Comparison

Matthew	Mark	Luke
Three servants (beaten, killed, stoned)	One servant (beaten, sent away)	One servant (beaten, sent away)
	One servant (struck head, treated shamefully)	One servant (beaten, treated shamefully, sent away)
	One servant (killed)	One servant (wounded, cast out of vineyard)
More than three servants (beaten, killed, stoned)	Many others (beaten, killed)	
Son (cast out of vineyard, killed)	Son (killed, cast out of vineyard)	Son (cast out of vineyard, killed)
Jesus asked; others answered	Jesus asked and answered	Jesus asked and answered
Ps. 118:22–23	Ps. 118:22–23	Ps. 118:22–23
Kingdom given to others		
Those falling on the stone		Those falling on the stone
. . .		. . .

#12 (#306, 114, 267) Anointing in Bethany (Mark 14:3–9; Matt. 26:6–13; John 12:1–8; cf. Luke 7:36–50)

Narrative

A few days before Passover, Jesus was in Bethany at the house of Simon the leper. While at the table eating, a woman took an alabaster flask of expensive ointment and poured it on Jesus. When the others witnessed what she had done, they protested that it was a waste and that the ointment could have been sold for a large sum and the proceeds given to the poor. But Jesus told them to leave the woman alone because she had done a beautiful thing for him, preparing him for burial. The poor would always be with them, so they could help them whenever they wanted. But he would not always be with them. Wherever the gospel was proclaimed in the whole world, what she did would be told in memory of her.

Analysis

There are a number of differences in how this narrative appears in the four Gospels. Some of the details differ to an extent that we may ask whether

Luke and John are reporting the same event that we read in Mark and Matthew. We will first consider whether John is reporting the same event and then address the differences in Luke.

Two elements suggest John is reporting a different event: (1) In Mark and Matthew, the anointing occurs two days prior to the Passover, whereas it is six days prior to the Passover in John. (2) The woman appears to have been known by Jesus in John, but there is no indication she was known by him in Mark, Matthew, and Luke.

However, there are so many elements in John's account that are strikingly similar to what we observe in the accounts by Mark and Matthew that it is very likely that John's account is referring to the same event: (1) The anointing is immediately preceded by the Jewish leaders plotting to kill Jesus. (2) The anointing occurs during the Passover week. (3) It happens in Bethany. (4) A woman pours costly ointment on Jesus. (5) The ointment is worth the same amount. (6) Some of those in the room object to her act and suggest that she could have sold the ointment and given the proceeds to the poor. (7) Jesus's response is the same, "Leave her alone. The poor will always be among you but I will not. She has anointed me for burial." And (8) the anointing is followed by further plans by the Jewish leadership to kill Jesus. These similarities mount a strong case that John was reporting the same event as Mark and Matthew, a case that is much stronger than the one we could mount against it.[63] As a result, we will look for differences in how John reports the anointing differently than Mark and Matthew.

It is more difficult to discern whether Luke is reporting the same event. The following suggest that he is: (1) The event occurs in the house of "Simon." (2) An anonymous woman anoints Jesus. (3) She uses an alabaster flask.

However, there are reasons to suspect Luke is referring to a different event: (1) Luke's event occurs in a different context than in the other three Gospels. (2) Luke will mention Mary the sister of Martha later (Luke 10:38–42) but does not link her to the woman who had anointed Jesus earlier in Luke 7:36–50 (see John 11:2). (3) Jesus's host, Simon, is a Pharisee in Luke 7:36, 40, whereas he appears to have been a leper (perhaps he was healed by Jesus) in Mark 14:3 // Matt. 26:6. (4) Luke's Simon is indignant for a different reason than we find in Mark // Matthew // John. In Luke 7:39, Simon thinks that if Jesus were a true prophet, he would know the woman anointing him was a sinner and, accordingly, would not allow her to anoint him. In Mark // Matthew and John, it is because the woman could have sold the ointment and given the proceeds to the poor. It is difficult to decide if Luke is referring to a different event or has redacted the same event narrated by the other Gospels.[64] If Luke preserves a different event, some of the similarities, and especially those with John but differing from Mark, may be plausibly understood as the two events becoming confused, resulting in details that have cross-pollinated.[65]

Since we are seeking to identify clear examples of compositional devices discussed in previous chapters, we will proceed with the understanding that Mark, Matthew, and John all refer to the same event while not considering Luke. Numerous differences appear between these three accounts. The woman is anonymous in Mark 14:3 // Matt. 26:7,[66] while John 12:3 (cf. 11:1–2; 12:1–2) identifies her as Mary the sister of Lazarus and Martha.[67] In Mark 14:3 // Matt. 26:6, the host is identified as Simon the leper, whereas he is anonymous in John.[68]

Mark 14:1 // Matt. 26:2 place the anointing two days prior to Passover, while John 12:1 says it occurred six days before Passover. Either Mark (followed by Matthew) or John have displaced the event. Mark may have done so in order to bring the symbolic anointing of Jesus for his burial closer to the event itself.[69] However, it may be that John displaced the event. Not only does he probably displace an event elsewhere (see pericope #10 earlier in this chap.), but it would have been proper practice for him to displace the anointing from its original context and transplant it here. We recall Lucian recommending that stories should be joined together in a narrative like links in a chain and with overlapping material when possible.[70] Just prior to the anointing in John, Jesus raised Lazarus from the dead in the presence of the latter's sisters, Mary and Martha (11:1–44). Perhaps John recalled at this point that he had a story about Mary to which he had already alluded (11:1–2), so he tells it here, linking the two with Mary serving as the overlap.[71]

In Mark 14:3, 5, the alabaster jar and pure nard ointment were "expensive" (πολυτελοῦς, *polutelous*), worth "more than 300 denarii." In John 12:3, 5, it was an "expensive" (πολυτίμου, *polutimou*) pound of pure nard ointment worth "300 denarii."[72] We observed differences in numerical specificity in pericope #26 in the previous chapter, where Plutarch reports that Caesar subdued "300 nations" in *Caes.* 15.3 but "more than 300 nations" in *Pomp.* 67.6. Matthew 26:7 describes the product as "expensive" (βαρυτίμου, *barutimou*)[73] ointment without specifying its contents or monetary value.[74]

In Mark 14:3 // Matt. 26:7, she pours the ointment on Jesus's head, whereas she pours it on his feet in John 12:3.[75] As mentioned above, John may have cross-pollinated some of the details from a different event we observe in Luke. Whether John did this intentionally cannot be determined.

Those named who were offended by her act differ. In Mark 14:4, it is "some [of those present]." In Matt. 26:8, it is the disciples. In John 12:4–5, it is Judas Iscariot. Mark is not specific and may have had in mind a group consisting only of some of Jesus's disciples or also included others who were not his disciples. Matthew is perhaps more specific than Mark, while John may be shining his literary spotlight on Judas Iscariot, who may have been the one to express what several of them were thinking.

Summary

- Mark or John displace an event from its original context and transplant it in another either to raise tension in Mark's narrative or to link it with another story involving the same characters in John.
- Differences in numerical specificity are present.
- John may cross-pollinate details from a different event.
- Mark perhaps shines a literary spotlight on Judas.

#13 (#309–12) The Last Supper (Mark 14:17–25; Matt. 26:20–29; Luke 22:14–23; John 13:1–30; 1 Cor. 11:21–23)
Narrative

While Jesus was eating the Passover meal with his disciples one evening, he rose from the table, took off his outer robe, tied a towel around himself, and poured water into a basin. He then began to wash the disciples' feet and dry them with the towel he had wrapped around himself. When he came to Simon Peter, Peter said, "Lord, are you going to wash my feet?" Jesus answered, "You do not understand now what I am doing. But you will understand afterward." Peter said, "You will never wash my feet." Jesus answered, "If I do not wash you, you have no part in me." Peter said, "Lord, not my feet only but also my hands and my head." Jesus said to Peter, "The one who has bathed does not need to wash, except for his feet. But he is clean all over. And you [plural] are clean. But not all of you." He said this because he knew one of them was going to betray him.

After he had washed all of their feet, he put on his robe, returned to his place at the table, and said, "Do you know what I have done to you? You call me Teacher and Lord. And you are correct. If then I, your Lord and Teacher, have washed your feet, you ought to wash one another's feet. I have given you an example. And a servant is not greater than his master. You are blessed if you do these things."

Then he said to them, "Truly, I tell you, one of you will betray me." His disciples were sorrowful and looked at one another. They asked Jesus, "Is it I?" Jesus answered, "It is one of the Twelve; one who is dipping bread into the dish with me. The Son of Man goes as it is written of him. But woe to the man who betrays him! It would have been better for that man if he had not been born." Judas said, "Is it I, Master?" Jesus answered, "Yes." Judas immediately left, and it was night.

Jesus said to his disciples, "I have earnestly desired to eat this Passover meal with you before I suffer. For I will not eat it again until it is fulfilled in God's kingdom." While they were eating, he took bread, blessed, and broke it, then gave it to the disciples and said, "Take. Eat. This is my body, which is for you. Do this in remembrance of me." He then took a cup, gave thanks, gave it to them and said, "All of you, drink it. This is my blood of the covenant, which is poured out for you. Truly, I tell you that I will not drink again from the fruit of the vine until I drink it new in God's kingdom."

Analysis

There are several differences in this pericope. Only John narrates Jesus washing the feet of his disciples. All four Gospels have Jesus tell his disciples that one of them eating with him that evening will betray him. Only in John 13:18 does Jesus quote Ps. 41:9, "The one eating my bread has lifted up his heel against me."

In Mark 14:18, Matt. 26:21, and John 13:21, Jesus said, "Truly, I tell you that one of you eating with me will betray me."[76] In Mark 14:19–20 and Matt. 26:22–23, the disciples asked Jesus one after another, "It is not me, is it [the Greek suggests a negative answer]?" Jesus tells them, it is one of the Twelve, one who is dipping bread in the dish with him. Only Matt. 26:25 adds that Judas then asked Jesus, "It is not me, is it, Rabbi [the Greek likewise suggests a negative answer]?" Jesus answered, "You have said so" (an idiom for "yes").[77] Mark 14:21 // Matt. 26:24 then have Jesus say, "For the Son of Man goes as it is written of him," while Luke 22:22 has, "For the Son of Man goes as it has been determined" (substitution).

John narrates the scene slightly differently. After Jesus tells his disciples that one of them will betray him, his disciples look around at one another, wondering who it is. The Beloved Disciple (who was the primary source if not the author of John's Gospel) was reclining at the table next to Jesus. Peter nodded to that disciple, prodding him to ask Jesus who it is. The Beloved Disciple asked Jesus, "Lord, who is it?" Jesus answered, "It is the one to whom I will give this piece of bread after I have dipped it." He then dipped it and gave it to Judas and said to him, "What you are going to do, do quickly." John then adds that no one at the table knew why Jesus had said this to Judas. This suggests that Jesus's statement about dipping a piece of bread and giving it to the one who was about to betray him may have been said only for the Beloved Disciple to hear. After taking the piece of bread, Judas immediately left. Thus, Matt. 26:25 has Jesus identify Judas as his betrayer by having Judas ask if it is he and Jesus answers that it is, while John 13:26 has Jesus tell the Beloved Disciple it is the one to whom he gives a piece of bread and then proceeds to hand it to Judas.

Luke narrates Jesus's statement that someone will betray him and woe to that man as being said after he had given the Eucharist, whereas Mark // Matthew locate it prior to the Eucharist. Luke 22:18 narrates Jesus saying he will not drink from the fruit of the vine again until God's kingdom arrives prior to his breaking bread, whereas Mark 14:25 // Matt. 26:29 narrate this logion after the bread had been eaten.

Jesus's logia differ slightly when administering the Eucharist. Luke preserves an oral tradition also found in 1 Cor. 11:23–25 (written by Paul). Mark, followed by Matthew, preserves a different tradition or has redacted one.

> 1 Corinthians 11:24b: "This is my body, which is for you. Do this in my remembrance." (τοῦτό μού ἐστιν τὸ σῶμα τὸ ὑπὲρ ὑμῶν· τοῦτο ποιεῖτε εἰς τὴν ἐμὴν ἀνάμνησιν, *touto mou estin to sōma to huper humōn. touto poieite eis tēn emēn anamnēsin.*)

> 1 Corinthians 11:25b: "This cup is the new covenant in my blood. Do this as often as you drink in my remembrance." (τοῦτο τὸ ποτήριον ἡ καινὴ διαθήκη ἐστὶν ἐν τῷ ἐμῷ αἵματι· τοῦτο ποιεῖτε, ὁσάκις ἐὰν πίνητε, εἰς τὴν ἐμὴν ἀνάμνησιν, *touto to potērion hē kainē diathēkē estin en tō emō haimati. touto poieite, hosakis ean pinēte, eis tēn emēn anamnēsin.*)

> Luke 22:19b: "This is my body, which is given for you. Do this in my remembrance." (τοῦτό ἐστιν τὸ σῶμά μου τὸ ὑπὲρ ὑμῶν διδόμενον· τοῦτο ποιεῖτε εἰς τὴν ἐμὴν ἀνάμνησιν, *touto estin to sōma mou to huper humōn didomenon. touto poieite eis tēn emēn anamnēsin.*)

Luke 22:20b: "This cup which is poured out for you is the new covenant in my blood." (τοῦτο τὸ ποτήριον ἡ καινὴ διαθήκη ἐν τῷ αἵματί μου τὸ ὑπὲρ ὑμῶν ἐκχυννόμενον, *touto to potērion hē kainē diathēkē en tō haimati mou to huper humōn ekchunnomenon.*)

The differences between the renditions offered by Paul and Luke are miniscule. Luke 22:19b adds "given" (διδόμενον, *didomenon*) (addition) and relocates "my" (μου, *mou*) from prior to the verb in 1 Cor. 11:24b to after it (syntax). Luke 22:20b omits the verb (ἐστὶν, *estin*) (subtract), alters the syntax of "in my blood," adds "which is poured out" (ἐκχυννόμενον, *ekchunnomenon*) for clarification and to parallel "which is given" (διδόμενον, *didomenon*) in Luke's previous logion (22:19b). Luke omits, "Do this as often as you drink in my remembrance."

Because the logia in 1 Cor. 11:24–25 are certainly oral tradition (11:23), the verbal similarities here between Paul and Luke guarantee either that they both drew from the same tradition or that Luke used 1 Cor. 11:24–25 as his source.[78] I have proposed above that Luke added, subtracted, and altered the syntax by assuming Paul preserved the same oral tradition. However, it is entirely possible that Luke preserved an earlier form than Paul or that one or both had slightly redacted the same form. What is noteworthy is that these logia of Jesus in Paul and Luke are so similar that we can be certain they both drew from the same tradition.

We find parallels to these logia in Mark 14:22b, 24–25 // Matt. 26:26b, 27b–29. Although they differ from what we read in 1 Corinthians and Luke, Mark and Matthew are nearly word-for-word.

Mark 14:22b: "Take. This is my body." (λάβετε, τοῦτό ἐστιν τὸ σῶμά μου, *labete, touto estin to sōma mou.*)

Mark 14:24–25: "This is my blood of the covenant which is poured out for many. Truly, I tell you I will not drink again of the fruit of the vine until that day when I drink it new in the kingdom of God." (τοῦτό ἐστιν τὸ αἷμά μου τῆς διαθήκης τὸ ἐκχυννόμενον ὑπὲρ πολλῶν. ἀμὴν λέγω ὑμῖν ὅτι οὐκέτι οὐ μὴ πίω ἐκ τοῦ γενήματος τῆς ἀμπέλου ἕως τῆς ἡμέρας ἐκείνης ὅταν αὐτὸ πίνω καινὸν ἐν τῇ βασιλείᾳ τοῦ θεοῦ, *touto estin to haima mou tēs diathēkēs to ekchunnomenon huper pollōn. amēn legō humin hoti ouketi ou mē piō ek tou genēmatos tēs ampelou heōs tēs hēmeras ekeinēs hotan auto pinō kainon en tē basileia tou theo.*)

Matt. 26:26b: "Take. Eat. This is my body." (λάβετε φάγετε, τοῦτό ἐστιν τὸ σῶμά μου, *labete phagete, touto estin to sōma mou.*)

Matt. 26:27b–29: "Drink it, all of you. For this is my blood of the covenant, which for many is poured out for the forgiveness of sins. And I tell you from this moment I will never drink from this fruit of the vine until that day when I drink it with you new in the kingdom of my Father." (πίετε ἐξ αὐτοῦ πάντες, τοῦτο γάρ ἐστιν τὸ αἷμά μου τῆς διαθήκης τὸ περὶ πολλῶν ἐκχυννόμενον εἰς ἄφεσιν ἁμαρτιῶν. λέγω δὲ ὑμῖν, οὐ μὴ πίω ἀπ᾽ ἄρτι ἐκ τούτου τοῦ γενήματος τῆς ἀμπέλου ἕως τῆς ἡμέρας ἐκείνης ὅταν αὐτὸ πίνω μεθ᾽ ὑμῶν καινὸν ἐν τῇ βασιλείᾳ τοῦ πατρός μου, *piete ex autou pantes, touto gar estin to haima mou tēs diathēkēs to peri pollōn ekchunnomenon eis aphesin hamartiōn. legō de humin, ou mē piō ap arti ek toutou tou genēmatos tēs ampelou heōs tēs hēmeras ekeinēs hotan auto pinō meth humōn kainon en tē basileia tou patros mou.*)

Assuming Matthew is here using Mark as his source, he edits Mark by adding the command not only to take the bread but to eat it, which is only implied in Mark. Where Mark says all of the disciples drank from the cup, Matthew has Jesus tell them, "Drink it, all of you." In Mark, Jesus says his blood will be poured out "for [ὑπὲρ, *huper*] many," whereas Matthew says it will be poured out "for [περὶ, *peri*] many for the forgiveness of sins." Matthew substitutes a different preposition and adds "for the forgiveness of sins" for clarity. Matthew also substitutes "the kingdom of my Father" for Mark's "the kingdom of God."[79]

The most important difference in the logia, however, concerns how the logia in 1 Corinthians // Luke differ from their parallels in Mark // Matthew. Either Mark (followed by Matthew) has paraphrased the tradition in 1 Corinthians // Luke, or they are independent traditions.[80]

The most profound difference pertains to the day on which Jesus's last meal with his disciples is said to have occurred. In the Synoptics, it is clear that the Last Supper is a Passover meal that was eaten on the first day of Unleavened Bread, which is the typical day to eat it (Mark 14:12–16; Matt. 26:17–19; Luke 22:7–13). However, there are several elements in John's Gospel that suggest he has located the Last Supper a day earlier than what is portrayed in the Synoptics. First, in John 13:1, the Last Supper is eaten "before the Feast of the Passover."[81] Second, there is nothing in John's account of the meal that suggests it was a Passover meal (13:2–16:26). Third, in 18:28, in the morning the Jewish leaders led Jesus, whom they had arrested the previous evening, into the Praetorium (i.e., the governor's residence). But they did not enter with Jesus in order to avoid being defiled and, therefore, prevented from eating the Passover meal that evening. Fourth, in 19:14, John identifies the day Jesus was handed over to Pilate as the day of preparation of the Passover. Mark 15:42 says it was a day of preparation, "which is, the day before the Sabbath." However, John 19:31 says, "For the day of that Sabbath was great" (ἦν γὰρ μεγάλη ἡ ἡμέρα ἐκείνου τοῦ σαββάτου, ēn gar megalē hē hēmera ekeinou tou sabbatou), perhaps suggesting that this was no ordinary Sabbath, which would be consistent if the Passover meal fell on that Sabbath. John appears deliberate in his attempts to lead his readers to think the Last Supper was not a Passover meal. And if we were to read John's Gospel apart from any knowledge of the Synoptics, we would regard John as reporting that Jesus was crucified prior to the celebration of the Passover meal. There is a plausible reason for this, which we will consider in pericope #15 below. For now, we may suggest that John may have displaced the celebration of the Passover meal to have occurred one day later than we find in the Synoptics.[82]

Summary

- Luke compresses dialogue and substitutes terms.
- Luke (or the tradition from which he drew) presents the relationship of Jesus informing his disciples of his betrayal by one of them and his administering the Eucharist in opposite order to how they are narrated by Mark // Matthew.
- Matthew adds to clarify and substitutes terms.

#14 (#332–33) Jesus before the Sanhedrin and Peter's Denial (Mark 14:53–72; Matt. 26:57–75; Luke 22:55–71; John 18:13–27)
Narrative

After being arrested, Jesus was taken to the house of Caiaphas, who was the high priest at the time. The chief priests, scribes, and elders had assembled there. Simon Peter and another disciple followed Jesus but at a distance.[83] A former high priest named Annas was the father-in-law of Caiaphas.[84] Annas knew the other disciple, so he was able to enter the court of the high priest while Peter remained outside. The other disciple went out and spoke to the woman guarding the door and brought Peter inside.

While Peter warmed himself by the fire, one of those present recognized him and said, "He was also with Jesus." But Peter denied it. A little later, someone else saw Peter and likewise accused him of being with Jesus. Once again Peter denied it. Still later, another accused Peter of being with Jesus, and he denied it a third time. Immediately, a cock crowed. Jesus turned and looked at Peter. Then Peter left and wept bitterly.

Jesus appeared before Annas, who questioned him about his disciples and his teaching. Jesus answered that he had spoken widely and openly, in their synagogues and in the temple. Nothing had been said in secret, so Annas should ask others who had heard him. One of the officers standing near Jesus struck him and said, "This is how you answer the high priest?" Jesus replied, "If I have spoken wrongly, testify concerning the wrong. But if truthfully, why do you strike me?" Annas then sent Jesus to Caiaphas.

Now those who had assembled sought testimony against Jesus in order to have grounds to put him to death. But only false witnesses came forward, and their testimonies did not agree. The high priest stood up and asked Jesus if he had anything to say, but he remained silent. The high priest then commanded Jesus to tell them if he was the Messiah, the Son of God. Jesus answered, "I am. And you will see the Son of Man seated at the right hand of Power and coming on the clouds of heaven." The high priest tore his clothes and charged Jesus with blaspheming. And they condemned him of deserving death. They spat in Jesus's face, blindfolded him, and then hit him saying, "Prophesy, Messiah, and tell us who hit you!" Others hit him and spoke against him.

Analysis

Only John mentions Jesus before Annas and narrates the story as though it had occurred while Peter was denying Jesus. However, he omits the story of Jesus appearing before the Jewish counsel with Caiaphas. Only Luke 22:61 tells us that after Peter denied Jesus a third time, Jesus turned and looked at him.

In all three Synoptics, Peter sat with others by the fire: Mark 14:54 (συγκαθήμενος, *sugkathēmenos*), Matt. 26:58 (ἐκάθητο, *ekathēto*), Luke 22:55 (συγκαθισάντων ἐκάθητο, *sugkathisantōn ekathēto*). In John 18:18, he "stands" (ἑστὼς, *hestōs*) with others by the fire. This may not be a discrepancy, since "stands" (ἑστὼς, *hestōs*), from the Greek word ἵστημι, *histēmi*, can mean to remain in the same place, and John may elsewhere use it in this sense (e.g., 6:22; 8:44).

In Mark 14:54 // Matt. 26:58, Peter sat with the servants/guards (ὑπηρέτης, *hupēretēs*). In John 18:18, the slaves (δοῦλος, *doulos*) and servants/guards (ὑπηρέτης, *hupēretēs*) had built a fire and were warming themselves by it.

The time, location, and identity of those accusing Peter of his affiliation with Jesus differ slightly (Mark 14:66–72 // Matt. 26:69–74 // Luke 22:55–60 // John 18:17–18, 25–27). In all four Gospels, the first person to accuse Peter of being one of Jesus's followers was a female servant. In Mark, she said, "You were also with *Jesus the Nazarene*," whereas Matthew substituted, "You were also with *Jesus the Galilean*." Luke has the woman address those around the fire rather than Peter directly, "This man was also with him." John has the woman ask Peter a question, "You are not also one of this man's disciples, are you?" In Mark // Matthew, after being accused by the woman, Peter left his immediate company and relocated himself near the gate (Matthew provides a synonym for "gate" by substituting τὸν πυλῶνα, *ton pulōna*, for Mark's τὸ προαύλιον, *to proaulion*).

In Mark, the second accusation comes from the same female servant: "This man is from them." But in Matthew, "another woman" (ἄλλη, *allē*) accused Peter to the others of having been with Jesus the Nazarene. In Luke, another person—this time a male (ἕτερος, *heteros*)—accused Peter, "You are also from them." In John, a group asked Peter, "Are you not also from his disciples?" In Mark and Matthew, Jesus was by the gate during the second accusation, while in John he was still by the fire. In Mark and Matthew, the woman addressed the bystanders, whereas the man / the group accused him directly in Luke and John.

In Mark, the bystanders were Peter's third accusers, "Truly, you are from them. For you are also a Galilean." In Matthew, bystanders said to Peter, "Truly, you are also from them. For even your accent gives you away." In Luke, a "certain other man" (ἄλλος τις, *allos tis*) insisted, "Truthfully, this man was also with him. For he is also a Galilean." In Luke, the man accusing Peter for the third time was different than the man accusing him the second time. In John, the "certain other man" in Luke is identified as being one of the male slaves (δοῦλος, *doulos*) of the high priest and a relative of the man whose ear Peter had cut off. Instead of accusing Peter with a statement, as we observe in the Synoptics, John has the accuser ask Peter, "Did I not see you in the orchard with him?" Moreover, the man addressed Peter directly in Mark, Matthew, and John, whereas he addressed the others in Luke.[85]

According to Mark 14:72, a cock crowed twice, whereas it is once in Matt. 26:74 // Luke 22:60 // John 18:27. It is here that we can observe one of the most strained attempts at harmonization to resolve an apparent contradiction in the Gospels. Harold Lindsell attempted to resolve the discrepancy by suggesting that Peter denied Jesus three times before the rooster crowed, then denied him another three times before it crowed a second time. Therefore, Peter denied Jesus a total of six times rather than three, something none of the Gospels say.[86] Gleason Archer opines, "We may be very sure that if the rooster crows twice, he has at least crowed once."[87] Some scholars have posited that the "twice" (δίς, *dis*) in Mark is probably a textual corruption.[88] Others have contended that the "twice" is probably original and could be a figure of speech.[89] It could also be that "twice" is original and both Matthew and Luke have simplified with a single cock's crow.[90] Whether the "two" in Mark is a textual corruption or Matthew and Luke were either simplifying or correcting Mark's "two" is difficult to determine.

The interaction between Jesus and the high priest also differs. In Mark 14:61, after numerous witnesses provided false and contradictory testimony, Caiaphas asked Jesus, "Are you the Christ, the Son of the Blessed One?" In Matt. 26:63, after numerous witnesses provided false and contradictory testimony, Caiaphas said to Jesus, "I adjure you according to the living God that you tell us if you are the Christ, the Son of God!" Given verbal similarities throughout this pericope, Matthew appears to use Mark as his primary source and changes a question to a command. In Luke 22:67, the Jewish leaders (rather than only Caiaphas, whom Luke does not mention—the reverse of spotlighting) likewise put the matter to Jesus as a command: "If you are the Christ, tell us."[91]

In Mark 14:62, Jesus answered, "I am. And you will see the Son of Man seated at the right hand of Power and coming *with* [μετὰ, *meta*] the clouds of heaven" (emphasis added). In Matt. 26:64, Jesus answered, "You have said so. Only I tell you from now on you will see the Son of Man seated at the right hand of Power and coming *on* [ἐπὶ, *epi*] the clouds of heaven" (emphasis added). In Luke 22:67–69, Jesus answered, "If I tell you, you will never believe. And if I ask you, you will never answer. But from now on, the Son of Man will be seated at the right hand of the powerful God."[92] The council then asked Jesus, "Are you, therefore, the Son of God?" And Jesus said to them, "You say that I am."

The response of the Jewish counsel differs. In Mark 14:63 // Matt. 26:65, Caiaphas tore his own clothes (Mark: τοὺς χιτῶνας, *tous chitōnas;*

Matthew: τὰ ἱμάτια, *ta himatia*) and then charged Jesus with blasphemy. The counsel then judged him as deserving death. In Luke 22:71, there was no tearing of clothing or a charge of blasphemy. Luke's Gentile readers may not have been familiar with the divine Son of Man figure in Judaism or have understood why Jesus's claim to be that figure was so offensive to the Jewish leaders that they would want him dead. So for clarity, Luke may have translated the final portion of the exchange into a concept more clearly understood by his Gentile readers by creating the additional exchange where they asked Jesus if he was the Son of God, since Gentiles would understand that as a claim to being divine in a sense similar to the Jewish Son of Man.[93] Thus, Luke's redaction preserves the essence of the exchange. Another possibility is that Luke narrates an event only alluded to by Mark 15:1 // Matt. 27:1: the morning meeting at which the Jewish leaders consulted and decided to have Jesus put to death. Although Jesus's confession is very similar, it is possible that the council put the same question to him, giving him a final opportunity to repudiate any lofty claims about his identity. It is also possible that Luke conflates portions of the first meeting into a second one.

In Mark 14:65 // Matt. 26:67–68, they beat, spit upon, and mock Jesus after the counsel condemned him. In Luke 22:63–65, it is prior to meeting with the counsel.

Summary

- Matthew substitutes by using a synonym.
- In all of the Synoptics, the accusations against Peter are offered as a statement. In John, they are always offered in the form of a question.
- Luke may have translated the dialogue between Jesus and the Jewish leaders into terms that would have been clearer to his Gentile readers.
- Luke reverses Mark's order of Jesus being condemned and the abuse given him afterward, placing the abuse prior to his condemnation. This is similar to his apparent reversal of the order in which Matthew narrates the second and third temptations[94] and when the veil of the temple was torn from top to bottom.[95]
- The discrepancies in details between Mark and Luke pertaining to who accused Peter of being affiliated with Jesus and the specific locations where the accusations occurred suggest the event itself was remembered while some of the peripheral details were not. Thus, one or more of the evangelists reported the details as he or his sources

recalled them, crafted, or creatively reconstructed them as part of their literary artistry.

#15 (#344–48) The Crucifixion and Death of Jesus (Mark 15:22–41; Matt. 27:33–56; Luke 23:33–49; John 19:17–37)
Narrative

As Jesus was being led away to his execution, some women along the way were weeping. Jesus told them not to weep for him but rather for themselves and their children because very tough times were coming. They arrived at a place called "Golgotha," which translated means "Skull Place."[96] They offered Jesus wine mixed with myrrh, but he declined. At 9 a.m., they crucified Jesus with two thieves, one on each side of him. The four soldiers divided his clothes among themselves and cast lots for a nice tunic that remained. A tablet with the charge against Jesus was placed above his head on the cross. The charge was written in Aramaic, Latin, and Greek and read, "The King of the Jews." The Jewish chief priests went to Pilate and asked him to change the charge to "this man said, 'I am King of the Jews.'" But Pilate declined their request.

Some of those present were insulting him, yelling, "Aha! You who were going to destroy the temple and rebuild it in three days, save yourself and come down from the cross!" The Jewish leaders present were mocking him to one another, saying, "He saved others, but is unable to save himself! Let the Messiah, the king of Israel come down from the cross now that we may see and believe!" Those crucified with him also reviled him.

Numerous women had come with Jesus and his disciples from Galilee to Jerusalem, following and serving him. Some of them came and viewed Jesus's crucifixion from a distance. Among them were Mary Magdalene, Mary the wife of Zebedee, whose sons James and John were disciples of Jesus, Mary the mother of James and Joses, and Salome. A few of them came near Jesus. When he observed that one of them was his mother, he said, "Woman, behold your son." Then he said to his Beloved Disciple, who was also present, "Behold your mother." From that point, that disciple took Jesus's mother under his care.

At noon, darkness fell over the land for three hours, after which Jesus cried out in Aramaic, "My God! My God! Why have you forsaken me?" Some of those nearby thought he was calling for Elijah. One of them quickly filled a sponge with sour wine and offered it to Jesus to drink and said, "Let us see if Elijah will come and take him down." Jesus then uttered a loud cry and died. The centurion present observed the manner in which Jesus had died and said, "This man was truly the Son of God!" The temple curtain was torn in two from top to bottom. There was an earthquake, the rocks split, tombs were opened, and many saints who had died were raised. After Jesus's resurrection, they came out of their tombs, walked into Jerusalem, and appeared to many.

Analysis

Numerous differences appear in this pericope, and some are especially interesting. In Mark 15:23 Jesus is offered "wine" (οἶνον, oinon) "mixed with myrrh" (ἐσμυρνισμένον, esmurnismenon),[97] whereas in Matt. 27:34 it is mixed with "gall" (χολῆς, cholēs). Matthew appears to have substituted "gall" for "myrrh" in order to reflect Ps. 68:22 (LXX; 69:21 MT): "And they put gall in my food and gave me sour wine for my thirst" (καὶ ἔδωκαν εἰς τὸ βρῶμά μου χολὴν καὶ εἰς τὴν δίψαν μου ἐπότισάν με ὄξος, kai edōkan eis to brōma mou cholēn kai eis tēn dipsan mou epotisan me oxos).[98]

Mark 15:24 and Matt. 27:35 report that soldiers divided Jesus's clothing among themselves by casting lots. Both state that the soldiers cast lots for his clothing (plural) in order to decide who would take which garment. However, in John they cast lots for a specific piece of Jesus's clothing. In John 19:23–25a, the number of soldiers is specified at four, and they divided Jesus's clothes into four parts, one for each of them. Apparently, Jesus's tunic was left over, and it was of a high quality. So they decided to cast lots for it rather than tear it into four pieces. John adds this was in fulfillment of Ps. 21:19 (LXX), which is quoted verbatim: "They divided my clothing [plural] among them and cast lots on my clothing [singular]" (διεμερίσαντο τὰ ἱμάτιά μου ἑαυτοῖς καὶ ἐπὶ τὸν ἱματισμόν μου ἔβαλον κλῆρον, diemerisanto ta himatia mou heautois kai epi ton himatismon mou ebalon klēron).

The largest difference in this pericope pertains to the time at which Jesus was crucified. Mark 15:25 says it was the third hour (i.e., 9 a.m.). However, in John 19:14, Jesus was still on trial before Pilate at the sixth hour (i.e., noon). Moreover, recall that a discrepancy likewise appears to exist pertaining to the day on which Jesus had his Last Supper with his disciples (see #13). The Synoptics appear to narrate Jesus being crucified after the Passover meal, while John speaks of a Passover meal to be eaten on the day of Jesus's crucifixion. Thus, there are discrepancies pertaining to both the time and day of Jesus's crucifixion.

Bock refers to this as "one of the most complex chronological issues in the NT,"[99] while Raymond Brown writes, "This is perhaps the most disputed calendric question in the NT."[100] Some have proposed that John is following the time used by the Romans for their civil day while the Synoptics are following a different timetable in which the workday begins at 6 a.m.[101] Others suggest the Passover was often celebrated on different days, since there were disputes over the proper day on which the Passover fell[102] or because of the different times at which days started and ended for Galilean and Jerusalem Jews.[103] Still others suggest that any meal during the week of Passover could be referred to as a Passover meal and that the discrepancy in time (i.e., third versus sixth hour) could result from John rounding up and Mark rounding down.[104] Robert Stein considers these as well as a few other explanations and concludes, "[I]t is doubtful that any of the explanations has a particularly high degree of certainty."[105]

Some scholars think John altered the day and time of Jesus's crucifixion in order to emphasize theological points, specifically that Jesus is the burnt offering for sins and the Passover Lamb.[106] In this view, John has displaced the day and time of Jesus's crucifixion. Plutarch may have made a similar chronological move in reference to Julius Caesar. Plutarch, Suetonius, and Cassius Dio report how Caesar once wept while at the statue of Alexander.[107] When asked why he wept, Caesar answered that he was now the same age as was Alexander when he had conquered the world while he, Caesar, had yet to accomplish any great deed. Suetonius and Dio place the event in Spain during Caesar's quaestorship in 69–68 BCE. Plutarch also locates the event in Spain; however, he places it immediately after Caesar's praetorship, which ended six years later in December 62.

Since Alexander was thirty when he invaded India during his final campaign, and Caesar was thirty-one or thirty-two when quaestor and thirty-eight when his term as praetor expired, the timing of the event is more at home in the context described by Suetonius and Dio. Pelling thinks that "Plutarch may well be up to something here,"[108] for it is here and the period that follows when Caesar's ambitions for power became central in Plutarch's *Caesar*.[109] Thus, it appears that Plutarch has displaced the story and transplanted it around seven years later in order to draw attention to the beginning of Caesar's quest for power. If Plutarch can alter the year in which Caesar wept when considering the inferiority of his own accomplishments in comparion to those of Alexander in order to emphasize Caesar's ambitious character, John could alter the day and time of Jesus's crucifixion to symbolize the sacrificial quality of Jesus's death. And we have previously observed how either Mark or John changed the day when the woman anointed Jesus.[110]

In Mark 15:26, the tablet on Jesus's cross read, "The King of the Jews." In Matt. 27:37b, it is "This is Jesus, the King of the Jews"; in Luke 23:38, "This is the King of the Jews." In John 19:19b, it is "Jesus of Nazareth, the King of the Jews." Archer proposes this reflects three messages in three languages on the tablet: Aramaic, Latin, and Greek.[111] This will not do, since there are four versions. It is preferable to recognize that paraphrasing and/or imprecise memory is responsible for the differences in wording.

In Mark 15:40–41, Matt. 27:55–56, and Luke 23:49, women who had followed Jesus from Galilee stood at a distance from his cross. In John 19:25–27, they were standing "by the cross of Jesus" (παρὰ τῷ σταυρῷ τοῦ Ἰησου, *para tō staurō tou Iēsou*) and conversing with him. John is not necessarily in tension with the Synoptics here; the women are near Jesus while he is alive. In the Synoptics, the women view him from a distance after he had died.

Those of the party of Jesus who were present at Golgotha differ. In Luke 23:49, they are all of Jesus's acquaintances and women who had followed him from Galilee. In John 19:25, four women are said to have been standing by Jesus's cross, and their names are provided. In the following verse (19:26), we learn that Jesus's Beloved Disciple is also there. Accordingly, John's naming of the women present is not meant to be an exhaustive list. This is strengthened by Mark, who names three of the women present at the cross and then adds that many other women who had come to Jerusalem with Jesus were also present (15:40–41). Thus, some of the differences in those named to be present at Golgotha need not be held in tension. I have provided a fuller treatment of the women present at Jesus's crucifixion, burial, and empty tomb in appendix 3.

The logia of the Jewish leaders at Golgotha differ slightly. In Mark 15:31b–32 they say, "He saved others; he is not able to save himself. [He is] the Messiah, the King of Israel! Let him come down from the cross now, in order that we may see and believe." Matthew 27:42–43 is similar to Mark with only slight alterations but then elaborates, "He saved others; he is not able to save himself. He is the King of Israel. Let him come down from the cross now and we will believe in him. He has trusted in God. Let God rescue him now if He wants. For he said, 'I am God's Son.'" In Luke 23:35b, they say, "He saved others; let him save himself if he is God's Christ, the Chosen One."[112] Only Luke also portrays a soldier saying, "If you are the King of the Jews, save yourself."

Mark 15:32b and Matt. 27:44 state that the two thieves who had been crucified on each side of Jesus also reviled him. But Luke 23:39–40 states that one of the thieves rebuked the other, saying, "Do you not fear God, since you are under the same death sentence? And we rightly so. For we are getting what we deserve for the deeds we did. But this man did nothing wrong." Then he said to Jesus, "Remember me when you come into your kingdom." Does Mark // Matthew or Luke or both preserve the true account of the thieves? The tension vanishes if we propose that both thieves initially reviled Jesus but one later had a change of heart and repented. Such is plausible given deathbed conversions. On the other hand, all three Synoptics place the response of the thieves in the same location of their narrative: The three have just been crucified, lots were cast for Jesus's clothing, the Jewish leaders are mocking him, and even one or both thieves mock him. This is immediately followed by darkness covering the land beginning at noon. Thus, Luke appears to be reporting the same incident as Mark // Matthew. Luke may have displaced the act of the repentant thief from a later time that day, or Mark—followed by Matthew—left the thief unrepentant in order to highlight Jesus being rejected by all. As a historical question, it is impossible to determine what occurred with the available data. Accordingly, it would appear that either displacement or the altering or omission of narrative details has occurred.

Although the evangelists attribute additional statements to Jesus while on the cross, they appear earlier, and we will interest ourselves here only with Jesus's final two utterances, which are reported differently. Jesus's two final utterances are reported by Mark 15:33–37 and Matt. 27:45–50 as him crying out with a "loud voice" (φωνῇ μεγάλῃ, *phōnē megalē*), "My God! My God! Why have you forsaken me?" Some of the bystanders thought he was calling for Elijah. One of them ran and filled a sponge with "sour wine" (ὄξους, *oxous*), put it on a reed, and gave it to him to drink. Jesus then cried out with a loud voice (φωνῇ μεγάλῃ, *phōnē megalē*) and died. In John 19:28–30, Jesus said, "I am thirsty." Some of those present soaked a sponge in sour wine (ὄξους, *oxous*), put it on a hyssop branch, and put it to Jesus's mouth.[113] When Jesus received the sour wine, he said, "It is finished," and died. Luke does not provide the next-to-last logion, but Luke 23:46 tells us Jesus cried out loudly (φωνῇ μεγάλῃ, *phōnē megalē*), " 'Father, into your hands I entrust my spirit.'[114] And having said this, he died [τοῦτο δὲ εἰπὼν ἐξέπνευσεν, *touto de eipōn exepneusen*]."

In Jesus's next-to-last statement on the cross, Mark // Matthew have Jesus say, "My God! My God! Why have you forsaken me?"[115] But John appears to substitute "I am thirsty." In Jesus's final statement on the cross, Mark // Matthew report that Jesus then cried out loudly and died; Luke reports that Jesus cried out loudly, "Father, into your hands I entrust my spirit," then died; and John reports that Jesus said, "It is finished," then died. These are quite different renditions. Since Luke does not provide a next-to-last statement from Jesus on the cross and one could quite plausibly suggest Mark // Matthew simply did not provide the words of Jesus's final statement when he cried out loudly, the differences could be said to appear between Mark // Matthew and John in Jesus's next-to-last statement and between Luke and John in Jesus's final statement.

Virtually all specialists of John's Gospel acknowledge that the evangelist often adapted the traditions about Jesus.[116] These two utterances of Jesus may be an instance when we can observe the extent to which John redacted existing tradition.

For the next-to-last logion, it appears that John has redacted "My God! My God! Why have you forsaken me?" (Mark // Matthew) to say, "I am thirsty." Daniel Wallace proposes that since every occurrence of "thirst" in John carries the meaning of being devoid of God's Spirit,[117] the evangelist has reworked what Jesus said "into an entirely different form." It is "a *dynamic equivalent transformation*" of what we read in Mark // Matthew. Accordingly, in John, Jesus is stating that God has abandoned him. In Mark 15:34, Jesus quotes Ps. 22:1: "My God! My God! Why have you forsaken me?" Thus, John can write, "Knowing that everything had now been accomplished, *in order that the Scripture may be fulfilled* [i.e., Ps. 22:1], Jesus said, "I am thirsty" (John 19:28, emphasis added).[118] John has redacted Jesus's words but has retained their meaning.[119]

Jesus's final logion in Luke 23:46, "Father, into your hands I entrust my spirit" (a quote from Ps. 31:5, LXX), becomes "it is finished" in John 19:30. What is finished? John says Jesus had come to "take away the sin of the world" by laying down his life for it (John 1:29; cf. 3:17; 10:15, 17; 12:47). His redemptive work on the cross was now complete (John 19:28, 30), and he could return to his Father (John 7:33; 14:12, 28; 16:5, 10; 20:17). John redacts Jesus's words, and although he maintains their gist, he adds some theological flavoring that is consistent with the portrait of Jesus he has painted from the very beginning: Jesus is the Lamb of God, sacrificed for the sins of others.

Of interest are the portents reported to have occurred surrounding Jesus's death. Mark 15:33–39, Matt. 27:46–54, and Luke 23:44–45 report

(a) darkness from noon until 3 p.m., and (b) that the veil in the temple is torn in two from top to bottom. Only Matthew adds that the earth shook, the rocks split, the tombs were opened, and many bodies of the dead saints were raised. These came out of the tombs after Jesus's resurrection, went into Jerusalem, and appeared to many.[120]

Mark 15:38 // Matt. 27:51 narrate the temple veil tearing in two after Jesus's death, whereas Luke 23:45 narrates its occurrence prior to his death. Perhaps Luke has altered the order in which he presents events in order to change things up slightly.[121]

Mark 15:39 reports that when the centurion observed how Jesus had died, he proclaimed that Jesus was "truly" (ἀληθῶς, *alēthōs*) the "Son of God." Matthew 27:54 is similar, except it is the centurion and those guarding Jesus with him who observe and proclaim. Luke 23:47 has only the centurion say Jesus was "certainly [ὄντως, *ontōs*] innocent/righteous [δίκαιος, *dikaios*]."

Summary

- Matthew substitutes a word in order to allude to Ps. 68 (LXX), which describes a man who cries out to God, having been rejected by all.
- John may have altered the day and time of Jesus's crucifixion to symbolize the sacrificial quality of Jesus's death.
- Paraphrasing and/or imprecise memory or reporting is responsible for differences in wording.
- John does not intend to provide a complete list of Jesus's followers at the cross.
- Either Luke displaces an event or Mark // Matthew alter details.
- John redacts Jesus's words yet retains their meaning (*ipsissima vox*). He sometimes adds theological flavoring.
- Luke appears to reverse the order in which he presents some events.

#16 (#352–53, 356) The Resurrection (Mark 16:1–8; Matt. 28:1–10, 16–20; Luke 24:1–51; John 20:1–29; 21:1–24)[122]

Narrative

Early on the Sunday morning after Jesus's crucifixion, there was an earthquake and an angel rolled the stone away from Jesus's tomb and sat upon it. Those guarding the tomb were terrified, and at some point they fled. Shortly thereafter, a number of Jesus's women followers went to the tomb where Jesus had been buried. When they arrived, they found the stone had been rolled away.

The women fled from the tomb and reported these things to the disciples, who found it difficult to believe them. So Peter and the Beloved Disciple ran to the tomb and entered it. Jesus's body was not there, just as the women had claimed. However, they noticed the linen cloths in which Jesus had been buried were folded neatly. The two disciples went home.

Mary Magdalene, however, remained at the tomb and was weeping. Stooping into the tomb, she saw two angels who asked her why she wept. She said someone had taken her Lord and she did not know where his body now was. When she turned around, she saw Jesus standing there but did not recognize him. He, too, asked her why she wept and whom she sought. Mary thought he was the gardener and told him that if he had taken Jesus's body to let her know where he had placed it and she would go and get it. Jesus said, "Mary." Then she knew it was him and exclaimed, "Rabbi!" Mary ran to the disciples and informed them she had seen Jesus. The guards reported what had occurred at the tomb to the Jewish chief priests, who bribed them to say the disciples had stolen Jesus's body while they slept.

Later that day, two of Jesus's followers were walking toward their town of Emmaus, which was a little less than seven miles outside Jerusalem. One of them was named Cleopas. Jesus joined them along the way, but they were kept from recognizing him. They appeared quite sad, and Jesus asked why. They answered they had hoped Jesus was the Messiah who would free them from Rome, but the Jewish leaders had handed him over to the Romans, who had crucified him only three days prior. They added that some of their women folk had gone to the tomb that morning, discovered it empty, and reported to Jesus's disciples that angels there told them Jesus had risen from the dead. As a result, some of the disciples ran to the tomb and also found it as the women had said but did not see Jesus there. Jesus then explained to the Emmaus disciples from the Scriptures that the Messiah had to die and be glorified. Since evening was near, they invited him to stay with them. And when they reclined for a meal, Jesus blessed some bread and distributed it to them. They then recognized him, and he vanished from their sight. So they got up and left for Jerusalem to inform Jesus's disciples what had occurred.

When they arrived, the disciples were gathered in a room behind locked doors, hiding in fear of the Jewish leaders. They explained to the disciples that Jesus had appeared to them. The disciples replied that Jesus had also appeared to Peter sometime earlier that day. While they were still conversing, Jesus appeared in their presence and said, "Peace be with you." They were stunned. He showed them his hands and side and invited them to touch him. He then asked for some food to prove he was not a ghost. They gave him a piece of broiled fish, which he ate. And he explained the Scriptures to them how the Messiah had to suffer and rise from the dead on the third day. One of Jesus's disciples named Thomas was not present on that occasion. So when he joined them later, they told him they had seen Jesus. But he did not believe them and said he would not believe unless he saw and touched the nail prints in Jesus's hands and his side where a Roman guard had stabbed him with a spear.

Eight days later, the disciples were gathered in a room, and this time Thomas was with them. Jesus appeared among them and said, "Peace be with you." He then invited Thomas to touch his hands and side and believe. Jesus appeared to his disciples a third time by the Sea of Galilee. Peter, Thomas, Nathanael, James and John the sons of Zebedee, and two other disciples had been fishing all night and had caught nothing. As the sun was rising, Jesus stood on the beach about 100 yards away and yelled out to them, "Children, do you not have any fish?" When they answered, "No," he told them they would find some if they cast their net on the right side of the boat. So they did and caught so many fish that they were unable to haul in the net. The Beloved Disciple said to Peter, "It is the Lord!"

When they reached land, they saw that Jesus had started a charcoal fire and laid some fish and bread on it. He asked them to bring some of the fish they had caught and to come have breakfast. Afterward, Jesus had a discussion with Peter as they walked along the shore pertaining to his leading the new church and his eventual martyrdom.

At a later time, Jesus commissioned his disciples to go make disciples of all peoples, beginning with Jerusalem, teaching them to repent for the forgiveness of sins through him and to keep his commandments. Jesus then blessed them and was taken up into heaven while they watched.

A Few Preliminary Comments

The discipline of New Testament studies is comprised of a heterogeneous community of scholars that includes atheists such as Gerd Lüdemann and

Joseph Hoffmann, agnostics such as Bart Ehrman and James Crossley, liberals such as John Dominic Crossan and Stephen Patterson, moderates such as James Charlesworth and Luke Timothy Johnson, conservatives such as Craig Blomberg and Lynn Cohick, and those of the Jewish faith such as Amy Jill-Levine and Geza Vermes. Those outside the field of New Testament studies may be surprised to learn that the question of whether Jesus actually rose from the dead is a topic on which there is an abundance of academic literature. Gary Habermas has compiled a bibliography of approximately 3,400 academic journal articles and books that touch on the subject between 1975 and 2016.[123] The prominent historian of Jesus, Dale Allison, referred to the question of Jesus's resurrection as the "prize puzzle of New Testament research."[124]

I have written on the matter of the historicity of Jesus's resurrection elsewhere and have no objective to treat it here.[125] Yet it need be said that those who dismiss Jesus's resurrection as a myth must a priori regard many elements in the resurrection narratives as wholesale invention. Readers should keep in mind, however, that the Gospels are not the earliest literature to report the resurrection of Jesus. Before the first Gospel was written, Paul mentioned Jesus's resurrection and his appearance to others (1 Cor. 15:3–8; ca. 53–56 CE). There is a consensus among scholars today that 1 Cor. 15:3–7 is an oral tradition Paul embedded in his letter and that the content of that tradition is much earlier. This oral tradition mentions Jesus's death, burial, resurrection, and six of his post-resurrection appearances to others, several of whom were personally acquainted with Paul.[126] Paul said he had delivered this tradition to the church in Corinth while with them, which most scholars date ca. 50–51 CE and, of course, he had received it from others at an earlier date. Thus, with Jesus having been crucified in April of 30 or 33 CE, this means Paul delivered the story of Jesus's resurrection to the church in Corinth no less than seventeen and no more than twenty-one years after Jesus's death. And he received that tradition earlier still. Therefore, irrespective of what one thinks pertaining to the degree of flexibility each evangelist may have taken when writing his resurrection narrative, none of them invented the core story. Moreover, despite the fact that many Christians soon came to regard the Gospels as being divinely inspired, the literary genres of and compositional devices employed in the Gospels and Plutarch's *Lives* are more similar than different. Accordingly, we can still attempt to assess the resurrection narratives for standard compositional devices that resulted in differences between the accounts.

Earlier we observed that Plutarch's treatment of the events of December 50 through early January 49 BCE are often impossible to harmonize and observed him reworking his material in ways that are sometimes difficult to discern.[127] We will observe some similar reworking of the resurrection narrative by the evangelists that are every bit as perplexing. In a few instances, they are even more so. The analysis that follows can only attempt to provide various proposals for the differences, in which we may have varying degrees of confidence.

Analysis

Matthew 28:1 uses a generic term for "grave" (τάφος, *taphos*), whereas the terms used by Mark 16:2 // John 20:1 (μνημεῖον, *mnēmeion*) and Luke 24:1 (μνῆμα, *mnēma*) are more specific and refer to a tomb for remembrance or a monument.

The time at which the women arrived at Jesus's tomb differs. In Mark 16:2, it is "very early . . . after the sun had risen" (λίαν πρωΐ, *lian prōi* . . . ἀνατείλαντος τοῦ ἡλίου, *anateilantos tou hēliou*).[128] However in John 20:1, it is "early while it was still dark" (πρωΐ σκοτίας ἔτι οὔσης, *prōi skotias eti ousēs*).[129] It is *possible* that it was "still dark" (per John) when the women left for the tomb, and they arrived "after the sun had risen" (per Mark).[130] Everyone who has taken time to view a sunrise knows that the amount of daylight changes significantly between ten minutes prior to sunrise and ten minutes after. When reading John, one is left with the impression that it was dark when the women arrived at the tomb. But the evangelists, no different than Plutarch and other ancient authors, had no objective of narrating events with photographic precision. Nor did they have in mind twenty-first century readers who would be comparing their accounts under a microscope (as we are doing!).

The number and identity of the women who went to the tomb differ.[131] While the Synoptics report multiple women who discovered the empty tomb, only Mary Magdalene is mentioned in John 20:1. However, John appears to know of other women present, since Mary goes on in the next verse to tell Peter and the Beloved Disciple, "They have taken the Lord from the tomb and *we* do not know where they have laid him!" (emphasis added). To whom does the "we" refer? It is possible she is including Peter and the Beloved Disciple with herself. However, that would be entirely redundant, since the two men would not even have known the tomb was empty until the very moment she informed them. Since all three

Synoptics report the presence of multiple women at the discovery of the empty tomb, it seems more likely that John is aware of the presence of other women and is shining his literary spotlight on Mary Magdalene in his narrative.

Plausibility for this conclusion is increased when we consider the evangelist's use of literary spotlighting elsewhere. Even at the crucifixion scene, John shines a spotlight on the women. For in 19:25, he names those "standing by Jesus's cross" as "his mother, his mother's sister, Mary the wife of Clopas, and Mary Magdalene." Yet in the next sentence he mentions someone else who was present: "So, when Jesus saw his mother *and the disciple whom he loved* standing there, he said to his mother, 'Woman, behold your son'" (emphasis added). Lest one be unknowingly influenced by the novel *The Da Vinci Code* and think "the disciple whom Jesus loved" was Mary Magdalene, "the disciple" (τὸν μαθητὴν, *ton mathētēn*) is masculine in Greek and is mentioned as a man elsewhere in John's Gospel (13:23; 21:7, 20; cf. 21:2 if John is one of the two sons of Zebedee as tradition has him). Even stronger is that Mary Magdalene announces her discovery of the empty tomb to "the disciple whom Jesus loved" in John 20:2! Moreover, Mark 15:41 names three of the women present at the cross and then adds that many other women who had come to Jerusalem with Jesus were also present. And Luke 23:49 tells us that all of Jesus's acquaintances[132] and women who had followed him from Galilee stood at a distance. Thus, some of the differences in those named as being present at Golgotha need not be held in tension. However, this does not necessarily explain why Mark names three women, Matthew names two, and Luke names four. Perhaps some of the evangelists were not attempting to be thorough; perhaps they were using different sources; or perhaps they were identifying the women who were their sources.

Luke informs us that when the women announced that the tomb was empty, Peter ran to the tomb and found it as they had said (Luke 24:12).[133] At first look, this may appear inconsistent with John 20:3–20, which says Peter and the Beloved Disciple ran to the empty tomb upon the women's report. However, only twelve verses later in Luke 24:24, the two Emmaus disciples reported that "*some of those with us* went away to the tomb and found it just as the women had said" (emphasis added). Thus, Luke appears to be shining his literary spotlight on Peter in 24:12.

Mark 16:5 and Matt. 28:2–4 mention one angel at the tomb, while Luke 24:4 and John 20:12 mention two. Mark and Matthew may be shining their literary spotlight on the angel making the announcement.

Mark 16:5 refers to the angel as a "young man [νεανίσκον, *neaniskon*] dressed in a white robe," while Luke 24:4 describes the angels as "two men [ἄνδρες δύο, *andres duo*] in dazzling/lightning-like clothing" (ἐν ἐσθῆτι ἀστραπτούσῃ, *en esthēti astraptousē*). It is obvious that Luke has angels in mind, since he goes on to call them "angels" (24:22–23). Moreover, white or shining clothing in the New Testament are often the mark of a heavenly visitation.[134]

The location of the angel(s) at the moment of initial contact with the women differs. In Mark 16:5, Luke 24:3–4, and John 20:11–12, he/they is inside the tomb. However, in Matt. 28:2–6, readers get the impression the angel is sitting on the stone he had rolled away from the tomb when the women see him. One might reasonably posit that Matthew has skipped forward in time when the angel speaks to the women and that they may all have been inside the tomb when the angel appeared to them.[135] However, Matt. 28:6 has the angel say, "Come! See the place where he was laid." The "Come! See" (δεῦτε ἴδετε, *deute idete*) probably suggests movement to somewhere else in this context. Mark 16:6 has the angel inside the tomb say, "See [ἴδε, *ide*] the place where they have laid him." In Mark, there is no need for the women to "Come!" for they are already there. However, in the Bible, the phrase "Come. See" (δεῦτε ἴδετε, *deute idete*) also appears in 2 Kings 6:13, Ps. 46:8 LXX (45:9), and John 4:29. In 2 Kings and John, it clearly means to go to another location. In Ps. 45, it is used in the sense of "to consider," which would also work in this context: "Consider the place where he was laying."[136]

The posture of the angel(s) is described differently. In Matt. 28:2, he is "sitting" (ἐκάθητο, *ekathēto*), presumably on the stone. In Mark 16:5, he is "sitting" (καθήμενον, *kathēmenon*) inside the tomb and on the right. In John 20:12, they are "sitting" (καθεζομένους, *kathezomenous*) where Jesus had once laid; one at the head, one at the feet. But in Luke 24:4, the angels "stood beside" (ἐπέστησαν, *epestēsan*) the women. The *standing* need not be in conflict with the *sitting* in the other Gospels, since the Greek ἐπέστησαν, *epestēsan* (from ἐφίστημι, *ephistēmi*), often means *to appear or be present* without any hint of the posture taken. And Luke clearly employs the term often in this sense elsewhere.[137] Thus, while it is quite possible that Luke intended to imply the angels were standing erect, he may have intended to communicate nothing more than that the angels appeared to the women without any reference to whether they were sitting or standing erect.

The message of the angel(s) to the women is stated differently. In John 20:13, the angels asked Mary Magdalene, "Woman, why are you weeping?"

No further correspondence between the angels and Mary is mentioned. However, a fuller discourse is found in the Synoptics:

> Do not be amazed. You are seeking Jesus the Nazarene who was crucified. He has been raised. He is not here. Behold, the place where they laid him. But go tell his disciples and Peter that he is going ahead of you to Galilee. There you will see him, just as he told you.[138] (μὴ ἐκθαμβεῖσθε Ἰησοῦν ζητεῖτε τὸν Ναζαρηνὸν τὸν ἐσταυρωμένον· ἠγέρθη, οὐκ ἔστιν ὧδε· ἴδε ὁ τόπος ὅπου ἔθηκαν αὐτόν. ἀλλ᾽ ὑπάγετε εἴπατε τοῖς μαθηταῖς αὐτοῦ καὶ τῷ Πέτρῳ ὅτι προάγει ὑμᾶς εἰς τὴν Γαλιλαίαν· ἐκεῖ αὐτὸν ὄψεσθε, καθὼς εἶπεν ὑμῖν. / mē ekthambeisthe. Iēsoun zēteite ton Nazarēnon ton estaurōmenon. ēgerthē, ouk estin hōde. ide ho topos hopou ethēkan auton. all' hupagete eipate tois mathētais autou kai tō Petrō hoti proagei humas eis tēn Galilaian. ekei auton opsesthe, kathōs eipen humin.) (Mark 16:6–7)

> Do not be afraid. For I know that you are seeking Jesus who was crucified. He is not here, for he has been raised just as he said.[139] Come! See the place where he was laid. Now go quickly and tell his disciples that he has been raised from the dead, and behold, he is going ahead of you to Galilee. There you will see him. Behold, I told you. (μὴ φοβεῖσθε ὑμεῖς, οἶδα γὰρ ὅτι Ἰησοῦν τὸν ἐσταυρωμένον ζητεῖτε· οὐκ ἔστιν ὧδε, ἠγέρθη γὰρ καθὼς εἶπεν· δεῦτε ἴδετε τὸν τόπον ὅπου ἔκειτο. καὶ ταχὺ πορευθεῖσαι εἴπατε τοῖς μαθηταῖς αὐτοῦ ὅτι ἠγέρθη ἀπὸ τῶν νεκρῶν, καὶ ἰδοὺ προάγει ὑμᾶς εἰς τὴν Γαλιλαίαν, ἐκεῖ αὐτὸν ὄψεσθε· ἰδοὺ εἶπον ὑμῖν. / mē phobeisthe humeis. oida gar hoti Iēsoun ton estaurōmenon zēteite. ouk estin hōde, ēgerthē gar kathōs eipen, deute idete ton topon hopou ekeito. kai tachu poreutheisai eipate tois mathētais autou hoti ēgerthē apo tōn nekrōn, kai idou proagei humas eis tēn Galilaian, ekei auton opsesthe idou. eipon humin.) (Matt. 28:5–7)

> Why are you seeking the living among the dead? He is not here but has been raised. Remember how he spoke to you while still in Galilee, saying that it is necessary for the Son of Man to be delivered into the hands of sinful men and to be crucified and to be raised on the third day.[140] (τί ζητεῖτε τὸν ζῶντα μετὰ τῶν νεκρῶν; οὐκ ἔστιν ὧδε, ἀλλ᾽ ἠγέρθη. μνήσθητε ὡς ἐλάλησεν ὑμῖν ἔτι ὢν ἐν τῇ Γαλιλαίᾳ λέγων τὸν υἱὸν τοῦ ἀνθρώπου ὅτι δεῖ παραδοθῆναι εἰς χεῖρας ἀνθρώπων ἁμαρτωλῶν καὶ σταυρωθῆναι καὶ τῇ τρίτῃ ἡμέρᾳ ἀναστῆναι. / ti zēteite

ton zōnta meta tōn nekrōn? ouk estin hōde, all' ēgerthē. mnēsthēte hōs
elalēsen humin eti ōn en tē Galilaia legōn ton huion tou anthrōpou hoti
dei paradothēnai eis cheiras anthrōpōn hamartōlōn kai staurōthēnai kai
tē tritē hēmera anastēnai.) (Luke 24:5–7)

Matthew has slightly paraphrased Mark. He substitutes the more appropriate "afraid" (φοβεῖσθε, *phobeisthe*) for Mark's "amazed" (ἐξεθαμβήθησαν, *exe thambēthēsan*).[141] Whereas Mark says, "He has been raised. He is not here. . . . There you will see him, *just as he told you*," Matthew says, "He is not here. For he has been raised *just as he said*. . . . There you will see him. *Behold, I told you*." Luke 24:5–9 either paraphrases Mark more freely than Matthew or has drawn from a different source.[142] Luke has changed the angel's statement to a question: "You are seeking Jesus the Nazarene who was crucified. He has been raised. He is not here" (Mark 16:6) becomes "Why are you seeking the living among the dead? He is not here but has been raised" (Luke 24:5–6). In Luke, Galilee is mentioned as the place where Jesus had predicted his betrayal, crucifixion, and resurrection, whereas it is where the disciples are to go promptly in Mark and Matthew. One could attempt to reconcile the differences in the angel's message by conflating every element of the message as reported in all of the Synoptics.[143] It would seem odd, however, that Luke or his source would report only that which Mark and Matthew have omitted, since there is little overlap between them. Thus, paraphrasing or a different source is a more plausible explanation.

The location of where Mary Magdalene first encountered Jesus differs. In John 20:14–18 she conversed with two angels at the tomb and then turned around and saw Jesus behind her, although she did not recognize him and thought he was the gardener. Jesus asked her why she was weeping and whom she sought. She answered, "Sir, if you have carried him away, tell me where you have laid him and I will take him." Jesus said, "Mary!" She turned to him and exclaimed, "Rabbi!" Jesus then told her, "Do not hold me. For I have not yet ascended to my Father. But go to my brothers and tell them that I am going to my father and to your father, to my God and to your God."

The story differs in Matt. 28:8–10 in which upon hearing the message of the angel at the tomb, the group of women, which included Mary Magdalene, left quickly with fear and trembling and ran to tell Jesus's disciples. Jesus met them along the way and said, "Greetings!" And they came to him, took hold of his feet, and worshipped him. Jesus then said to them, "Do not be afraid. Go tell my brothers to depart to Galilee. They will see me there." Thus, in Matthew, Mary Magdalene first encountered Jesus when she was running away from the tomb to deliver the angel's message to the disciples, whereas in John it was at the tomb. Moreover, in Matthew, Jesus told the women to deliver the message to his male disciples that he is going ahead of them to Galilee, whereas in John the message is that he is going to his Father and God. At minimum, it appears that either Matthew or John has relocated the appearance to Mary Magdalene. This shows the extent to which at least one of the evangelists or the sources from which he drew felt free to craft the story.[144]

It is noteworthy that in all three Synoptics, Mary Magdalene's name appears first among those who discovered the empty tomb. And in Matthew she is named first among those who encountered the risen Jesus. That John shined his literary spotlight on her as the first to discover the empty tomb and to see the risen Jesus suggests the earliest tradition concerning the resurrection of Jesus included a prominent role played by Mary Magdalene on Easter morning.

Moreover, the traditions in all three Synoptics have angels appearing to multiple women and announcing Jesus's resurrection. This element, though absent in John, must likewise be regarded as being very early. The early Christians preserved the story of the appearance of angels to Jesus's women disciples at the empty tomb and an appearance of Jesus to at least one of them, Mary Magdalene, before appearing to any of his male disciples. This is intriguing given the credibility challenges they could anticipate because of their culture's aversion to an appeal to women witnesses.[145]

It is also worth observing that if Matt. 28:8–10 and John 20:14–18 are reporting Jesus's initial appearance to Mary Magdalene, his message differs slightly. In Matthew, it is (1) not to fear and (2) to tell his brothers to go to Galilee where they will see him. In John, it is (1) to stop holding him because he had not yet ascended to his Father, and (2) to tell his brothers that he is ascending to his and their Father and God. Again we observe the extent to which one or more of the evangelists or their sources apparently felt free to vary the tradition.

The narratives differ pertaining to whether an angel was at the tomb during the initial visit of the women. Whereas all three Synoptics report the presence of one or more angels at the empty tomb when the women arrived, John's account suggests no angels were present until Mary's second visit.[146]

Is John's account closer to what was originally taught, while the resurrection narratives in the Synoptics have conflated and greatly compressed various elements? Matthew has compressed elsewhere when he narrates the centurion going to Jesus and petitioning him to heal his servant rather than sending two separate sets of emissaries while never seeing Jesus himself as in Luke.[147] However, if the resurrection narratives in the Synoptics have not been conflated and greatly compressed, why is the initial appearance of the angels to the women absent in John? If Matthew (and the Synoptics) conflated and compressed elements in the narrative, of necessity they would have needed to redact other elements in order to improve the flow of the narrative.

In Mark 16:8, the women fled from the tomb in fear and astonishment. And they said nothing to anyone, because they were afraid. However, in Matthew, Luke, and John, the women informed the disciples of the empty tomb. This appears to be a contradiction. However, a resolution is certainly possible; for example, earlier in Mark 1:44, Jesus told a man whom he had just healed of leprosy, "See that you say nothing to anyone. But go show yourself to the priest." The command in both instances is very similar.[148] Thus, it could be that Mark is saying, as implied in 1:44, that the women did not stop along the way to speak with anyone else but went directly to the disciples.

There is a difference pertaining to the length of time Jesus remained with his disciples after his resurrection. In Matt. 28:7, 10, first the angel and then Jesus instructed the women to tell his disciples that he was going before them to Galilee, where they would see him. Depending on the precise location where they were to meet, Galilee was approximately eighty miles north and was a three-day walk at minimum before they would see him. In John 20:1–21:25, Jesus appeared to his disciples in Jerusalem on the same day he had risen. He appeared to them again eight days later at an undisclosed location. Sometime afterward, it is not said when, he appeared to them a third time by the Sea of Galilee. So in John there is an absolute minimum of nine days in which Jesus remained on earth after his resurrection. In Luke 24:1–53, Jesus's resurrection, all of his appearances, and his ascension to heaven are narrated as though having occurred on that Sunday. That Luke compressed the events in this manner is clear, since in the sequel to his Gospel, Luke says Jesus appeared to his disciples over a period of forty days before ascending to heaven (Acts 1:3–9).

Moreover, with Judas now dead, there were eleven main disciples. Thus Luke 24:33 can speak of Jesus's first appearance to a group of his male disciples as including "the eleven and those with them." However, John 20:19–24 tells us Thomas was absent during that event. Thus, only ten of the main disciples would have been present. Accordingly, either Luke conflated the first and second appearances to the male disciples, or John crafted the second appearance in order to rebuke those who, like Thomas, heard about Jesus's resurrection and failed to believe. Some have suggested that the "eleven" may have been a way of referring to the core of the apostolic body.[149] However, while scholars generally agree that "the Twelve" became a nickname for Jesus's main disciples (e.g., 1 Cor. 15:5), there is no indication that "the eleven" was ever used in a similar sense. Thus, it seems more probable in this instance that Luke has conflated the first and second appearances of Jesus to his male disciples.

A major difference in the resurrection narratives pertains to where Jesus first appeared to a group of his male disciples. Matthew and Mark locate this appearance in Galilee, whereas Luke and John place it in Jerusalem (Matt. 28:10, 16–17; 26:32 // Mark 16:7 [implied; cf. 14:28]; Luke 24:33–36; John 20:19). In fact, in Luke and John, the words of neither the angels nor Jesus at the tomb provide any hint of any appearance in Galilee.

Some have suggested that the first appearance occurred in Jerusalem and that the command to go to Galilee was to prepare them to meet Jesus there eventually, perhaps after the completion of the Festival of Unleavened Bread when Galilean pilgrims would return home.[150] However, this does not appear to be what is being communicated in Mark and Matthew. In Matthew, the angel instructed the women to "go quickly" to the disciples with the message that Jesus had been raised and was going before them to Galilee, where they would see him (28:7). There was a sense of urgency since Jesus had already left for Galilee. Only three verses later, the women were running from the tomb to relay the news to the disciples when Jesus met them and reiterated the instructions: "Tell my brothers to go to Galilee. They will see me there" (28:10). The Greek ἐκεῖ, *ekei* ("there"), appears first in the sentence for emphasis: "There [in Galilee] you will see him," says the angel (28:7). Then Jesus reiterates with "there [κἀκεῖ, *kakei*; in Galilee] they will see me" (28:10). Indeed, in Mark and Matthew, this is what Jesus had told them he would do (Mark 14:28 // Matt. 26:32), and Matt. 28:16–17 informs us that the disciples proceeded to Galilee as instructed and Jesus appeared to them there as promised.[151] There is no hint that the disciples delayed. Finally, we may ask why Matthew narrated both the angel and Jesus instructing the disciples to go to Galilee in order to meet him there if he was going to appear to them in Jerusalem in only a few hours. Such a command does not seem to be of such importance that it needed to be reported by Mark // Matthew at that point in the narrative.

There is another element that suggests Matthew located Jesus's first appearance to his male disciples in Galilee: The appearance in Galilee in Matt. 28:16–17 is almost certainly a parallel to the appearance in Jerusalem in Luke 24:36–49, which is narrated as the first appearance to the male disciples as a group. Matt. 28:16–17 informs us that upon seeing Jesus in Galilee, some worshipped him but others "doubted" (ἐδίστασαν, *edistasan*). The term used here for "doubt" appears on only one other occasion in the New Testament, and it is also in Matthew (14:31). On that occasion, the disciples were in a boat one night on a stormy Sea of Galilee when they saw Jesus walking on water. Peter said to Jesus, "Lord, if it is you, command me to come to you on the water!" Jesus said, "Come." So Peter got out of the boat and began walking on the water toward Jesus. But when he became frightened, he began to sink and cried out to Jesus for help. Jesus grabbed him and asked why he had "doubted" (ἐδίστασας, *edistasas*). The term means to have two (δίς, *dis*) thoughts on a matter. This is what we observe here with Peter. His faith, which led him to walk on water, is accompanied by doubt: "I can do this because of Jesus. But how is this even possible? If something goes wrong, I will drown in this deep water!" In Matt. 28:16–17, when the disciples saw Jesus, some worshipped him, but some others were having two thoughts: "He's alive and well! But how can this be, since he was crucified just the other day?"[152]

Luke 24:37–41 expresses the experience in different terms, saying the disciples were startled and fearful, thought they were seeing a ghost (could this be why Matthew says some doubted?), were troubled, and had questions in their hearts (i.e., doubts). Of special interest is verse 41: "And still unbelieving from their joy and marveling" (ἔτι δὲ ἀπιστούντων αὐτῶν ἀπὸ τῆς χαρᾶς καὶ θαυμαζόντων, *eti de atistountōn autōn apo tēs charas kai thaumazontōn*). It seems clear that the "unbelieving" in Luke 24:41 is an idiom similar to what we use today to describe an event eliciting great surprise, such as a final play that wins a ballgame: *unbelievable!* The "unbelief" elicited by "joy and marveling" could carry no other meaning in this context.[153]

Thus, Luke uses an even stronger term than Matthew's "doubt" when describing the initial response of the male disciples when Jesus first appeared to them after his resurrection: "unbelieving." Yet it is clear that we are not to imagine those experiencing "unbelief" in Luke 24:41 as though they were standing there looking at Jesus with arms crossed and lips pressed. My mom and dad have both died. If they were to appear before me alive today, I would have a response that could be described in terms similar to what Matthew and Luke employed. I would feel joy and wonder at seeing them. But that would be accompanied by questions in my heart, "How can this be? I held my dad's hand the moment he died and I buried both!" I would exclaim, "Unbelievable!" and have two thoughts—"Wow!" and "How?" If Matt. 28:17 and Luke 24:41 are, as it seems, describing the same event, we have one more reason for understanding Matthew to have located the first appearance of Jesus to a group of his male disciples in Galilee while Luke locates it in Jerusalem.

It is noteworthy that while in Mark // Matthew the disciples are instructed to go to Galilee where they will see Jesus, in Luke, Galilee is mentioned only as the location where Jesus had predicted his betrayal, crucifixion, and resurrection. This is not as insignificant as it may appear at first look but is only one element of a larger picture involving redaction in the Synoptics. As we observed above, Luke compresses all of the appearances and the ascension to have occurred on the same day as Jesus's resurrection. So there is no time to have the disciples go to Galilee. Thus, Luke may have redacted the message of the angel in Mark // Matthew by eliminating a trip to Galilee. However, if the first appearance to the male disciples was in Jerusalem (per Luke and John), Mark // Matthew may have redacted the message to direct our focus on Galilee. In any sense, it seems clear that Matthew narrates the first appearance of Jesus to his male disciples to have been in Galilee. And Mark implies such. But why do Mark and Matthew do so while Luke and John locate it in Jerusalem? It is difficult to determine. Perhaps Mark and Matthew either preferred or knew only sources that located the appearance in Galilee, whereas the source(s) preferred by Luke and John put the appearance in Jerusalem.[154]

There is a slight difference in what is reported that Jesus showed his disciples when he first appeared to them. In Luke 24:40, he showed them his hands and feet, while in John 20:20, he showed them his hands and side. That John substituted Jesus's side for his feet is understood, since only John had earlier narrated a guard piercing Jesus's side at the crucifixion site in order to verify Jesus had already died.

In John 20:17, Jesus told Mary Magdalene to stop "clinging" (ἅπτου, *haptou*) to him because he had not yet ascended to the Father. However, in Matt. 28:9–10, he gave no such instruction when the women (i.e., Mary Magdalene and "the other Mary") fell down at his feet and held onto them (ἐκράτησαν, *ekratēsan*) upon seeing him. Moreover, only ten verses later Jesus invited Thomas to touch him (lit. "put" [βάλε, *bale*] his hand in his side, John 20:27). Why, in John, did Jesus forbid Mary from clinging to him and speak of his ascension? Various proposals have been offered with no consensus opinion emerging. However, most agree that John was at least communicating that Jesus's renewed relationships with his followers would not be on the same terms as before, for very soon Jesus would relate to them through his Spirit.[155] Pertaining to Jesus's breathing on his disciples and saying, "Receive the Holy Spirit" (John 20:22), perhaps John, knowing he would not be writing a sequel as had Luke, desired to allude to the event at Pentecost.[156] So he wove mention of the ascension into his communications with Mary Magdalene (20:17) and of the Holy Spirit at Pentecost into his communications with his male disciples (20:22).[157]

In Luke 24:50–52, Jesus ascended from Bethany, whereas in Acts 1:9–12, he ascended from the Mount of Olives. This is not a discrepancy, since Bethany is located on the Mount of Olives.[158]

We have observed a number of differences in this pericope. Although many of them can be easily understood in light of the compositional devices we have observed being used by Plutarch and the evangelists elsewhere, there are a several that leave us bewildered: (1) the location where Mary Magdalene first encountered the risen Jesus, (2) Jesus's message to Mary Magdalene, (3) whether there were angels at the tomb during the initial visit by the women, (4) the number of Jesus's male disciples who were present when Jesus first appeared to them, and (5) whether Jesus first appeared to the male disciples in Jerusalem or in Galilee. It is of interest that all but the first of these differences can be resolved quite easily if John's Gospel were removed from our consideration.

Should John's Gospel be excluded from our analysis of the resurrection narratives? Almost all scholars think John has exercised greater flexibility in the manner that he relayed stories about Jesus and that it was the last of the four Gospels to be written. However, John contains a few traditions found in only one of the Synoptics' resurrection narratives, such as the visit of Peter and others to Jesus's tomb after the women announced that his body was gone (Luke), Jesus's appearance to Mary Magdalene (Matt.), and Jesus's first appearance to a group of his male disciples in Jerusalem (Luke). If John wrote independent of the Synoptic traditions as most scholars think, these multiple points of contact with unique Synoptic traditions caution us against dismissing John. Therefore, the tensions remain.

Summary

- Luke and John shine their literary spotlights, and it is likely that Mark and Matthew do likewise.
- Paraphrasing and the use of different sources are likely the cause of certain differences.
- Matthew or John relocated an appearance of Jesus to Mary Magdalene.
- It is possible that Matthew (and the Synoptics) have conflated and compressed numerous elements in the narrative and were forced to redact other elements in order to improve the narrative flow or that one or more of the evangelists have engaged in a bit of creative reconstruction.
- Either Luke conflated two appearances into one or John has crafted an appearance.

Chapter Summary

Since the Gospels bear a strong affinity to Greco-Roman biography, we might anticipate that their authors would employ at least some of the literary conventions of that genre. In this section on the Gospels, we have focused our attention on sixteen pericopes appearing in two or more of the Gospels (three more are considered in chap. 5). Although there are many more, I have limited myself to those pericopes I regard as having the best chance of containing differences resulting from the same type of compositional devices described in the compositional textbooks and inferred from the pericopes we examined in Plutarch's *Lives*.

The literature is vast pertaining to the literary relationships that exist between the Gospels. We proceeded with the assumption accepted by the overwhelming majority of New Testament scholars that Mark wrote first and that Matthew and Luke made robust use of Mark as their primary source. Accordingly, in pericopes where substantial verbal correspondences exist between Mark and Matthew or between Mark and Luke or among Mark, Matthew, and Luke but differences are present, we are fairly safe in concluding that Matthew or Luke or both have either redacted Mark or have drawn from one or more sources in addition to Mark.

To be expected, the evangelists employ numerous techniques observed in the compositional textbooks. We observed that they substitute words and phrases, alter syntax, change the inflection of a term from singular to plural (or vice versa), add in order to intensify, clarify, translate, or expand upon the thought. They, especially Luke, also change a statement to a question or a command. It is possible in a few instances that a question has been changed to a statement. On two occasions, Matthew converts Jesus's one-sided address to his antagonists to a dialogue with them. On several occasions, the evangelists invert the order of events. Luke appears to have been the primary evangelist to do this. Of course, we must keep in mind that our sampling is small. So it would be premature to conclude that only Luke or only Matthew does something. The evangelists' use of these devices most often appear to have no objective other than to follow the literary conventions of their day. However, there are exceptions. For example, John often redacts Jesus's words in order to add theological flavoring.

Of particular interest is our observation that the evangelists occasionally omit and substitute words, even when quoting the Scriptures they regard as holy (see pericope #1 in chap. 4). Matthew also substitutes one of Mark's words with his own in order to prompt his readers to recall a psalm that readers could now use to think of Jesus's crucifixion. We also observed that Mark mentions a prophecy by Isaiah then proceeds to quote Malachi and then Isaiah (Mark 1:2).

Noticeably absent are clear examples where we can recognize the evangelists following the law of biographical relevance. The reason is because all four Gospels feature the same main character, Jesus. It is not as though we can compare how the story of Peter denying Jesus is reported by the Gospels and by a *Life of Simon Peter* or how the ministry of John the Baptist is reported by the Gospels and by a *Life of John the Baptist*.[159] So everything the Gospels report about Jesus is biographically relevant to Jesus.

In one instance, there is a very slight difference in numerical specificity. In another instance, we observed that a list of names provided by the evangelist was not meant to be exhaustive.

We observed the evangelists employing several of the compositional devices we inferred in our analysis of Plutarch's *Lives*. The evangelists occasionally displace an event from its original context and transplant it in another either to raise tension in the narrative or to link it with another story involving the same characters. They simplify, though not often. More than the other evangelists, Matthew occasionally transfers what one person said to the lips of another. And the evangelists occasionally change the recipients being addressed. They compress and probably conflate stories. Because Matthew is known to abbreviate often, it should come as no surprise to observe that he compresses more often than the other evangelists. Luke and John make use of literary spotlighting, and Mark and

Matthew probably do. However, spotlighting is not nearly as prominent in the Gospels as we observed in Plutarch's *Lives*. Yet, spotlighting may be occurring more often than is within our ability to recognize it, since Jesus is the main character in all four Gospels.

In a few instances, it is difficult to determine which evangelist may be employing a compositional device. For example, in assessing whether the earliest version of the story included one or two blind men whom Jesus healed, one is hard-pressed to adjudicate whether the two blind men in Matthew resulted from him doubling up and conflating two healings, which would be consistent with his tendency to abbreviate, or that the single blind man in Mark resulted from Mark's knowledge of two blind men being present while shining a spotlight on a person known to his readers or identifying his source, or because Matthew preferred a version of the story that differed from Mark's.

In the pericopes with notable differences we assessed, only a handful of instances cannot be plausibly understood in light of the specific compositional devices we are considering: Mark and Luke provide descriptions of the location of the feeding of the five thousand that puzzle, Mark // Matthew narrate a woman pouring expensive perfume on Jesus's head while John has her pouring it on his feet, the persons who accused Peter of being affiliated with Jesus leading to his denials and the specific locations where the accusations occurred, the location of Jesus's post-resurrection appearance to Mary Magdalene, and whether Jesus first appeared to a group of his male disciples in Jerusalem or in Galilee. However, as we observed in a few of the pericopes in our analysis of Plutarch's *Lives*, these sorts of discrepancies could suggest the event itself was remembered while some of the peripheral details were not.[160] As a result, ancient authors, including the evangelists, may have reported the peripheral details either as they or their sources recalled them, crafted them, or even creatively reconstructed them as part of their literary artistry in writing a quality narrative.[161]

In short, a very large majority of the differences we have observed could be the result of an evangelist using a different source or employing the compositional devices that were standard conventions for writing history and biography in his day. Moreover, these differences almost always appear in the peripheral details.

5

Synthetic Chronological Placement in the Gospels

EARLIER WE OBSERVED a number of pericopes in which one or more authors altered the chronological placement of an event.[1] In this section we will assess a few more examples and determine whether assigning a synthetic chronology or timing of events was a compositional device employed in ancient biography. Since that will be our focus in this section, a portion of Lucian's instructions pertaining to writing history properly is worth repeating:

> Now after the preface, the transition to the narrative, whether long or short, should be unforced and compliant, proportionate to the content. For all of the remaining body of a history is simply a long narrative. So, let it be adorned with the virtues of narrative, writing in a manner that is smooth, even, and consistent, not with bumps or potholes. Then, for style, let its clarity bloom, as I said, having been engineered even in the interconnection of its content matter. For the historian will make everything distinct and complete. And after he has described the first topic he will introduce the second, holding and linking both together as a chain, neither with breaks nor as merely a collection of many stories. Instead, the first and second topics should not only be neighbors but also share content and overlap to the uttermost.[2]

Lucian's point is that historians should connect pericopes with literary artistry, interweaving content and linking one story to another. This interweaving and linking could be especially useful when the order of events was unknown. But there are other reasons why an author might have chosen to link events. Rather than presenting a collection of anecdotes, synthetic chronological placement may be used to present a nicely flowing narrative using chronological progression.

In what follows, I will provide five examples in classical literature where the author uses a synthetic chronology and five examples in the Gospels where their authors may be doing likewise. We observed Plutarch's editorial hand at work in pericope #32 in chapter 3, where he arranged events using a synthetic chronology. In Plutarch's *Caesar* (60.3–5), Caesar offered his neck after realizing his gaffe at the procession. Because Antony did not play a significant role at that event, Plutarch did not include the procession in his *Antony*. However, Plutarch appears to like the element in that story of Caesar offering his neck. So when describing Antony's attempt to place a diadem on Caesar in his *Antony* (12.1–4), Plutarch has Caesar offer his neck as he leaves, disappointed by the people's lack of enthusiasm for him to be made king. Plutarch most likely has displaced Caesar's offering his neck from the story of the procession and transplanted it to the Lupercalia event, synthetically linking a portion of one event with another in order to highlight the extent of Caesar's disappointment.[3]

This synthetic chronology was observed when comparing Plutarch's *Caesar* with Plutarch's *Antony*. When we added reports of the same events reported by Cicero, Nicolaus of Damascus, Livy, Velleius Paterculus, Suetonius, Appian, and Cassius Dio, we observed an abundance of discrepancies of details, chronological and otherwise. And when we assessed those differences carefully, we got the impression the authors were clearly aware of certain things that had taken place while recollections of the precise details were fuzzy. As a result, each author composed his narrative placing various elements where he thought most plausible or expedient for emphasizing a point,[4] and in a manner that assisted the narrative to progress smoothly. Pelling comments, "There are so many uncertainties in sequence about these incidents that it is likely that they were remembered as free-floating individual stories, and each narrator imposed his own order."[5] This is creative reconstruction.

A second example we examined involves comparing how Plutarch, Suetonius, and Cassius Dio report how Caesar once wept while at the statue of Alexander.[6] It seems that Plutarch displaced the story and transplanted it about seven years later in order to draw attention to the beginning of Caesar's quest for power.

Earlier we examined Plutarch's account of the Catilinarian Conspiracy of 63–62 BCE.[7] Here we will draw attention to an element not covered by Plutarch for our third example.[8] When Catiline stood for a consulship in 63, at a meeting of the senate that took place about mid-July, on the day on which the consular elections were originally to have been held, Catiline uttered an ominous and memorable threat, warning that he would bring about general destruction if Cato carried out his intention to indict and prosecute him. In Cicero's words, Catiline is reported to have said that "if his own fortunes should be set on fire, he would put out the flames not with water but by destruction" (Cicero, *Mur.* 51).[9] When Catiline lost his bid for the consulship soon afterward, he gathered a significant band of conspirators. Cicero received word of his plans from spies within the conspiracy and summoned the senate on 7 or 8 November, on which occasion he questioned Catiline about his nefarious activities. Since the senate was still not prepared at that time to take action against Catiline, Cicero urged Catiline to dispel the cloud of suspicion that hung over him by voluntarily departing from Rome.

Our account of the earlier meeting in July and Catiline's threat is owed to Cicero's eyewitness report. It is preserved in his defense speech for Lucius Murena (consul-elect for 62) at a trial a mere four months later (late November).[10] There can be little doubt that the context Cicero assigns to Catiline's threat is trustworthy, since Cicero provides a detailed account of the meeting in July in a speech delivered to a jury, one-third of whom were senators who could readily have detected Cicero in a fabrication.

Catiline's bold and outrageous bluster was apparently so well known and memorable that it did not escape the notice of the historian Sallust, who worked those words of Catiline into his account of the conspiracy. He recounts the treasonous threat in language very similar to the version reported in the speech for Murena: "Inasmuch as I have been cornered and am being driven to desperation by my enemies, I shall put out the fire besetting me with demolition" (Sall. *Cat.* 31.9 [Rolfe/Ramsey, LCL]). However, Sallust explicitly assigns those words to the meeting of the senate on 8 November, some four months after the occasion on which, according to Cicero, Catiline actually made the outburst. One possibility that must be considered is that Catiline perhaps repeated himself at the second meeting so that both Cicero and Sallust preserve the true historical picture. However, this is highly unlikely because the bold metaphor of pulling the whole state down in retaliation for an attack on his personal fortunes (characterized as "fire") is such a unique formulation that it does not lend itself to repetition. It was undoubtedly highly effective the first time it was uttered for its shock value. The same effect would not have been achieved if it were uttered more than once. However, the following observation should dispel any notion that Sallust and not Cicero placed Catiline's threat in its true historical context. If Sallust's context (at the meeting on 8 November) were the correct one, it would have played into Cicero's hands when he was defending his client Murena just a week or two later. Cicero would undoubtedly have seized upon those words, holding them up to the jury as the last, mad words of the villain Catiline before he stormed out of the senate and left Rome to join his rebel army.

In fact, if we consider how tempting it would have been to shift those chilling words of Catiline to the later occasion, we can readily understand why Sallust chose to tell the story the way he does. For Ramsey,

> Sallust . . . can't resist postdating Catiline's threat from July to make it fall precisely on November 8th so that it will have the greatest impact . . . by having Catiline utter his chilling threat as his *last*, parting words. Sallust as a creative writer saw the possibility of making a good story better by tweaking it. What harm is done, he could argue. Catiline did in fact utter a threat likening an attack by a political enemy to "fire" which he would extinguish not with water but by means of general destruction (*ruina*, the word found in both Cicero's and Sallust's version). Further, he made that threat at a meeting of the senate in 63 BCE, in response to a threat from a political enemy (Cato/Cicero).[11]

A fourth example of historical displacement is furnished by Sallust's account of an impassioned speech of Catiline to his supporters, which Sallust claims was delivered about 1 June 64 (*Cat.* 17.1). That speech, scholars conclude, was almost certainly modeled on a revolutionary speech that Catiline is alleged to have delivered to his supporters shortly before the July elections in 63 BCE (Cicero, *Mur.* 50).[12] The two occasions bear a striking resemblance to each other in both the content and physical setting of the speech itself. Sallust tells us that Catiline delivered his remarks in June 64 at a meeting of his followers behind closed doors, with all outsiders excluded,[13] whereas Cicero describes the meeting in July 63 as a "*contione domestica*," a "harangue to his private circle" (*Mur.* 50).[14] Sallust chose to place Catiline's revolutionary speech of 63 one year earlier, at the time of his first failed candidacy for the consulship because, as Ramsey comments, Sallust decided to present Catiline as a wild-eyed revolutionary as early as the elections of 64. We know, however, that at that time Catiline was far from being the down-and-out, desperate politician he is made out to be in the Sallustian speech. Rather, in 64 he stood a good chance of being elected consul for 63 and had the backing of senior political figures like Marcus Crassus and even Julius Caesar. Sallust distorts the true picture to cast Catiline as a villain even before he resorted to desperate measures after his second defeat, at the election in 63, more than one year later.[15]

Sallust was regarded as one of Rome's greatest historians. Addressing students of rhetoric, Quintilian wrote,

> For my part I would have them read the best authors from the very beginning and never leave them, choosing those, however, who are simplest and most intelligible. For instance, when prescribing for boys, I should give Livy the preference over Sallust; for, although the latter is the greater historian, one needs to be well-advanced in one's studies to appreciate him properly. (*Inst.* 2.5.19 [Butler, LCL])[16]

We can observe a fifth example of synthetic chronological placement in Tacitus. Ronald Mellor writes of a

> recently discovered bronze text. . . . This senatorial decree, set up around the Empire to announce the suicide and condemnation of Piso in 20 CE, shows . . . that Tacitus seems to have moved the trial from December to the previous spring. If that reconstruction is correct, he presumably did it for the sake of a better narrative. He would regard the precise date of an event as of no greater importance to an historian who seeks to convey moral truth through a persuasive narrative.[17]

Like Sallust, Tacitus is regarded as one of Rome's finest historians. Thus, Plutarch's use of synthetic chronological placement was not sloppy writing. Rather, it seems that synthetic chronological placement was a compositional device in both biographical and historical writing and was employed by those held to be among the finest historians and biographers of that era. By contrast, the Roman historian Asconius, who wrote in the age of Nero, adopted methods that we associate with the science of modern historical investigation, always aiming to report events as they actually had occurred and providing accurate dates. However, the ancients did not hold Asconius in the same high regard they had for Sallust and Tacitus because Asconius did not aspire to write artful prose that could be valued as literature in its own right. Ramsey comments, "As a reliable source Asconius is without equal. As a writer held in high regard as a literary figure, he is way down at the bottom of the heap."[18]

Having noted these five examples from classical literature of authors using the compositional device of synthetic chronology, for contrast and comparison, we will now consider five instances where synthetic chronological placement in the Gospels seems likely. Before assessing them, I want to describe three ways in which chronology is usually narrated. Although stories can be grouped in a variety of ways, I am interested here only in chronological arrangement. Some pericopes are free-floating, orphaned from a particular context. We often observe the evangelist introducing these with "On one day" (e.g., Luke 5:17; 8:22; 20:1), or "On a Sabbath" (e.g., Mark 2:23; Luke 6:1, 6; 13:10), without specifying that the event had occurred subsequently to the event preceding it in the narrative.[19] We will refer to instances of this first way of narrating as *floating chronology*.

More frequently, an evangelist mentions an event in a manner that leaves the impression that it occurred subsequently to the event preceding it in the narrative but does not require that it occurred at that time. For example, immediately after narrating Jesus healing a paralytic, Mark says Jesus went out again by the sea and taught a crowd (2:13). Although readers will get the impression Jesus did this after healing the paralytic, Mark's language does not *require* such a chronological progression.[20] We will refer to instances of this second way of narrating as *implied chronology*.

There are also occasions when an evangelist presents a chronology of events in which the timing is specified. For example, Mark says Jesus healed Simon's mother-in-law; then he says, "When the sun set that evening," they brought to him all those having sicknesses and demons (1:30–32). Mark is not vague pertaining to the time at which Jesus healed the sick and demon-possessed. It occurred on the same day Jesus healed Simon's mother-in-law. We will refer to instances of this third way of narrating as *explicit chronology*.

For our purposes then, we will speak of three types of chronology: floating, implied, and explicit. Although these types can be helpful, the degree to which chronology is *implied* will vary. In some cases, the chronology may be so strongly implied that it is close to being *explicit*. Thus, an explicit chronology in one Gospel could be considered to be in conflict with the same events presented in a strongly implied chronology in another Gospel. And it is here that we will focus our attention.

Our first and perhaps best candidate for synthetic chronological placement in the Gospels is found in a pericope we previously examined of a woman in Bethany who anointed Jesus.[21] Mark 14:1, followed by Matthew 26:2, locates the anointing two days prior to Passover and after Jesus's triumphal entry, while John 12:1 says it occurred six days before Passover and prior to the triumphal entry. Either Mark or John appear to have changed the day, using synthetic chronological placement in order to bind the anointing explicitly to a different context than where it actually occurred. Lucian would have smiled with approval. The event is presented as historical, but the stated chronology is artificial.[22]

As a second example of synthetic chronological placement, we also observed that the Gospels appear to differ on the day and time that Jesus was crucified.[23] The Synoptics state clearly that Jesus was crucified after the Passover meal had been eaten, whereas John seems to suggest that his crucifixion occurred prior to the Passover meal. Opinions differ regarding how best to explain this difference.

In my view, Keener's suggestion that John changed the day and time that Jesus was crucified in order to make a theological point seems most plausible, because no one reading John's account independently of the Synoptics would get the impression the Last Supper was a Passover meal. In fact, they would get precisely the opposite impression. However, in the end, I do not think certainty on the matter is possible.

For the remaining three examples of synthetic chronological placement in the Gospels, we will now consider three pericopes not previously discussed.

#17 (#42, 84) The Cleansing of the Leper (Mark 1:40–45; Matt. 8:1–4; Luke 5:12–16)

A leper approached Jesus, knelt before him, and said, "Lord, you can make me clean if you are willing." Jesus touched the man and said, "I am willing. Be cleansed." Immediately, the leprosy left the man. Jesus then instructed him to say nothing to anyone but rather to go show himself to the priest and offer the gift Moses commanded as proof to others.

This pericope appears in all three Synoptics. Luke narrates it using a floating chronology, introducing the story with, "While he was in one of the cities" (Luke 5:12), and following it with, "One day while he was teaching" (Luke 5:17). Mark places the leper's cleansing in a context with an explicit chronology. Jesus heals Peter's mother-in-law (Mark 1:30–31). Mark follows this with "When evening came and the sun had set," people came to Jesus, bringing the sick and demon-possessed (Mark 1:32–34). "In the early morning while it was still dark," Jesus got up and went to a secluded place to pray (Mark 1:35–38). He then left Capernaum and went throughout Galilee preaching in their synagogues (Mark 1:39). It is in the course of this journey that Jesus heals the leper who is our subject (Mark 1:40–45). For in Mark 2:1, Jesus returned to Capernaum "after some days" (δι᾽ ἡμερῶν, di hēmerōn). Therefore, Mark's chronology is explicit that Jesus healed the leper after he had healed Peter's mother-in-law.

Matthew likewise places Jesus healing the leper in a context with an explicit chronology. But it differs from Mark's. In Matthew, the healing of the leper likewise occurs as Jesus was traveling throughout Galilee and preaching in their synagogues (Matt. 4:23–25). Matthew locates the Sermon on the Mount during this trip (Matt. 5:1–7:29). After the sermon, Matthew reports that large crowds were following Jesus when the leper approached him and was healed (Matt. 8:1–4).[24] Jesus then returned to Capernaum, where he healed a centurion's servant (Matt. 8:5–13) and then healed Peter's mother-in-law (Matt. 8:14–17). Thus, in Matthew, Jesus healed the leper prior to healing Peter's mother-in-law, whereas Mark places it afterward. And both Mark and Matthew use explicit chronologies.

Who then is responsible for altering the chronology? Additional details provided in all three Synoptics may provide a clue. Jesus told the now-healed leper not to tell anyone what he had done for him. In Mark and Luke there is nothing to suggest this healing had occurred somewhere other than a private or semi-private setting. However, Matthew implies that Jesus healed him in front of a *large crowd* (ὄχλοι πολλοί, *ochloi polloi*).[25] Why would Jesus heal a man and then tell him not to tell anyone if the healing had occurred in front of many people? It makes more sense that the healing was done in a private or semi-private setting as allowed by Mark and Luke and that Matthew has placed it in a different context. This conclusion is strengthened when we consider why Matthew may have done so. Earlier, we observed Jesus healing two blind men (see pericope #7 in chap. 4). In that pericope, healing the leper is the first in a long string of miracles performed by Jesus and narrated to support Jesus's message to John the Baptist in Matt. 11:4–6: "Go and report to John what you hear and see: the blind receive sight and the lame are walking, lepers are cleansed and the deaf hear, even the dead are raised and the poor have the good news proclaimed to them."

Using literary artistry, Matthew has placed the story of Jesus healing a leper in a context that draws attention to Jesus performing the very signs expected of the Messiah. Again, the events are presented as historical whereas the chronological placement of the leper being healed is artificial.

There are other chronological differences occurring here worth observing.[26] In all three Synoptics, Jesus healed Peter's mother-in-law and then healed a crowd of people that evening. But after that, the evangelists part ways pertaining to what happened next. In Mark and Luke, Jesus remained in Capernaum that night and then rose early the next morning to pray. When his disciples found him, they informed him others were looking for him, and Jesus told them they must leave at once and go throughout Galilee so he could also preach in their synagogues. And they left.

Matthew narrates the events differently. After healing Peter's mother-in-law and then interacting with a crowd that evening, Jesus ordered his disciples to get in a boat and cross the lake. But before they could cross, a man approached Jesus and said he would follow him. Jesus told him that foxes have holes and birds have nests, while he and his disciples had no home. Then another man approached Jesus and said he would follow him, but first he wanted to bury his father. Jesus told him to follow him now and let the dead bury their dead. They then got into the boat and crossed the lake. Jesus fell asleep in the boat and had to be awakened in order to calm the wind and waves. In Matthew, Jesus crossed the lake only hours after healing Peter's mother-in-law, whereas in Mark and Luke, he remained overnight in Capernaum.[27]

In addition, Matthew explicitly locates the two people telling Jesus they want to follow him in Capernaum on the evening of the day he healed Peter's mother-in-law, which was near the very beginning of Jesus's ministry (Matt. 8:14–23). But Luke places them explicitly in the context of Jesus's final journey to Jerusalem, while he and his disciples were walking along the road (Matt. 9:51–62, esp. 51, 57).[28] Whether we are seeing a floating anecdote that the evangelists explicitly connect to contexts they deemed appropriate, or whether one of them displaced the event from its historical context and transplanted it in another, it seems likely that synthetic chronological placement is being employed.

#18 (#33, 139) Jesus Is Rejected at Nazareth
(Mark 6:1–6a; Matt. 13:53–58; Luke 4:16–30)

When was Jesus rejected at Nazareth? Luke locates it at the beginning of Jesus's ministry, shortly after he was tempted in the desert (Luke 4:15–30), while Mark and Matthew place it later in Jesus's ministry (Mark 6:1–6 // Matt. 13:53–58). Are different events being narrated? Or has Luke conflated this rejection with another in the same town (see Matt. 4:13–17; 13:53–58 // Mark 6:1–6)? Or has either Luke or Mark displaced the story to a different time? Certainty eludes us. Notwithstanding, there are good reasons to think Luke has displaced the story and linked it explicitly to the beginning of Jesus's ministry.

Mark reports the following string of events: Jesus calms a stormy Sea of Galilee, cures a demoniac named Legion, heals a hemorrhaging woman, raises Jairus's daughter, is rejected at Nazareth, sends out the Twelve, is inquired about by Herod, is briefed by his disciples, who have now returned, then feeds the five thousand.[29] This long string of events is mentioned by Luke and in the same order as they appear in Mark with only one exception—Jesus's rejection at Nazareth—which is missing from Luke's string. Luke has instead placed that event earlier in Jesus's ministry.

So we will travel back to the beginning of Jesus's ministry and view what is going on there in the Synoptics. All three narrate Jesus being tempted in the desert and then returning to Galilee. Matthew and Luke then say Jesus left Nazareth and went to Capernaum (Matt. 4:13 // Luke 4:16–31).[30] But Luke provides more details, informing us that Jesus left Nazareth because he was rejected there and almost killed (Luke 4:16–30). Of course, it is possible that Jesus was rejected twice at Nazareth.[31] However, consider the following: First, as previously observed, Luke follows Mark in a long string of stories in which only this one is missing but appears in a different context. Second, there are strong parallels between the story in all three Synoptics: Jesus was preaching in their synagogue on a Sabbath (Mark 6:2 // Matt. 13:54 // Luke 4:16); the people's response was "Hey, we know this fellow's family" (Mark 6:3 // Matt. 13:55–56 // Luke 4:22); and Jesus's reply to them was that a prophet is not accepted in his own town (Mark 6:4 // Matt. 13:57 // Luke 4:24). These suggest either Mark or Luke displaced the story and placed it in a different context using a synthetic chronology.[32]

#19 (#25, 271, 273; cf. 276) The Cleansing of the Temple (Mark 11:1–17, 27–33; Matt. 21:1–27; Luke 19:28–20:8; John 12:12–22)

When did Jesus cleanse the temple? John 2:11–13 places it explicitly at the beginning of Jesus's ministry, shortly after his first miracle in Cana of Galilee.[33] However, all three Synoptics explicitly place it within a week of his death. Were there two temple cleansings, or did either John or the Synoptics displace the event? Most exegetes think there was only one temple cleansing and that the chronology in the Gospels was often determined by literary considerations other than actual timing.[34] Keener suggests that when combined with the final Passover (John 13:1; 18:28, 39; 19:14), the temple cleansing at the beginning of Jesus's ministry frames "Jesus' entire ministry [as] the Passion Week, overshadowed by his impending 'hour.'"[35] Brown also thinks there was one temple cleansing. Rather than literary artistry, Brown explains the different timings of the cleansing by suggesting that Jesus warned of the temple's destruction early in his ministry (Mark 14:57–59) but cleansed the temple precincts during his final days and that John has conflated the two events by transplanting the temple cleansing to the early part of Jesus's ministry.[36] Regardless of how one arrives at the conclusion that there was only one temple cleansing, if the conclusion is correct, Mark or John displaced the event from its original context and transplanted it in another.

If literary artistry on John's part is responsible here for differing chronologies, such work is by no means unique to John's Gospel. The New Testament begins with a genealogy in Matthew. Careful readers will notice that Matthew divided the genealogy into three sets of fourteen generations (Matt. 1:17). However, not only does Matthew omit some generations mentioned in the Old Testament, there are only thirteen new names in the third set. For some reason, the number fourteen is important to Matthew. A number of scholars have suggested that Matthew is employing a device known as *gematria* in which Hebrew letters are assigned numerical values. For example, *dalet* (ד, *d* or "D") is the fourth letter of the Hebrew alphabet while *vav* (ו, *v* or "V") is the sixth. Since there are no separate letters for vowels in Hebrew, the name "David" (דוד, *david*) has a numerical value of fourteen (D = 4, V = 6, D = 4). Thus, in arranging his genealogy in three sets of fourteen, Matthew was probably emphasizing Jesus's Davidic ancestry: Jesus is the son of David, the Messiah. This is literary artistry,

Matthew shaping his genealogy of Jesus to make a theological point. And this is precisely what some scholars suggest John has done here and elsewhere in his Gospel in order to emphasize Jesus's role as the sacrificial Passover Lamb who takes away our sins.[37] While certainty is not possible, the timing of the temple cleansing in John is a candidate for synthetic chronological placement.

Summary

In this chapter, I have provided five examples in which Plutarch, Sallust, and Tacitus appear to have altered the chronology of an event and five examples where the evangelists may have done likewise. We observed three types of chronology in the Gospels: floating, implied, and explicit. Lucian taught that the proper method for writing history is not to provide a collection of stories in a disjointed manner but instead to connect the stories like links of a chain, using overlapping material when possible. We observed Matthew doing this more than the other evangelists and Luke doing it least often, at least if we are thinking of linking events in a chronological manner. Luke may have instead preferred to link events thematically. On occasion, the explicit chronology presented in one Gospel appears in tension with the strongly implied or even explicit chronology presented in another Gospel. In most of these instances, it appears that one of the evangelists altered the chronology of an event. In some of these, the reasons for doing so can be plausibly surmised to produce a smooth-flowing narrative, highlight a point the evangelist desired to make, provide a contextual home for an orphaned story, or for reasons not apparent to us.[38] Having examined numerous pericopes in Plutarch's *Lives* and the Gospels, we are now prepared to summarize our findings and draw some final conclusions.

Conclusion

BY THE BEGINNING of the twenty-first century, a paradigm shift had occurred. No longer viewing the Gospels as *sui generis* (i.e., of a unique genre), the majority of New Testament scholars had embraced the view of Richard Burridge and others before him that the Gospels belong to the genre of Greco-Roman biography, as noted in our introduction. This genre permitted a degree of elasticity in how stories were reported.

Very little to date has been written pertaining to how reading the Gospels in view of their biographical genre can shed light on the multitude of differences in their reports. We sought in chapters 1–2 to identify specific compositional devices employed in ancient biographical literature by first considering the progymnasmata (preliminary exercises in rhetoric) taught in the compositional textbooks in antiquity. These instructed aspiring rhetoricians and writers how to paraphrase texts using a number of techniques such as the following: addition to clarify, intensify, or expound upon certain points; omission for brevity; substituting a different term, usually a synonym; altering the inflection of a word (e.g., changing a singular to a plural or vice versa); creating a dialogue from a speech or teaching; and changing a question to a statement or a command, or vice versa.

We then turned our attention in chapter 3 to nine of Plutarch's *Lives*, which provide modern historians with a rare opportunity to examine how one author narrates the same story differently in different contexts. Like the Gospels, these *Lives* belong to Greco-Roman biography, were written in the same language, Greek, and were written within only a few decades of the Gospels. We identified thirty-six pericopes Plutarch narrates in two or more of the nine *Lives* and then observed that Plutarch compresses stories, conflates them, transfers what one character said to the lips of a different person, inverts the order of events, rounds numbers, simplifies, and displaces a story or an element of a story from its original context and then transplants it in a different one, occasionally using a synthetic chronology. The most common device we observed Plutarch using was literary spotlighting.

Plutarch often adapts his narrative in accordance with the law of biographical relevance. He paraphrases logia and larger blocks of content. On most occasions, his paraphrasing appears to have no objective behind it other than to follow the literary conventions of his day. He occasionally crafts peripheral details in a creative reconstruction when they were unknown in order to move the narrative along smoothly or perhaps to assist him in making a point that was generally accurate pertaining to the situation though not technically precise. Still, even the crafted details are usually not far from the truth. Although Plutarch errs on occasion, the differences we observe almost always seem to result from Plutarch's use of the compositional devices that have been posited by classical scholars as being standard conventions for writing ancient history and biography.

We then turned our attention in chapters 4–5 to the canonical Gospels and assessed nineteen pericopes that appear in two or more of them. We examined the differences and discovered that the evangelists appear to have made frequent use of nearly all of the compositional devices upon which we focused in the previous chapters. Accordingly, our study has revealed quite clearly that each of the evangelists had some level of rhetorical education.[1]

During the age when the Gospels were written, the finest historians and biographers did not practice writing with the same commitment to precision as us moderns. They wanted to tell a story in a manner that entertained, provided moral guidance, emphasized points they regarded as important, and paint a portrait of important people. If they had to adapt some details on occasion, it was permissible. Such adapting was not intended to distort the truth but to communicate it more effectively. Modern itinerate speakers, teachers, preachers, and even professors often do this in their lectures and homilies for emphasis or to make a point more clearly. In fact, most of us have done it for similar reasons when telling a personal story.

Similarly, when a photographer takes a photograph of a couple holding hands while walking through a meadow of flowers, she may edit the photo by adding a slight haze. The haze was not actually present at the time the photo was taken. Neither was the sky as blue as it appears in the edited photo. However, no one objects to those alterations, since they were done to emphasize the romantic element of that moment, which was actually present. The photo is a "true representation" in its message, even if not in every detail. True representation is the objective of many photographers. And so it was with the finest historical and biographical writers when the Gospels were written.

Kurt Aland's *Synopsis of the Four Gospels* is an indispensable source for serious students of the Gospels, for it assists readers in comparing how a pericope is reported in two or more Gospels. Those making use of this resource are surprised to observe how closely and frequently the verbal correspondences are between the parallel accounts. There are numerous examples, in fact, where the correspondence is either word-for-word or nearly so.[2] This frequent verbal correspondence often avails itself of a line-by-line comparison.

When I set out on this research project, I had thoughts of creating a *Synopsis of Nine of Plutarch's* Lives—a resource comparable to Aland's *Synopsis of the Four Gospels*. In it, I would have juxtaposed the pericopes appearing in two or more of those nine *Lives*. However, as I progressed through the various pericopes, I came to realize such a synopsis, while of value, would not lend itself to a line-by-line comparison. The reason is because Plutarch paraphrases consistently and more freely than we find in the Gospels.

This led me to an interesting observation. Despite the fact that the evangelists employ many of the same compositional devices that were taught in the compositional textbooks and others that were employed by Plutarch, the extent of editing by the evangelists is minimal by ancient standards. As interesting as the differences in the Gospels may be, it is the refusal of their authors to paraphrase more freely that is striking to those readers familiar with both the Gospels and Plutarch's *Lives*. This is especially true of the Synoptic Gospels. I am not the first to make this observation. Gerald Downing writes,

> It is because people were taught to "say the same thing in other words" that close repetition of the same words among our sources [i.e., the Gospels] ... appears so striking and so much in need of comment. ... With so much pressure in favour of paraphrase, and so common a conviction of its validity, it really does seem very strange that we find so much identical wording among our Synoptic Gospels.[3]

Elsewhere, having compared Josephus's use of his sources with how the authors of the Synoptic Gospels use theirs, Downing writes,

> It is not the divergencies among the synoptists (or even between them and John), in parallel contexts, that are remarkable: it is the extraordinary extent of verbal similarities. The question is, Why were they content to copy so much? rather than, Why did they bother to change this or that? The procedure is not however mechanical, and there *are* considerable divergencies. But it has to be recognized that the relationship may betoken a much greater respect, one for the other, even than Josephus' for Scripture.[4]

Similar to Plutarch, the differences in the Gospel pericopes we examined occur almost always in the peripheral details. Of course, our samplings of pericopes from Plutarch and the Gospels are limited, and more robust samplings could reveal exceptions.[5] In our limited sampling, we observed a pericope in which the Gospels narrate a few broader differences than we find in those *Lives* we examined and cannot be explained by appealing to the compositional devices we identified in them.[6]

Our analysis of thirty-six pericopes that appear on two or more occasions in Plutarch's *Lives* supports the conclusions of classical scholars that the type of compositional devices we have identified were standard practice in writing biographical literature in that era. When this background knowledge is added to the fact that the Gospels share close affinity to Greco-Roman biography, the same genre in which Plutarch's *Lives* fit, and that a significant amount of the differences in the Gospels can be easily understood in light of this background knowledge, it becomes quite plausible that the evangelists were aware of and made use of many of the compositional devices we inferred from Plutarch's *Lives* as well as those prescribed in the compositional textbooks. Thus, the suspicions of many New Testament scholars that the evangelists used compositional devices similar to those we have identified in this book are correct. Accordingly, we now have some more clearly defined and assured ideas pertaining to how the flexibility of ancient biography impacts our understanding of the Gospels.

Our findings also have practical implications for a number of readers. Since the early days of the Christian church, many, though by no means all, devout believers have been troubled by the differences in the Gospels. They have often responded with harmonization efforts, some of which have bordered on subjecting the Gospel texts to a sort of hermeneutical waterboarding until they tell the exegete what he or she wants to hear. Doing such violence to the texts is unnecessary, since a large majority of the differences can quite easily and rightly be appreciated and/or resolved in light of the literary conventions of ancient biography and history writing. For many, this will require a paradigm shift, especially for those outside academia who may tend to read the Gospels anachronistically as though ancient biographers and historians wrote with the same objectives and conventions as their modern cousins.

Many who believe the biblical authors were divinely inspired also assume those authors must have written with the degree of accuracy and almost forensic precision we desire and expect today. However, this would require those authors to have stepped out of their culture and to have thought in terms of literary conventions that were in existence—as we see in the work of Asconius—but not valued as highly as other conventions. Fortunately, historical nearsightedness can be corrected with the proper glasses. We craft the proper lenses by reading a significant amount of literature from the period, which improves our understanding of the genre to which the Gospels belong. Like anyone who begins to wear glasses, some initial discomfort and adjusting will occur. But a truly high view of the Gospels as holy writ requires us to accept and respect them as God has given them to us rather than to force them into a frame shaped by how we think he should have.

Devout Christians are not alone among those who may be in need of a paradigm shift. Critics of a cynical type have often appealed to Gospel differences as a means for not taking seriously what they report. It seems to me those critics also fall prey to reading the Gospels anachronistically. History writing has much depth. What our study reveals is that there are many things that can be and are going on in a text. The crude thing to say is that we have a contradiction, since a difference is not necessarily a contradiction. A critic may dispute theism or contend that the Gospels do not represent an accurate representation of Jesus's teachings and deeds. Those issues are important objections to consider and are subject matters in discussions related to philosophy and the historical Jesus. However, if our assessments in this volume are correct, appealing to Gospel differences as a reason for dismissing the general historical accuracy of what they report should be abandoned.

One does not need to be a student of the late Roman Republic or the early Christian church to recognize that the two centuries spanning from

100 BCE through 100 CE must be regarded as two of the most interesting and world-changing centuries in all of human history. It is during this period that Jesus of Nazareth lived. His life could be said to have impacted world history in a manner that has been far more reaching than the life of Julius Caesar or any other person who lived during those years and perhaps at any other time. Our best sources about Jesus are found in the New Testament. The most comprehensive of those sources are the four Gospels. In them we learn how Jesus was remembered by many of his early followers.

As with all ancient literature, there are many challenges historians encounter in their inquiries into the past. One Christmas morning when I was a child, I discovered a set of walkie-talkies that had been placed for me under the Christmas tree. I gave one to a family member and went outside with the other. In an age prior to mobile phones and Wi-Fi, I was fascinated with the ability to communicate with another person who was not present in a wireless manner. I walked farther and farther away from the other family member only to observe that, as I did, an increasing amount of static made it increasingly difficult to understand what the other person was saying. Similarly, historians encounter an increasing amount of "noise" as they travel further into the past in order to study its people, events, and cultures, due to the differences between our culture and theirs. This noise often renders it difficult to understand the texts, which are our best connection to the past. But as historians learn more about the ancients, the amount of noise can be reduced, allowing us to hear what the ancient authors are saying with greater clarity. It is my hope that this study will reduce historical noise by helping us become better attuned to compositional devices and Gospel differences.

Thirty-Six Pericopes Appearing Two or More Times in the Nine Lives of Plutarch Examined

Not all of the following pericopes appear in chapter 3 of our text. Those that contain no differences (1, 2, 4, 5, 14, and 21) are marked with an asterisk (*).

1. Sulla Gives the Name "Magnus" to Pompey (*Pomp.* 13.4–5; *Sert.* 18.2; *Crass.* 7.1)*
2. Death of Sulla in 78 BC (*Pomp.* 15.3–16.1; *Cic.* 4.3; *Luc.* 5.1)*
3. Pompey Fights Sertorius (*Sert.* 12.1–5; 19.1–6; 21.5–6; 23.1–24.4; 26.1–27.3; *Pomp.* 10.1; 17.1–18.1; 19.1–5; 20.1–3; *Luc.* 5.1–2; 8.5)
4. Caesar and Pirates (*Caes.* 1.1–2.4; *Crass.* 7.5)*
5. Servile War with Spartacus (*Crass.* 8.1–11.8; *Pomp.* 21.1–5; *Cat. Min.* 8.1–2)*
6. Pompey and Crassus Serve as Consular Colleagues for the First Time (*Pomp.* 22.1–23.2; *Crass.* 12.1–4)
7. Pompey Replaces Lucullus (*Luc.* 21–35; *Pomp.* 30–31)
8. Antioch's Faux Pas with Cato (*Pomp.* 40.1–3; *Cat. Min.* 13.1–3)
9. Sayings about Cato (*Cat. Min.* 19.4–5; *Luc.* 40.1–3)
10. Lucullus's Triumph (*Luc.* 37.1–4; *Cat. Min.* 29.3–4)
11. Catilinarian Conspiracy (*Cic.* 10.1–22.5; 23.1–3; *Caes.* 7.1–8.4; *Cat. Min.* 22.1–24.3; 26.1–4; *Crass.* 13.2–4; *Brut.* 5.2–3; *Ant.* 2.1–2; *Luc.* 38.3)
12. Cicero Defends Murena (*Cic.* 35.3; *Cat. Min.* 21.5)
13. Pompey Attempts to Form a Marriage Alliance with Cato (*Pomp.* 44.1–5; *Cat. Min.* 30.2–5; 45.1)
14. Publius Clodius and Pompeia (*Caes.* 10.1–5; *Cic.* 28.1–3)*
15. Pompey Was Sick and Refused to Get a Thrush from Lucullus (*Pomp.* 2.5–6; *Luc.* 40.2)

16. Caesar, Pompey, and Crassus Form a Coalition; Caesar's First Consulship (*Caes.* 13.1–14.9; 15.3; *Pomp.* 46.2–4; 47.1–48.7; *Crass.* 14.1–3; *Cat. Min.* 31.1–35.5; *Luc.* 42.4–6; 43.1; *Cic.* 26.3)

17. The Tribune P. Clodius Pulcher Abuses Cicero, Cato, and Pompey (*Cic.* 30.1–33.2; *Cat. Min.* 31.2; 32.5; 33.3–4; 34.1–39.4; *Caes.* 14.9; *Pomp.* 46.4–7; 48.5–7; *Brut.* 3.1–2)

18. Pompey Returns Cicero from Banishment; Cicero Reconciles Pompey to the Senate; Cicero Wants to Nullify Deeds of Clodius, but Cato Objects (*Pomp.* 49.1–7; *Cat. Min.* 40.1–2; *Cic.* 33.1–34.2)

19. Luca Meeting; Carrying Out the Agreement (*Caes.* 21.1–4; *Pomp.* 51.1–52.3; *Crass.* 14.5–15.5; *Cat. Min.* 41.1–43.6)

20. Caesar Conquers Germans during a Truce (*Caes.* 22.1–4; *Cat. Min.* 51.1); Pompey Loans Troops to Caesar (*Caes.* 25.1; *Pomp.* 52.3; *Cat. Min.* 45.3)

21. Caesar's Daughter Julia (Pompey's Wife) Dies (*Caes.* 23.4; *Pomp.* 53.4–5)*

22. Crassus and His Son Publius Are Killed by Parthians (*Crass.* 25.1–12; 30.1–33.5; *Cic.* 36.1; *Caes.* 28.1; *Pomp.* 53.6; *Ant.* 34.1–2; 37.1)

23. Rome in Chaos; Pompey Elected Sole Consul to Establish Order; Pompey Delivers Illegal Encomium (*Caes.* 28.1–5; *Pomp.* 53.1–55.7; *Cat. Min.* 47.1–48.5)

24. No Compromise Reached between Caesar, Pompey, and the Senate (*Caes.* 29.1–31.2; *Pomp.* 56.1–59.4; *Ant.* 5.1–4; *Cat. Min.* 51.4–5; *Cic.* 36.6–37.1)

25. Caesar Crosses the Rubicon and Attacks Ariminum; Rome in Panic (*Caes.* 32.1–34.4; *Pomp.* 60.1–61.4; *Cat. Min.* 52.1–5; *Ant.* 6.1–3; *Cic.* 37.1–3)

26. Caesar Conquers Italy, Pursues Pompey, and Ends Up Being Pursued by Him (*Caes.* 15.3; 35.1–37.5; 39.1–41.3; *Pomp.* 62.1–67.6; *Cat. Min.* 53.3–55.2; *Ant.* 6.1–4; 8.1–2; *Cic.* 38.1–6; *Brut.* 4.1–4)

27. Caesar Defeats Pompey at Pharsalus; Pompey Flees; Brutus Goes Over to Caesar; Cato Rescues Cicero from Pompey's Son; Caesar Pardons Cicero (*Caes.* 42.1–47.2; *Pomp.* 68.1–73.7; *Cat. Min.* 55.2–3; *Brut.* 5–6; 8.3; *Cic.* 39.1–5; *Ant.* 8.2–3)

28. Pompey Killed; Caesar in Egypt; Caesar Defeats Pharnaces (*Caes.* 48.1–50.2; *Pomp.* 74.1–80.6; *Cat. Min.* 56.1–4; *Brut.* 33.1–4)

29. Caesar Returns to Rome during His Second Dictatorship; Caesar Elected to Third Consulship (*Caes.* 51.1–2; 57.4; *Cic.* 40.1–4; *Ant.* 10.1–3; 21.2)

30. Scipio Ignores Cato's Advice Not to Attack Caesar and Is Defeated; Cato Commits Suicide; Deaths of Cato's Son, His Daughter Porcia, and His Friend Statilius (*Caes.* 52.1–54.3; *Cat. Min.* 58.1–66.7; 73.3–4; *Brut.* 49.5; 51.4; 53.4–5)

31. More Victories and Challenges for Caesar (*Caes.* 56–57, 62; *Cic.* 40.4; *Brut.* 7.1–9.3; 10.2–4; *Ant.* 11)

32. Caesar Hailed as King; Lupercalia Festival; Diadems Placed on Statues of Caesar; Caesar Removes Marullus and Flavius from Their Offices; Caesar Insults Politicians Honoring Him; Exposes His Neck and Invites Another to Kill Him (*Caes.* 60.2–61.5; *Ant.* 12.1–4; *Brut.* 9.4)

33. Conspiracy against and Assassination of Caesar; Aftermath with Assassins (*Caes.* 64.1–68.1; *Cic.* 39.5b–6; 42.3; *Ant.* 13.2–15.1; *Brut.* 11.1–21.1)

34. Octavian Arrives in Rome, Disputes with Antony, and Forms Friendship with Cicero (*Cic.* 43.6–45.2; *Brut.* 22.1–4; *Ant.* 16.1–4)

35. Antony Declared a Public Enemy and Driven Out of Italy; The Triumvirate Is Formed; Cicero Is Killed; The Conspirators Are Condemned (*Cic.* 45.3–46.4; 48.4–49.1; *Ant.* 17.1; 19.1–20.2; *Brut.* 24.2; 26.2–27.5)

36. Deaths of Gaius, Cassius, and Brutus (*Brut.* 25.2b–3a; 26.2–5; 27.5–28.2a; 36.3–4; 41.1, 4; 42.2b–3a; 43.5–6; 48.1; 52.4b–5; 53.3; *Caes.* 69.3–8; *Ant.* 19.1–20.2; 22.1–4)

Nineteen Pericopes Appearing Two or More Times in the Canonical Gospels Examined

As noted in chapter 4 at the first of the canonical Gospel pericopes, the numbers in parentheses for each pericope represent the numbers of the pericope(s) as it/they appear in Aland's *Synopsis of the Four Gospels*. Note that the final three pericopes are examined in chapter 5 and thus are not listed in ascending order with the rest.

1. (#13–16, 18) John the Baptist and Jesus's Baptism (Mark 1:2–11; Matt. 3:1–17; Luke 3:1–18, 21–22; John 1:19–34)
2. (#20) The Temptation of Jesus (Mark 1:12–13; Matt. 4:1–11; Luke 4:1–13)
3. (#47, 112) The Man with the Withered Hand (Mark 3:1–6; Matt. 12:9–14; Luke 6:6–11)
4. (#85) Healing the Centurion's Servant (Matt. 8:5–13; Luke 7:1–10)
5. (#91, 137) The Gadarene Demoniacs (Mark 5:1–20; Matt. 8:28–34; Luke 8:26–39)
6. (#95, 138) Jairus's Daughter and the Woman with a Hemorrhage (Mark 5:21–43; Matt. 9:18–26; Luke 8:40–56)
7. (#96, 264) Two Blind Men (Mark 10:46–52; Matt. 20:29–34; Luke 18:35–43; cf. Matt. 9:27–31)
8. (#146–48) Feeding the Five Thousand; Walking on Water; Healings at Gennesaret (Mark 6:31–56; Matt. 14:13–36; Luke 9:10b–17; John 6:1–25)
9. (#166, 263, 313, 253) Who Is the Greatest? (Mark 9:33–37; 10:13–16, 35–45; Matt. 18:1–6; 19:13–15; 20:20–28; Luke 9:46–48; 18:15–17; 22:24–30)
10. (#271–76 [cf. #25]) Jesus in Jerusalem (Cleansing of the Temple); Cursing a Fig Tree; Return to Bethany (Mark 11:12–14, 20–26; Matt. 21:18–22; Luke 19:45–46)

11. (#278) Parable of the Vineyard and Wicked Tenants (Mark 12:1–12; Matt. 21:33–46; Luke 20:9–19)

12. (#306, 114, 267) Anointing in Bethany (Mark 14:3–9; Matt. 26:6–13; John 12:1–8; Cf. Luke 7:36–50)

13. (#309–12) The Last Supper (Mark 14:17–25; Matt. 26:20–29; Luke 22:14–23; John 13:1–30; 1 Cor. 11:21–23)

14. (#332–33) Jesus before the Sanhedrin and Peter's Denial (Mark 14:53–72; Matt. 26:57–75; Luke 22:55–71; John 18:13–27)

15. (#344–48) The Crucifixion and Death of Jesus (Mark 15:22–41; Matt. 27:33–56; Luke 23:33–49; John 19:17–37)

16. (#352–53, 356) The Resurrection (Mark 16:1–8; Matt. 28:1–10, 16–20; Luke 24:1–51; John 20:1–29; 21:1–24)

17. (#42, 84) The Cleansing of the Leper (Mark 1:40–45; Matt. 8:1–4; Luke 5:12–16)

18. (#33, 139) Jesus Is Rejected at Nazareth (Mark 6:1–6a; Matt. 13:53–58; Luke 4:16–30)

19. (#25, 271, 273; cf. 276) The Cleansing of the Temple (Mark 11:1–17, 27–33; Matt. 21:1–27; Luke 19:28–20:8; John 12:12–22)

Which Women Were Present at the Cross, Burial, and Empty Tomb?

Crucifixion (Mark 15:40–41)	Burial (Mark 15:47)	Empty Tomb (Mark 16:1)
Mary Magdalene	Mary Magdalene	Mary Magdalene
Mary mother of James the Younger and Joses	Mary mother of Joses	Mary mother of James
Salome		Salome

Crucifixion (Matt. 27:56)	Burial (Matt. 27:61)	Empty Tomb (Matt. 28:1)
Mary Magdalene	Mary Magdalene	Mary Magdalene
Mary mother of James and Joseph	"the other Mary"	"the other Mary"
Mother of the sons of Zebedee		

Crucifixion (Luke 23:49)	Burial (Luke 23:55–56)	Empty Tomb (Luke 24:10–11)
Women are present but not named	Women are present but not named	Mary Magdalene
		Joanna[1]
		Mary mother of James
		"others with them"

Crucifixion (John 19:25)	Burial (John 19:38–42)	Empty Tomb (John 20:1)
Mary mother of Jesus	No mention of women present	
Mary's sister		
Mary Magdalene		Mary Magdalene
Mary wife of Clopas[2]		

Nearly 30 percent of women in Palestine (the Roman name for Judea) in late antiquity were named Mary or Salome,[3] so it is logical to expect to observe a number of women named Mary in the Gospels. Mark and Matthew mention three women named Mary throughout their Gospels: the mother of Jesus, the mother of James the Younger and Joses/Joseph, and Mary Magdalene. Luke mentions four women named Mary: the mother of Jesus, Mary Magdalene, the sister of Martha, and the mother of James.[4] John mentions four women named Mary: the mother of Jesus, Mary Magdalene, the sister of Martha and Lazarus, and the wife of Clopas.

The following women are named as those present at the crucifixion, burial, and/ or resurrection narratives:

- Mary Magdalene: Mark // Matthew and John report that Mary Magdalene was at the crucifixion scene. Mark // Matthew report that she was also at the burial. All four Gospels report that Mary Magdalene was at the empty tomb.
- Mary the mother of James and Joses/Joseph: At Jesus's crucifixion, Mark names her as "Mary the mother of James the Younger and Joses." At the burial scene, he abbreviates by omitting the mention of "James the Younger" and identifies her as "Mary the mother of Joses." And at the empty tomb scene, he abbreviates by omitting the other brother, Joses, and identifies her as Mary the mother of James. Matthew appears to be mentioning the same Mary but uses Joseph as a variation of Joses: "Mary the mother of James and Joseph."[5] He then abbreviates at the burial and empty tomb scenes by referring to her as "the other Mary." Luke mentions a plurality of women who were present at the crucifixion and burial scenes but does not provide their names. However, Luke names three of the women present at the empty tomb—Mary Magdalene, Joanna, and *Mary the mother of James*—and says there were "other women with them." Although there are two mothers of a son named James who are mentioned in Matt. 27:56,[6] only the mother of James and Joseph/Joses is specifically named "Mary."
- Salome: Mark reports that Salome was present at the crucifixion and empty tomb.
- The mother of the sons of Zebedee: Only Matthew mentions her presence at the crucifixion.
- Joanna: Only Luke mentions Joanna and places her at the empty tomb.
- Mary the wife of Clopas: Only John mentions this Mary and places her at Jesus's crucifixion.

- Mary the mother of Jesus: Only John mentions this Mary and places her at Jesus's crucifixion.
- The sister of Mary the mother of Jesus: Only John mentions this woman and places her at Jesus's crucifixion.

Are these eight different women, or are a few of the same women named differently in different Gospels?

Mark mentions three women present at the crucifixion scene: Mary Magdalene, Mary the mother of James and Joses, and Salome. Matthew provides the names of the first two Marys and in a similar order. However, he names "the mother of the sons of Zebedee" as the third woman. Since Matthew largely uses Mark as his source and neglects to mention Salome, it is possible that "the mother of the sons of Zebedee" in Matthew is named Salome in Mark. However, it is likewise possible Matthew has substituted a different woman witness for Salome if he had heard directly from her.

Is "Mary the mother of James and Joses/Joseph" in Mark (15:40–41, 47; 16:1) and Matthew (27:56, 61; 28:1) "the mother of Jesus" in John 19:25?[7] Mark always refers to Jesus's brother and the brother of James the Younger as "Joses," while Matthew uses the variant "Joseph" for both men.[8] At first look, it would appear that we should answer affirmatively, since Jesus is reported to have had brothers named James, Joses/Joseph, Simon, and Judas (Mark 6:3 // Matt. 13:55). Thus, Mark gives the name "Joses" to (a) Jesus's brother and (b) the brother of James and son of Mary who was at the cross, burial, and empty tomb (Matthew uses the variant "Joseph" in both cases). Moreover, if one desires to harmonize the names of the women at Jesus's crucifixion reported by Mark // Matthew, and John, Mary the mother of Jesus is the only candidate.

However, there are a few factors weighing against this connection. First, it would be odd for Jesus's mother to appear second in the list.

Second, it would be odd for the Synoptics to refer to the mother of Jesus as "the mother of James and Joses/Joseph" (Mark // Matt.), "the other Mary" (Matt.), and probably "the mother of James" (Luke). However, perhaps there was a tendency among some of the early Christians to exalt Jesus's mother and the Synoptics countered that tendency by being intentional in downplaying her after giving birth to Jesus (see also Mark 3:21, 31–35 // Matt. 12:46–50 // Luke 8:19–21; cf. Luke 2:42–49; 11:27–28). Moreover, it is worth observing how letters whose authorship have been traditionally attributed to Jesus's brothers begin. In Jude 1:1, the author refers to himself as "Jude, a slave of Jesus Christ and brother of James" while James 1:1 begins as "James, a slave of God and of the Lord Jesus Christ." Thus, one could argue that hesitancy existed among some of the early Christians to identify Jesus with his earthly family, perhaps out of reverence for the exalted Jesus.

Third, it is possible they were protecting Mary's identity with anonymity. Yet this is doubtful, since Mary had probably died by the time the Gospels were written, although certainty is not possible.

Fourth, since Jesus's brother James later became the leader of the Jerusalem church, it would be odd for Matthew to distinguish him from another James by referring to him as "the Younger/Lesser/Smaller" (τοῦ μικροῦ, *tou mikrou*). However, in addition to James the son of Zebedee, James the son of Alphaeus is listed as one of Jesus's twelve chosen disciples (Mark 3:18 // Matt. 10:3 // Luke 6:15; cf. Acts 1:13). And it is probably true that in the earliest days of the church the "Twelve" held a more prominent place than being a brother of Jesus who had apparently come late to the party, since the data suggests that none of Jesus's brothers followed him until after his death.[9] Yet Eusebius preserves a fragment from the fifth book of Hegesippus's memoirs (second century and no longer extant) in which he speaks of the martyrdom of James the brother of Jesus: "He has been called the Just by all from the time of our savior to the present day." Hegesippus explains the reasons for this are there were many who had the name James, and from a very early age James had lived a life of exceeding piety for his Jewish faith.[10] If Hegesippus is correct, we might expect to see "Mary the mother of James the Just and Joses" if this Mary was the mother of Jesus.

Could Mary the mother of James the Younger and Joses/Joseph be "the wife of Clopas"? It is possible. But since nothing is known of Clopas, it is impossible to know. We might also ask whether Mary the mother of James the Younger and Joses/Joseph was the sister of Jesus's mother, but this would require two sisters being named Mary.[11]

In the end, one can only speculate pertaining to whether some of the women mentioned in one Gospel are variants of women mentioned in the parallel accounts. The differences notwithstanding, one is hard-pressed to conclude that the accounts stand in contradiction, since Luke mentions "women" at the crucifixion and burial without providing the number and names three women and "others with them" at the empty tomb. Each evangelist may have included the names of the women from whom came the testimony upon which their narrative relied.

Biosketches of the Main Characters in Plutarch's Lives

ANTONY

Marcus Antonius, or Mark Antony, was born in ca. 83 BCE and was the grandson of the famous orator and consul of 99 BCE bearing the same name.[1] Antony served as consul in 44 and 34, and was consul-designate in 31. From 57 to 55, he served with distinction as a cavalry officer in Syria, prior to joining Caesar in his Gallic campaigns in 54. He was elected quaestor in 52, then augur and tribune of the plebs in 50.

In December 50, Antony unsuccessfully attempted to broker a deal with the senate that would thwart attempts to give Pompey the upper hand over Caesar. When all attempts finally failed, Antony and his fellow tribune Quintus Cassius fled Rome in early January 49 and joined Caesar, claiming that they feared for their lives at the hands of Caesar's political enemies in the senate. Caesar used this apparent violation of the sacrosanctity of the Tribunes as an excuse to begin the civil war by invading Italy.

Antony played a major role in assisting Caesar to defeat Pompey and become dictator. When Caesar left Rome in April 49 to neutralize Pompey's forces in Spain, he put Antony in charge of all Italy except Rome. Later Antony helped Caesar defeat Pompey at the Battle of Pharsalus on 9 August 48 and served as Caesar's chief deputy as Master of the Horse, administrating Italy during Caesar's absence in Egypt and the Middle East from ca. October 48 to September 47. Antony was Caesar's consular colleague in 44 at the time of Caesar's murder on 15 March.

In November 43, Antony joined Marcus Lepidus and Octavian Caesar (the future emperor Augustus) to form a coalition known as the "triumvirate," to which a law granted absolute power for five years. As part of Antony's conditions for joining the triumvirate, he insisted that Cicero's name be added to the proscription list on which the three dynasts placed their political enemies with a bounty for their murder. Octavian reluctantly agreed, and Cicero was hunted down by soldiers and killed. Antony ordered that Cicero's head and right hand be cut off and displayed on the Rostra in the Forum.

Antony and Octavian eventually fought a war against each other. On 2 September 31, Octavian defeated Antony in the Battle of Actium off the west coast of Greece, from which Antony escaped to Egypt with his mistress Cleopatra, who was the queen. When Octavian entered Alexandria on 1 August 30, Antony committed suicide.

BRUTUS

Marcus Junius Brutus was born ca. 85 BCE.[2] Some believed he was a descendant of Lucius Junius Brutus, the founder of the Republic who drove Rome's last king, the tyrant Tarquinius Superbus, into exile and was elected to the first consulship in 509. In 77, his father, who fought in an uprising, surrendered to Pompey, who put him to death despite promising to spare him. So Cato (Uticensis) raised the young orphaned son. Brutus's mother Servilia was Cato's half-sister and a reputed mistress of Julius Caesar. Given his love for the Republican cause, Brutus took the side opposed to Caesar in the civil war, despite the bad blood between himself and Pompey, his father's executioner. After Pompey's defeat in the Battle of Pharsalus on 9 August 48, Brutus made his peace with Caesar, who welcomed him and advanced his career, in part out of Caesar's regard for Brutus's mother Servilia.

Brutus divorced his first wife and married Cato's daughter Porcia, who had been widowed when her husband, Caesar's consular colleague Calpurnius Bibulus, died in 48. Caesar saw to it that Brutus secured the urban praetorship for 44 in place of the less prestigious peregrine praetorship, which fell to the lot of Gaius Cassius. Caesar also designated Brutus for a future consulship in 41, with Cassius as his colleague. However, during their praetorships in 44, Brutus and Cassius formed a conspiracy that carried out the assassination of Caesar on 15 March.

Although Antony allowed the senate to pass a decree granting amnesty to Brutus and the conspirators, he went on to incite the people against them, forcing them to leave Rome. Brutus and Cassius were able to amass funds and build up armies in Greece and Asia, while Cicero was successful in getting the senate to back them. In October 42, Brutus and Cassius met Antony and Octavian twice in battle at Philippi in eastern Macedonia. In the first battle, Brutus defeated Octavian, while Cassius was defeated by Antony. Wrongly believing that Brutus had also been defeated, Cassius committed suicide. Brutus was defeated in the second battle and committed suicide.

CAESAR

Gaius Julius Caesar was born in 100 BCE and was the nephew of the Roman general and political leader Gaius Marius (consul 107, 104–100, 86).[3] Lucius Cornelius Cinna (consul 87–84) gave Caesar his daughter Cornelia in marriage and designated him for the priestly office of *Flamen Dialis*. After Cinna was murdered in a mutiny in 84 and Cinna's followers were crushed by Sulla in a civil war (83–82), Sulla annulled Caesar's appointment to the priesthood and ordered him to divorce Cornelia. Caesar refused to do so and was fortunate that Sulla spared his life, thanks to the intervention of powerful nobles on Caesar's behalf.

In ca. 69, Caesar held a quaestorship in Further Spain. His wife died prior to his leaving for his province. He then married Sulla's granddaughter Pompeia. In 63, Caesar was elected to the chief pontificate and a praetorship, winning the former through massive bribery. Caesar is likely to have supported the first consular candidacy of Catiline in 64, but distanced himself from him when Catiline formed a conspiracy in 63 after a second unsuccessful bid to be elected consul. Caesar divorced Pompeia when she fell under the suspicion of having an affair with Publius Clodius Pulcher in late 62.

Caesar chose to stand for a consulship in 60, forfeiting the right to celebrate a triumph, which would have prevented him from entering Rome in time to meet the requirement of professing his candidacy to the magistrate conducting the elections. He won the consulship by allying himself with Pompey and Crassus. Pompey married Caesar's daughter Julia, and Caesar married Calpurnia, the daughter of Calpurnius Piso (consul 58). In 56, Caesar, Pompey, and Crassus met several times at Luca during which they renewed their political pact, and Caesar helped Pompey and Crassus to be elected consuls for 55 in exchange for their commitment to sponsor legislation to extend his provincial command in Gaul for another five years beyond March 54. The ties that bound the alliance between Caesar and Pompey began to dissolve when Julia died in 54 and Crassus was killed in his war against the Parthians in 53. In 52, Pompey married the daughter of Metellus Scipio, who was an enemy of Caesar, and Pompey selected Scipio to serve as his consular colleague during the last five months of that year.

In 50, Caesar insisted that he be allowed to stand for the consulship in absentia the following year, as he had been authorized to do by a law sponsored by all ten tribunes in 52. But many in the senate were now alarmed by Caesar's power and would not permit the privilege granted to Caesar to be honored. They demanded instead that he hand over his armies to a successor and return to Rome. Caesar proposed a compromise, which was rejected. When all negotiations failed, Caesar crossed the boundary of his province formed by the Rubicon River and quickly gained control of Rome and Italy. Caesar pursued Pompey to Greece, where Pompey mustered the forces he had evacuated from Italy. After Caesar defeated Pompey at Pharsalus in August 48, Cicero and Marcus Brutus abandoned their opposition to Caesar and made peace with him. Caesar pursued Pompey, who had fled to Egypt in the hope of raising fresh forces there. Upon his arrival, Caesar learned of Pompey's treacherous murder, punished those involved, overthrew the Egyptian boy-king Ptolemy XIII and set Cleopatra VII, Antony's future mistress, on the throne. While in Egypt, Caesar had an affair with Cleopatra, and she allegedly bore him a son named Ptolemy XV Caesar (nicknamed "Caesarion"). Upon his return to Italy in late 47, Caesar turned his attention to defeating formidable forces arrayed against him under the command of Cato, Scipio, and Juba, king of Numidia, in North Africa. News of the defeat of Scipio and Juba at the Battle of Thapsus on 6 April 46 drove Cato to commit suicide a few days later in the city of Utica in order to avoid living under Caesar's dictatorship. The last round of fighting took place in Spain, where in 45 Caesar defeated the remnants of the Republic forces that were marshaled under the generalship of Pompey's two sons Gnaeus and Sextus.

Caesar was voted numerous great honors, including "dictator for life" and even deification. He introduced reforms and granted pardons to many who had fought against him. But he had made many enemies during his rise to power. Marcus Brutus, whom Caesar had pardoned, led a conspiracy against Caesar and assassinated him on 15 March 44. Because Caesar had no children, he adopted his great-nephew Gaius Octavius (the future emperor Augustus), who avenged his uncle's murder.

CATO MINOR (CATO THE YOUNGER)

Marcus Porcius Cato (Uticensis), known as Cato the Younger, was born in 95 BCE and was the great-grandson of Cato the Censor (also known as Cato the Elder), who had served as consul in 195 and censor in 184.[4] Cato Uticensis was a leading conservative who wielded great influence in the Roman senate. Guided by Stoic philosophy, he lived by a strict moral code. He served as tribune in 62, stood firmly against the coalition of Caesar, Pompey, and Crassus in the 50s, unsuccessfully opposed both Caesar's agrarian legislation in 59 and the election of Pompey and Crassus to a second consulship in 55. In 58, the tribune Publius Clodius Pulcher sent Cato on two missions outside Italy in order to remove him and his influence from Rome. When he returned in 56, Cato stood for a praetorship, but his bid was thwarted by the coalition of Pompey, Crassus, and Caesar. However, he stood for it again the following year and was successful. In early 52, Cato supported a motion in the senate that authorized the election of Pompey as sole consul for that year. Later he blocked attempts to avert civil war by negotiation between Pompey and Caesar in early January 49, and then joined Pompey against Caesar when civil war broke out later that month. After Caesar defeated Pompey at Pharsalus on 9 August 48, Cato led his troops to the province of Africa. When at the Battle of Thapsus on 6 April 46 Caesar crushed the forces in Africa, Cato realized that the Republican cause was lost. He chose to commit suicide in Utica on ca. 10 April hence his surname, "Uticensis," rather than live under the tyranny of Caesar. His daughter married Marcus Brutus, who later led the conspiracy to assassinate Caesar in 44, and his son joined the forces of Brutus against Antony and Octavian and was killed in battle in 42.

CICERO

Marcus Tullius Cicero was born on 3 January 106 BCE into a well-to-do family belonging to the upper class known as equestrian.[5] As a young man, he successfully defended some major clients and by the age of thirty-six gained the reputation of being Rome's foremost orator. Cicero was the first in his family to hold public office and was eventually elected to the highest office in Rome, the consulship, which he held in 63. During his consulship, his leadership was responsible for crushing a conspiracy aimed at toppling the Roman government. The ringleader was a patrician senator named Lucius Sergius Catilina (known in English as Catiline). In early December 63, Cicero secured written evidence against five of the leading conspirators, caused them to be placed under house arrest, and carried out a decree of the senate authorizing their execution. However, four years later, in March 58, an aggressive tribune named Publius Clodius Pulcher passed a law banishing Cicero from Italy for executing the conspirators, who were Roman citizens, without trial. Cicero returned to Rome in September 57 after Pompey and others pushed successfully to have him recalled.

Upon returning, Cicero found that Caesar, Pompey, and Crassus were now exercising enormous political control thanks to the coalition formed in 60. Because of this, Cicero could play only a limited role in politics during the 50s. On the eve of civil war between Pompey and Caesar in December 50, Cicero's instinct was to try to work out a settlement. At first, he hesitated to support either party but ended up siding with Pompey. When Pompey was defeated at Pharsalus in August 48 and betrayed and killed in Egypt the next month, Cicero made peace with Caesar.

During the continuation of the civil war and the dictatorship of Caesar, Cicero retreated from politics and focused on his literary career from 46 to 45. When Caesar was assassinated on 15 March 44, Cicero was drawn back into politics late in the year, and in 43 led efforts in alliance with Octavian (i.e., the future emperor Augustus) against Antony, Caesar's consular colleague. Antony was defeated in battle in April 43, declared an "Enemy of the State," and forced to flee Italy. However, when the senate attempted to deprive Octavian of the supreme command of the army that had fallen to him thanks to the deaths of the two consuls in the fighting with Antony, Octavian responded by forming a coalition with Antony and Lepidus. That coalition, known as the Triumvirate, was granted by legislation unlimited power to govern for a term of five years. When the three initiated proscriptions, posting the names of their political enemies with a bounty for their murders, Octavian yielded to Antony's demand that Cicero's name be included among the first victims. On Antony's orders, soldiers were dispatched, and Cicero was killed on 7 December 43, roughly one month shy of his sixty-fourth birthday. At Antony's further instructions, they cut off Cicero's head and hand that he had used to write his polemics against Antony, the *Philippics*, and displayed those grizzly trophies on the Rostra in the Forum.

CRASSUS

Marcus Licinius Crassus was born ca. 115 BCE.[6] He was the general most responsible for crushing in 71 the uprising of slaves led by Spartacus, extending from 73–71; he crucified six thousand of Spartacus's followers along the Appian Way.[7] Crassus was skilled in finance and amassed great wealth for himself through the purchase of property confiscated from the victims of Sulla's proscriptions from 82 to June 81. He was consul in 70 and 55, both times with Pompey. At the urging of Caesar in 60, he set aside his long-standing rivalry with Pompey and formed a coalition with Caesar and Pompey. This political alliance dominated Roman politics until Crassus perished while leading an ill-fated campaign against the Parthians in the Middle East. After Crassus's defeat at the Battle of Carrhae in June 53, the Parthian general Surena offered a truce guaranteeing Crassus and his army safe passage out of Parthian territory. But Crassus was familiar with Parthian treachery and would have declined, had he not felt pressured by his troops who had grown impatient with his leadership and desired a truce. He reluctantly agreed to a meeting with Surena, who proceeded to deceive and kill him, just as Crassus had feared. Surena had Crassus beheaded and his right hand cut off, both of which trophies he delivered to the Parthian king Hyrodes as proof of Crassus's death.

LUCULLUS

Lucius Licinius Lucullus was born ca. 118 BCE.[8] He was a strong supporter of Sulla and served as praetor in 78 and consul in 74. In 74, while Pompey was in Spain, fighting Sertorius, Lucullus coveted a command in the East against Mithridates, king of Pontus. So, as consul, he met Pompey's demands for additional supplies and reinforcements to battle Sertorius in order to keep him occupied in Spain. Lucullus went on to defeat Mithridates and his ally Tigranes, king of Armenia, in a series of battles stretching from 73–68 but was unable to gain complete victory. Eventually, Pompey was sent to relieve him of his command in 66. Lucullus returned to Rome and celebrated a long-delayed triumph in 63, while Pompey went on to conclude the war and celebrate a magnificent triumph in 61.

After returning to Rome, Lucullus divorced his wife, a sister of the demagogue Publius Clodius Pulcher, for adultery. He then married Cato's niece. But that marriage likewise failed. After his return from the Mithridatic War, Lucullus largely refrained from politics, choosing instead to live luxuriously from the spoils of war he had amassed. He succumbed to insanity and died in 57 or 56.

POMPEY

Gnaeus Pompeius Magnus (Pompey the Great), known as Pompey (POM-pee), was born in 106 BCE.[9] He first demonstrated his talent in military leadership when he led a private army to several victories in the civil war of 83–82 at the conclusion of which Publius Sulla was named dictator. Sulla reluctantly awarded Pompey a triumph in 81 and later the senate sent him in 77 against Sertorius, who had fought on the side opposed to Sulla and had fled to Spain. Pompey struggled mightily against Sertorius but could not crush him. Eventually Sertorius perished in a conspiracy formed against him by some of his followers, led by Perperna, who was then defeated and killed by Pompey, who took command of the Sertorian forces in 72.

Although Crassus deserved the major credit for crushing in 71 the Slave War led by Spartacus, Pompey's forces on their return to Italy from Spain intercepted and defeated some of the fleeing slaves, permitting Pompey to lay claim to a share in the victory. In 67, Pompey was given a command for three years to eradicate piracy from the Mediterranean, and he cleared the seas in only three months. Lucullus, consul in 74, achieved great successes in the Third Mithridatic War during the years 73–68, but command in the war was eventually transferred to Pompey in 66, who three years later brought the war to a conclusion with the death of Mithridates, king of Pontus. Pompey also subdued Judea in 63, and when he returned to Rome, he celebrated a magnificent triumph in September 61 for his conquests in the Mithridatic War.

Pompey served as consul three times, twice with Crassus as his co-consul (70, 55) and once as sole consul during the first part of the tumultuous year 52. Pompey's first marriage was to Sulla's stepdaughter Aemilia. When she died, he married Mucia Tertia, whom he divorced in 62 for allegedly committing adultery with Caesar. In late 60, Pompey joined a coalition with Caesar and Crassus, commonly and incorrectly referred to as the "First Triumvirate," and married Caesar's daughter Julia in 58, who was much younger than him.

Shortly after betraying his friend Cicero in 58 by allowing the populist tribune Publius Clodius Pulcher to banish him from Italy, Clodius turned his attention to undermining Pompey's power. Although Clodius gained the upper hand in 58, Pompey was able to regain power in the following year. The coalition with Caesar and Crassus was renewed in 56 through a series of meetings at Luca, and Caesar assisted Pompey and Crassus to obtain the consulships for 55, although illegal force had to be employed. Pompey's marriage with Julia was a happy one. When she died in childbirth in 54 and Crassus was killed by the Parthians in 53, Pompey continued to support Caesar, although there were now fewer ties binding them, while each vied to occupy the position of Rome's most powerful figure.

With violence increasing in Rome, Pompey was authorized by the senate to be elected sole-consul for 52, with the hope of restoring order and peace. During the course of that year, he married his fourth wife, Cornelia, the widow of Crassus's son Publius Crassus who, like his father, had recently died in the war against the

Parthians. Cornelia was the daughter of Quintus Caecilius Metellus Pius Scipio, whom Pompey chose to be his consular colleague for the last five months of 52.

When negotiations with Caesar broke down in January 49, the senate authorized Pompey to lead forces against him. Pompey enjoyed a few initial victories in 48 but was finally defeated at Pharsalus in Thessaly on 9 August. He escaped and fled to Egypt, where he was treacherously murdered on 28 September by order of the chief ministers of the Egyptian boy-king Ptolemy XIII, brother of Cleopatra VII.

SERTORIUS

Quintus Sertorius was born ca. 126 BCE.[10] After Sulla frustrated his attempt to be elected tribune in 89 or 88, Sertorius joined Sulla's adversary Cinna, who was consul in 87 and had been driven from Rome by his political enemies. Then with Sertorius and others, Cinna successfully marched on Rome in late 87 and purged it of his opponents. After Cinna's dominance ended with his death in a mutiny in early 84, Sulla invaded Italy the following year and took Rome in late 82 with the help of Quintus Caecilius Metellus Pius, Crassus, and Pompey. During the course of the war, Sertorius went abroad to govern one or both of Rome's Spanish provinces, from which he was expelled by the Sullan government in 81 but returned the next year to lead a native uprising. Thanks to superior generalship and the use of guerrilla warfare to which Roman armies were unaccustomed, Sertorius managed to hold his own against the generals Metellus Pius and Pompey, who were sent against him. Finally, in 73 or 72, he was murdered in a conspiracy formed by one of his lieutenant generals, Perperna.

Notes

INTRODUCTION

1. An asterisk (*) appears after the first occurrence of terms included in a glossary provided for nontechnical readers.

2. Celsus may be referring to inconsistencies and contradictions in the Gospels when he says Christians have corrupted the Gospels by changing them several times: ἵν᾽ ἔχοιεν πρὸς τοὺς ἐλέγχους ἀρνεῖσθαι, *hin' echoien pros tous elegchous arneisthai.* (Origen, *Cels.* 2.27; Greek text taken from Origenes [Origen], *Contra Celsum Libri VIII*, ed. M. Marcovich, *VigChrSup* 54 [Leiden: Brill, 2001], 105). The phrase in Greek is both vague and ambiguous. R. J. Hoffmann renders it "in order to be able to deny the contradictions in the face of criticism" (R. J. Hoffmann, *Celsus on the True Doctrine: A Discourse against the Christians* [New York: Oxford University Press, 1987], 64). Frederick Crombie renders it "so that they might be able to answer objections" (Origen, *Cels.* 2.27 [*ANF* 4:443]).

3. F. Gerald Downing, "Redaction Criticism: Josephus' *Antiquities* and the Synoptic Gospels (I)," *JSNT* 2, no. 8 (1980): 45–65, and "Redaction Criticism: Josephus' *Antiquities* and the Synoptic Gospels (II)," *JSNT* 3, no. 9 (1980): 29–48; R. A. Derrenbacker Jr., *Ancient Compositional Practices and the Synoptic Problem*, BETL 186 (Leuven: Peeters, 2005); Jordan Henderson, "Josephus's *Life* and *Jewish War* Compared to the Synoptic Gospels," *JGRChJ* 10, no. 5 (2014): 113–31.

4. Brian McGing, "Philo's Adaptation of the Bible in His *Life of Moses*," in *The Limits of Ancient Biography*, ed. Brian McGing and Judith Mossman (Swansea: Classical Press of Wales, 2006), 117–40.

5. D. A. Russell, "Plutarch's Life of Coriolanus," *JRS* 53, parts 1 and 2 (1963): 21–28.

6. Charles E. Hill, "'In These Very Words': Methods and Standards of Literary Borrowing in the Second Century," in *The Early Text of the New Testament*, ed. Charles E. Hill and Michael J. Kruger (Oxford: Oxford University Press, 2012), 261–81.

7. Craig S. Keener, "*Otho*: A Targeted Comparison of Suetonius's Biography and Tacitus's *History*, with Implications for the Gospels' Historical Reliability," *BBR* 21, no. 3 (2011): 331–56.

8. In the education process, a heavy emphasis was placed on memory, and aspiring authors were taught to rely extensively on it. But memory is not always reliable to the detail. Therefore, J. C. Rolfe cautions those who look for "lost sources" behind a text, opining this is "a point to which students of source-criticism do not always give enough attention" (Suetonius, *Lives of the Caesars*, trans. J. C. Rolfe, 2 vols., rev. ed., LCL 31 [1914; Cambridge: Harvard University Press, 1998], Logos 6, 1:13–14).

9. The literature is vast. For a recent and impartial summary on the present state of discussions pertaining to oral tradition in antiquity, see Eric Eve, *Behind the Gospels: Understanding the Oral Tradition* (Minneapolis, MN: Fortress, 2014).

10. See David B. Gowler, "The Chreia," in *The Historical Jesus in Context*, ed. Amy-Jill Levine, Dale C. Allison Jr., John Dominic Crossan (Princeton, NJ: Princeton University Press, 2006), 132–48. See also Ronald F. Hock, *The Chreia and Ancient Rhetoric: Commentaries on Aphthonius's* Progymnasmata, WGRW 31 (Atlanta, GA: Society of Biblical Literature, 2012), http://www.sbl-site.org/assets/pdfs/pubs/061631C.front.pdf.

11. In such instances, harmonization can be the most appropriate solution. Some interesting examples may be found in Eric Lounsbery, *J. J. Blunt's Undesigned Scriptural Coincidences: The Proof of Truth* (Maitland, FL: Xulon Press, 2005).

12. One example appears in Luke 21:16–19, where Jesus tells his disciples that some of them will be killed, yet not a hair on their heads will perish. Whatever Jesus meant by this statement, it is doubtful he was assuring them that while the Romans may mutilate their bodies and execute them in various brutal manners, God would see to it that their hair remained unharmed!

13. I am indebted to Christopher Pelling for suggesting this possibility (e-mail message to author, 20 July 2015).

14. Derrenbacker (*Ancient Compositional Practices and the Synoptic Problem*, 3) speaks of "scholarship's virtually complete silence on the physical conditions and literary methods of ancient authors" and says that "little attention has been paid to the compositional methods of ancient writers that may have been employed by the evangelists in the construction of their gospels. Similar literary methods of ancient authors are often overlooked by most Synoptic source critics, with virtually no investigation into the methods of authors and their sources in antiquity being attempted by source (or redaction) critics. In other words, while 'compositional analyses' of the Gospels seem to abound, typically these analyses make little attempt to find compositional conventions that are historically analogous to the production of the Gospels" (5). Eric Eve (*Behind the Gospels*, 184) opines, "[T]he Synoptic Problem needs rethinking in terms . . . of ancient compositional practices."

15. These are also referred to as rhetorical handbooks. For work that interacts with the compositional textbooks, see Burton L. Mack and Vernon K. Robbins, *Patterns of Persuasion in the Gospels* (1989; repr., Eugene, OR: Wipf and Stock, 2008). Mack and Robbins offer interesting proposals pertaining to the evangelists' use of the compositional textbooks in general and, more specifically, chreia. However, in my opinion, several of their examples seemed forced and their excitement about chreia often leads them to imagine their presence where others may not be so sanguine.

16. Alex Damm, "Ancient Rhetoric and the Synoptic Problem," in *New Studies in the Synoptic Problem: Oxford Conference, April 2008; Essays in Honour of Christopher M. Tuckett*, ed. P. Foster, A. Gregory, J. S. Kloppenborg, and J. Verheyden, BETL 239 (Leuven: Peeters, 2011), 491.

17. Charles H. Talbert, *What Is a Gospel? The Genre of the Canonical Gospels* (Philadelphia, PA: Fortress, 1977); David E. Aune, *The New Testament in Its Literary Environment*, Library of Early Christianity 8 (Philadelphia, PA: Westminster Press, 1987).

18. Richard A. Burridge, *What Are the Gospels? A Comparison with Graeco-Roman Biography*, 2nd ed. (Grand Rapids, MI: Eerdmans, 2004).

19. Darrell L. Bock, "Precision and Accuracy: Making Distinctions in the Cultural Context That Give Us Pause in Pitting the Gospels against Each Other," in *Do Historical Matters Matter to Faith? A Critical Appraisal of Modern and Postmodern Approaches to Scripture* (Wheaton, IL: Crossway, 2012), 367–81, esp. 368; Steve Walton, "What Are the Gospels? Richard Burridge's Impact on Scholarly Understanding of the Genre of the Gospels," *Currents in Biblical Research* 14, no. 1 (2015): 81–93, esp. 86–87.

20. Burridge, *What Are the Gospels?*, 114–15; Richard A. Burridge, "Reading the Gospels as Biography," in *The Limits of Ancient Biography*, ed. Brian McGing and Judith Mossman (Swansea: Classical Press of Wales, 2006), 31–49. Burridge says between 10,000 to 20,000 words (32).

21. Burridge, "Reading the Gospels as Biography," 33.

22. Burridge, "Reading the Gospels as Biography," 33.

23. These are only some of the qualities of Greco-Roman biography. For a complete list, see Burridge, *What Are the Gospels?*, 10–23.

24. Burridge, *What Are the Gospels?*, 301. Phillip Alexander's quote is from P. S. Alexander, "Rabbinic Biography and the Biography of Jesus: A Survey of the Evidence," in *Synoptic Studies: The Ampleforth Conferences of 1982 and 1983*, ed. C. M. Tuckett, Journal for the Study of the New Testament Supplement Series 7 (Sheffield: JSOT Press, 1984), 40.

25. J. Neusner, *The Incarnation of God: The Character of Divinity in Formative Judaism* (Philadelphia, PA: Fortress, 1988), 213, quoted in Burridge, *What Are the Gospels?*, 302.

26. Christopher Pelling refers to this as "the most-quoted passage in Plutarch" (Christopher Pelling, *Plutarch and History: Eighteen Studies* [Swansea: Classical Press of Wales, 2002], 259).

27. Translation by Christopher Pelling in Plutarch, *Rome in Crisis: Nine Lives*, trans. Ian Scott-Kilvert and Christopher Pelling (New York: Penguin Books, 2010), 214. See also Plutarch, *Mor.*, bk. 3, *Mulier. virt.*, where Plutarch explains that his objective behind providing the *Comparisons* that accompany most of the *Parallel Lives* is to bring out for clearer viewing the qualities of the main characters.

28. That historical writing contained moral objectives may be observed in Polybius, *Hist.* 2.61, and Tacitus, *Ann.* 3.65. Also see Rhiannon Ash, Judith Mossman, and Frances B. Titchener, eds., *Fame and Infamy: Essays for Christopher Pelling on Characterization in Greek and Roman Biography and Historiography* (Oxford: Oxford University Press, 2015). Unfortunately, this book was published too late during my research phase to be included.

29. See, for example, Burridge, *What Are the Gospels?*, 62–65; Adela Yarbro Collins, *Mark*, Hermeneia (Minneapolis, MN: Fortress, 2007), 22–33.

30. Beth M. Sheppard, *The Craft of History and the Study of the New Testament*, Resources for Biblical Study 60 (Atlanta, GA: Society of Biblical Literature, 2012), 112.

31. See Christopher Pelling, "Breaking the Bounds: Writing about Julius Caesar," in *The Limits of Ancient Biography*, ed. Brian McGing and Judith Mossman (Swansea: Classical Press of Wales, 2006), 266–67.

32. See Andrew W. Pitts, "Source Citation in Greek Historiography and in Luke(-Acts)," in *Christian Origins and Greco-Roman Culture: Social and Literary Contexts for the New Testament*, ed. Stanley E. Porter and Andrew W. Pitts, Texts and Editions for New Testament Study 9 (Leiden: Brill, 2013), 349–88; Andrew W. Pitts, "The Genre of the Third Gospel and Greco-Roman Historiography: A Reconsideration" (paper presented in the "Paul J. Achtemeier Award for New Testament Scholarship" section of the Annual Meeting of the Society of Biblical Literature, Atlanta, GA, 22 November 2015); and Ben Witherington III, *The Acts of the Apostles: A Socio-Rhetorical Commentary* (Grand Rapids, MI: Eerdmans, 1998), 1–39. Craig S. Keener (*The Historical Jesus of the Gospels* [Grand Rapids, MI: Eerdmans, 2009], 85–94) regards Luke's Gospel as biography when taken alone but that it "becomes a biographic component in a larger history" when read in combination with its sequel Acts (85–86).

33. Collins (*Mark*, 42–84) argues that Mark's Gospel is an "Eschatological Historical Monograph."

34. Richard A. Burridge and Graham Gould, *Jesus: Now and Then* (Grand Rapids, MI: Eerdmans, 2004), 51.

35. Pelling, *Plutarch and History*, 160. Bock ("Precision and Accuracy," 370) speaks in terms of being "accurate without being precise."

36. On Philostratus's *Vit. Apoll.*, see Christopher P. Jones, introduction to *The Life of Apollonius of Tyana*, by Philostratus, vol. 1, *Books 1–4*, ed. and trans. Christopher

P. Jones, Loeb Classical Library 16 (Cambridge: Harvard University Press, 2005), Logos 6, 1–30; C. P. Jones, *Plutarch and Rome* (Oxford: Clarendon Press, 1971), 126–28. See also Craig S. Keener, *Acts: An Exegetical Commentary*, vol. 1, *Introduction and 1:1–2:47* (Grand Rapids, MI: Baker Academic, 2012), 332–33.

37. See Pelling, *Plutarch and History*, 143–70, esp. 156–62. Pelling observes that Plutarch's concept of "truth" when writing of historical events and people "is less alien to us than we readily admit" (157). In support he provides a few examples in modern biographies (157–58).

38. *Perseus Digital Library*, ed. Gregory R. Crane (Medford/Somerville, MA: Tufts University), http://www.perseus.tufts.edu.

39. Eberhard Nestle, Erwin Nestle, Barbara Aland, Kurt Aland, and Holger Strutwolf, eds., *Novum Testamentum Graece* (NA[28]), 28th rev. ed. (Stuttgart: Deutsche Bibelgesellschaft, 2013); Barbara Aland, Kurt Aland, Johannes Karavidopoulos, Carlo M. Martini, and Bruce M. Metzger, eds., *The Greek New Testament* (UBS[5]), 5th rev. ed. (Stuttgart: Deutsche Bibelgesellschaft, 2014); and Michael W. Holmes, ed., *The Greek New Testament: SBL Edition* (Atlanta, GA: Society of Biblical Literature, 2010).

40. I am indebted to Daniel Wallace for this information.

41. Bruce M. Metzger and Bart D. Ehrman, *The Text of the New Testament: Its Transmission, Corruption and Restoration*, 4th ed. (New York: Oxford University Press, 2005), 55–56. See also Charles E. Hill, and Michael J. Kruger, eds., *The Early Text of the New Testament* (Oxford: Oxford University Press, 2012).

42. Acts 16:12 and 2 Peter 3:10 are the only two that appear in the NA[28]. I am indebted to Daniel Wallace for this information (e-mail message to author, 8 December 2014).

CHAPTER 1

1. See George A. Kennedy, trans., *Progymnasmata: Greek Textbooks of Prose Composition and Rhetoric*, WGRW 10 (Atlanta, GA: Society of Biblical Literature, 2003), 1. Malcolm Heath ("Theon and the History of the Progymnasmata," *Greek, Roman, and Byzantine Studies* 43, no. 2 [2003]: 129) argues for the fifth century. In essays appearing in Matthew Ryan Hauge and Andrew W. Pitts, *Ancient Education and Early Christianity*, LNTS 533 (London: T&T Clark, 2016), Ronald F. Hock ("Observing a Teacher of *Progymnasmata*," 39–70) is persuaded by Heath (see p. 43), whereas Andrew W. Pitts ("The Origins of Greek Mimesis, Ancient Education, and Gospel of Mark: Genre as a Potential Constraint in Assessing Markan Imitation," 107–36) favors the first century (see p. 111).

2. Kennedy, *Progymnasmata*, 73, 89, 129, 130.

3. See especially Quintilian, *Inst.* Although Quintilian provides a lot of content similar to the Greek textbooks, the passages especially helpful for our research include 1.9.2; 2.4.1–41; 10.5.1–3, 11; cf. Kennedy, *Progymnasmata*, ix.

4. When citing Theon throughout this book, I will be using the page numbering system of Spengel, *Rhet.* (vol. 2), which is the standard. However, since Kennedy's volume is widely used, I will include in parentheses the page number on which the text is found in that volume. Thus, 59 above refers to volume 2, page 59 of Spengel, while [3] refers to page 3 in Kennedy. All English translations of Theon are from George A. Kennedy's *Progymnasmata*, unless otherwise indicated. Kennedy's English translation of Hermogenes and Aphthonius is based on the Greek texts provided by Hugo Rabe, *Prolegomenon Sylloge* (Leipzig: Teubner, 1931). For more detail on Rabe, see Kennedy, *Progymnasmata*, 90–91. Kennedy's English translation of Nicolaus is based on the Teubner text provided by Joseph Felton, ed., *Nicolai Progymnasmata* (Leipzip: Teubner, 1913. Citations in the notes of other translations than the LCL are therefore referring to the introductions, notes, or commentary of those translators on a given ancient text or its English translation.

5. Libanius, *Progymnasmata*, "The Exercise in Anecdote: Anecdote 2." See Craig A. Gibson, trans., *Libanius's* Progymnasmata: *Model Exercises in Greek Prose Composition and Rhetoric*, Writings from the Greco-Roman World 27 (Atlanta, GA: Society of Biblical Literature, 2008), 55–64.

6. See also 60 (4).

7. Cf. Hermogenes, 6 (76); Aphthonius, 23, 3–4R (97). The "3–4R" refers to pages 3–4 in Rabe, which provides additional text for Theon not found in Spengel. Aphthonius provides additional ways for paraphrasing chreia in 23–25, 4–6R (98–99); Nicolaus, 19–20 (139–40). See also Nicolaus, 21–25 (141–43). Pelling says, "Plutarchans tend to refer to these chreiai as apophthegmata" (e-mail message to author, 20 July 2015).

8. Cf. Hermogenes, 4 (75); Aphthonius, 22 (96); and Nicolaus, 11–17 (136–39).

9. Theon discusses this further in "On Prosopopoeia," 115–18 (47–49). Related to speeches, Hermogenes discusses *prosopopoeia* and *ethopoeia* in 20–22 (84–85). See also Nicolaus, 63–67 (164–66) and 194–200 (213–17). Although Josephus claimed great accuracy in his reporting, he felt free to invent speeches (see A. W. Mosley, "Historical Reporting in the Ancient World," *NTS* 12, no. 1 [1965]: 23–24). Polybius (*Hist.* 2.56.10–12) had a stricter practice of reconstructing speeches than Thucydides, Plutarch, and most other historians of that era. Even in view of his statement that the only task of the historian is to relate events as they had occurred, Lucian permitted the historian to use his oratorical skills in order to improve a speech (*Hist. conscr.* 39, 58).

10. Kennedy notes that 99–112 are based on a French translation by Michel Patillon and Giancario Bolognesi of an Armenian translation of a Greek *vorlage* (*Progymnasmata* 2003, 64).

11. Somewhat related is Hermogenes (*Inv.* 3.15.167), who describes the practice of *diatypōsis*, which Kennedy defines as the "vivid or emotional description of an action or the state of mind of someone" (George A. Kennedy, *Invention and*

Method: Two Rhetorical Treatises from the Hermongenic Corpus [Atlanta, GA: Society of Biblical Literature, 2005], 129n182).

12. F. Gerald Downing, "Compositional Conventions and the Synoptic Problem," *JBL* 107, no. 1 (1988): 71.

CHAPTER 2

1. D. A. Russell, "Plutarch (L.(?) Mestrius Plutarchus)," *OCD*, 1165; Christopher P. Jones, *Plutarch and Rome* (Oxford: Clarendon Press, 1971), 13.

2. John Buckler, "Chaeronea," *OCD*, 303; John F. Lazenby, "Chaeronea, battles of," *OCD*, 303; and Guy Thompson Griffith, "Archelaus," *OCD*, 139.

3. Jones, *Plutarch and Rome*, 22.

4. Russell, "Plutarch," *OCD*, 1165; Brian Campbell, "Sosius (*RE* 11) Senecio, Quintus," *OCD*, 1386 . Duff comments, "The first pair of *Parallel Lives*, that of Epaminondas and one of the Scipios, is no longer extant; but it probably contained a dedication to Sosius Senecio, who is addressed frequently in the surviving *Lives*" (Timothy E. Duff, *Plutarch's Lives: Exploring Virtue and Vice* [New York: Oxford University Press, 1999], 2).

5. Jones, *Plutarch and Rome*, 56. That Plutarch was appointed as a procurator is disputed and known only from the Byzantine historian George Syncellus (d. early ninth century). See Simon Swain, "Plutarch, Hadrian, and Delphi," *Historia* 40, no. 3 (1991): 318–30. I am grateful to Christopher Pelling for referring me to this journal article.

6. The Lamprias Catalogue is alleged to have been written by Plutarch's grandson. However, its date of composition rules out such a possibility. It is, therefore, pseudonymous.

7. M. J. Edwards, *Plutarch: The Lives of Pompey, Caesar and Cicero* (London: Bristol Classical Press, 1991), 1; Russell, "Plutarch," *OCD*, 1165.

8. Russell, "Plutarch," *OCD*, 1165.

9. Plutarch, *Life of Cicero* (Moles), 5.

10. Russell, "Plutarch," *OCD*, 1165.

11. Plutarch, *Life of Cicero* (Moles), 48.

12. Plutarch, *Life of Cicero* (Moles), 48.

13. Pelling, *Plutarch and History*, 144.

14. Pelling, *Plutarch and History*, 156, cf. 162, 210; Scott-Kilvert and Pelling, *Rome in Crisis*, xxxvii–xxxviii; Christopher Pelling, *Literary Texts and the Greek Historian* (New York: Routledge, 2000), 46.

15. Plutarch, *Caesar*, trans. Christopher Pelling, Clarendon Ancient History Series (Oxford: Oxford University Press, 2011), 14.

16. Scott-Kilvert and Pelling, *Rome in Crisis*, xxxvii; Pelling, *Plutarch and History*, 162; cf. 159 for Tacitus acting in a similar manner; Plutarch, *Life of Antony*, ed. C. B. R. Pelling, Cambridge Greek and Latin Classics (New York: Cambridge University Press, 1988), vii; and Plutarch, *Life of Cicero* (Moles), 33, 42.

17. Plutarch (*Cat. Min.* 23.3) reports what must have been a rare exception when Cicero arranged for several scribes known for their speed in using a very primitive version of shorthand symbols to be placed around the senate house in order to record what was said at the Catilinarian debate over the punishment of the conspirators on 5 December 63 BCE. See Pelling's comments in Scott-Kilvert and Pelling, *Rome in Crisis*, 563n103.

18. See Keener, *Acts: An Exegetical Commentary* (Grand Rapids, MI: Baker Academic, 2012), 1:258–319; Marion L. Soards, *The Speeches in Acts: Their Content, Context, and Concerns* (Louisville, KY: Westminster/John Knox, 1994), 134–61; and Witherington, *Acts of the Apostles: A Socio-Rhetorical Commentary* (Grand Rapids, MI: Eerdmans, 1998), 32–39.

19. Pelling, *Plutarch and History*, 62n28; Anthony A. Barrett, introduction to *The Annals: The Reigns of Tiberius, Claudius, and Nero*, by Tacitus, trans. J. C. Yardley (New York: Oxford University Press, 2008), xxiii–xxiv.

20. Pelling, *Plutarch and History*, 156, 161.

21. Plutarch, *Life of Cicero* (Moles), 39, 41–42, 44; Edwards, *Plutarch*, 3.

22. Plutarch, *Life of Cicero* (Moles), 44.

23. Jones, *Plutarch and Rome*, 85.

24. Pelling, *Plutarch and History*, 158; Plutarch, *Life of Cicero* (Moles), 41.

25. Pelling, *Plutarch and History*, 158.

26. Russell, "Plutarch," *OCD*, 1165.

27. Pelling, *Plutarch and History*, 2–11.

28. Pelling, *Plutarch and History*, 35n68. In the same note, Pelling admits that he did not include *Sertorius* in his analysis of Plutarch's methods of composition in his Roman *Lives* since "its content affords little basis for comparison with other *Lives*." While there is far less material in *Sertorius* that has parallels in the other *Lives*, I found enough to benefit the present project.

29. Scott-Kilvert and Pelling, *Rome in Crisis*, 527n10; Plutarch, *Life of Cicero* (Moles), 6.

30. Plutarch, *Caesar* (Pelling), 36.

31. Plutarch, *Life of Cicero* (Moles), 40.

32. See Plutarch, *Caesar* (Pelling), 56–57; Russell, "Plutarch's Life of Coriolanus," *Journal of Roman Studies* 53, parts 1 and 2 (1963): 22; Edwards, *Plutarch*, 3; Plutarch, *Life of Cicero* (Moles), 36–39.

33. Translation by Pelling in Scott-Kilvert and Pelling, *Rome in Crisis*, 203.

34. I have here conflated two compositional devices described by Pelling, *Plutarch and History*, 94–96: "the *expansion* of inadequate material, normally by the fabrication of circumstantial detail" and "the *fabrication of a context*."

35. See Pelling, *Plutarch and History*, 153–54, 161.

36. Kurt Aland, ed. *Synopsis of the Four Gospels: Greek-English Edition of the* Synopsis Quattuor Evangeliorum, 12th ed. (Stuttgart: German Bible Society, 2001).

37. This phrase was first used by Duane Reed Stuart, *Epochs of Greek and Roman Biography*, Sather Classical Lectures 4 (1928; repr., New York City: Biblo and

Tannen Booksellers and Publishers, 1967), 78, as cited in Plutarch, *Caesar* (Pelling), 22.

38. See Plutarch, *Caesar* (Pelling), 22–23.

39. A few examples are provided in the next section.

40. F. Gerald Downing says there are "frustratingly few . . . instances of specific writings together with their acknowledged or clearly arguable source materials as data dateable from our period, few examples even of works with single sources, let alone plural ones" (F. Gerald Downing, "Writers' Use and Abuse of Written Sources," in *New Studies in the Synoptic Problem*, ed. P. Foster, A. Gregory, J. S. Kloppenborg, and J. Verheyden, BETL 239 [Leuven: Peeters, 2011]), 524).

41. Pelling, *Literary Texts and the Greek Historian*, 49; Pelling in Scott-Kilvert and Pelling, *Rome in Crisis*, 37–38.

42. Pelling, *Plutarch and History*, 91–115; Plutarch, *Life of Cicero* (Moles), 36–39. See also Edwards, *Plutarch*, 3.

CHAPTER 3

1. Please remember that the text quoted is the most recent Teubner whereas the references are those found in the LCL.

2. See Plutarch, *Caesar* (Pelling), 183–84.

3. Russell, "Plutarch's Life of Coriolanus," 53. Pelling adds, "Similar is the debt to Thucydides in, for instance, his account of the Sicilian campaign at *Nicias* 12– 29: at *Plutarch and History*, 119, I estimate that 'rather over half' of that comes from Thucydides, rising to 'over two-thirds' for the detail of the campaign itself" (Plutarch, *Caesar*, 40n90).

4. Moles recognizes the immensity of a comprehensive treatment pertaining to "how Plutarch's handling of a given incident or character varies from *Life* to *Life*," asserting that it "is simply too large a topic" for his commentary on Plutarch's *Life of Cicero* (1).

5. See, for example, the story of Domitius drinking poison to escape the consequences of being defeated by Caesar at Corfinium in Plutarch, *Caesar* (Pelling), 327–28, or Trebonius sharing a tent with Antony (*Ant.* 13.1; see Pelling, *Plutarch and History*, 95; Plutarch, *Life of Antony* [Pelling], 147–49) or a friend holding up his toga in order to catch Antony's vomit after a night of drinking (*Ant.* 9.6; see Pelling, *Plutarch and History*, 94; Plutarch, *Life of Antony* [Pelling], 137–38, comment on 5–9). Pelling (*Plutarch and History*, 153–54) refers to this practice as "creative reconstruction" rather than fabrication, invention, and fiction.

6. Proscriptions were lists containing the names of Romans who were declared outlaws. The property of those on the list was forfeited and put up for sale to the public. Moreover, rewards were offered for the death of those on the list.

7. So spelled by Plutarch. However, the more correct spelling is "Perperna."

8. The Third Mithridatic War.

9. Caesar would enter the competition later. Plutarch tells us Caesar stated that he would rather be the leading person of a small village than be second in Rome (*Caes.* 11.2).

10. The Teubner text is cited here and differs slightly from the older LCL (translation mine).

11. The text is the most recent Teubner and differs only in a few accent marks from the older LCL (translation mine).

12. I am indebted to John Ramsey for alerting me to this difference.

13. Henderson, "Josephus's *Life* and *Jewish War* Compared," 123. According to Paul Maier, *J. W.* was published in Greek in 77 or 78 CE from the Aramaic in which Josephus had composed it, while *Life* was attached as an appendix to *Ant.* and written in 93–94 CE (Josephus, *Josephus, the Essential Works: A Condensation of Jewish Antiquities and the Jewish War*, trans. and ed. Paul L. Maier, rev. ed. [Grand Rapids, MI: Kregel, 1994], 11–12).

14. In Roman naming conventions, the *praenomen* was the person's personal name. The *nomen* identified one's family, clan, or race. And the *cognomen* was a characteristic that would distinguish one person further from another.

15. See the comments on the differing names of the tribunes in the analysis portion of pericope #32.

16. Pelling notes that Amnaeus is an otherwise unknown figure (Scott-Kilvert and Pelling, *Rome in Crisis*, 561n79).

17. Scott-Kilvert and Pelling, *Rome in Crisis*, 561n79.

18. The first triumph occurred on 12 March 81, grudgingly allowed by Sulla for Pompey's victories in Africa and Sicily over Cn. Papirius Carbo, Cn. Domitius Ahenobarbus, and King Iarbas. The second occurred on 29 December 71 for ending the war against Sertorius. Pompey would celebrate his third on 28–29 September 61 for defeating Mithridates VI in the Third Mithridatic War.

19. Patricians were a privileged class of Roman citizens comprised of approximately fifty clans who had once monopolized Roman magistracies and priesthoods. By the Late Republic, they had lost their monopoly of power and only fourteen patrician clans survived (Arnaldo Momigliano and Tim Cornell, "patricians," *OCD*, 1091–92).

20. Ramsey in Sallust, *The War with Catiline; The War with Jugurtha*, trans. J. C. Rolfe, rev. John T. Ramsey, LCL 116 (Cambridge: Harvard University Press, 2013), 10.

21. Edwards, *Plutarch*, 26; Ramsey in Sallust, *War with Catiline* (Rolfe/Ramsey, LCL), 10–11.

22. See Plutarch, *Life of Cicero* (Moles), 164–65; Pelling in Scott-Kilvert and Pelling, *Rome in Crisis*, 562n94; Plutarch, *Caesar* (Pelling), 162; Ramsey in Sallust, *War with Catiline* (Rolfe/Ramsey, LCL), 11.

23. Plutarch is mistaken here (and in 54.1 and *Brut.* 5.3) in his description of Servilia as the sister of Cato. She was actually Cato's niece. See Pelling in Scott-Kilvert and Pelling, *Rome in Crisis*, 563–64n106.

24. Lucullus later divorced Servilia for infidelity (*Cat. Min.* 24.3; *Luc.* 38.1). It is striking that Plutarch neglects to mention Caesar's affair with Servilia in his *Life of
Caesar* (*Caesar* [Pelling], 460).

25. Pelling in Scott-Kilvert and Pelling, *Rome in Crisis*, 562n95; Ramsey in Sallust,
War with Catiline (Rolfe/Ramsey, LCL), 14.

26. Roman citizens who were members of the lower social orders, which constituted
the demos (i.e., common people, populace), were called the "plebs." These were
distinct from aristocrats.

27. Cicero (*Cat.* 4.8–10), Cassius Dio (*Hist. rom.* 37.36.1–2), and Sallust (*Cat.* 51.43)
differ from Plutarch's accounts, describing Caesar's proposed punishment as
the confiscation of the conspirators' property and sentencing them to life imprisonment without any chance of release. Pelling (Scott-Kilvert and Pelling, *Rome
in Crisis*, 563n99) and Moles (Plutarch, *Life of Cicero*, 169, note on 21.1) opine that
Plutarch's rendition is probably mistaken.

28. See Plutarch, *Caesar* (Pelling), 56, 163–64, esp. 164: In reality, "the conspirators
were denounced in the senate on 3 December, Crassus was attacked [in an oration by Cicero] on the 4th, and the final debate on punishment took place on
the 5th. P. knew that the sittings of 3 and 5 December were distinct (*Cic.* 19.14,
20.421.5), and he already knew of the sitting of the 4th as well (*Crass.* 13.3)."
The reference numbering provided by Pelling in this citation is that of the most
current Teubner rather than the older LCL. See also Ramsey in Sallust, *War with
Catiline* (Rolfe/Ramsey, LCL), 13–14.

29. A *drachma* was a Greek coin. A *talent* was a certain massed weight of gold or
silver.

30. Pelling, *Plutarch and History*, 53–54.

31. Edwards says the latter was "their professed motive," but "the official reason for
Pompey's recall was to defeat Catiline" (*Plutarch*, 131). See also Plutarch, *Life of
Cicero* (Moles), 171, comment on 23.4.

32. It is also worth observing that in *Lucullus*, the name "Lucullus" is spelled
Λούκουλλος, *Loukoullos*, whereas in *Pompey*, it is Λευκολλος, *Leukollos*. In
fact, "Lucullus" appears in *Pompey* 26 times and is always spelled Λευκολλος,
Leukollos. However, in *Lucullus*, "Lucullus" appears 170 times, and it is always
spelled Λούκουλλος, *Loukoullos*. This difference appears only in the LCL Greek
text. The most recent Teubner has amended the *Lucullus* text throughout to be
consistent with Λευκολλος, *Leukollos* in *Pompey*. I am grateful to John Ramsey
for bringing this to my attention.

33. See pericope #13 above in which Pompey was prohibited from entering the city
and supporting Piso's candidacy for consul in 62 BCE, since he was outside waiting to celebrate his third triumph.

34. Pelling (Plutarch, *Caesar*) says this "famous coalition of the three" was "long
mis-called 'the first triumvirate'" (188), mis-called since "contemporaries did
not regard any such triple coalition as being of central importance" (190). "The
agreement at Luca in 56 was probably more far-reaching" (191).

35. Fasces were symbols of the authority of a political office. They were "a bound bundle of elm- or birch-wood rods about five feet long, with an ax projecting from their middle, were carried before higher magistrates by attendants known as lictors, twelve in number for each consul. The axes were removed when magistrates (other than dictators and triumphing generals) were within the city to signify a citizen's right to appeal magisterial verdicts of corporal or capital punishment" (Ramsey in Sallust, *War with Catiline* [Rolfe/Ramsey, LCL], 48–49n29). Lictors were attendants who carried the fasces of magistrates, cleared paths for approaching magistrates, and carried out arrests.

36. Pelling in Scott-Kilvert and Pelling, *Rome in Crisis*, 569n161.

37. Henderson ("Josephus's *Life* and *Jewish War* Compared," 124) observes a number of incidences in which Josephus either inverts the order of events or links events closely together in one account that he narrates to have occurred on different occasions in another. See *J. W.* 2.570–75 // *Life* 79, 187–89; *J. W.* 2.595–613 // *Life* 85, 126–48; and *J. W.* 624–31 // *Life* 190–335, 368–72.

38. In Scott-Kilvert and Pelling, *Rome in Crisis*, 570–71n174, Pelling says Plutarch is probably mistaken on the timing in *Cat. Min.*, since according to other sources it occurred on a different occasion, probably earlier in the year. He also notes that Cicero said Cato ended up boycotting the senate that year (Cic. *Sest.* 63). Elsewhere Pelling says, "We cannot be sure of the precise occasion; the anecdote may well have been timeless in the source that Dio, Suet., and P. share" (Plutarch, *Caesar*, 201). The story of Cato's arrest is given in Dio (*Hist. rom.* 38.3.2–3), who reports the event and places it—with Plutarch's *Caesar*—at the time of the first agrarian law. But Dio (38.7.4) likewise reports that Cato opposed the second agrarian law.

39. Plutarch, *Caesar* (Pelling), 201. The reference numbers provided reflect the LCL.

40. The transfer took place by early April 59, and the tribunicial elections took place in July or probably later (Scott-Kilvert and Pelling, *Rome in Crisis*, 571n176).

41. Cicero wrote that this banishment prohibited him from coming within 400 miles (644 km) of Italy (*Att.* 3.4).

42. I am indebted to John Ramsey for alerting me to this example. So also Ernst Badian, in "Iunius (*RE* 53) Brutus (2), Marcus," *OCD*, 765. Pelling considers this as a possibility but is uncertain. He writes, "While in Cyprus Brutus dealt with the city of Salamis in a way that told heavily to his own financial advantage, in a manner that seems most discreditable to a modern reader (Cic. *Att.* 5.21, 6.1–3). If Plutarch knew of this (a big "if"), he may have suppressed it as discordant from his picture of the high-principled young student of ethics" (Scott-Kilvert and Pelling, *Rome in Crisis*, 591n31).

43. Pelling in Scott-Kilvert and Pelling, *Rome in Crisis*, 597n82.

44. See Plutarch, *Life of Cicero* (Moles), 181, in reference to 33.4.

45. See Plutarch, *Life of Cicero* (Moles), 181, in reference to 33.5.

46. Cassius Dio (*Hist. rom.* 21.1–22.1) reports that Cicero was accompanied by Milo and some of the tribunes.

47. At least according to Plutarch in *Cat. Min.* 41.1.

48. It was standard practice for the consuls to be assigned provinces for one year. Plutarch does not mention the point of contention being that the law assigned the provinces to Pompey and Crassus for five years.

49. In the text, the law giving an extension of Caesar's provinces (*lex Licinia Pompeia*) appears prior to the law awarding provinces to the consuls (*lex Trebonia*). See Plutarch, *Caesar* (Pelling), 247, comment on 21.6; and Edwards, *Plutarch*, 49.

50. Pelling (Plutarch, *Caesar*, 253). Plutarch also provides the 300,000 figure in *Comp. Nic. Crass.* 4.3.

51. Pelling (Plutarch, *Caesar*, 262), notes related to 25.3–27; and Pelling (Plutarch, *Life of* Antony, 127–28), notes related to 5.4–5.

52. T. Robert S. Broughton, with Marcia L. Patterson, *Magistrates of the Roman Republic*, vol. 2, 99 B.C., Philological Monographs 15 (New York: American Philological Association, 1951). See Pelling in Scott-Kilvert and Pelling, *Rome in Crisis*, 638n208.

53. Although each of the three was suspected of having such an ambition, Plutarch may have exaggerated their actual plans.

54. Plutarch, *Caesar* (Pelling), 258, 275.

55. Valerius Maximus (*Mem.* 6.2.5) mentions Pompey's illegal action and Cato's objection but does not specifically name Plancus. Cassius Dio, *Hist. Rom.* 40.55.1–4 adds Pompey's intervention in the trial of Milo. Both inform us that Pompey had not actually attended Plancus's trial, in agreement with Plut. *Cat. Min.* 48.4. Moreover, Stone argues for a trial date of sometime between January and early February 51. If so, by then Pompey would have stepped down as consul and taken his proconsulship. This would mean he would most likely have left the city by the time of Plancus's trial, which provides further reason to favor Plutarch's version in *Cat. Min.* 48.4. See A. M. Stone, "*Pro Milone*: Cicero's Second Thoughts," *Antichthon* 14 (1980): 88–111. I am grateful to John Ramsey for alerting me to these references and to Stone's essay.

56. Cicero was actually outside of the city walls waiting for a senate decision on whether to grant him a triumph. See Plutarch, *Life of Cicero* (Moles), 185, comment on 37.1.

57. Pelling, *Plutarch and History*, 107.

58. Elected tribunes normally assumed their new office on 10 December while elected consuls started on 1 January.

59. Pelling (Plutarch, *Caesar*, 305) opts for the latter while Raaflaub opts for the former (see K. Raaflaub, "Zum politischen Wirken der caesarfreundlichen Volkstribunen am Varaben des Bürgerkrieges," *Chiron* 4 [1974]: 293–326, esp. 306–11).

60. Scott-Kilvert and Pelling, *Rome in Crisis*, 621n28; possibly on 21 December.

61. Plutarch does not connect Lentulus's statement in *Caes.* 30.3 to have occurred during the same senate sitting in which Scipio introduced his motion in 30.2.

62. In *Pomp.* 58.6, Metellus says he will send someone against Caesar in order to defend Rome, although this is portrayed as occurring on a later occasion.

63. Plutarch, *Caesar* (Pelling), 305; Pelling, *Plutarch and History*, 107.

64. Plutarch, *Caesar* (Pelling), 306; Plutarch, *Life of Antony* (Pelling), 126–30.

65. Plutarch, *Life of Antony* (Pelling), 129.

66. Plutarch, *Life of Antony* (Pelling), 130. See also Plutarch, *Caesar* (Pelling), 309.

67. For a few examples, see Plutarch, *Caesar* (Pelling), 305–7.

68. Pelling, *Plutarch and History*, 108.

69. Caesar, *Bell. civ.* 1.33.2. See Plutarch, *Caesar* (Pelling), 325.

70. Spain was the ultimate destination. However, Caesar headed first to Gaul. See Plutarch, *Caesar* (Pelling), 334 and comments related to 36.1.

71. Shortly after Caesar left for Spain, Cicero decided to join Pompey in Illyricum. Plutarch also reports that he was quite pessimistic while there (*Cic.* 38.1–6).

72. Pelling (Plutarch, *Caesar*, 349–50) explains that Pompey was not actually in Dyrrhachium but in nearby Asparagium, then on the hill of Petra.

73. Plutarch, *Caesar* (Pelling), 330.

74. It is worth observing that numerical differences exist in the writings of Josephus. Henderson ("Josephus's *Life* and *Jewish War* Compared," 123–24) observes that 600 gold pieces were taken at Dabaritta in *J. W.* 2.595, whereas it is 500 in *Life* 127. In *J. W.* 2.610, 2,000 soldiers surround the house of Josephus, whereas it is 600 in *Life* 145. In *J. W.* 2.628, John of Gischala receives 2,500 reinforcements, whereas it is 1,000 in *Life* 200–201. John's followers are given an ultimatum of 5 days to surrender in *J. W.* 2.624, whereas it is 20 days in *Life* 370. Three thousand soldiers desert John and 2,000 remain in *J. W.* 2.625, whereas 4,000 desert him and 1,500 remain in *Life* 371–72.

75. Plutarch, *Caesar* (Pelling), 335–36.

76. As noted above in our analysis of the Catilinarian conspiracy, Plutarch is mistaken in his description of Servilia as the sister of Cato. She was Cato's niece.

77. Master of the Horse was an emergency magistrate chosen by the dictator and who served as his lieutenant. He was the most powerful person in the city of Rome when the dictator was absent (A. N. Sherwin-White/Andrew Lintott, "*magister equitum*," *OCD*, 885).

78. So also Lucan, *De bello civili* (or *Pharsalia*) 7.471.

79. Pelling's translation of *Caes.* 45.9 (most current Teubner numbering).

80. See Pelling in Scott-Kilvert and Pelling, *Rome in Crisis*, 609n198). It is also of interest that Appian reports that Cassius is the one who discovered Theodotus and crucified him (*Bell. civ.* 2.90). Plutarch is not entirely committed to simplification in *Brutus*, for in 46.1–5, he reports that Brutus allowed his soldiers to plunder the cities of Thessalonica and Lacedaemon (i.e., Sparta). He adds that this was the only inexcusable act of Brutus during his entire life (46.2).

81. Pelling (Plutarch, *Caesar*, 386–87, §49.4, §49.5) comments that Plutarch is here mistaken, since Ptolemy was at war with his sister Cleopatra, and Achillas would

have been with his army preparing for an attack from Cleopatra's forces rather than inside the city with Potheinus and Caesar. Achillas was killed in his own camp as a result "of a plot of the eunuch Ganymedes and the princess Arsinoe." Moreover, according to Caesar (*Bell. civ.* 3.112.12), he did not have Potheinus killed until after the fighting with Achillas had started.

82. That Antony was in possession of Pompey's house is mentioned by Plutarch in *Ant.* 10.2, 21.2, 32.3.

83. The Greek text actually says "Corfinius" rather than Antony. Koraes amends the Teubner text to instead read "Antony." Although there are no manuscripts with this reading, Pelling (Plutarch, *Caesar*, 398) says this amendment "seems correct," since this is the report of Plutarch in *Antony* and by Cicero (*Phil.* 2.64). In *Ant.* 21.3, Plutarch is clear that Antony acquired the house as a result of the proscriptions, suggesting he was at least the initial buyer. In *Ant.* 32.3, Plutarch reports that Antony was still living in the house when Pompey's younger son, Sextus, met with Antony and Octavian in the summer of 39, nine years after Pompey's death. So unless Antony had initially purchased Pompey's house, then gave or sold it to Corfinius, and then later reacquired it, it would appear either that Plutarch contradicted himself or that at some time the manuscripts were corrupted. In *Pomp.* 40.5, Plutarch notes that the unnamed purchaser of Pompey's house is unimpressed by its size.

84. Although beyond the scope of this project, Pelling takes into consideration other sources and opines that *Ant.* 21 is "a remarkable passage, revealing the freedom with which P. adapts his material" (Plutarch, *Life of Antony*, 169).

85. The battle occurred on 6 April 46 (Ramsey in Sallust, *War with Catiline* [Rolfe/ Ramsey, LCL], xxv). Pelling writes, "There is indeed a good case for regarding Thapsus rather than Pharsalus as the decisive battle of the war" (Plutarch, *Caesar*, 398).

86. This is the same city to which the apostle Paul wrote a letter to the church residing there.

87. Pelling (Plutarch, *Caesar*, 416) comments that Plutarch's sequence of Caesar being declared consul for the fourth time prior to leaving for Spain is incorrect, since he was not declared consul for 45 until the end of 46.

88. Tradition regards Superbus as the last king of Rome (534–510 BCE). He was tyrannical in the manner in which he ruled and was expelled by Lucius Iunius Brutus, who was one of Rome's first two consuls in 509 (Badian, "Iunius [*RE* 52] Brutus [1], Marcus," *OCD*, 765; Tim Cornell, "Tarquinius Superbus, Lucius," *OCD*, 1432).

89. Regarding graffiti, see Plutarch, *Caesar* (Pelling), 462–63.

90. See Pelling in Scott-Kilvert and Pelling, *Rome in Crisis*, 595n66.

91. See Plutarch, *Caesar* (Pelling), 461–62.

92. See Plutarch, *Caesar* (Pelling), 447, comment on 60.3.

93. See Plutarch, *Caesar* (Pelling), 458–59.

94. Plutarch does not inform us when this event occurred. Nicolaus of Damascus (*Vit. Caes.* 130.22) situates it shortly after the Lupercalia festival that year. However, he does not mention Caesar's invitation to strike his neck at this event or the earlier Lupercalia festival.

95. The timing is not stated by Appian (*Bell. civ.* 2.108) or Plutarch (*Brut.* 9.4; *Ant.* 12.1–4; *Caes.* 61.4).

96. Plutarch does not name the tribunes in *Ant.* 12.4.

97. Plutarch, *Brut.* 9.4 also has diadems on Caesar's statues.

98. Appian (*Bell. civ.* 2.108) and Velleius Paterculus (*Hist. rom.* 68.4) leave the timing unstated.

99. Pelling (Plutarch, *Caesar*, 448) comments, "There are so many uncertainties in sequence about these incidents that it is likely that they were remembered as free-floating individual stories, and each narrator imposed his own order."

100. See Plutarch, *Caesar* (Pelling), 448–49, for comments related to 60.4 and 60.6.

101. Lucian, *How to Write History*, 55 (translation mine, from the Greek text in *Lucian*, vol. 6, LCL 430 [1959; repr., Cambridge: Harvard University Press, 2006], 67).

102. Quintilian, *The Institutio Oratoria of Quintilian*, trans. H. E. Butler, LCL 127 (London: Heinemann, 1921), Logos 6, 4:579–81 (I have slightly modified Butler's translation).

103. See Pelling, *Plutarch and History*, 94–96; Plutarch, *Life of Cicero* (Moles), 36–39, esp. b, d, l, m; and Edwards, *Plutarch*, 3.

104. Caesar's logion, "You, too, my son?" is absent in Plutarch but reported by Suetonius, *Caes.* 82.2 (Rolfe, LCL), and Cassius Dio, *Hist. rom.* 44.19.5. However, Dio doubts the authenticity of the logion, and Suetonius appears to as well.

105. Nicholas Horsfall, "The Ides of March: Some New Problems," *Greece and Rome* 21, no. 2 (1974): 191–99. Horsfall only gives consideration to a few problems. For a treatment that focuses on the hour at which the conspirators met, see John Ramsey, "At What Hour Did the Murderers of Julius Caesar Gather on the Ides of March 44 B.C.?," in *In Pursuit of Wissenschaft: Festschrift für William M. Calder III zum 75. Geburtstag*, Spudasmata 119, ed. Stephan Heilen, Robert Kirstein, R. Scott Smith, Stephen M. Trzaskoma, Rogier L. van der Wal, and Matthias Vorwerk (New York: Olms, 2008), 351–63.

106. Pelling in Scott-Kilvert and Pelling, *Rome in Crisis*, 596n71. See also Theodore John Cadoux and Robin J. Seager, "Ligarius (*RE* 4), Quintus," *OCD*, 836.

107. Appian (*Bell. civ.* 2.117.490, 3.26.101), Cassius Dio, *Hist. rom.* 44.19.1–3, Cicero (*Fam.* 10.28; *Phil.* 2.34).

108. Plutarch, *Caesar* (Pelling), 479, comment on 66.4.

109. After Caesar was assassinated, Dolabella became consul in his place. See Broughton and Patterson, *Magistrates of the Roman Republic*, vol. 2, 99 *B.C.*, year 44 BC.

110. Pelling (Scott-Kilvert and Pelling, *Rome in Crisis*, 601n116) is uncertain whether there was one or two senate sittings but leans toward only one (see Plutarch, *Caesar* [Pelling], 490, comment on 67.8).

111. In *Cic.* 42.3, there is no mention of Antony's eulogy. However, in that text, Antony shows (δείξαντος, *deixantos*) Caesar's torn and bloody clothing (τήν ἐσθῆτα, *tēn esthēta*).

112. Pelling says, "The nature and motives of A.'s speech are controversial" (Plutarch, *Life of Antony*, 153). He then cites differences in reports of the speech by Cicero, Appian, Cassius Dio, Suetonius, and Plutarch (153–54).

113. A drachma was equal to four sesterces. During the reign of Augustus, the ordinary Roman legionary made 900 sesterces a year (or 225 drachma), and there is no evidence Augustus had given an increase. According to Matt. 20:1–9, the daily wage for a vineyard laborer was 1 denarius, which was nearly equal in value to the drachma (see Colin M. Wells, "Roman Empire," *AYBD* 5:805, comment under "F. Social Inequalities"; also see Brian Campbell, "*stipendium*," *OCD*, 1402, comment under "stipendium"). Thus, Caesar's gift amounted to approximately three to four months wages for the common Roman citizen.

114. To the Greeks and Romans in the first century, a δαίμων, *daimōn* (Greek for "demon") was a supernatural being that held an intermediate position between God and humans and could bring luck or harm to an individual. For Jesus and the early Christians, all daimons were servants of Satan and, thereby, evil. In order to avoid confusion, I have maintained *daimon* when used by Plutarch but render *demon* in the context of the Gospels.

115. Pelling in Scott-Kilvert and Pelling, *Rome in Crisis*, 607n175. The triumvirate was legalized on 27 November by the *lex Titia*.

116. Pelling observes that "App. *Civil Wars* 4.7 also has '300', and that was probably Pollio's number: Plutarch may have misremembered here." See Scott-Kilvert and Pelling, *Rome in Crisis*, 607n176.

117. Shane Butler (*The Hand of Cicero* [New York: Routledge, 2002], 124n2), writes, "Except for Plut. *Cic.* 48.6, all who mention two hands do so as interlocutors in Seneca the Elder's *Suasoriae*: the historian Livy (*Suas.* 6.17), the poet Cornelius Severus (*Suas.* 6.26), the orator Bruttedius Niger (*Suas.* 6.20). One hand only is mentioned by Plutarch, *Ant.* 20.2; Liv. *Per.* 120; App. *B Civ.* 4.19.77; Val. Max. 5.3; Dio Cass. 47.11.2; the historian Aulus Cremutius Cordus in Sen. *Suas.* 6.19; the rhetor Aulus Porcius Latro in Sen. *Contr.* 7.2.9." I am indebted to John Ramsey for referring me to Butler.

118. See Pelling in Scott-Kilvert and Pelling, *Rome in Crisis*, 611n222; Plutarch, *Caesar* (Pelling), 500, comment on 69.12.

119. See Plutarch, *Caesar* (Pelling), 500, comment on 69.13; and Scott-Kilvert and Pelling, *Rome in Crisis*, 630n133.

120. Suetonius (*Caes.* 89) says some of the conspirators took their own lives with the daggers they had used to kill Caesar.

121. Pelling in Scott-Kilvert and Pelling, *Rome in Crisis*, 609n206.

122. Plutarch, *Caesar* (Pelling), 500, comment on 69.14.

123. Plutarch, *Life of Antony* (Pelling), 172, comment on 22.3; Plutarch, *Caesar* (Pelling), 403, comment on 53.5–6.

124. Pelling in Scott-Kilvert and Pelling, *Rome in Crisis*, 612n228.

125. D. Brutus Albinus was the conspirator who persuaded a hesitating Caesar to go on with his plans to meet with the senate on the Ides of March. On Antony's orders, a Gallic chieftain killed this conspirator in the summer of 43. See Pelling in Scott-Kilvert and Pelling, *Rome in Crisis*, 607n179.

126. See discussion of literary techniques or compositional devices in chapter 1.

CHAPTER 4

1. Bart D. Ehrman, *The New Testament: A Historical Introduction to the Early Christian Writings* (Oxford: Oxford University Press, 2008), 229.

2. Ehrman, *New Testament*, 221.

3. Luke Timothy Johnson, *The Real Jesus: The Misguided Quest for the Historical Jesus and the Truth of the Traditional Gospels* (San Francisco, CA: HarperSanFrancisco, 1996), 89.

4. Craig S. Keener, *Historical Jesus of the Gospels* (Grand Rapids, MI: Eerdmans, 2009), 349.

5. It is possible that the Q source was one of the accounts referred to in Luke 1:1.

6. Austin Farrer, "On Dispensing with Q," in *Studies in the Gospels: Essays in Memory of R. H. Lightfoot*, ed. D. E. Nineham (Oxford: Basil Blackwell, 1955), 55–88.

7. A few scholars hold a variant of this view, contending that it was Matthew who used Luke as a source rather than the other way around.

8. Only a few sources can be mentioned here. In favor of the Two-Source Hypothesis, see Robert H. Stein, *Studying the Synoptic Gospels: Origin and Interpretation*, 2nd ed. (Grand Rapids, MI: Baker Academic, 2001). In favor of the Farrer Hypothesis, see Mark Goodacre, *The Case Against Q: Studies in Markan Priority and the Synoptic Problem* (Harrisburg, PA: Trinity Press International, 2002). In favor of the Griesbach Hypothesis, see William R. Farmer, *The Synoptic Problem: A Critical Analysis*, 2nd ed. (Macon, GA: Mercer University Press, 1976).

9. Michael R. Licona, *The Resurrection of Jesus: A New Historiographical Approach* (Downers Grove, IL: IVP Academic, 2010), 281–83.

10. Raymond E. Brown, *An Introduction to the Gospel of John*, ed. Francis J. Moloney, AYBRL (New York: Doubleday, 2003), Logos 6, 195–96; Craig S. Keener, *The Gospel of John: A Commentary* (Peabody, MA: Hendrickson, 2003), 1:52, 114–15. Even such a conservative Christian scholar as F. F. Bruce can speak of Shakespeare's rendition of Antony's eulogy at Caesar's funeral reported in Plutarch's *Brutus*, "a translation of the freest kind, a transposition into another key," and write, "What Shakespeare does by dramatic insight (and, it may be added, what many a preacher does by homiletical skill), all this and much more the Spirit of God accomplished in our Evangelist [i.e., John]. It does not take divine inspiration to provide a verbatim transcript; but to reproduce the words which were spirit and life to their first believing hearers in such a way that they continue to

communicate their saving message and prove themselves to be spirit and life to men and women today, nineteen centuries after John wrote—that is the work of the Spirit of God" (F. F. Bruce, *The Gospel and Epistles of John* [Grand Rapids, MI: Eerdmans, 1983], 16–17).

11. Richard Burridge, *Four Gospels, One Jesus? A Symbolic Reading,* 3rd ed. (Grand Rapids, MI: Eerdmans, 2014), 133–63.

12. Keener, *Gospel of John,* 1:114; Mark Allan Powell, *Introducing the New Testament: A Historical, Literary, and Theological Survey* (Grand Rapids, MI: Baker Academic, 2009), 175. Dale Allison holds that, although the traditional author, John the son of Zebedee, did not write the Gospel attributed to him, he was the major source behind it. (Allison stated this opinion in a paper titled " 'Jesus Did Not Say to Him That He Would Not Die': John 21:20–23 and Mark 9:1," presented in the "John, Jesus and History" section of the Annual Meeting of the Society of Biblical Literature, Chicago, IL, 17 November 2012, which is to be published in *Jesus Remembered in the Johannine Tradition,* vol. 5 of *John, Jesus, and History,* ed. Paul N. Anderson, Felix Just, and Tom Thatcher, ECL 5, SymS [Atlanta: SBL Press, forthcoming].) Richard Bauckham believes the author was John the Elder, a minor disciple of Jesus who had traveled with him (see Richard Bauckham, *The Testimony of the Beloved Disciple: Narrative, History, and Theology in the Gospel of John* [Grand Rapids, MI: Baker Academic, 2007], 33–72). Craig Blomberg and Craig Keener both favor the traditional authorship of John the son of Zebedee (see Craig L. Blomberg, *The Historical Reliability of John's Gospel* [Downers Grove, IL: IVP Academic, 2001], 22–41; and Keener, *Gospel of John,* 1:81–139). Brown thought the Beloved Disciple was an "eyewitness who was responsible for the basic testimony/witness that was incorporated into the Fourth Gospel. But others were responsible for composing the written Gospel and redacting it" somewhat similar to how Peter had been the eyewitness source behind Mark's Gospel (Brown, *Introduction to the Gospel of John,* 195–96 and n. 15). Ben Witherington argues for Lazarus as the author (see Ben Witherington, III, *Invitation to the New Testament: First Things* [New York: Oxford University Press, 2013], 124–30).

13. For example, Craig Keener writes, "[A]ll [Johannine] scholars acknowledge *some* adaptation and conformity with Johannine idiom" (*Gospel of John,* 1:52). I have read John's Gospel and 1 John many times in their original language, Greek. It is clear to me, at least, that the vocabulary and style of both strongly suggest that the same person composed them. If I am correct, one must choose either that John conformed his language to sound like Jesus in his letter or that John has recast Jesus's teachings in his own words. Since Jesus in John's Gospel teaches with an idiom that differs from how he sounds in the Synoptics about as much as British English differs idiomatically from the English of North Americans living in the Deep South, the latter option seems more plausible.

14. N. T. Wright, *Following Jesus: Biblical Reflections on Discipleship,* 2nd ed. (Grand Rapids, MI: Eerdmans, 2014), 35.

15. πνευματικὸν ... εὐαγγέλιον, *pneumatikon ... euangelion* (from Eusebius, *Hist. eccl.* 6.14.7, who is aware of Clement's *Hypotyposeis*, which is no longer extant).

16. Origen, *Commentary on the Gospel according to John*, 10.2, 4, 15 (vol. 9 of ANF).

17. We observe something similar only a few verses later in Luke 23:18–25. Here Pilate releases Barabbas at the crowd's request and has Jesus crucified. But Luke does not mention Pilate's custom of releasing a prisoner whom the Jews requested at their Passover feast. Thus, if Luke alone is read, Pilate's releasing Barabbas at the crowd's request could appear implausible.

18. For (d), I am indebted to Darrell Bock (e-mail message to author, 11 November 2015).

19. Bock, "Precision and Accuracy," 367.

20. Kurt Aland, ed. *Synopsis of the Four Gospels: Greek-English Edition of the* Synopsis Quattuor Evangeliorum, 12th ed. (Stuttgart: German Bible Society, 2001).

21. The theological point behind this redaction of the recipient of God's announcement is obvious. (The same may be said of Mark's redaction of Isa. 40:3.) Mark is certainly communicating that the messenger is preparing the way for Jesus and in so doing takes a text clearly referring to God and applies it to Jesus. Of course, Mark could be thinking of Jesus as God's emissary without at all requiring that he be divine in an ontological sense. However, that Mark was speaking of Jesus in terms of ontological divinity is a reasonable option. When we recall that the objective of ancient biography is to illuminate the character of the biography's subject, the illumination of Jesus's identity in Mark is profound. In addition to the text under current consideration, Jesus forgives the sins of and heals a paralytic in Mark 2:1–12. The Jewish scribes think Jesus is committing blasphemy, since only God can forgive sins. In Mark 3:22–27, the scribes assert Jesus is able to exorcise demons because he is demon-possessed. But Jesus answers that Satan does not cast out himself, since a house divided against itself cannot stand. Rather, his exorcisms are his binding Satan and plundering his kingdom. What man can bind Satan? In Mark 4:37–39, Jesus calms the wind and the waves by his command, which is something God does (Pss. 89:9; 107:28–29; Eccles. 8:8). In Mark 6:45–51, Jesus walks on water, which is something only God can do (Job 9:8). In Mark 5:22–24, 35–43, Jesus raises someone from the dead, which is something only God does (Eccles. 8:8). Although a few others in the Bible raised the dead, in every case it was God doing it in answer to their prayers (1 Kings 17:17–24; 2 Kings 4:17–37; Acts 9:36–42). Jesus, however, raises the dead by his own power. In Mark 9:14–29, Jesus casts out a demon while his disciples were unable. When his disciples ask why they were unable, he answers, "This kind is not able to be cast out except by prayer." Jesus, however, was able to cast out the demon without prayer. Moreover, others could cast out demons in the name of Jesus (Mark 9:38–39). In Mark 12:1–12; 13:32, Jesus stands in a special relationship with God as his Son in a manner that is above all prophets and even angels. In Mark 12:35–37, the Messiah is not only David's son but also his Lord.

In Mark 13:24–27; 14:61–64, Jesus is the apocalyptic Son of Man to whom God will give all authority to judge the world and who will be worshipped and served in a manner that should otherwise be given only to God (see Deut. 6:13; 10:20; Dan. 7:13–14; 1 En. 38:1–6; 40:4; 45:3; 46:1–3; 48:5; 49:2, 4; 51:1–3; 61:8; 62:5–6, 9, 11; 69:27–29; 4 Ezra 13:8–12, 37–38; 14:3). While scholars debate what Jesus claimed about his identity, when the biographical genre of Mark's Gospel is recognized, it is quite clear that Mark's portrait of Jesus is that of a being who is, in some sense, God.

22. One may also observe how Luke narrates John the Baptist's statement in Acts 13:25: "Who do you suppose that I am? I am not he. But, behold, one is coming after me, the sandal [singular] of his feet [plural] I am not worthy to untie." Although the singular/plural combination of sandal/feet and strap/sandals is a grammatical mismatch in English, it was apparently an idiom in Greek. See Mark 1:7; Luke 3:16; Acts 13:25. John 1:27 does not use this idiom but has "thong" and "sandal" both in the singular. Matt. 3:11 only mentions removing his sandals rather than untying them.

23. In John 1:21, John the Baptist denies being Elijah. The Synoptics report later that some were saying Jesus is John the Baptist risen from the dead, Elijah, Jeremiah, or one of the prophets (Mark 6:14–16; Matt. 14:1–2; Luke 9:7–9). The disciples later inform Jesus of this (Mark 8:27–28; Matt. 16:13–14; Luke 9:18–19). They also ask Jesus why others anticipate the coming of Elijah. Jesus answers that John the Baptist was Elijah (i.e., he preached with the spirit of Elijah; see Mark 9:11–13; Matt. 11:14; 17:10–12). In Luke 1:17, the angel tells Zacharias that his son will preach with the spirit of Elijah and to make ready a people who are prepared for the Lord.

24. Bock ("Precision and Accuracy," 371) writes, "One of the writers is likely giving the significance of what took place (probably Matthew with his 'this')." Collins (*Mark*, 150) thinks Mark may have altered the logion to reflect Ps. 2:7. See a similar discrepancy with the heavenly voice that spoke at Jesus's transfiguration; cf. Mark 9:7 // Matt. 17:5 // Luke 9:35.

25. See John 3:34; 7:37–39; 14:16–17, 26; 16:13–14; 20:22.

26. Additional examples of inflection not observed in the pericopes that follow in the main text can be observed in Matt. 4:3 // Luke 4:3 ("these stones" // "this stone") and Mark 4:1–20 // Matt. 13:1–23 // Luke 8:4–15 (those receiving the seed are in the plural in Mark and Luke but in the singular in Matthew; also, μέριμναι, *merimnai* // μεριμνῶν, *merimnōn*, "cares" [Mark // Luke] and μέριμνα, *merimna*, "care" [Matt.]).

27. In the NT, the phrase καὶ μεταβὰς ἐκεῖθεν, *kai metabas ekeithen*, also appears in Matt. 15:29 and Acts 18:7, both carrying the sense of immediate succession.

28. W. D. Davies and Dale C. Allison Jr., *A Critical and Exegetical Commentary on the Commentary on the Gospel according to Saint Matthew*, vol. 2, *Commentary on Matthew VIII–XVIII*, ICC (1991; repr., London; New York: T&T Clark, 2004), Logos 6, 317.

29. See pericope #11 below, the parable of the vineyard and the wicked tenants.

30. One need not reject this solution because it involves Jesus's knowledge of the thoughts of the Jewish leaders in Mark 3:2–5 // Luke 6:7–10. Such knowledge may not necessarily be attributed to supernatural powers. After Jesus's previous encounters with Jewish leaders pertaining to his actions on a Sabbath, it would not have been difficult for him to discern what the Jewish leaders in the synagogue that Sabbath were thinking while observing whether he would heal the man with a withered hand.

31. Dropsy is a condition in which the afflicted body part is swollen because of an abnormal collection of fluid underneath the skin. This is pericope #214 in Aland, *Synopsis of the Four Gospels*.

32. Luke reports both stories (6:6–11; 14:1–6), and there are many differences between them. The event in Luke 6 occurred in a synagogue; in Luke 14, the event occurred in the house of one of the leaders of the Pharisees. In Luke 6, the man Jesus healed had a withered hand; in Luke 14, the man suffered from dropsy. In Luke 6, Jesus told the man to stretch out his hand. When he does, his hand is healed. In Luke 14, Jesus took hold of the man and healed him. In Luke 14:5, Jesus added a question preserved with a few differences in Matt. 12:11. The healing of the man with dropsy is unique to Luke.

33. This is the view of Davies and Allison, *Commentary on the Gospel according to Saint Matthew*, 2:320; John Nolland, *The Gospel of Matthew: A Commentary on the Greek Text*, NIGTC (Grand Rapids, MI: Eerdmans; Bletchley, Paternoster, 2005), Logos 6, 487–88; and Robert H. Gundry, *Matthew: A Commentary on His Handbook for a Mixed Church under Persecution*, 2nd ed. (Grand Rapids, MI: Eerdmans, 1994), 226.

34. Of interest to the reader of Greek is that the word "destroy" (ἀπολέσωσιν, *apolesōsin*) in Mark and Matthew is in the subjunctive mood (connoting *probability*), while in Luke 6, "do" (ποιήσαιεν, *poiēsaien*) is in the optative mood (connoting *possibility*). In this instance, there is no appreciable difference in meaning.

35. Many scholars, perhaps a slight majority, think John 4:46b–54 presents another version of the same story. The similarities are interesting: The one who is sick is in Capernaum, and a person of rank in Capernaum asks Jesus to heal one for whom he cares and that is near death with sickness. Jesus heals the person from a distance. The healing occurs toward the beginning of Jesus's ministry. John 4:54 says this was the second sign Jesus did while in Galilee, the first being when he turned water into wine (2:1–11; 4:46). But there are many differences: In John, the one entreating is "a certain royal official" (τις βασιλικὸς, *tis basilikos*) rather than a centurion, and the person sick is his son rather than his slave. The official leaves Capernaum, goes to Jesus in Cana, and asks him to come to Capernaum rather than make the request when Jesus was in Capernaum. The royal official wants Jesus to come to his house, whereas the centurion regards himself unworthy for Jesus to come to his house. Also, Jesus does not commend

the official for his faith. If the healing in John is a separate event, it could be included in Matt. 4:23–25. A few scholars favoring the same event are Blomberg, *Historical Reliability of John's Gospel*, 107; Raymond E. Brown, *The Gospel according to John (I–XII): Introduction, Translation, and Notes*, ABC 29 (1966; repr., New Haven, CT; London: Yale University Press, 2008), Logos 6, 193; and Craig A. Evans, *Matthew*, NCBC (New York: Cambridge University Press, 2012), 186. Ben Witherington, III (*John's Wisdom: A Commentary on the Fourth Gospel* [Louisville, KY: Westminster John Knox, 1995], 127) favors a different event, while Keener (*Gospel of John*, 1:632) does not take a position. Blomberg writes, "If they are variant accounts of the same event, as I have tentatively favoured, then ... we have a good example of the freedom that John felt to bring out different details and emphases in stories already commonly known from early Christian oral tradition, if not from the final form of the Synoptics themselves" (*Historical Reliability of John's Gospel*, 107).

36. See Aland, *Synopsis of the Four Gospels*, pericope #90/136. This pericope is not assessed in the present volume.

37. A few plausible explanations exist for the difference, but they are speculative. See Darrell L. Bock, *Luke 9:51–24:53*, BECNT (Grand Rapids, MI: Baker Academic, 1996), 782–84; and Davies and Allison, *Commentary on the Gospel according to Saint Matthew*, 2:78–79.

38. See pericope #7 below.

39. The word count is the number of Greek words, including definite articles. Luke uses 293 words in his parallel narrative (Luke 8:26–39).

40. Willoughby C. Allen, *A Critical and Exegetical Commentary on the Gospel according to St Matthew*, 3rd ed., ICC (Edinburgh: T&T Clark, 1912), Logos 6, 84.

41. Mark 5:23: "is at the point of death" (lit. "finally has," ἐσχάτως ἔχει, *eschatōs echei*); Luke 8:42: "was dying" (ἀπέθνῃσκεν, *apethnēsken*).

42. Matt. 9:18: "just now died" (ἄρτι ἐτελεύτησεν, *arti eteleutēsen*).

43. More examples of an evangelist changing a question to a statement or vice versa will be provided in the text below. A few additional examples in the Gospels that will not be cited are Mark 2:7 // Luke 5:21 // Matt. 9:3; Mark 2:18 // Matt. 9:14 // Luke 5:33; Mark 4:28 // Matt. 8:25 // Luke 8:24; Mark 8:12b // Matt. 16:4; Mark 12:24 // Matt. 22:29; and Mark 14:12–17 // Matt. 26:17–20 // Luke 22:7–14.

44. For a number of these, see Darrell L. Bock, *Luke 9:51–24:53*, BECNT (Grand Rapids, MI: Baker Academic, 1996), 1502–4.

45. Mark 10:13–52 // Luke 18:15–43: the little children and Jesus, the rich and the kingdom of God, Jesus predicts his death, the request of James and John (absent in Luke), and a blind beggar receives sight. The location (Jericho), the context in which the story appears in Mark and Matthew, and the verbal agreement between the two accounts make it clear that Matthew is not narrating a different event.

46. Luke states the purpose of his Gospel in 1:3: "to write for you in an orderly manner" (καθεξῆς σοι γράψαι, *kathexēs soi grapsai*). In the New Testament and LXX,

only Luke uses the term "orderly" (καθεξῆς, *kathexēs*) (Luke 1:3; 8:1; Acts 3:24; 11:4; 18:23). In the Apostolic Fathers, see 1 Clem. 37:3; Mart. Pol. 22:3. Many have understood Luke to mean he intended to narrate events with a keener interest in their precise chronology than had previous authors who wrote about Jesus. Although the term usually refers to a successive chronological order, an examination of what Luke proceeds to do in Luke and Acts allows us to rule out such a meaning in Luke 1:3. More than the other Synoptic Gospels, Luke narrates events using an unstated chronology where Mark or Matthew are specific (e.g., cf. Mark 4:35 with Luke 8:22). Moreover, we can sometimes observe Luke breaking up tradition and placing portions in a different context (e.g., cf. Mark 9:33–49 // Matt. 18:1–22 with Luke 9:46–50 and 17:1–4). That Luke has done this here is evident from the editorial fatigue present in Luke 17:2, where Luke mentions "one of these little ones." However, there are no "little ones" in this context. In fact, the closest references to a child are in Luke 11:11–13; 18:15. Marshall suggests Luke is thinking in terms of arranging events in a broad rather than precise chronological order (I. H. Marshall, *The Gospel of Luke: A Commentary on the Greek Text*, NIGTC [Carlisle: Paternoster; Grand Rapids, MI: Eerdmans, 1978], Logos 6, 43). If this is all Luke had in mind in 1:3, he was not distinguishing his account from those who had written before him (1:1–2), since Luke's order is quite similar to Mark's. Bock thinks Luke means chronological, geographical ("from Galilee, to Samaria, Jerusalem, Judea-Samaria, and then Rome"), and "salvation-historical in that it shows the progress of salvation under God's direction. ... Thus, the order of Luke's account works on many levels. It is broadly chronological and geographic, and deals with sacred history" (Bock, *Luke 9:51–24:53*, 62–63). Joseph Fitzmyer understands Luke to be referring to "a systematic presentation; that is a veiled reference to the Period of Israel, the Period of Jesus, and the Period of the Church" (Joseph A. Fitzmyer, *Gospel according to Luke I–IX: Introduction, Translation, and Notes*, ABC 28 [1970; repr., New Haven, CT: Yale University Press, 2008], Logos 6, 299).

47. The location (Jericho), the context in which the story appears in Mark and Matthew, and the verbal agreement between the two accounts make it clear that Matthew is not narrating a different event.

48. Craig S. Keener, *Matthew*, IVPNTC 1 (Downers Grove, IL: InterVarsity Press, 1997), 306–7.

49. In Matt. 9:27 they were following Jesus, whereas they were sitting beside the road in 20:30. In 9:28, they followed Jesus into a house, whereas Jesus summoned them to come to him on the road in 20:32.

50. We previously read of Cyrene. After learning of Pompey's death, Cato took command of Pompey's fleet and sailed to Cyrene. See pericope #28 in chapter 3.

51. Collins (*Mark*, 734) writes, "The mention of Simon of Cyrene is likely to be historical reminiscence. The memory of his forced service was maintained because his sons, Alexander and Rufus, were known to the earliest audiences of the

narrative. The fact that Mark retains the reference to the sons suggests that they were known to the evangelist and to at least some members of his audiences."

52. The mention of spending 200 denarii for food is doubly attested by Mark 6:37 and John 6:7, although mentioned differently in each. Thus, it appears to have been an element in the story Matthew and Luke chose to omit.

53. Luke does not narrate Jesus walking on water but transitions to a different story that is not chronologically linked to what precedes it.

54. The Plain of Gennesaret was quite fertile and produced fruits such as walnuts, olives, figs, grapes, and vegetables. In Jesus's time, the Sea of Gennesaret and the Sea of Tiberias were alternate names for the Sea of Galilee (Luke 5:1; 1 Macc. 11:67; John 6:1; 21:1). W. A. Elwell and B. J. Beitzel, "Gennesaret," in *BEB*, 856; Douglas R. Edwards, "Gennesaret (Place)" in *AYBD*, 2:963.

55. And Capernaum is where the people found Jesus (John 6:24–25).

56. Paul J. Achtemeier ("Toward the Isolation of Pre-Markan Miracle Catenae," *JBL* 89, no. 3 [1970]: 265–91), argues that the feeding of the five thousand and Jesus's walking on water were independent stories that Mark connected artificially in a sandwiching fashion with the walking (6:45–51a) sandwiched between 6:44 and 6:53, and 6:51b–52 serving to link the stories (281–84). This could explain why Luke does not mention Jesus's walking on water after the feeding. However, Achtemeier's solution, though possible, does not adequately account for the same connection of the feeding and the walking on water in John, who is typically regarded as being independent of Mark.

57. Evans and Marcus hold the latter. See Evans, *Matthew*, 353; Joel Marcus, *Mark 8–16: A New Translation with Introduction and Commentary*, ABC 27A (New Haven, CT: Yale University Press, 2009), Logos 6, 747. I prefer the former option, since Mark elsewhere does not hesitate to report Jesus's disciples in a less than attractive light (e.g., 4:40; 8:17, 33; 9:32; 10:13–15; 14:37–42, 50, 66–72).

58. Most scholars regard Matthew's use of "heaven" as a circumlocution* for where Mark and Luke render "God," since many Jews of that time resisted uttering the name of God out of respect. For a few examples, compare Matt. 4:17 // Mark 1:15; Matt. 5:3 // Luke 6:20; Matt. 11:12 // Luke 16:16; Matt. 13:24 // Mark 4:26; Matt. 13:31 // Mark 4:30 // Luke 13:18; Matt. 13:33 // Luke 13:20–21; Matt. 19:14; cf. 18:3 // Mark 10:14–15 // Luke 18:16–17; Matt. 19:21–23 // Mark 10:23–24 // Luke 18:24–25.

59. Luke does not report Jesus cursing the fig tree.

60. This phrase also appears in Luke 5:17 and 8:22 but nowhere else in the New Testament.

61. This is more than a *quid pro quo*, for they may find the answer to their question by recognizing that John baptized on God's authority and prepared the way for Jesus (Mark 9:11–13 // Matt. 17:10–13; cf. 11:12–14; John 1:32–36).

62. This is not the place to discuss the authenticity of this logion of Jesus. However, whether Jesus said it here or John has displaced it from another context,

paraphrased, then transplanted it at the beginning of Jesus's ministry, there seems to be a historical kernel behind it, given Mark 14:58; 15:29, and Acts 6:13–14. John 2:11–13 describes Jesus's turning water into wine as the beginning of the signs (σημείων, *sēmeiōn*) he performed in Cana (the second occurred later in John 4:46–54), and Jesus left there and went to Capernaum, where he stayed for only a few days. From there, he went to Jerusalem for the Passover and cleansed the temple. Accordingly, when John 2:23 speaks of the people believing in him because of the *signs* (σημείων, *sēmeiōn*) he was doing, it suggests he is referring to the same event in the Synoptics and has displaced it. See Luke 19:37, where the people were praising God during Jesus's triumphal entry because of the miracles (δυνάμεων, *dunameōn*) they had witnessed. John 12:17–18 tells us the people went to see Jesus during his triumphal entry because they had heard he raised Lazarus from the dead.

63. Blomberg (*Historical Reliability of John's Gospel*, 175) opines that Mark and John are "almost certainly referring to the same event" and that "Mark has thematically relocated (and Matthew has simply copied him) what John narrates in its correct chronological sequence" in order to foreshadow Jesus's death more closely to the event itself. Witherington likewise thinks "Mark may have placed this story here for theological reasons . . . [and] the Johannine placement of the story in Bethany prior to the triumphal entry seems historically more probable" (Ben Witherington, III, *The Gospel of Mark: A Socio-Rhetorical Commentary* [Grand Rapids, MI: Eerdmans, 2001], 366).

64. Fitzmyer thinks the story of a woman anointing Jesus at a dinner setting assumed various forms in the oral tradition about Jesus (*Gospel according to Luke I–IX*, 686), while Marshall regards the anointing in Luke as a different event (*Gospel of Luke*, 306).

65. Blomberg (*Historical Reliability of John's Gospel*, 176, 176n259), Brown (*Gospel according to John [I–XII]*, 449–53), Evans (*Matthew*, 425), and Witherington (*Gospel of Mark*, 365) think Luke is reporting a separate event and that some of the details have cross-pollinated. This may especially be observed when reading the anointing in John (see pericope #12 in chap. 4).

66. So also Luke 7:37.

67. It is of interest that, in Mark // Matthew, Jesus said the woman's act of kindness would be taught all over the world in memory of her, while her name is only mentioned in John. Why not mention her name? Richard Bauckham observes three instances in which persons who are anonymous elsewhere are named in John. He asserts there is little evidence of a tendency to invent and add names to the tradition prior to the fourth century. It is more likely that Mark was preserving the story using anonymous persons in order to protect them. By the time John's Gospel was written, there was no longer a need to protect the identity of the anonymous figures since they had died by then. See Richard Bauckham, *Jesus and the Eyewitnesses: The Gospels as Eyewitness Testimony* (Grand Rapids, MI: Eerdmans, 2006), 194–97.

68. It is possible that "Simon the leper" was deceased or had been healed by Jesus. See Blomberg, *Historical Reliability of John's Gospel*, 176n259; Evans, *Matthew*, 425; Keener, *Gospel of John*, 2:863.

69. Preferring John's chronology over Mark's is Blomberg, *Historical Reliability of John's Gospel*, 175; Marcus, *Mark 8–16*, 932, and Witherington (note 63 above).

70. In Lucian, *How to Write History*, 67.

71. Michael Chung ("A Bracketed Bethany Anointing," *BBR* 25, no. 3 [2015]: 359–69) likewise argues that John has changed the day. However, he gets there by another route, arguing that John has moved the anointing and placed it in the middle of a sandwich "to add emphasis to the overall message of the Jewish leaders' desire to kill Lazarus" (362).

72. A Roman pound (λίτραν, *litran*) was slightly less than 12 US ounces or 324 grams. See Keener, *Gospel of John*, 2:862.

73. The term appears only here in the New Testament, LXX, Apostolic Fathers, Josephus, and Philo.

74. In Luke 7:37, it is an alabaster flask of nonspecified ointment without a general or specific monetary value assigned to it.

75. So also Luke 7:38. Moreover, in John 12:3, she anointed his feet and wiped them with her hair, whereas in Luke 7:38 she wet his feet with her tears, wiped them with her hair, kissed, and anointed them.

76. Matthew 26:21 and John 13:21 omit "eating with me" and John 13:21 renders "truly, truly" for emphasis.

77. See also Matt. 26:64; 27:11; Mark 15:2; Luke 23:3.

78. Most scholars think Paul wrote 1 Corinthians sometime between 52 and 56 CE and date Luke's Gospel between 70 to 85 CE, although some date it to between the late 50s and very early 60s. Fewer still are those who date it after 85. Thus, we may say that Luke's Gospel was written between five to thirty-five years after Paul wrote 1 Corinthians. Therefore, if Luke relies on oral tradition at this point, it is remarkable to observe how well the integrity of the tradition had been preserved by the time Luke used it!

79. Mark has "kingdom of God" whereas Matthew renders "kingdom of my Father," which appears only here (Matt. 26:29). Elsewhere, Matthew similarly uses "kingdom of their Father" (13:43). Whereas "kingdom of God" is found in abundance in Mark and Luke, it is rare in John (3:3, 5) and only appears four times in Matthew (12:28; 19:24; 21:31, 43). By far, Matthew prefers "kingdom of heaven" (3:2; 4:17; 5:3, 10, 19 [2x], 20; 7:21; 8:11; 10:7; 11:11–12; 13:11, 24, 31, 33, 44–45, 47, 52; 16:19; 18:1, 3–4, 23; 19:12, 14, 23; 20:1; 22:2; 23:13; 25:1) and substitutes the term for "kingdom of God" in 4:17 // Mark 1:15 and 19:14 // Mark 10:14. There are additional differences in syntax and a few additional words in Matthew I have not mentioned.

80. Joseph A. Fitzmyer (*Gospel according to Luke X–XXIV: Introduction, Translation, and Notes*, ABC 28A [1985; repr., New Haven, CT: Yale University Press, 2008],

Logos 6, 1393) suggests the formula in 1 Corinthians // Luke derives from an Antiochene liturgy while the formula in Mark // Matthew derives from a Jerusalem liturgy.

81. One could argue that John is somewhat vague and does not explicitly link 13:2 with 13:1 chronologically. While such a reading is not impossible, it requires some forcing.

82. Bock (*Luke 9:51–24:53*, 2:1951–60) provides a nice overview of the main solutions proposed to account for this difference.

83. One can only guess the identity of the anonymous disciple. It may be the Beloved Disciple, but there is no requirement that it be.

84. Annas had been high priest prior to Caiaphas (Luke 3:2; Acts 4:6). He became high priest in 6 CE and remained in that office until deposed in 15 CE (Josephus, *Ant.* 18:26, 34). See Keener, *Gospel of John*, 2:1089.

85. In Mark and Matthew, Peter's accuser(s) address(ed) Peter, then others, then Peter again. In Luke, the accuser(s) address(ed) others, then Peter, then others. In John, all of Peter's accusers addressed him directly.

86. Harold Lindsell, *The Battle for the Bible* (Grand Rapids, MI: Zondervan, 1976), 174–76. Lindsell claims to have received this idea through personal communication with J. M. Cheney in 1965. Cheney went on to publish his hypothesis in Johnston M. Cheney, *The Life of Christ in Stereo: The Four Gospels Combined as One*, rev. ed. (Portland, OR: Western Baptist Seminary Press, 1969), 189–92, 257–58.

87. Gleason L. Archer, *Encyclopedia of Bible Difficulties* (Grand Rapids, MI: Zondervan, 1982), 339.

88. W. D. Davies and Dale C. Allison Jr., *A Critical and Exegetical Commentary on the Commentary on the Gospel according to Saint Matthew*, vol. 3, *Commentary on Matthew XIX–XXVIII*, ICC (London; New York: T&T Clark, 2004), Logos 6, 487, on comment related to Matt. 26:34, n. 36. See also Bruce M. Metzger, *A Textual Commentary on the Greek New Testament*, 2nd ed. (New York: American Bible Society, 1994), 96–98.

89. See Craig A. Evans, *Mark 8:27–16:20*, WBC 34B (Dallas, TX: Word, 2001), Logos 6, 402, who in support cites Aristophanes, *Eccl.* 390–91: "when the rooster calls the second time."

90. Collins, *Mark*, 672.

91. Perhaps Matthew and Luke had access to a source (i.e., Q) who narrated a command and they preferred the command over the question in Mark.

92. Mark // Matthew use "Power" as a circumlocution for "God." Luke's audience, probably a patron named Theophilus, was Greek. So Luke redacts Mark's circumlocution while preserving "power" and renders "powerful God" (τῆς δυνάμεως τοῦ θεοῦ, *tēs dunameōs tou theo*). See also note 58 above about Matthew's use of "heaven" versus Mark and Luke's use of "God."

93. Luke may engage in contextual translation elsewhere. In the story of Jesus healing a paralytic who has been lowered through the roof, Mark 2:4 says, "They removed the roof . . . having dug [it] out" (ἀπεστέγασαν τὴν στέγην, *apestegasan tēn stegēn* . . . ἐξορύξαντες, *exoruxantes*), whereas Luke 5:19 speaks of removing "tiles" (τῶν κεράμων, *tōn keramōn*) from the roof (see Robert H. Stein, *Difficult Passages in the New Testament: Interpreting Puzzling Texts in the Gospels and Epistles* [Grand Rapids, MI: Baker, 1990], 42–46). Fitzmyer writes, "The roof of the common Palestinian house was made of wooden beams placed across stone or mudbrick walls; the beams were covered with reeds, matted layers of thorns, and several inches of clay. It was sloped and usually rolled before the rainy season. Such a roof could have been dug through (see Mark 2:4). Luke, however, has changed the description, introducing the tiled roof of Hellenistic houses in the eastern Mediterranean area—making the action more intelligible to Greek-speaking Christian readers outside of the Palestinian context" (Fitzmyer, *Gospel according to Luke I–IX*, 582). Bock, however, does not think a discrepancy is necessarily present since τῶν κεράμων, *tōn keramōn*, can also mean clay, "and Luke may be describing the removed lumps of clay with a word that also indicated their function" (Bock, *Luke 9:51–24:53*, 1:480–81). And Marshall says tiled roofs existed in Palestine at that time (Marshall, *Gospel of Luke*, 213).

94. See Matt. 4:5–11 // Luke 4:5–13.

95. See pericope #15 that follows.

96. The Latin term for "skull" is *calvaria*, from which the English name "Calvary" is derived.

97. The comments on Mark's text by Craig A. Evans and R. T. France are of interest. According to Pliny the Elder (*Nat.* 14.15), wine mixed with myrrh was most esteemed among the Romans. France argues it was probably offered by sympathetic bystanders (b. Sanhedrin 43a) who were most likely part of Jesus's women followers in order to help with the pain. Joel Marcus agrees. Evans argues there is no evidence of the pain-relieving properties in myrrh and suggests the wine was probably offered by the soldiers as part of their mockery. This would be closer to the parallel account in Matt. 27:34. Davies and Allison agree. See Davies and Allison, *Commentary on the Gospel according to Saint Matthew*, 3:612–13; Evans, *Mark 8:27–16:20*, 500–501; R. T. France, *The Gospel of Mark: A Commentary on the Greek Text*, NIGTC (Grand Rapids, MI: Eerdmans; Carlisle: Paternoster, 2002), Logos 6, 642–43; Marcus, *Mark 8–16*, 1042–43.

98. Whereas οἶνος, *oinos*, was a general term for "wine," ὄξος, *oxos*, was a sour wine. It was more effective than water for relieving thirst and was a less expensive type used by people of low means and soldiers.

99. Bock, *Luke 9:51–24:53*, 1951.

100. Brown, *Gospel according to John (XIII–XXI)*, 555.

101. See, for example, Archer, *Encyclopedia of Bible Difficulties*, 363–64. Appealing to Pliny the Elder (*Nat.* 2.77), Archer suggests the Roman civil day began at midnight. Therefore, Jesus was brought before Pilate around the sixth hour (i.e., 6 a.m.), in agreement with John 19:14. This would fit nicely with Mark's claim that Jesus was crucified at the third hour (or 9 a.m. according to his timetable; Mark 15:25). At best, this proposal only accounts for the time discrepancy and does not touch on the different days. But it is doubtful that it solves the time discrepancy. When John 19:14 says it was about the sixth hour when Jesus was before Pilate, if the Gospels are correct, a lot had already taken place that morning before arriving at that point in the narrative. The first thing that morning, the Jewish leaders made plans concerning what to do with Jesus (Matt. 27:1 // Mark 15:1 // Luke 22:66), brought him before them, and questioned him (Luke 22:66-71). They then bound and led him to Pilate (Matt. 27:2 // Mark 15:1 // Luke 23:1 // John 18:28-29). The Jewish leaders accused Jesus before Pilate (Matt. 27:11-12 // Mark 15:2-3 // Luke 23:2-3, 5 // John 18:29, 19:12). Then Pilate and Jesus had a personal conversation (John 18:33-38). Pilate sent Jesus to Herod (Luke 23:6-7), who questioned and mocked Jesus before having him returned to Pilate (Luke 23:8-12). Pilate then had further interaction with the Jewish leaders and the crowd and offered to release a prisoner to them, hoping they would choose Jesus. But the crowd instead requested Barabbas (Luke 23:13-25 // John 18:39-40). Pilate then had Jesus scourged, after which the soldiers abused him. Then Pilate presented Jesus to the crowd and debated with the Jewish leaders over Jesus's fate (John 19:1-8). Pilate and Jesus then had a second personal conversation (John 19:9-11), after which Pilate debated with the Jewish leaders again (John 19:12-16). It is this final debate with the Jewish leaders that John says occurred around the sixth hour (i.e., 6 a.m.). Thus, in order for the proposal of different timetables to be correct, the ordeal had to begin *very* early that morning, well before 6 a.m. And it is doubtful that Pilate or Herod would have accommodated the Jewish leaders by getting up that early. In fact, Roman matters such as court often started at the third hour (i.e., 9 a.m.) (Martial, *Spect.* 4.8.2).

102. For a proponent of this view, see David Instone-Brewer, *Traditions of the Rabbis from the Era of the New Testament*, vol. 2A, *Feasts and Sabbaths: Passover and Atonement* (Grand Rapids, MI: Eerdmans, 2011), 115–200.

103. Harold W. Hoehner, *Chronological Aspects of the Life of Christ* (Grand Rapids, MI: Zondervan, 1977), 65–90.

104. For a proponent of this view, see Blomberg, *Historical Reliability of John's Gospel*, 187–88, 237–39, 246–47; and Bock, *Luke 9:51–24:53*, 2:1954–55, 2:1956. Blomberg observes that when specific times are provided in the Gospels and Acts, they almost always are said to have occurred at the third, sixth, or ninth hour. Accordingly, he proposes that the evangelists mentioned time within three-hour increments in keeping with Roman watches (Blomberg, *Historical Reliability of*

John's Gospel, 247). A specific hour is named in the Gospels and Acts: Mark 15:25, 33–34; Matt. 20:3, 5–6, 9; 27:45–46; Luke 23:44; Acts 2:15; 3:1; 10:3, 9, 30; 23:23; John 1:39; 4:6; 19:14. Admittedly, the number of occasions is limited at nineteen. The hours are mentioned as being the third, sixth, or ninth in all except Matt. 20:6, 9 (eleventh hour), and John 1:39 (tenth hour). Although military operations played a main part in the nine *Lives* of Plutarch we have examined, Plutarch does not make mention of specific time often: *Cat. Min.* 15.1 (third hour); *Ant.* 65.4 (sixth hour); *Ant.* 68.1 (tenth hour); *Crass.* 17.1 (twelfth hour); *Brut.* 36.2 (third watch); *Caes.* 43.3 (morning watch); *Pomp.* 68.3 (morning watch).

105. Stein, *Difficult Passages in the New Testament*, 65. Stein does not consider the view that follows in this volume.

106. For a proponent of this view, see Keener, *Gospel of John*, 2:1097–1103, 1129–31. Jesus is said to be the Passover Lamb elsewhere in the New Testament (1 Cor. 5:7; 1 Pet. 1:19). Bock (*Luke 9:51–24:53*, 1960) regards the position held by Keener to be a "likely alternative" to his own. Collins (*Mark*, 746–47), is undecided pertaining to whether Mark or John reports the correct day and suspects the precise timing may not have been known.

107. Plutarch, *Caes.* 11.1–3; Suetonius, *Jul.* 7; Cassius Dio, *Hist. rom.*37.52.2.

108. Pelling, *Plutarch and History*, 257. Pelling likewise suggests that Plutarch altered Caesar's weeping at the statue of Alexander to weeping when reading about him, since Plutarch's readers have just read about him and are now reading of Caesar. "The beginning of [Plutarch's] *Pericles* is explicit on the way in which written narrative is a more powerful incentive to virtue and achievement than any statue" (257).

109. Plutarch, *Caesar* (Pelling), 183, comments on 11.5–6.

110. See pericope #306/114/267. Evans (*Mark 8:27–16:20*) thinks John with Paul (1 Cor. 5:7) presents the correct chronology and that Mark has confused the day. Evans names several scholars who agree (369–72).

111. Archer, *Encyclopedia of Bible Difficulties*, 346.

112. "Chosen one" (ὁ ἐκλεκτός, *ho eklektos*). Earlier in Luke 9:35, God calls Jesus "my Son, my Chosen One" (ὁ υἱός μου ὁ ἐκλελεγμένος, *ho huios mou ho eklelegmenos*).

113. John adds that this was in fulfillment of Scripture. He probably had in mind Ps. 69:21 (68:22 LXX): "They gave me sour wine [ὄξους, *oxous*] for my thirst," and Ps. 22:15 (21:16 LXX): "My strength is dried up as a potsherd. My tongue sticks to my throat and you lay me in the dust of death."

114. Ps. 31:5.

115. In Mark 15:34, ελωι ελωι, *elōi elōi*, Eloi! Eloi! In Matt. 27:46, ηλι ηλι, *ēli ēli*, Eli! Eli! Evans (*Matthew*, 463) thinks "Matthew transliterates Jesus' words into Hebrew, perhaps to match the Hebrew text of Ps 22:1 but perhaps also to show more clearly why bystanders (v. 47) thought Jesus was calling out to Elijah (i.e., the sound of *eli* ['my God'] is closer to *elia* ['Elijah'], a shortened form of the prophet's name)."

116. Keener, *Gospel of John*, 1:52.

117. See also John 4:13–15; 6:35; 7:37.

118. See Daniel B. Wallace, "*Ipsissima Vox* and the Seven Words from the Cross: A Test Case for John's Use of the Tradition" (paper presented at the Annual Meeting of the Society of Biblical Literature Southwestern Region, Dallas, TX, 5 March 2000).

119. And John has done so while softening the tension created with what Jesus says earlier in John 16:32: "Behold, an hour is coming and has come that you will be scattered, each to his own home, and I will be alone. Yet I am not alone, because my Father is with me." However, this does not rule out Jesus feeling that even his Father had now abandoned him on the cross. If John is independent of the Synoptic tradition as many scholars hold, we may have multiple independent sources pertaining to this logion with Mark's version being closer to what Jesus may have uttered.

120. Much has been written pertaining to the other portents appearing in Matt. 27:51b–53. It is difficult to determine whether Matthew intended for his readers to understand these phenomena as historical events that had occurred in space-time or included them as "special effects" similar to what we observe in other literature of that era, whether Greco-Roman or Jewish, although I favor the latter option. See Licona, *Resurrection of Jesus*, 548–53. For taking this position, I was scolded on the Internet by some ultra-conservative Christians. In response, the *Southeastern Theological Review* 3, no. 1 (Summer 2012), provided several reviews of my book and had "A Roundtable Discussion with Michael Licona on *The Resurrection of Jesus: A New Historiographical Approach* (Danny Akin, Craig Blomberg, Paul Copan, Michael Kruger, Michael Licona, and Charles Quarles)" that discussed the "special effects" interpretation I had proposed (71–98). This roundtable discussion is available to view online at http://www.risenjesus.com/wp-content/uploads/a-roundtable-discussion-with-michael-licona-on-the-resurrection-of-jesus.pdf. Evans (*Matthew*, 466) regards Matt. 27:52–53 as "probably a post-Matthean gloss."

121. See similar altering of the order of the presentation of events in Matt. 4:5–10 // Luke 4:5–13 (pericope #20 in Aland, *Synopsis of the Four Gospels*) and Matt. 12:41–42 // Luke 11:31–32 (pericope #119 in Aland, *Synopsis of the Four Gospels*).

122. Although Jesus's appearances to Mary Magdalene, the Emmaus disciples, and the eleven disciples in Mark 16:9–20 have parallels in the other Gospels, I have not included that text in my analysis, since almost all scholars hold that Mark's Gospel ended at 16:8 and Mark 16:9–20 is spurious and was added later, perhaps in the second century. However, there is no consensus pertaining to why Mark ended his Gospel abruptly with the women fleeing from the tomb and saying nothing to anyone. Almost all scholars hold one of three positions: (1) Mark intended for his Gospel to end at 16:8; (b) he was unable

to complete it due to sickness, death, or imprisonment; or (c) the ending he wrote was lost.

123. Habermas is in the process of writing a massive work on Jesus's resurrection that will include this research.

124. Dale C. Allison Jr., *Resurrecting Jesus: The Earliest Christian Tradition and Its Interpreters* (New York: T&T Clark, 2005), 200.

125. See Licona, *Resurrection of Jesus*.

126. Gal. 1:18–19; 2:1–14; Acts 15:1–22; 21:18. On 1 Cor. 15:3–7 as oral tradition, its origin, and dating, see Licona, *Resurrection of Jesus*, 223–35.

127. See pericope #24 in chapter 3.

128. Similarly are Matt. 28:1, "at dawn" (lit. "the beginning": τῇ ἐπιφωσκούσῃ, *tē epiphōskousē*), and Luke 24:1, "at early dawn" (ὄρθρου βαθέως, *opthrou batheōs*).

129. See Mark 1:35 // Luke 4:42 (#39 in Aland, *Synopsis of the Four Gospels*) for a similar difference in the times given.

130. Evans (*Mark 8:27–16:20*, 534) suggests either a textual corruption with an οὔπω, *oupō* ("not yet")—i.e., the sun having *not yet* risen—having dropped out of the text or a mistranslation of an original Aramaic tradition that connects "the sun having risen" in 16:2 instead of with the beginning of 16:3: "the sun having risen, they were saying to one another, 'Who will for us roll away the stone from the tomb's entrance?'"

131. See appendix 3 for a detailed comparison of the women present at the scenes of Jesus's crucifixion, burial, and empty tomb.

132. Here the word "acquaintances" is masculine in the Greek: πάντες οἱ γνωστοὶ αὐτῷ. *pantes hoi gnōstoi autō* (lit. "all those known to him").

133. There is some dispute over whether Luke 24:12 was part of Luke's original text. The RSV omitted the verse, but the NRSV, along with almost all English translations, has included it. Metzger (*Textual Commentary on the Greek New Testament*, 157–58) explains why the textual committee included it and assigned it a certainty grade of "B." The textual notes for Luke 24:12 in the NET says that "the MS evidence for omission is far too slight for the verse to be rejected as secondary. It is included in P[75] and the rest of the MS tradition." (P[75] is one of the earliest manuscripts of the Gospel of Luke and is dated to the early third century.)

134. See Mark 9:3; Matt. 28:3; John 20:12; Acts 1:10; 10:30. See also Dan. 7:9; 2 Macc. 3:26, 33; 2 En. 1:4–11; Gos. Pet. 36, 55; Joseph. *Ant.* 5:277. At his transfiguration, Jesus's clothing became intensely white (Mark 9:2–3 // Matt. 17:1–2 // Luke 9:28–29).

135. Indeed, this is what we read in Luke 24:3–4, that after entering the tomb, the women "did not find the body of the Lord Jesus. And while they were perplexed about this, two men in dazzling clothing suddenly appeared near them."

136. The phrase does not appear in the Apostolic Fathers, Philo, or Josephus. It is also absent in Plutarch. It appears in Athenaeus, *Deipn.* 11.97 [497d], a third-century

CE Greek rhetorician who quotes from the Epigrams of Hedylus, in which readers are invited to enter the temple of Arsinoe and drink wine. The phrase also appears in the pseudepigraphal *Acts of Pilate* 13.1, which has borrowed directly from Matthew and has the same meaning. John Wenham suggests the invitation of Matthew's angel to "Come! See" "is not an invitation to enter the tomb, but to put away their fears and take a close look at the grave space (now empty save for burial linen)" (John Wenham, *Easter Enigma: Are the Resurrection Accounts in Conflict?* [1992; repr., Eugene, OR: Wipf & Stock, 2005], 86). The use of the phrase in Ps. 45:9 (LXX) gives plausibility to such an explanation. However, read most naturally, Matthew's narrative suggests the angel was sitting on the large stone outside of the tomb when issuing the invitation to enter the tomb and see the place once occupied by Jesus's corpse. While a natural reading is by no means decisive, since all historians are select in the details they report, it is unlikely that the women, while inside the tomb, had to be directed to the particular spot where Jesus had been laid. Although many tombs were hewn to accommodate the remains of an entire family, the women had observed Jesus's burial, and Jesus had been the first and only person to have been buried in that tomb at that time (Luke 23:53; Matt. 27:60; John 19:41). Moreover, Luke 24:3 says that, after entering the tomb, the women "did not find the body of the Lord Jesus." Accordingly, they apparently knew where it had been laid.

137. Luke 2:9, 38; 10:40; 20:1; 21:34; 28:2. Moreover, the term derives from ἵστημι, *histēmi*, which is often used in the sense of being in a static position. There are twenty-six occurrences of ἵστημι, *histēmi*, in Luke's Gospel and thirty-five in Acts (Luke 1:11; 4:9; 5:1, 2; 6:8 [2x], 17; 7:14, 38; 8:20, 44; 9:27, 47; 11:18; 13:25; 17:12; 18:11, 13, 40; 19:8; 21:36; 23:10, 35, 49; 24:17, 36; Acts 1:11, 23; 2:14; 3:8; 4:7, 14; 5:20, 23, 25, 27; 6:6, 13; 7:33, 55, 56, 60; 8:38; 9:7; 10:30; 11:13; 12:14; 16:9; 17:22, 31; 21:40; 22:25, 30; 24:20, 21; 25:10, 18; 26:6, 16, 22; 27:21). Luke employs ἵστημι, *histēmi*, in the sense of "stopped" (Luke 5:2; 7:14; 8:44; 18:40; 19:8; 24:17; Acts 8:38; similar to a soldier's response when ordered to "stand down"), being stationary or in a fixed position (Luke 7:38), to be present (Luke 9:27), to put forward (Acts 1:23), to remain intact (Luke 11:18), and to appoint or hold to one's account (Acts 7:60; 17:31). In Luke 7:38 while Jesus is reclining to eat in the house of Simon the Pharisee, an immoral woman stood (στᾶσα, *stasa*) behind him and wet his feet with her tears, dried them with her hair, kissed them, and anointed them with perfume. Since Jesus is reclining, it is difficult to interpret the woman's position of στᾶσα, *stasa*, as "standing erect" while she is honoring Jesus. She would need to be an extraordinary gymnast to kiss his feet while standing erect! The meaning of remaining in a particular location is to be preferred. Of the sixty-one occurrences of ἵστημι, *histēmi*, in Luke/Acts, 16 percent refer to being stopped, in a stationary or fixed position, present, or together (Luke 5:2; 7:14, 38; 8:44; 9:27; 11:18; 18:40; 19:8; 24:17; Acts 8:38).

138. See Mark 14:28.
139. See Matt. 26:32.
140. See Luke 18:31–33.
141. Luke 24:5 (ἐμφόβων, *emphobōn*) agrees with Matt. 28:5.
142. That another source is behind Luke's account may be suggested by Luke's inclusion of Joanna and "the other women with them," who are not mentioned in the parallel accounts by Mark // Matthew. Moreover, Mark // Matthew do not include some of the disciples running to the tomb or some of the appearances in Jerusalem, which are all mentioned by Luke and John. And only Luke includes Jesus's appearance to the Emmaus disciples.
143. Wenham, *Easter Enigma*, 84–85, esp. 88.
144. Wenham (*Easter Enigma*) engages in a commendable effort to harmonize the many differences in the resurrection narratives by conflating all four Gospels into a single, coherent account. He regards his attempts as "reasoned conjecture" and disciplined imagination (122). See also Archer, *Encyclopedia of Bible Difficulties*, 347–56, for a similar effort to harmonize the resurrection narratives via extensive conflation. Because one historian often selects material another may not find as important or as interesting, we should not expect that parallel accounts will always include the same details. Accordingly, harmonizing the accounts through conflation is a reasonable exercise. However, as observed in pericope #14 above, such efforts to harmonize parallel accounts can go too far. Although the overall renditions offered by Wenham and Archer are not impossible, their solutions include numerous elements that require either straining the texts or ignoring details that resist being harmonized with others. For the present discrepancy being considered, Wenham proposes that the women to whom Jesus appeared in Matt. 28:8–10 were Salome and Mary the mother of James the Younger and did not include Mary Magdalene, since according to John, she alone had run to tell the disciples Jesus's body was gone (Wenham, *Easter Enigma*, 95–96). Blomberg, (*Historical Reliability of John's Gospel*, 261) thinks Mary Magdalene may have gone ahead of the other women to the tomb, saw it empty, and ran to inform the disciples before the other women arrived and saw the angels. Yet these scenarios are not at all the impression readers receive when reading Matt. 28:1–10. Moreover, it does not square with Luke 24:1–12, since Peter ran to the tomb when the women (including Mary Magdalene; vv. 9–10) made the announcement to the disciples. Wenham thinks Luke has conflated the announcement of Mary Magdalene with a separate announcement by Joanna and the other women who were with her (Wenham, *Easter Enigma*, 89). Archer likewise imagines Mary Magdalene separating herself from Salome and the other Mary while they are returning to inform the male disciples. He then imagines Mary Magdalene returning to the tomb a second time (per John). When the angels delivered the message of Jesus's resurrection to her during the first visit, she did not comprehend it. Therefore, she

thought the gardener might have reburied Jesus's body. After she encounters Jesus during the second visit, she runs to inform his male disciples but does not see Salome and the other Mary, who are now returning to the tomb for a second visit when they encounter Jesus for the first time (Archer, *Encyclopedia of Bible Difficulties*, 348–50). This is quite creative, but it goes against the text that has the women encountering Jesus for the first time while they are fleeing from the tomb rather than going to it (Matt. 28:8–9). Accordingly, I see no reason for employing both the degree and frequency of conflation required by the proposals of Wenham and Archer, instead being more persuaded that one or more of the evangelists have creatively reconstructed the events of that watershed Sunday morning and the weeks that followed. Darrell L. Bock comments, "The exact sequence of resurrection events remains obscure because of the variety of witnesses to the event and the variety of perspectives from which the details are presented. It is possible to harmonize the traditions, but it is evident that literary variation is required to see a fit" (Bock, *Luke 9:51–24:53*, 1888).

145. Little weight was given to a woman's testimony in antiquity, including first-century Judaism (Joseph. *Ant.* 4.8.15 [or 4.219 per Loeb citation numbering]; b. Rosh Hashanah 1.8; Plutarch, *Publ.* 8.4; Justinian, *Inst.* 2.10.6; *Sipra VDDeho. pq.* 7.45.1.1. I am indebted to Craig Keener for the latter three references.). Indeed, Celsus, who wrote an attack on Christianity titled *The True Word*, noted that the person supposed to have seen the risen Jesus was a "frenzied woman" (γυνὴ πάροιστρος, *gunē paroistros*). Celsus's book is no longer extant but has been preserved almost in its entirety in Origen's *Contra Celsum*. Celsus's reference to Mary Magdalene as a "frenzied woman" is in *Cels.* 2.55 (Greek text taken from Origenes [Origen], *Contra Celsum Libri VIII*, 127 [Marcovich]).

146. William Lane Craig proposes, "There was no running account of all the appearances, just separate stories. Different evangelists knew or chose different stories. This is one reason why the course of events is so difficult to reconstruct" (William Lane Craig, *Assessing the New Testament Evidence for the Historicity of the Resurrection of Jesus*, Studies in the Bible and Early Christianity 16 [Lewiston, NY: Edwin Mellen Press, 1989], 258). Craig thinks that since Matthew did not include the women reporting the empty tomb and the angel's message to the disciples and their trip to the tomb, Jesus's appearance to Mary Magdalene and the other Mary "gives the illusion that the appearance occurred before the women reached the disciples, which Luke and John tell us is not so. The appearance did not occur until the disciples and women had all returned to the tomb" (256). This is possible. However, differences are still present, such as the following: (1) Jesus appears to the women during their trip to tell the disciples in Matthew, whereas it is at the tomb in John. (2) The demeanor of the women when Jesus appears to them differs. In Matt. 28:8, they had left the tomb quickly "with fear and great joy," whereas Mary Magdalene is weeping with sorrow in John 20:11–15. (3) Jesus's message to the women differs slightly.

147. See pericope #4 in this chapter.

148. Mark 16:8: οὐδενὶ οὐδὲν εἶπαν, *oudeni ouden eipan*; Mark 1:44: μηδενὶ μηδὲν εἴπῃς, *mēdeni mēden eipēs*.

149. Wenham, *Easter Enigma*, 106; and Archer, *Encyclopedia of Bible Difficulties*, 356.

150. See, for example, Craig L. Blomberg, *Matthew: An Exegetical and Theological Exposition of Holy Scripture*, NAC 22 (Nashville, TN: Broadman & Holman, 1992), Logos 6, 427–28.

151. Some scholars have suggested that the "going before" (προάγει, *proagei*) in Mark // Matthew is not to be understood in a chronological sense that Jesus will arrive in Galilee prior to his disciples but is referring to Jesus's leadership by gathering together his scattered flock in Galilee (Davies and Allison, *Commentary on the Gospel according to Saint Matthew*, 3:486). He will recommission them there and send them out to continue his ministry (Nolland, *Gospel of Matthew*, 1090). Others see both meanings present: "going before" and "leading them there" (Evans, *Mark 8:27–16:20*, 537–38). Given the reasons stated above, it is difficult to imagine the chronological sense being absent. It is plausible that Matthew (perhaps reflecting Mark's lost ending, since Mark's narrative infers an initial appearance in Galilee) has compressed and telescoped the events after Jesus's resurrection and redacted certain elements in order to render a coherent account. Accordingly, the "going before" (προάγει, *proagei*) in this context would possess a surface meaning of "going before," but the meaning of "leading" could likewise be present in order to carry the symbolism of Jesus gathering his scattered flock in Galilee and continuing his ministry.

152. It is possible to understand "the others" who doubted in Matt. 28:17 as some who were not part of the apostolic group. But this is not the impression readers of Matthew get, since no others are mentioned.

153. The term carries the same sense in Mark 9:24, where a man says to Jesus, "I believe. Help my unbelief" (ἀπιστίᾳ, *apistia*). It is obvious that "unbelief" in this context is not absolute but, much like Peter's doubt, includes some belief.

154. While scholars disagree on the extent to which John was familiar with the Synoptics, a very large majority of scholars agree that Luke used Mark's Gospel extensively though not exclusively.

155. Witherington, *John's Wisdom*, 331. Raymond Brown thinks John has creatively foreshadowed the ascension (*Gospel according to John [XIII–XXI]*, 1012, 1014–15). We might also interpret Jesus as saying, "Stop clinging to me. I have not yet ascended and will be around for a while. So hurry now and tell my disciples that I have risen." This option is also entertained by Bruce, *Gospel and Epistles of John*, 389; and J. H. Bernard, *A Critical and Exegetical Commentary on the Gospel according to St. John*, vol. 2, ed. A. H. McNeile (New York: Scribner, 1929), Logos 6, 670.

156. Luke describes the Pentecost event in Acts 2.

157. G. R. Beasley-Murray, *John*, WBC 36 (Dallas, TX: Word, 2002), Logos 6, 382; Brown, *Gospel according to John (XIII–XXI)*, 1023, 1030; and Keener, *Gospel of John*, 2:1199–1200, cf. 1194–95. Witherington (*John's Wisdom*) thinks John 20:22 "portrays a prophetic sign act or parable on a par with the sort of gesture we saw Jesus perform in John 13 when he washed the disciples' feet. The gesture then does not entail an actual bestowal of the Holy Spirit at that moment" (340) but foreshadows the equipping for ministry (341). Blomberg (*Historical Reliability of John's Gospel*, 266–67) regards as separate events Jesus's breathing on his disciples in John and the bestowing of the Holy Spirit at Pentecost.

158. Bock, *Luke 9:51–24:53*, 1944. On 1944n22, he likewise notes that ἕως, *heōs* can refer to "the area of."

159. There are no reports of a *Life of Simon Peter* or a *Life of John the Baptist* being written.

160. See esp. pericopes #32 and #33 in chapter 3.

161. That the evangelists crafted or creatively reconstructed some peripheral details on occasion seems likely. In Matt. 10:29, Jesus asks, "Are not two sparrows sold for a penny," while Luke 12:6 renders it as "Are not five sparrows sold for two pennies?" Perhaps Matthew, Luke, or the oral tradition from which they drew knew the concept and general details behind Jesus's teaching and crafted some of the precise details. One may also compare the location where Jesus informs Peter he will deny him three times before the night is over. In Mark 14:26–32 // Matt 26:30–36, Jesus and his disciples had left the room where they had just eaten the Last Supper and went to the Mount of Olives. It is there and before they entered Gethsemane that Jesus informs Peter he will deny him three times. However, in Luke 22:31–39, it occurs before they go to the Mount of Olives. And in John 13:33–38; 18:1, it is while they are eating the Last Supper. It may be that the relative rather than the specific time was remembered when Jesus predicted Peter would deny him thrice and the evangelists felt free to locate it where they thought most appropriate or desirable. Keener comments that John's account differs due to "John's literary artistry" (*Gospel of John*, 2:927) while Brown (*Gospel according to John [XIII–XXI]*, 609) regards John's account as a "composite" of material the Synoptics locate at the Last Supper and themes unique to John, such as "glorification, departure, fraternal love." Brown asserts that it is difficult to determine how much of the material "belongs in the historical setting of the Last Supper and how much has been imported from the public ministry." Consider also Peter's accusers in pericope #14 above.

CHAPTER 5

1. See pericope #32 in chapter 3 and pericopes #7, 10, 12, and 15 in chapter 4. Also, this chapter is an expanded version of a paper titled "Synthetic Chronological Placement in Ancient Biographical Literature" that I read in the "Synoptic

Gospels: Issues in the Gospels" section of the Annual Meeting of the Evangelical Theological Society in Atlanta, Georgia, on 18 November 2015. Craig Blomberg and Darrell Bock read response papers (see bibliography). Although I was not in agreement with all of their criticisms, I found several of them quite helpful and have updated this chapter accordingly.

2. Lucian, *How to Write History*, 55 (translation mine, from chap. 4).

3. It is likewise possible that Caesar's offering his neck was a floating anecdote that Plutarch has linked to the procession in *Caesar* and the Lupercalia event in *Antony*. In any sense, synthetic chronological placement is involved.

4. See Plutarch, *Caesar* (Pelling), 448–49, comments related to 60.4 and 60.6.

5. Plutarch, *Caesar* (Pelling), 448, comment on 60.4.

6. Suetonius, *Jul.* 7; Cassius Dio, *Hist. rom.* 37.52.2; and Plutarch, *Caes.* 11.1–3. See pericope #15 in chapter 4.

7. See chapter 3, pericope #11.

8. I am indebted to John Ramsey for providing this example and the one that follows.

9. Catiline, quoted in Cicero, *Defence Speeches*, trans. D. H. Berry, Oxford World Classics (Oxford: Oxford University Press, 2000), 90.

10. Cicero, *Mur.* 25.51. For the date, see Michael C. Alexander, "Trials in the Late Roman Republic, 149 BC to 50 BC," *Phoenix*, suppl. vol. 26 (1990): 111–12. Consular elections were usually held in July and the winners assumed their office on 1 January of the following year.

11. John Ramsey (e-mail message to author, 14 November 2015).

12. See J. T. Ramsey, ed., *Sallust's* Bellum Catilinae, 2nd ed., American Philological Association Texts and Commentaries (Oxford: Oxford University Press, 2006), 117, note on §20.1.

13. Regarding the location for the delivery of Catiline's remarks, Sallust said, "He withdrew to an out-of-the-way room in the house, and there, after sending far away all witnesses, he delivered a speech of this sort" (*Cat.* 20.1, Rolfe/Ramsey, LCL).

14. The Latin text "*contione domestica*" is taken from Cicero, *In Catilinam 1–4. Pro Murena. Pro Sulla. Pro Flacco*, trans. C. Macdonald, Loeb Classical Library 324 (Cambridge: Harvard University Press, 1977), but the translation provided is from John Ramsey (e-mail message to author, 14 November 2015).

15. John Ramsey (e-mail message to author, 14 November 2015).

16. Quintilian, *Institutio Oratoria*, 1:255.

17. Ronald Mellor, *The Roman Historians* (London: Routledge, 1999), 93.

18. John Ramsey (e-mail message to author, 12 November 2015).

19. Matthew does not prefer to narrate events in the free-floating manner we often observe in Mark and especially in Luke.

20. See also Mark 3:1; 6:7.

21. See chapter 4, pericope #12 (Mark 14:3–9 // Matt. 26:6–13 // John 12:1–8; cf. Luke 7:36–50).

22. One might argue that chronology is not present here, since we observe one of Mark's so-called "sandwiches" in which he follows an A-B-A pattern (see Craig L. Blomberg, "Dealing with Gospel Differences: Can We Still Believe the Bible?" [paper presented in the "Synoptic Gospels: Issues in the Gospels" section of the Annual Meeting of the Evangelical Theological Society, Atlanta, GA, 18 November 2015]). But this observation changes nothing. Mark has seven clear sandwiches in his Gospel: 3:20–35; 5:21–43; 6:7–32 (cf. Matt. 14:13, who makes an explicit chronological link); 11:12–21; 14:1–11, 17–31, 53–72. Bracketing this one, it is quite interesting to observe that, of the other six, all but one are crystal clear that the event being sandwiched occurred either in-between the events on each side or simultaneously with them. In other words, the chronology is explicit. For example, Jairus came to Jesus and asked him to heal his daughter. Then a hemorrhaging woman was healed when she snuck up and touched Jesus's robe. *While Jesus is still speaking to her,* people come from Jairus's house and tell him his daughter had just died. Jesus then went and raised her. The hemorrhaging woman is explicitly linked to the timeframe in which Jesus interacted with Jairus (Mark 5:22–43; see pericope #6 above). Since almost every sandwich in Mark ties events together chronologically, even if thematically, one need not choose between thematic and chronological arrangements. Both can be and are present. The example not abundantly clear is Mark 6:7–30. Notwithstanding, it is worth observing the parallel in Matt. 14:13 makes an explicit chronological link, even if Mark does not.

23. See chapter 4, pericope #15 (Mark 15:22–41 // Matt. 27:33–56 // Luke 23:33–49 // John 19:17–37).

24. In Matt. 8:1, Jesus came down from the mountain and a large crowd was following him. Matthew 8:2 begins with "and behold" (καὶ ἰδού, *kai idou*). This phrase occurs twenty-eight times in Matthew (2:9; 3:16, 17; 4:11; 7:4; 8:2, 24, 29, 32, 34; 9:2, 3, 10, 20; 12:10, 41, 42; 15:22; 17:3, 5; 19:16; 20:30; 26:51; 27:51; 28:2, 7, 9, 20) of which twenty-three clearly refer to the event occurring within a tight chronology. The five exceptions are 8:2, 9:2, 9:20, 19:16, 20:30. Of these, only 19:16 is clearly not chronological. Moreover, like Matt. 8:1–5, Luke 7:1 reports that Jesus entered Capernaum after he had preached his sermon.

25. Although the term ὄχλοι πολλοί, *ochloi polloi*, is plural, in the New Testament it almost always refers to a single crowd (Matt. 4:25; 8:1; 12:15; 13:2; 15:30; 19:2; Luke 5:15; 14:25). The term does not appear in the Apostolic Fathers, Philo, or Josephus.

26. For what follows, see Mark 1:29–38; 4:35–41 // Matt. 8:14–27 // Luke 4:38–43; 8:22–25; 9:57–62.

27. It will not do to claim that Matthew does not explicitly link the crossing to have occurred that same day. For Mark says the whole town had gathered to see Jesus that evening (Mark 1:33–34). And he healed the sick and cast out demons. In Matthew, the people came to him that evening, and he healed the sick and cast

out demons. Matthew then adds, "Now seeing a crowd around him, Jesus gave orders to cross to the other side of the lake" (Matt. 8:18).

28. So also Mark 8:27–30 // Matt. 16:13–20 // Luke 9:18–21 (pericope #158 in Aland, *Synopsis of the Four Gospels*) where Jesus asked his disciples who others are saying he is. In Mark 8:27, Jesus asked them while they were walking between villages, but in Luke 9:18 he asked them while he was praying alone and his disciples were nearby.

29. Mark 4:35–6:44 // Luke 8:22–9:17.

30. Luke 4:31 begins with "and he went down" (Καὶ κατῆλθεν, *kai katēlthen*) to Capernaum. Marshall (*Gospel of Luke*, 191) says Luke's term "is the appropriate word to use for a descent from Nazareth in the hills (over 1200 ft. high) to the lakeside (686 ft. below sea level)." Nolland makes the same observation and adds that Luke has also changed Mark's (1:21) plural "they entered" (εἰσπορεύονται, *eisporeuontai*) to the singular "he entered" (κατῆλθεν, *katēlthen*), since Jesus's disciples had yet to be introduced in his narrative (John Nolland, *Luke 1:1–9:20*, WBC 35A [Dallas, TX: Word, 1989], Logos 6, 205). This term, κατῆλθεν, *katēlthen*, appears only sixteen times in the NT (Luke 4:31; 9:37; Acts 8:5; 9:32; 11:27; 12:19; 13:4; 15:1, 30; 18:5, 22; 19:1; 21:3, 10; 27:5; James 3:15). See esp. Luke 9:37 and James 3:15. So also Fitzmyer, *Gospel According to Luke I–IX*, 543–44. Bock likewise recognizes the geographical implications of the term here (Darrell L. Bock, *Luke 1:1–9:50*, BECNT [Grand Rapids, MI: Baker Academic, 1994], 428–29). Alfred Plummer says "went down" or "came down" is "the probable meaning" (Alfred Plummer, *A Critical and Exegetical Commentary on the Gospel According to St. Luke*, 5th ed., International Critical Commentary [1896; London; New York: T&T Clark, 1989], 131).

31. To support this approach, one could posit that there may be some overlap between two strings of events reported by the same author, since Mark reports many events using an implied rather than explicit chronology. Whether this solution is more probable than Matthew's use of synthetic chronological placement would need to be pursued.

32. In favor of one rejection at Nazareth and that Luke has displaced the story to an earlier time is Blomberg, *Matthew*, 227; Bock, *Luke 1:1–9:50*, 397; Davies and Allison, *Commentary on the Gospel According to Saint Matthew*, 2:452; Fitzmyer, *Gospel According to Luke I–IX*, 526–30; William Hendriksen, *Exposition of the Gospel of Luke*, NTC (Grand Rapids, MI: Baker Academic, 1978), Logos 6, 249–50; Marshall, *Gospel of Luke*, 179; Nolland, *Luke 1:1–9:20*, 191. In favor of two rejections at Nazareth is Plummer, *Commentary on the Gospel According to St. Luke*, 118.

33. Luke 3:1 dates the beginning of Jesus's ministry "in the fifteenth year of the reign of Tiberius Caesar." Since Tiberius began his reign after Augustus's death in 14 CE, this allows us to date the beginning of Jesus's ministry sometime in 28–29 CE.

34. John F. McHugh, *A Critical and Exegetical Commentary on John 1–4*, ed. G. N. Stanton, ICC (London, New York: T&T Clark, 2009), Logos 6, 202. Bock initially favored two events (Bock, *Luke 9:51–24:53*, 2:1577) but now thinks there was only one and that John displaced it to the early part of Jesus's ministry (e-mail message to author, 10 April 2015). Gerald Borchert says, "The familiar argument of two cleansings is a historiographic monstrosity that has no basis in the texts of the Gospels" (Gerald L. Borchert, *John 1–11*, NAC 25A [Nashville: Broadman & Holman, 1996], Logos 6, 160).

35. Keener, *Gospel of John*, 1:518–19. He regards two cleansings as "unlikely" (1:518).

36. Brown says, "That we cannot harmonize John and the Synoptics by positing two cleansings of the temple precincts seems obvious. Not only do the two traditions describe basically the same actions, but also it is not likely that such a serious public affront to the Temple would be permitted twice" (Brown, *Gospel According to John*, 117–18). D. A. Carson favors two cleansings, contending that the two primary objections to two cleansings are "weak and subjective" (D. A. Carson, *The Gospel According to John*, PNTC [Leicester: Inter-Varsity Press; Grand Rapids, MI: Eerdmans, 1991], Logos 6, 177–78, esp. 178). Carson says the first objection involves a scholarly resistance to acknowledging "doubles of anything in Scripture, primarily because of the desire to tease out trajectories of developments." The second objection is that the Jewish authorities would not have let Jesus get away with a second cleansing. But Carson answers that the second cleansing would have occurred a few years after the first and would probably have caught the Jewish authorities off guard. While Carson's first objection is legitimate, it does not follow that one should resist seeing an occurrence of synthetic chronological placement in a particular instance if there are good reasons for thinking it has occurred there. Carson's second reason seems plausible. Also favoring two cleansings is E. Randolph Richards, "An Honor/Shame Argument for Two Temple Clearings," *TJ* 29, no. 1 (2008): 19–43. Unfortunately, I learned of this article too late to include it in my research.

37. Of course, literary artistry does not require the events to be fictitious.

38. Derrenbacker (*Ancient Compositional Practices and the Synoptic Problem*, 88) notes Bosworth's study on Strabo and Arrian (A. B. Bosworth, *From Arrian to Alexander: Studies in Historical Interpretation* [Oxford: Oxford University Press, 1988], esp. chap. 3, "The Handling of Sources," 38–60). In that source, Bosworth writes referring to Strabo, "He can also take great liberties with the arrangement of the material, varying the order of presentation for no apparent reason" (46).

CONCLUSION

1. Damm, "Ancient Rhetoric and the Synoptic Problem," 485–86.

2. Just a sampling includes the following: Matt. 3:7–10 // Luke 3:7–9; Matt. 7:7–8 // Luke 11:9–10; Matt. 12:41–42 // Luke 11:31–32; Matt. 12:43–45 // Luke 11:24–26;

Matt. 23:37–39 // Luke 13:34–35; Mark 13:3–8 // Matt. 24:3–8 // Luke 21:7–11; Matt. 24:16–21 // Luke 21:21–23; and Matt. 24:46–51 // Luke 12:43–46.

3. Downing, "Writers' Use and Abuse of Written Sources," 529, 531, see also 523–45.

4. Downing, "Redaction Criticism: Josephus' *Antiquities* and the Synoptic Gospels (II)," 33.

5. Perhaps the greatest differences in the Gospels can be found in the infancy narratives reported by Matthew and Luke (see Aland, *Synopsis of the Four Gospels*, pericopes #3–4, 7–12). As Jonathan Pennington writes, "Despite our conflation of all these events at the annual church Christmas pageant, these stories do not in fact overlap at all. If Jesus did not appear as the named figure in both of these accounts, one would never suspect they were stories about the same person" (Jonathan T. Pennington, *Reading the Gospels Wisely: A Narrative and Theological Introduction* [Grand Rapids, MI: Baker Academic, 2012], 56).

6. See chapter 4, pericope #16, "The Resurrection."

APPENDIX 3

1. This is most likely the same Joanna mentioned in Luke 8:3 as being the wife of Chuza, Herod's household manager.

2. Who was Clopas? Appealing to his source Hegissipus (no longer extant), Eusebius says he was Jesus's uncle, the brother of Joseph, and that he had a son named Simeon (*Hist. eccl.* 3.11; 4.22.4). Is "Clopas" in John 19:25 a variation of "Cleopas" in Luke 24:18? Luke 24:24 suggests Cleopas may have been with the disciples when the women reported the empty tomb to them. It is worth noting that we observed similar minor variations in the spelling of names in the previous chapter of this study. See pericopes #27 (Crassianus vs. Crassinius vs. Crastinus), #32 (Flavius vs. Flavus), and possibly #15 (note 32) where "Lucullus" is spelled differently (Λούκουλλος, *Loukoullos*, vs. Λευκολλος, *Leukollos*). However, Bock argues that the names are not related since "Clopas" is the Greek form of a Semitic name whereas "Cleopas" is a short form of "Cleopatris," which is the masculine form of "Cleopatra," meaning "illustrious mother" (Bock, *Luke 9:51–24:53*, 2:1911). See also BDAG, 547; and Robert F. O'Toole, "Cleopas (Person)," in *AYBD*, 1:1063.

3. The exact number is 28.6 percent (Bauckham, *Jesus and the Eyewitnesses*, 72). For more on the women at Jesus's cross, burial, and empty tomb, see the same book, pp. 48–51.

4. Luke mentions a fifth Mary in Acts 12:12 who is said to be the mother of John who was also called Mark. This may be the John Mark who is said to have written the Gospel of Mark. John Mark is also mentioned in Acts 12:25; 15:37; Philem. 1:24; Col. 4:10; and 2 Tim. 4:11.

5. Acts 1:23 provides another name variant where we see "Joseph called Barsabbas also named Justus [Ἰοῦστος, *Ioustos*]." Thus, it appears that this "Joseph" was

also called "Justus" and "Barsabbas." In Acts 15:22 (cf. 15:27, 32) we find "Judas [Ἰούδας, *Ioudas*] called Barsabbas," which may have been Joseph's brother. "Barsabbas" or "son of the Sabbath," perhaps meant he was born on the Sabbath (Craig S. Keener, *Acts: An Exegetical Commentary*, vol. 3, *15:1–23:35* [Grand Rapids, MI: Baker Academic, 2014], 2281).

6. The sons of Zebedee were James and John (Matt. 4:21; 10:2; cf. Mark 1:19; 3:17; 10:35; Luke 5:10).

7. Although John never specifically names Jesus's mother as "Mary" (John 2:1, 3, 5, 12; 6:42; 19:25–26), the Synoptics do (Mark 6:3; Matt. 1:16, 18, 20, 24; 2:11; 13:55; Luke 1:27, 30, 34, 38–39, 46, 56; 2:5, 16, 19, 34). Yet it may be worth noting that in the Synoptics, after the infancy narratives, Jesus's mother is only mentioned related to three events: (1) Jesus staying behind in the temple when he was twelve (Luke 2:42–51), (2) when his mother and brothers came to get Jesus during his ministry (Mark 3:31–35 // Matt. 12:46–50 // Luke 8:19–21), and (3) indirectly when those in Nazareth spoke ill of Jesus (Mark 6:1–6 // Matt. 13:54–58). In John, Jesus's mother is only mentioned related to three events: (1) the very inception of Jesus's ministry (2:1–12), (2) when others spoke of her indirectly (6:42), and (3) at Jesus's crucifixion (19:25–26). That Jesus had brothers, one of whom was named James, is mentioned in literature that predates the Gospels (1 Cor. 9:5; Gal. 1:19; the James mentioned in the following is probably the brother of Jesus: 1 Cor. 15:7; Gal. 2:9, 12; Acts 12:17; 15:13–29; 21:18).

8. In fact, the name "Joses" never appears in Matthew, while the name "Joseph" appears only twice in Mark (15:43, 45), each referring to Joseph of Arimathea, who buried Jesus.

9. See Licona, *Resurrection of Jesus*, 440–58.

10. Eusebius, *Hist. eccl.* 2.23.4–7.

11. This would not be impossible. See Keener, *Gospel of John*, 2:1142.

APPENDIX 4

1. The biosketch "Antony" is based on a biosketch written by John T. Ramsey, "Who's Who in Caesar" in *The Landmark Edition of Caesar's Commentaries*, Kurt A. Raaflaub, ed and translator, Robert B. Strassler Series Editor (New York: Pantheon, forthcoming).

2. The biosketch "Brutus" is based on information provided by John Ramsey (e-mail message to author, 9 December 2015) and the following entries: Andrew Drummond, "Iunius (RE 46a in Suppl. 5. 356 ff.) Brutus, Lucius," *OCD*, 765; Ernst Badian, "Iunius (*RE* 52) Brutus (1), Marcus," *OCD*, 765; and Ernst Badian, "Iunius (*RE* 53) Brutus (2), Marcus," *OCD*, 765–66.

3. The biosketch "Caesar" is based on information provided by John Ramsey (e-mail message to author, 9 December 2015) and Ernst Badian, "Iulius (*RE* 131) Caesar, C.," *OCD*, 757–60.

4. The biosketch "Cato Minor (Cato the Younger)" is based on a biosketch written by Ramsey, "Who's Who in Caesar."

5. The biosketch "Cicero" is based solely on an unpublished biosketch written by John Ramsey. Used by permission of the author.

6. The biosketch "Crassus" is based on a biosketch written by Ramsey, "Who's Who in Caesar."

7. Appian, *Bell. civ.* 1.120.

8. The biosketch "Lucullus" is based on information provided by John Ramsey (e-mail message to author, 9 December 2015) and Ernst Badian, "Licinius (*RE* 104) Lucullus (2), Lucius," *OCD*, 834.

9. The biosketch "Pompey" is based on a biosketch written by Ramsey, "Who's Who in Caesar."

10. The biosketch "Sertorius" is based on information provided by John Ramsey (e-mail message to author, 9 December 2015) and the following entries: Christoph F. Konrad, "Sertorius Quintus," *OCD*, 1354; Ernst Badian, "Cornelius (*RE* 106) Cinna (1), Lucius," *OCD*, 377; and Ernst Badian, "Cornelius (*RE* 392) Sulla Felix, Lucius," *OCD*, 384–85.

Glossary

consul The chief magistrate during the Republic. Two consuls served simultaneously as colleagues. During the Late Republic, elections typically took place in July and the consuls-elect assumed their office on 1 January and served for one year.

chreia (pl. chreiai) A pithy anecdote about a person, usually focusing on a memorable act or saying.

circumlocution An indirect manner of description. For example, Jews in antiquity who would not utter any form of God's name would substitute words such as "Power" (Mark 14:62) or "heaven" (Mark 11:30).

demos The common people of the Greco-Roman world.

doublets One original tradition appears in two different settings within the same book as though occurring on separate occasions.

encomium A speech in which a person is praised. The good could be exaggerated while the bad might be downplayed.

evangelist Author of one of the canonical Gospels.

Forum The preeminent public square in Rome, it was the location of shops, temples, and the Rostra.

harmonize The approach that places all of the accounts of the same event on top of one another (as though layered with transparencies) in order to produce a single coherent account that includes all of the details found in all of the accounts.

historical verisimilitude An event narrated with the appearance of being true or real.

ipsissima verba Literally, "the very words." In other words, a direct quote.

ipsissima vox Literally, "the very voice."

logion (pl. logia) A saying or teaching.

pericope A selection from a larger narrative.

proscriptions Lists containing the names of Romans who were declared outlaws. The property of those on the list was forfeited and put up for sale to the public. Moreover, bounties were offered for the death of those on the list.

Rostra Platform in the Roman Forum from which Roman magistrates would address the people or sit during a public event.

sui generis Of its own kind, unique (in terms of genre).

tria nomina In Roman naming conventions, the *praenomen* was the person's personal name. The *nomen* identified one's family, clan, or race. And the *cognomen* was a characteristic that would distinguish one person further from another. For example, in the name Gaius Epidius Marullus, "Gaius" is the *praenomen*, "Epidius" is the *nomen*, and "Marullus" is the *cognomen*.

verisimilitude Having an appearance of truth.

Bibliography

Achtemeier, Paul J. "Toward the Isolation of Pre-Markan Miracle Catenae." *Journal of Biblical Literature* 89, no. 3 (1970): 265–91.

Aland, Barbara, Kurt Aland, Johannes Karavidopoulos, Carlo M. Martini, and Bruce M. Metzger, eds. *The Greek New Testament* (UBS⁵). 5th rev. ed. Stuttgart: Deutsche Bibelgesellschaft, 2014.

Aland, Kurt, ed. *Synopsis of the Four Gospels: Greek-English Edition of the* Synopsis Quattuor Evangeliorum. 12th ed. Stuttgart: German Bible Society, 2001.

Alexander, Michael C. "Trials in the Late Roman Republic, 149 BC to 50 BC." *Phoenix*, supplementary vol. 26 (1990): 1–233.

Alexander, P. S. "Rabbinic Biography and the Biography of Jesus: A Survey of the Evidence." In *Synoptic Studies: The Ampleforth Conferences of 1982 and 1983*, edited by C. M. Tuckett, 19–50. Journal for the Study of the New Testament Supplement Series 7. Sheffield: JSOT Press, 1984.

Allen, Willoughby C. *A Critical and Exegetical Commentary on the Gospel According to St Matthew*. 3rd ed. International Critical Commentary. Edinburgh: T&T Clark, 1912. Logos 6. First published in 1907.

Allison, Dale C., Jr. "'Jesus Did Not Say to Him That He Would Not Die': John 21:20–23 and Mark 9:1." Paper presented in the "John, Jesus and History" section of the Annual Meeting of the Society of Biblical Literature in Chicago, IL, 17 November 2012. In *John, Jesus, and History*, edited by Paul N. Anderson, Felix Just, and Tom Thatcher. Vol. 5, *Jesus Remembered in the Johannine Tradition*. Early Christianity and Its Literature 5. Symposium Series. Atlanta, GA: SBL Press, forthcoming.

Allison, Dale C., Jr. *Resurrecting Jesus: The Earliest Christian Tradition and Its Interpreters*. New York: T&T Clark, 2005.

Anderson, Paul N., Felix Just, and Tom Thatcher, eds. *John, Jesus, and History*. Vol. 5, *Jesus Remembered in the Johannine Tradition*. Early Christianity and Its Literature 5. Symposium Series. Atlanta, GA: SBL Press, forthcoming.

The Ante-Nicene Fathers. Edited by Alexander Roberts and James Donaldson. 10 vols. American ed. Buffalo, NY: Christian Literature Company, 1885–96. Logos 6.

Archer, Gleason L. *Encyclopedia of Bible Difficulties*. Grand Rapids: Zondervan, 1982.

Arndt, W., F. W. Danker, and W. Bauer. *A Greek-English Lexicon of the New Testament and Other Early Christian Literature*. 3rd ed. Chicago, IL: University of Chicago Press, 2000. Logos 6.

Ash, Rhiannon, Judith Mossman, and Frances B. Titchener, eds. *Fame and Infamy: Essays for Christopher Pelling on Characterization in Greek and Roman Biography and Historiography*. Oxford: Oxford University Press, 2015.

Aune, David E. *The New Testament in Its Literary Environment*. Library of Early Christianity 8. Philadelphia, PA: Westminster Press, 1987.

Barrett, Anthony A. Introduction to *The Annals: The Reigns of Tiberius, Claudius, and Nero*, by Tacitus, ix–xxix. Translated by J. C. Yardley. New York: Oxford University Press, 2008.

Bauckham, Richard. *Jesus and the Eyewitnesses: The Gospels as Eyewitness Testimony*. Grand Rapids, MI: Eerdmans, 2006.

Bauckham, Richard. *The Testimony of the Beloved Disciple: Narrative, History, and Theology in the Gospel of John*. Grand Rapids, MI: Baker Academic, 2007.

Bauckham, Richard, James R. Davila, and Alexander Panayotov, eds. *Old Testament Pseudepigrapha: More Noncanonical Scriptures*. 2 vols. Grand Rapids, MI: Eerdmans, 2013–.

Beasley-Murray, G. R. *John*. Word Biblical Commentary 36. Dallas, TX: Word, 2002. Logos 6.

Bernard, J. H. *A Critical and Exegetical Commentary on the Gospel According to St. John*, vol. 2. Edited by A. H. McNeile. New York: Scribner, 1929. Logos 6.

Blomberg, Craig L. "Dealing with Gospel Differences: Can We Still Believe the Bible?" Response presented in the "Synoptic Gospels: Issues in the Gospels" section of the Annual Meeting of the Evangelical Theological Society, Atlanta, GA, 18 November 2015.

Blomberg, Craig L. *The Historical Reliability of John's Gospel*. Downers Grove, IL: IVP Academic, 2001.

Blomberg, Craig L. *Matthew: An Exegetical and Theological Exposition of Holy Scripture*. New American Commentary 22. Nashville, TN: Broadman & Holman, 1992. Logos 6.

Bock, Darrell L. *Luke 1:1–9:50*. Baker Exegetical Commentary on the New Testament. Grand Rapids, MI: Baker, 1994.

Bock, Darrell L. *Luke 9:51–24:53*. Baker Exegetical Commentary on the New Testament. Grand Rapids, MI: Baker, 1996.

Bock, Darrell L. "Precision and Accuracy: Making Distinctions in the Cultural Context That Give Us Pause in Pitting the Gospels against Each Other." In *Do Historical Matters Matter to Faith?: A Critical Appraisal of Modern and Postmodern Approaches to Scripture*, edited by James K. Hoffmeier and Dennis R. Magary, 367–81. Wheaton, IL: Crossway, 2012.

Bock, Darrell L. "Response to Mike Licona's Plutarch and the Gospels Paper." Paper presented in the "Synoptic Gospels: Issues in the Gospels" section of the Annual Meeting of the Evangelical Theological Society, Atlanta, GA, 18 November 2015.

Borchert, Gerald L. *John 1–11.* New American Commentary 25A. Nashville, TN: Broadman & Holman, 1996. Logos 6.

Bosworth, A. B. *From Arrian to Alexander: Studies in Historical Interpretation.* Oxford: Oxford University Press, 1988.

Broughton, T. Robert S., with the collaboration of Marcia L. Patterson. *Magistrates of the Roman Republic.* Vol. 2, *99 B.C.–31 B.C.* Philological Monographs 15. New York: American Philological Association, 1952.

Brown, Raymond E. *The Gospel according to John (I–XII): Introduction, Translation, and Notes.* Anchor Bible Commentary 29. New Haven, CT; London: Yale University Press, 2008. Logos 6. Originally published 1996 by Doubleday.

Brown, Raymond E. *The Gospel according to John (XIII–XXI): Introduction, Translation, and Notes.* Anchor Bible Commentary 29A. New Haven, CT; London: Yale University Press, 2008. Logos 6. Originally published 1970 by Doubleday.

Brown, Raymond E. *An Introduction to the Gospel of John.* Edited by Francis J. Moloney. Anchor Yale Bible Reference Library. New York: Doubleday, 2003.

Bruce, F. F. *The Gospel and Epistles of John.* Grand Rapids: Eerdmans, 1983.

Burridge, Richard. *Four Gospels, One Jesus? A Symbolic Reading.* 3rd ed. Grand Rapids, MI: Eerdmans, 2014.

Burridge, Richard A. "Reading the Gospels as Biography." In *The Limits of Ancient Biography,* edited by Brian McGing and Judith Mossman, 31–49. Swansea: Classical Press of Wales, 2006.

Burridge, Richard A. *What Are the Gospels? A Comparison with Graeco-Roman Biography.* 2nd ed. Grand Rapids, MI: Eerdmans, 2004. First published 1992 by Cambridge University Press.

Burridge, Richard A., and Graham Gould. *Jesus: Now and Then.* Grand Rapids, MI: Eerdmans, 2004.

Butler, Shane. *The Hand of Cicero.* London: Routledge, 2002.

Carson, D. A. *The Gospel according to John.* Pillar New Testament Commentary. Leicester: Inter-Varsity Press; Grand Rapids, MI: Eerdmans, 1991. Logos 6.

Charlesworth, James H., ed. *Old Testament Pseudepigrapha.* 2 vols. Peabody, MS: Hendrickson, 2009. Originally published 1983–85 by Darton, Longman & Todd.

Charlesworth, James H., with James R. Mueller. *The New Testament Apocrypha and Pseudepigrapha: A Guide to Publications, with Excursuses on Apocalypses.* Chicago, IL: American Theological Library Association; Metuchen, NJ: Scarecrow Press, 1987.

Cheney, Johnston M. *The Life of Christ in Stereo: The Four Gospels Combined as One.* Rev. ed. Portland, OR: Western Baptist Seminary Press, 1969.

Chung, Michael. "A Bracketed Bethany Anointing." *Bulletin for Biblical Research* 25, no. 3 (2015): 359–69.

Cicero. *In Catilinam 1–4. Pro Murena. Pro Sulla. Pro Flacco.* Translated by C. Macdonald. Loeb Classical Library 324. Cambridge: Harvard University Press, 1977. Logos 6.

Cicero. *Defence Speeches.* Translated by D. H. Berry. Oxford World Classics. Oxford: Oxford University Press, 2000.

Collins, Adela Yarbro. *Mark.* Hermeneia. Minneapolis, MN: Fortress, 2007.

Craig, William Lane. *Assessing the New Testament Evidence for the Historicity of the Resurrection of Jesus.* Studies in the Bible and Early Christianity 16. Lewiston, NY: Edwin Mellen Press, 1989.

Cribiore, Raffaella. *Gymnastics of the Mind: Greek Education in Hellenistic and Roman Egypt.* Princeton, NJ: Princeton University Press, 2001.

Damm, Alex. "Ancient Rhetoric and the Synoptic Problem." In *New Studies in the Synoptic Problem: Oxford Conference, April 2008; Essays in Honour of Christopher M. Tuckett,* edited by P. Foster, A. Gregory, J. S. Kloppenborg, and J. Verheyden, 483–508. Bibliotheca Ephemeridum Theologicarum Lovaniensium 239. Leuven: Peeters, 2011.

Davies, W. D., and Dale C. Allison Jr. *A Critical and Exegetical Commentary on the Gospel according to Saint Matthew.* Vol. 1, *Introduction and Commentary on Matthew I–VII.* London; New York: T&T Clark, 2004. Logos 6. Originally published in 1988.

Davies, W. D., and Dale C. Allison Jr. *A Critical and Exegetical Commentary on the Gospel according to Saint Matthew.* Vol. 2, *Commentary on Matthew VIII–XVIII.* London; New York: T&T Clark, 2004. Logos 6. Originally published in 1991.

Davies, W. D., and Dale C. Allison Jr. *A Critical and Exegetical Commentary on the Gospel according to Saint Matthew.* Vol. 3, *Commentary on Matthew XIX–XXVIII.* International Critical Commentary. London; New York: T&T Clark, 2004. Logos 6. Originally published in 1997.

Derrenbacker, R. A., Jr. *Ancient Compositional Practices and the Synoptic Problem.* Bibliotheca Ephemeridum Theologicarum Lovaniensium 186. Leuven: Peeters, 2005.

Downing, F. Gerald. "Compositional Conventions and the Synoptic Problem." *Journal of Biblical Literature* 107, no. 1 (1988): 69–85.

Downing, F. Gerald. "Redaction Criticism: Josephus' *Antiquities* and the Synoptic Gospels (I)." *Journal for the Study of the New Testament* 2, no. 8 (1980): 46–65.

Downing, F. Gerald. "Redaction Criticism: Josephus' *Antiquities* and the Synoptic Gospels (II)." *Journal for the Study of the New Testament* 3, no. 9 (1980): 29–48.

Downing, F. Gerald. "Writers' Use or Abuse of Written Sources." In *New Studies in the Synoptic Problem: Oxford Conference, April 2008; Essays in Honour of Christopher M. Tuckett,* edited by P. Foster, A. Gregory, J. S. Kloppenborg, and

J. Verheyden, 523–45. Bibliotheca Ephemeridum Theologicarum Lovaniensium 239. Leuven: Peeters, 2011.

Duff, Timothy E. *Plutarch's Lives: Exploring Virtue and Vice.* New York: Oxford University Press, 1999.

Edwards, M. J. *Plutarch: The Lives of Pompey, Caesar and Cicero.* London: Bristol Classical Press, 1991.

Ehrman, Bart D. *The New Testament: A Historical Introduction to the Early Christian Writings.* Oxford: Oxford University Press, 2008.

Elwell, Walter A., ed. *Baker Encyclopedia of the Bible.* 2 vols. Grand Rapids, MI: Baker, 1988. Logos 6.

Evans, Craig A. *Mark 8:27–16:20.* Word Biblical Commentary 34B. Dallas, TX: Word, 2001. Logos 6.

Evans, Craig A. *Matthew.* New Cambridge Bible Commentary. New York: Cambridge University Press, 2012.

Eve, Eric. *Behind the Gospels: Understanding the Oral Tradition.* Minneapolis, MN: Fortress, 2014.

Farmer, William R. *The Synoptic Problem: A Critical Analysis.* 2nd ed. Macon, GA: Mercer University Press, 1976.

Farrer, Austin. "On Dispensing with Q." In *Studies in the Gospels: Essays in Memory of R. H. Lightfoot,* edited by D. E. Nineham, 55–88. Oxford: Basil Blackwell, 1955.

Felton, Joseph, ed. *Nicolai Progymnasmata.* Leipzip: Teubner, 1913.

Fitzmyer, Joseph A. *The Gospel according to Luke I–IX: Introduction, Translation, and Notes.* Anchor Bible Commentary 28. New Haven, CT: Yale University Press, 2008. Logos 6. Originally published 1970 by Doubleday.

Fitzmyer, Joseph A. *The Gospel according to Luke X–XXIV: Introduction, Translation, and Notes.* Anchor Bible Commentary 28A. New Haven, CT: Yale University Press, 2008. Logos 6. Originally published 1985 by Doubleday.

Foster, P., A. Gregory, J. S. Kloppenborg, and J. Verheyden, eds. *New Studies in the Synoptic Problem: Oxford Conference, April 2008; Essays in Honour of Christopher M. Tuckett.* Bibliotheca Ephemeridum Theologicarum Lovaniensium 239. Leuven: Peeters, 2011.

France, R. T. *The Gospel of Mark: A Commentary on the Greek Text.* New International Greek Testament Commentary. Grand Rapids, MI: Eerdmans; Carlisle: Paternoster, 2002. Logos 6.

Freedman, D. N., ed. *The Anchor Yale Bible Dictionary.* 6 vols. New York: Doubleday, 1992. Logos 6. Formerly called the *Anchor Bible Dictionary.*

Goodacre, Mark. *The Case Against Q: Studies in Markan Priority and the Synoptic Problem.* Harrisburg, PA: Trinity Press International, 2002.

Gowler, David B. "The Chreia." In *The Historical Jesus in Context,* edited by Amy-Jill Levine, Dale C. Allison Jr., and John Dominic Crossan, 132–48. Princeton, NJ: Princeton University Press, 2006.

Gundry, Robert H. *Matthew: A Commentary on His Handbook for a Mixed Church under Persecution*. 2nd ed. Grand Rapids, MI: Eerdmans, 1994.

Hauge, Matthew, and Andrew W. Pitts. *Ancient Education and Early Christianity*. Library of New Testament Studies 533. London: T&T Clark, 2015.

Heath, Malcolm. "Theon and the History of the Progymnasmata." *Greek, Roman, and Byzantine Studies* 43, no. 2 (2003): 129–60.

Henderson, Jordan. "Josephus's *Life* and *Jewish War* Compared to the Synoptic Gospels." *Journal of Greco-Roman Christianity and Judaism* 10, no. 5 (2014): 113–31.

Hendriksen, William. *Exposition of the Gospel of Luke*. New Testament Commentary. Grand Rapids: Baker Academic, 1978. Logos 6. Originally published in 1953.

Hill, Charles E. "'In These Very Words': Methods and Standards of Literary Borrowing in the Second Century." In *Early Text of the New Testament*, edited by Charles E. Hill and Michael J. Kruger, 261–81. Oxford: Oxford University Press, 2012.

Hill, Charles E., and Michael J. Kruger, eds. *The Early Text of the New Testament*. Oxford: Oxford University Press, 2012.

Hock, Ronald F. *The Chreia and Ancient Rhetoric: Commentaries on Aphthonius's Progymnasmata*. Writings from the Greco-Roman World 31. Atlanta, GA: Society of Biblical Literature, 2012. http://www.sbl-site.org/assets/pdfs/pubs/061631C.front.pdf.

Hock, Ronald F. "Observing a Teacher of *Progymnasmata*." In *Ancient Education and Early Christianity*, edited by Matthew Hauge, and Andrew W. Pitts, 39–70. Library of New Testament Studies 533. London: T&T Clark, 2015.

Hoehner, Harold W. *Chronological Aspects of the Life of Christ*. Grand Rapids, MI: Zondervan, 1977.

Hoffmann, R. J. *Celsus on the True Doctrine: A Discourse against the Christians*. New York: Oxford University Press, 1987.

Hoffmeier, James K., and Dennis R. Magary, eds. *Do Historical Matters Matter to Faith? A Critical Appraisal of Modern and Postmodern Approaches to Scripture*. Wheaton, IL: Crossway, 2012.

Holmes, Michael W., ed. *The Greek New Testament: SBL Edition*. Atlanta, GA: Society of Biblical Literature, 2010.

Horsfall, Nicholas. "The Ides of March: Some New Problems." *Greece and Rome* 21, no. 2 (1974): 191–99.

Instone-Brewer, David. *Traditions of the Rabbis from the Era of the New Testament*. Vol. 2A, *Feasts and Sabbaths: Passover and Atonement*. Grand Rapids, MI: Eerdmans, 2011.

Johnson, Luke Timothy. *The Real Jesus: The Misguided Quest for the Historical Jesus and the Truth of the Traditional Gospels*. San Francisco, CA: HarperSanFrancisco, 1996.

Jones, Christopher P. *Plutarch and Rome*. Oxford: Clarendon Press, 1971.

Jones, Christopher P. Introduction to *The Life of Apollonius of Tyana*, by Philostratus. Vol. 1, *Books 1–4*, 1–30. Edited and translated by Christopher P. Jones. Loeb Classical Library 16. Cambridge: Harvard University Press, 2005. Logos 6.

Josephus. *Josephus, the Essential Works: A Condensation of Jewish Antiquities and the Jewish War.* Translated and edited by Paul L. Maier. Rev. ed. Grand Rapids, MI: Kregel, 1994. First published 1988.

Keener, Craig S. *Acts: An Exegetical Commentary.* Vol. 1, *Introduction and 1:1–2:47.* Grand Rapids, MI: Baker Academic, 2012.

Keener, Craig S. *Acts: An Exegetical Commentary.* Vol. 2, *3:1–14:28.* Grand Rapids, MI: Baker Academic, 2013.

Keener, Craig S. *Acts: An Exegetical Commentary.* Vol. 3, *15:1–23:35.* Grand Rapids, MI: Baker Academic, 2014.

Keener, Craig S. *Acts: An Exegetical Commentary.* Vol. 4, *24:1–28:31.* Grand Rapids, MI: Baker Academic, 2015.

Keener, Craig S. *The Gospel of John: A Commentary.* 2 vols. Peabody, MA: Hendrickson, 2003.

Keener, Craig S. *The Historical Jesus of the Gospels.* Grand Rapids: Eerdmans, 2009.

Keener, Craig S. *Matthew.* IVP New Testament Commentary 1. Downers Grove, IL: InterVarsity Press, 1997.

Keener, Craig S. "*Otho*: A Targeted Comparison of Suetonius's Biography and Tacitus's *History*, with Implications for the Gospels' Historical Reliability." *Bulletin for Biblical Research* 21, no. 3 (2011): 331–56.

Kennedy, George A. *Invention and Method: Two Rhetorical Treatises from the Hermongenic Corpus.* Atlanta, GA: Society of Biblical Literature, 2005.

Kennedy, George A. *New Testament Interpretation through Rhetorical Criticism.* Chapel Hill, NC: University of North Carolina Press, 1984.

Kennedy, George A., trans. *Progymnasmata: Greek Textbooks of Prose Composition and Rhetoric.* Writings from the Greco-Roman World 10. Atlanta, GA: Society of Biblical Literature, 2003.

Levine, Amy-Jill, Dale C. Allison Jr., and John Dominic Crossan, eds. *The Historical Jesus in Context.* Princeton, NJ: Princeton University Press, 2006.

Libanius. *Libanius's* Progymnasmata: *Model Exercises in Greek Prose Composition and Rhetoric.* Translated by Craig A. Gibson. Writings from the Greco-Roman World 27. Atlanta, GA: Society of Biblical Literature, 2008.

Licona, Michael R. *The Resurrection of Jesus: A New Historiographical Approach.* Downers Grove, IL: IVP Academic, 2010.

Licona, Michael R. "Synthetic Chronological Placement in Ancient Biographical Literature." Paper presented in the "Synoptic Gospels: Issues in the Gospels" section of the Annual Meeting of the Evangelical Theological Society, Atlanta, GA, 18 November 2015.

Lindsell, Harold. *The Battle for the Bible.* Grand Rapids: Zondervan, 1976.

Lounsbery, Eric. *J. J. Blunt's Undesigned Scriptural Coincidences: The Proof of Truth.* Maitland, FL: Xulon Press, 2005.

Luce, T. J. *The Greek Historians.* New York: Routledge, 1997.

Lucian. *Lucian.* Vol. 6, *How to Write History,* translated by K. Kilburn. Loeb Classical Library 430. Cambridge: Harvard University Press, 2006. First published 1959 by Heinemann.

MacDonald, Dennis R. "The Synoptic Problem and Literary Mimesis: The Case of the Frothing Demoniac." In *New Studies in the Synoptic Problem: Oxford Conference, April 2008; Essays in Honour of Christopher M. Tuckett,* edited by P. Foster, A. Gregory, J. S. Kloppenborg, and J. Verheyden, 509–21. Bibliotheca Ephemeridum Theologicarum Lovaniensium 239. Leuven: Peeters, 2011.

Mack, Burton L., and Vernon K. Robbins. *Patterns of Persuasion in the Gospels.* Eugene, OR: Wipf and Stock, 2008. First published 1989 by Polebridge.

Marcus, Joel. *Mark 1–8: A New Translation with Introduction and Commentary.* Anchor Bible Commentary 27. New Haven, CT: Yale University Press, 2000. Logos 6.

Marcus, Joel. *Mark 8–16: A New Translation with Introduction and Commentary.* Anchor Bible Commentary 27A. New Haven, CT: Yale University Press, 2009. Logos 6.

Marshall, I. H. *The Gospel of Luke: A Commentary on the Greek Text.* New International Greek Testament Commentary. Carlisle: Paternoster; Grand Rapids, MI: Eerdmans, 1978. Logos 6.

McGing, Brian. "Philo's Adaptation of the Bible in His *Life of Moses.*" In *The Limits of Ancient Biography,* edited by Brian McGing and Judith Mossman, 117–40. Swansea: Classical Press of Wales, 2006.

McGing, Brian, and Judith Mossman, eds. *The Limits of Ancient Biography.* Swansea: Classical Press of Wales, 2006.

McHugh, John F. *A Critical and Exegetical Commentary on John 1–4.* Edited by Graham N. Stanton. International Critical Commentary. London; New York: T&T Clark, 2009. Logos 6.

Mellor, Ronald. *The Roman Historians.* London: Routledge, 1999.

Metzger, Bruce M. *A Textual Commentary on the Greek New Testament.* 2nd ed. New York: American Bible Society, 2002. Originally published 1971 by United Bible Societies..

Metzger, Bruce M., and Bart D. Ehrman. *The Text of the New Testament: Its Transmission, Corruption and Restoration.* 4th ed. New York: Oxford University Press, 2005.

Mosley, A. W. "Historical Reporting in the Ancient World." *New Testament Studies* 12, no. 1 (1965): 10–26.

Nestle, Eberhard, Erwin Nestle, Barbara Aland, Kurt Aland, and Holger Strutwolf, eds. *Novum Testamentum Graece* (NA[28]). 28th rev. ed. Stuttgart: Deutsche Bibelgesellschaft, 2013.

Neusner, Jacob. *The Incarnation of God: The Character of Divinity in Formative Judaism.* Philadelphia, PA: Fortress, 1988.

Nineham, D. E., ed. *Studies in the Gospels: Essays in Memory of R. H. Lightfoot.* Oxford: Basil Blackwell, 1955.

Nolland, John. *The Gospel of Matthew: A Commentary on the Greek Text.* New International Greek Testament Commentary. Grand Rapids, MI: Eerdmans; Bletchley: Paternoster, 2005. Logos 6.

Nolland, John. *Luke 1:1–9:20.* Word Biblical Commentary 35A. Dallas, TX: Word, 1989. Logos 6.

Nolland, John. *Luke 9:21–18:34.* Word Biblical Commentary 35B. Dallas, TX: Word, 1993. Logos 6.

Nolland, John. *Luke 18:35–24:53.* Word Biblical Commentary 35C. Dallas, TX: Word, 1993. Logos 6.

Novakovic, Lidija. Resurrection: A Guide for the Perplexed. New York: Bloomsbury T & T Clark, 2016.

Origen. *Commentary on the Gospel according to John,* bk. 10. In vol. 9 (5th ed.), edited by Allan Menzies, translated by Fredrick Crombie, of *Ante-Nicene Fathers.* Edited by Alexander Roberts and James Donaldson. American ed. 10 vols. Buffalo, NY: Christian Literature Company, 1897. Logos 6.

Origen. *Origen against Celsus.* In vol. 4., translated by Fredrick Crombie, of *Ante-Nicene Fathers.* Edited by Alexander Roberts and James Donaldson. American ed. 10 vols. Buffalo, NY: Christian Literature Company, 1885. Logos 6.

Origenes [Origen]. *Contra Celsum Libri VIII.* Edited by M. Marcovich. Vigiliae Christianae, Supplements (formerly Philosophia Patrum). Texts and Studies of Early Christian Life and Language 54. Leiden: Brill, 2001.

The Oxford Classical Dictionary. Edited by S. Hornblower, A. Spawforth, and E. Eidinow. 4th ed. Oxford: Oxford University Press, 2012.

Pelling, Christopher. "Breaking the Bounds: Writing about Julius Caesar." *The Limits of Ancient Biography,* edited by Brian McGing and Judith Mossman, 255–80. Swansea: Classical Press of Wales, 2006.

Pelling, Christopher. *Literary Texts and the Greek Historian.* New York: Routledge, 2000.

Pelling, Christopher. *Plutarch and History: Eighteen Studies.* Swansea: Classical Press of Wales, 2002.

Pennington, Jonathan T. *Reading the Gospels Wisely: A Narrative and Theological Introduction.* Grand Rapids, MI: Baker Academic, 2012.

Philostratus. *The Life of Apollonius of Tyana.* Edited and translated by Christopher P. Jones. 3 vols. Loeb Classical Library 16, 17, 458. Cambridge: Harvard University Press, 2005–6.

Pitts, Andrew W. "The Genre of the Third Gospel and Greco-Roman Historiography : A Reconsideration." Paper presented in the "Paul J. Achtemeier Award for New Testament Scholarship" section of the Annual Meeting of the Society of Biblical Literature, Atlanta, GA, 22 November 2015.

Pitts, Andrew W. "The Origins of Greek Mimesis, Ancient Education, and Gospel of Mark: Genre as a Potential Constraint in Assessing Markan Imitation." In *Ancient Education and Early Christianity,* edited by Matthew Hauge and Andrew W. Pitts, 107–36. Library of New Testament Studies 533. London: T&T Clark, 2015.

Pitts, Andrew W. "Source Citation in Greek Historiography and in Luke(-Acts)." In *Christian Origins and Greco-Roman Culture: Social and Literary Contexts for the New Testament*, edited Stanley E. Porter and Andrew W. Pitts, 349–88. Texts and Editions for New Testament Study 9. Leiden: Brill, 2013.

Plummer, Alfred. *A Critical and Exegetical Commentary on the Gospel according to St. Luke.* 5th ed. International Critical Commentary. London; New York: T&T Clark, 1989. Logos 6. Originally published by Charles Scribner's Sons, 1896.

Plutarch. *Caesar.* Translated by Christopher Pelling. Clarendon Ancient History Series. Oxford: Oxford University Press, 2011.

Plutarch. *Life of Antony.* Edited by C. B. R. Pelling. Cambridge Greek and Latin Classics. New York: Cambridge University Press, 1988.

Plutarch. *The Life of Cicero.* Translated by J. L. Moles. Warminster, Wiltshire: Aris & Phillips, 1988.

Plutarch. *Rome in Crisis: Nine Lives.* Translated by Ian Scott-Kilvert and Christopher Pelling. Rev. ed. New York: Penguin Books, 2010.

Powell, Mark Allan. *Introducing the New Testament: A Historical, Literary, and Theological Survey.* Grand Rapids, MI: Baker Academic, 2009.

Quintilian. *The Institutio Oratoria of Quintilian.* Translated by H. E. Butler. 4 vols. Loeb Classical Library 124–27. London: Heinemann, 1921–22. Logos 6.

Raaflaub, K. "Zum politischen Wirken der caesarfreundlichen Volkstribunen am Varaben des Bürgerkrieges." *Chiron: Mitteilungen der Kommission für Alte Geschichte und Epigraphik* 4 (1974): 293–326.

Rabe, Hugo. *Prolegomenon Sylloge.* Leipzig: Teubner, 1931.

Ramsey, J. T., ed. *Sallust's* Bellum Catilinae. 2nd ed. American Philological Association Texts and Commentaries. Oxford: Oxford University Press, 2006.

Ramsey, John. "At What Hour Did the Murderers of Julius Caesar Gather on the Ides of March 44 B.C.?" In *In Pursuit of Wissenschaft: Festschrift für William M. Calder III zum 75. Geburtstag,* edited by Stephan Heilen, Robert Kirstein, R. Scott Smith, Stephen M. Trzaskoma, Rogier L. van der Wal, and Matthias Vorwerk, 351–63. Spudasmata 119. New York: Olms, 2008.

Ramsey, John T. "Who's Who in Caesar." In *The Landmark Edition of Caesar's Commentaries* [working title]. Edited and translated by Kurt A. Raaflaub. Landmark series, edited by Robert B. Strassler. New York: Pantheon, forthcoming.

Richards, E. Randolph. "An Honor/Shame Argument for Two Temple Clearings." *Trinity Journal* 29, no. 1 (Spring 2008): 19–43.

"A Roundtable Discussion with Michael Licona on *The Resurrection of Jesus: A New Historiographical Approach* (Danny Akin, Craig Blomberg, Paul Copan, Michael Kruger, Michael Licona, and Charles Quarles)." *Southeastern Theological Review* 3, no. 1 (Summer 2012): 71–98. http://www.risenjesus.com/wp-content/uploads/a-roundtable-discussion-with-michael-licona-on-the-resurrection-of-jesus.pdf.

Russell, D. A. "Plutarch's Life of Coriolanus." *Journal of Roman Studies* 53, parts 1 and 2 (1963): 21–28.

Sallust. *The War with Catiline; The War with Jugurtha*. Vol. 1. Translated by J. C. Rolfe. Revised by John T. Ramsey. Loeb Classical Library 116. Cambridge: Harvard University Press, 2013.

Sheppard, Beth M. *The Craft of History and the Study of the New Testament*. Resources for Biblical Study 60. Atlanta, GA: Society of Biblical Literature, 2012.

Soards, Marion L. *The Speeches in Acts: Their Content, Context, and Concerns*. Louisville, KY: Westminster/John Knox Press, 1994.

Spengel, Leonardi, ed. *Rhetores Graeci*. 3 vols. Frankfurt: Minerva, 1966. Originally published 1853–56 by Teubner.

Stein, Robert H. *Difficult Passages in the New Testament: Interpreting Puzzling Texts in the Gospels and Epistles*. Grand Rapids, MI: Baker, 1990.

Stein, Robert H. *Studying the Synoptic Gospels: Origin and Interpretation*. 2nd ed. Grand Rapids, MI: Baker Academic, 2001.

Suetonius. *Lives of the Caesars*. Translated by J. C. Rolfe. Rev. ed. 2 vols. Loeb Classical Library 31, 38. Cambridge: Harvard University Press, 1998. Logos 6. Vol. 1 originally published 1914 by Macmillan. Vol. 2 originally published 1914 by Harvard University Press.

Stone, A. M. "*Pro Milone*: Cicero's Second Thoughts." *Antichthon: Journal of the Australian Society for Classical Studies* 14 (1980): 88–111.

Stuart, Duane Reed. *Epochs of Greek and Roman Biography*. Sather Classical Lectures 4. New York: Biblo and Tannen, 1976. First published 1928 by University of California Press.

Swain, Simon. "Plutarch, Hadrian, and Delphi." *Historia: Zeitschrift für Alte Geschichte* 40, no. 3 (1991): 318–30.

Tacitus. *The Annals: The Reigns of Tiberius, Claudius, and Nero*. Translated by J. C. Yardley. New York: Oxford University Press, 2008.

Talbert, Charles H. *What Is a Gospel? The Genre of the Canonical Gospels*. Philadelphia, PA: Fortress, 1977.

Tuckett, C. M., ed. "Synoptic Studies: The Ampleforth Conferences of 1982 and 1983." Journal for the Study of the New Testament Supplement Series 7 (1984): 1–231.

Wallace, Daniel B. "*Ipsissima Vox* and the Seven Words from the Cross: A Test Case for John's Use of the Tradition." Paper presented at the Annual Meeting of the Society of Biblical Literature Southwestern Region, Dallas, TX, 5 March 2000.

Walton, Steve. "What Are the Gospels? Richard Burridge's Impact on Scholarly Understanding of the Genre of the Gospels." *Currents in Biblical Research* 14, no. 1 (2015): 81–93.

Wenham, John. *Easter Enigma: Are the Resurrection Accounts in Conflict?* Eugene, OR: Wipf & Stock, 2005. This 2nd edition previously published in 1992 by Paternoster. Originally published in 1984. All citations are to the Wipf & Stock edition.

Witherington, Ben, III. *The Acts of the Apostles: A Socio-Rhetorical Commentary*. Grand Rapids, MI: Eerdmans, 1998.

Witherington, Ben, III. *The Gospel of Mark: A Socio-Rhetorical Commentary*. Grand Rapids, MI: Eerdmans, 2001.

Witherington, Ben, III. *Invitation to the New Testament: First Things*. New York: Oxford University Press, 2013.

Witherington, Ben, III. *John's Wisdom: A Commentary on the Fourth Gospel*. Louisville, KY: Westminster John Knox, 1995.

Wright, N. T. *Following Jesus: Biblical Reflections on Discipleship*. 2nd ed. Grand Rapids, MI: Eerdmans, 2014.

General Index

Michael R. Licona, *Why Are There Differences in the Gospels?*

Note: References to figures and tables are denoted by 'f' or 't' in italics following the page number.

Modern Names Index

Ancient Sources Index

Scripture Index